SCIENCE AND RELIGIOUS BELIEF 1600–1900: A SELECTION OF PRIMARY SOURCES

SCIENCE AND RELIGIOUS BELIEF 1600-1900

Edited by
D. C. Goodman
at The Open University

 John Wright and Sons Limited
in association with
The Open University Press

ISBN 0 7236 0360 X

Printed in Great Britain by
Henry Ling Ltd., a subsidiary
of John Wright & Sons Ltd.,
at the Dorset Press, Dorchester

Contents

INTRODUCTION

THIS collection of primary source material has been prepared for students taking the Open University course, 'Science and Belief: from Copernicus to Darwin' (AMST 283). It is a companion volume to other set books in the course (R. Hooykaas, *Religion and the Rise of Modern Science*, Scottish Academic Press, 1972; C. C. Gillispie, *Genesis and Geology*, Harper and Row, 1959; and an anthology of secondary sources, edited by C. A. Russell: *Science and Religious Belief: A Selection of Recent Historical Studies*, University of London Press, 1973), but as an anthology it stands independently, and it is hoped that it will be found useful by students and readers elsewhere.

In selecting the sources the aim has been to bring together into an accessible form texts which capture some of the major intellectual issues of the period, relating to scientific and religious thought. All of the sources are in English; where necessary I have drawn on existing translations. A few of the texts are very well known and have been readily accessible to students for some time (for example, Galileo's *Letter to the Grand Duchess Christina*, and Richard Bentley's sermon, *A Confutation of Atheism from the Origin and Frame of the World*). Because of their importance and for the convenience of the student, they have been reproduced here once again. Other texts are less well known and less accessible. In the case of Robert Boyle it was necessary to select extracts from his voluminous writing. I am grateful to Professor Hooykaas for suggesting the extract from Kepler's *Astronomia Nova*.

The period covered by the texts is a long one, spanning three centuries. However, it is possible to identify themes which persist over these centuries. Indeed the discussion of these themes has an even longer life, extending back to classical antiquity. The origin of the universe was one of these major problems. Was the world created by a divine power or was it the inevitable result of physical circumstances? Baron d'Holbach's answer to this is remarkable for its clarity and uncompromising stand. His was an extreme view, leading to conclusions totally different from those of almost all of the other authors represented here. Those who argued for a divine creation differed on the extent to which God continued to intervene in Nature. Had God retired after the act of creation, leaving the world to operate of its own accord, or was he an ever-present governor, as Maclaurin insisted?

What sort of evidence could be invoked in support of the creation? The Scriptures continued to be regarded as a true testimony by many of our authors who make frequent references to the sacred texts. Another source of evidence was Nature itself. Since the time of Plato it had been argued that the study of the natural world offered a way to approach the divine creator, by the discovery of the intelligent planning of the universe. This applied not only to the grand order in the cosmos at large, but also in its least details. The importance of this religious approach is apparent in most of the natural philosophers included in the anthology. Indeed, it became a matter of duty for them. For Kepler, man had been given an inquiring mind by God to acquire an understanding of the created world. Kepler could only speak disdainfully of those men who never became interested in natural phenomena. He said they were more like corpses than living men. Kepler's astronomical discoveries were the fruits of theoretical beliefs involving inseparable religious and scientific thought. Much later in the eighteenth century William Derham continued to insist on the investigation of natural phenomena as a religious duty.

If man had been given a mind or soul, capable of reasoning, was he the only creature with this advantage? In the seventeenth century the existence of souls in animals was debated by theologians and natural philosophers, as the extracts from Descartes and Boyle show. A question of greater importance on account of its implications for natural science was the power of the human intellect. Was man's attempt to discern God's planning through the discovery of the laws of nature a justifiable enterprise, or was it no more than human folly and arrogance, since it supposed man's puny mind might understand the infinite ingenuity of the Creator? The texts show in several places how natural philosophers dealt with this question.

The evidence for a created world, as well as for the existence of God, seemed obvious to those who were convinced that there were the clearest signs of design or purposeful activity in nature. Boyle, who argued for the study of final causes, marvelled over the construction of the eye of the fly. Newton saw the distant positions of Jupiter and Saturn as a wise divine contrivance to prevent disturbances in the solar system. John Ray found unmistakable signs of God's design in the body of the camel, in the instincts which allowed animals to escape from predators, caused birds to migrate, and guided the bee to employ the hexagon in the construction of the honeycomb. Derham found the same wise provisions in the longevity and fertility of animals, which prevented overpopulation. Indeed the signs were so clear throughout nature, that Derham said an atheist must be perverse and justly 'esteemed a monster among rational beings'. Such arguments continued into the nineteenth century with the Bridgewater Treatises, which are here represented by an extract from Thomas Chalmers.

But if God had designed the world, and if he was all good, why was there evil in the universe? The discussion of monstrous births was a major issue in the seventeenth and eighteenth centuries. Similarly why had God created venomous creatures harmful to man? In one passage John Ray gave his opinion why God should have created the insects.

The atheistic literature of the period is slight, and this is reflected in the contents of the anthology. However, the threat of atheism was keenly felt, and because of this feeling, the argument from design acquired greater importance. To deny design was to open the doors to the atheistic tendencies of Epicurean atomism. An account of the world in terms of mechanical causes seemed to leave no place for God or design. The image of a world resulting from collisions of material particles in motion, the supposition of chance instead of design, and the idea of necessity in the universe, depriving God and man of free will, were all abhorrent to the religious natural philosopher. Yet in the seventeenth century the mechanical philosophy became dominant, and was promoted by Robert Boyle. To reassure his contemporaries Boyle wrote *The Christian Virtuoso* to show that it was perfectly possible to be both a Christian and an adept of the new corpuscularian philosophy. In fact he believed that the rising science would be a bulwark against atheism. Accordingly Boyle left money for lectures to be given on the evidence of Christianity. The first Boyle lecturer was Richard Bentley, a great classical scholar. His sermon in this anthology shows the use he made of Newton's scientific work.

John Ray's insistence on design as a means to combat atheism is apparent in his discussion of fossils. To explain shells and other figured stones as useless productions would, he said, 'put a weapon into the Atheist's hands'. In the following century Priestley in similar vein ridiculed certain passages in Hume.

Finally, the problem remained of reconciling the evidence from the natural world with the evidence of the Scriptures. Passages in the Bible gave a detailed account of things which came increasingly within the realm of scientific debate: the genesis of the universe, the Flood, and the special creation of Man. Other passages contradicted two postulates of the Copernican theory by implying that the sun moved and the earth was stationary. In the seventeenth century this difficulty was elegantly resolved by Galileo and Wilkins. The rise of geological knowledge in the nineteenth century presented fresh problems for scriptural interpretation. The importance attached to achieving harmony between religion and geology is here illustrated by the Reverend Joseph Townsend and by William Buckland, who became convinced that he had found evidence for the Flood. In biology religious opposition to the idea of variation of species was given expression in Sedgwick's hostile review of Robert Chambers' *Vestiges of the Natural History of Creation*. The Darwinian theory of evolution raised further problems for religious natural philosophers. The closing sections of the anthology are from Charles Darwin and T. H. Huxley.

1. Johannes Kepler (1571-1630)

Mysterium Cosmographicum (Tübingen, 1596)
Dedication and Chapter 2
From Werner Heisenberg, *The Physicist's Conception of Nature*,
translated by A.J. Pomerans, (London, 1958), pp. 73-83

Dedication of the first edition of the Mysterium Cosmographicum

To their Illustrious, High-born, Noble and Righteous Lords, Sigismund Friedrich, Baron of Herberstein, Neuberg and Guttenhag; and Lankowitz, Lord Chamberlain and Lord High Steward of Corinthia, Councillor to His Imperial Majesty and to the Most Illustrious Archduke of Austria, Steward of the Province of Styria

and

to the Most Noble Lords of the Illustrious Estates of Styria, the Honourable Council of Five, my gentle and gracious Lords

Greetings and Humble Respects!

What I have promised seven months ago, to wit a work that according to the judgment of the learned will be elegant, impressive, and far superior to all annual calendars, I now present to your gracious company, my noble Lords, a work that though it be small in compass and but the fruit of my own modest efforts, yet treats of a wondrous subject. If you desire maturity—Pythagoras has already treated of it some 2000 years ago. If you desire novelty—it is the first time that this subject is being presented to all mankind by myself. If you desire scope—nothing is greater or wider than the Universe. If you desire venerability—nothing is more precious, nothing more beautiful than our magnificent temple of God. If you wish to know the mysteries—nothing in Nature is, or ever has been, more recondite. *It is but for one reason that my object will not satisfy everybody, for its usefulness will not be apparent to the thoughtless.* I am speaking of the Book of Nature, which is so highly esteemed in the Holy Scriptures. St. Paul admonished

73

74 PHYSICIST'S CONCEPTION OF NATURE

the Heathens to reflect on God within themselves as they
would on the Sun in the water or in a mirror. Why then
should we Christians delight the less in this reflection, seeing
that it is our proper task to honour, to revere and to admire
God in the true way? Our piety in this is the deeper the greater
is our awareness of creation and of its grandeur. Truly, how
many hymns of praise did not David, His faithful servant,
sing to the Creator, who is none but God alone! In this his
mind dwelled reverently on the contemplation of the
Heavens. The Heavens, he sings, declare the glory of God.
I will consider Thy heavens, the work of Thy hands, the
moon and the stars which Thou has ordained. God is our
Lord, and great is His might; He counteth the multitude of
the Stars, and knoweth them by their names. Elsewhere,
inspired by the Holy Ghost and full of joyousness, he exclaims
to the Universe: Praise ye the Lord, praise Him, Sun and
Moon, etc. Now, do the heavens or the stars have a voice?
Can they praise God as men do? Nay, when we say that they
themselves give praise to God, it is only because they offer
men thoughts of praise to God. Thus, in what follows, let
us free the very tongues of the heavens and of nature so that
their voices may resound all the louder; and when we do so
let no one accuse us of vain and useless efforts.

I need not stress how important a witness my subject is for
the act of creation, questioned as it is by philosophers. For
here we may behold how God, like a master-builder, has laid
the foundation of the world according to order and law, and
how He has measured all things so carefully, that we might
well judge it is not nature that human art copies, but that God
in His very creation was thinking of the way in which man
yet unborn would be building one day.

Indeed, must we assess the value of divine things like we
do a dessert, by the farthing? But, you may object, what
good is an understanding of nature, what good the whole of

THE BEGINNINGS OF MODERN SCIENCE 75

astronomy, when the stomach is empty? However, reasoning men will not listen to the clamours of the uneducated that we cease from such studies because of this. We tolerate the painter because he delights the eye, the musician because he delights the ear, even though they bring us no other benefits. Indeed, the delight caused by their works not only benefits man, but is his glory also. What lack of education, what stupidity is it then, to begrudge the mind its own honourable joy, when we allow it to the eyes and to the ears! He who attacks these delights attacks Nature herself. For has not the all-merciful Creator, who fashioned Nature out of the Void, given every creature all it needs, and beauty and pleasure beyond in overflowing measure? Would He then single out the mind of man, the crown of all creation and made in His own image, to be alone without inspired joy? Indeed, we do not ask for what useful purpose birds do sing, for song is their pleasure since they were created for singing. Similarly we ought not to ask why the human mind troubles to fathom the secrets of the heavens. Our Creator has added mind to our senses not simply so that man might earn his daily keep—many kinds of creatures possessing unreasoning souls can do this much more skilfully —but also so that from the existence of the things which we behold with our eyes, we might delve into the causes of their being and becoming, even if this might serve no further useful purpose. And just as the bodies of men and of all other creatures are maintained by food and drink, so man's soul, which is quite different from his body, is maintained, enriched and, as it were, helped in its growth, by the food of understanding. Therefore he who is disinterested in such matters, is more alike to a corpse than he is to a living man. Now, just as Nature sees to it that the living will not lack victuals, so we may say justly that the diversity in the phenomena of Nature is so great, and the treasures hidden in the heavens so rich, precisely in order that the human mind shall never be lacking

76 PHYSICIST'S CONCEPTION OF NATURE

in fresh nourishment, in order that man become not satiated with the old nor stay at rest, but rather that he find the world an ever-open workshop for matching his wits.

Now what little I have served myself from the all-too-splendid table of the Creator by no means loses in value because it is despised by the great majority. More people praise the goose than do the pheasant; for the former is known to all—the latter to but a few; yet no epicure will esteem the pheasant for less than the goose. Thus the worth of my subject is needs the greater the fewer will sing its praise, if only these few be connoisseurs. What is meet for a Prince by no means suits the multitude; astronomy is not food for everybody, without distinction, but only for the aspiring soul, and this not through any fault of mine, not because of its nature, nor yet because God is a jealous God, but because most men are stupid and craven. Princes are accustomed to introducing an especially delicate dish between courses which, in order to avoid repletion, they enjoy after they are satisfied. Thus even the most noble and the wisest of men will find this and similar research to his taste only when he leaves his dwelling, and when passing through villages, cities, lands and kingdoms, he raises an enquiring eye to the great sphere of the whole earth, wishing to acquire a precise knowledge of all things. If in this he should fail to discover inspiration or lasting value in any of man's work, anything to still his hunger and to satisfy him, then will he hasten to seek out better things, then will he rise from the earth to the heavens, then will he immerse his spirit, troubled by empty worries, into that great tranquillity and proclaim with Lucretius:

Happy the soul, whose duty it was, all this to uncover,
Who first rose up into the heavenly heights.

He will start despising what before he deemed important; now will he esteem fully the works of God's hands, and in

THE BEGINNINGS OF MODERN SCIENCE 77

their contemplation he will finally come upon undisturbed and pure joy. However much and however deeply this striving may be despised, however much men may seek wealth, treasures and happiness, astronomers want nothing but the glory of knowing that their writings are for the wise and not for the rabble, for Kings and not for shepherds. Without hesitation I proclaim that there will yet be men for whom this will be a solace in their old age, men who carry out their public duties so that later they may taste without qualms of conscience the joy of which I have spoken.

Yes, there will once again come a Charles, who as ruler of Europe will seek in vain that which he, tired of ruling, finds in the narrow cell of his monastery; who among all the festivities, titles, triumphs, riches, cities, and kingdoms, finds so great a joy in the planetary sphere constructed after Pythagoras and Copernicus, that he renounces the whole world for it and prefers ruling the heavenly orbits with his measuring instruments to governing people with his sceptre. . . .

Written on the 15th May, on which self-same day one year earlier I commenced my work.

Your Highnesses' most devoted servant
M. Joannes Keplerus of Wurttemberg
Mathematician at Your School in Graz.

✳ ✳ ✳ ✳

[p. 78]

Sketch of My Principal Proof

In order now to come to my subject, and to consolidate by means of a new proof the doctrines of Copernicus about the new world which we have just discussed, I wish to run briefly through the whole subject from the beginning.

In the beginning God created the body. If this is understood then it will be reasonably clear also why God began with the creation of the body and not with anything else. Quantity, I say, lay at God's hand, and for its realization He needed everything that is of the essence of bodies, so that, as it were, the quantity of a body, inasmuch as the latter is a body

THE BEGINNINGS OF MODERN SCIENCE 79

at all, becomes the form and foundation of this concept. God desired quantity to come into existence before all else, so that there could be a distinction between *the curved* and *the straight*. Cusanus and others seem to me so divinely great, precisely because they paid so much attention to the relationship between the straight and the curved, and because they dared to equate the curved with God, and the straight with His creations. Thus, the work of those who wish to understand the Creator through His creatures, God through men, and divine thought through human thought, is no more useful than that of those who wish to understand the curved through the straight, and the circle through the square.

Why is it that in adorning the world, God reflected on the differences between the curved and the straight, and preferred the nobility of the curved? Why, indeed? Only because the most perfect builder must needs produce a work of the greatest beauty, for it is not now, nor ever was, possible (as Cicero, following Plato's Timaeus, shows in his book on the Cosmos) that the best should ever be anything but the most beautiful. Now, since the Creator conceived the world in His mind (we speak after the manner of men so that we mortals may understand) and since as I have said previously, the idea itself had been present beforehand and had been complete in its content, for the form of the work about to be created to become perfect also, according to the laws which God prescribes for Himself in all His goodness, it is clear that He could not derive the idea for the foundation of the world from anything but His own essence. How excellent and divine this is can be appreciated in two ways: first in itself, since God is One in His essence and Three in Person, and secondly, in comparison with His creatures.

This picture, this idea, God wished to imprint upon the world. So that the world become a most perfect and most

80   PHYSICIST'S CONCEPTION OF NATURE

beautiful world, so that man could know of these ideas, the all-wise Creator created magnitude and designed quantities, whose whole essence, so to speak, lies in the distinction between the two concepts of the straight and the curved. We are thus to be made aware in the above-mentioned twofold way, that the curved represents God. Nor must we think that so purposeful a distinction in the representation of God took place as if God had not reflected on it and had created magnitude-as-body for quite different reasons and purposes, and that the distinction between straight and curved and the similarity of the latter to God came about by itself, as it were, by accident.

Rather is it probable that God from the very beginning and purposely has selected the curved and the straight for stamping the world with the divinity of the Creator; quantity had existed so that these two might be possible, and for quantity to be understood He created the body before all else.

Let us now see how the perfect Creator used these quantities in the building of the world and what, according to our lights, seems to have been His probable procedure. This then we wish to search out in hypotheses old and new, and we shall give the palm to him who will show us the way.

The fact that the whole world is circumscribed by a sphere has already been discussed exhaustively by Aristotle (in his book on the Heavens), who based his proof particularly on the special significance of the spherical surface. It is for this very reason that even now the outermost sphere of fixed stars has preserved this form, although no motion can be ascribed to it. It holds the Sun as its centre in its innermost womb, as it were. The fact that the remaining orbits are round can be seen from the circular motions of the stars. Thus we need no further proof that the curved was used for adorning the world. While, however, we have three kinds of quantity in the world, *viz.*, form, number, and content of bodies, the

THE BEGINNINGS OF MODERN SCIENCE 81

curved is found in form alone. In this, content is not important since one structure inscribed concentrically into a similar one (for instance, sphere into sphere, or circle into circle) either touches everywhere or not at all. The spherical, since it represents an absolutely unique quantity, can only be governed by the number Three. Thus, if, in His creation, God had been concerned with the curved alone, there would be nothing in the Cosmos except the Sun in the centre as the picture of the Father, the sphere of fixed stars (or the waters of the Mosaic story) on the surface as the picture of the Son, and the all-pervading heavenly ether, *i.e.*, extension and firmament, as the picture of the Holy Ghost. Now, since the fixed stars are innumerable while the planets have a very definite number, and since the magnitudes of the individual heavenly orbits are different, we must needs seek the cause for this in the concept of the straight. We should otherwise have to assume that God had created the world haphazard although He had the best and most reasonable plans at His disposal, and no one will be able to convince me of this even in the case of the fixed stars whose positions seem to be the most irregular, like seeds scattered at will.

Therefore let us transfer our attention to straight quantities. Just as previously we chose the spherical surface precisely because it was the most perfect quantity, so shall we now leap to those bodies which are the most perfect among straight quantities and which consist of three dimensions. It is, after all, a certain fact that the idea of the world is perfect. Thus we shall omit straight lines and surfaces, for since they are innumerable and therefore completely unsuitable for order, they are best left out of the finite, best-regulated and most perfectly beautiful of all worlds. We shall do no more than select from the infinitely many kinds of bodies some that have special characteristics; I am thinking of those whose angles, edges or side surfaces are equal either individually, in pairs, or

F

82 PHYSICIST'S CONCEPTION OF NATURE

according to some law, so that we might arrive with good reasons at some finite result. If now a class of body, defined by certain conditions, although having a finite number of types, nevertheless has a tremendous number of individual members, then whenever possible, we shall use the edges and mid-points of the faces of these bodies for the representations of the number, magnitude and position of the fixed stars. However, should this transcend our human powers we shall postpone any attempt to explain the number and position of the fixed stars until such a time as someone will be able to describe all of them without exception according to number and magnitude. Let us therefore omit the fixed stars, and leave them to the wisest of Master-builders Who alone knows the number of the stars, calling each by its name, and let us rather turn our glance towards the nearer planets which exist in much smaller numbers. If now in our final selection of bodies we omit the great mass of irregular ones, and only retain those whose faces are equal in side and in angle, there remain those five regular bodies to which the Greeks gave the following names: the Cube, or the hexahedron; the Pyramid, or the tetrahedron; the dodecahedron; the icosahedron; and the octahedron. That there can be no more than these five can be seen from Euclid, Book XIII, in the note on proposition 18.

Since the number of these bodies is well-determined and very small, while others are uncountable or infinite, there had to appear two kinds of stars which are distinguished by an obvious characteristic (such as are rest and motion). One kind must border on the infinite just as the number of fixed stars, the other must be closely limited, as is the number of the planets. Here it is not our task to find reasons why these move while those do not. However, once it is granted that planets require motion it follows that if they were to retain these, they had to be assigned curved orbits.

THE BEGINNINGS OF MODERN SCIENCE 83

Thus we come to curved orbits through motion, and to bodies through number and magnitude. We can but exclaim with Plato that *God is a great geometrician*, and in constructing the planets He inscribed bodies into circles and circles into bodies until there remained not a single body that was not endowed with movable circles internally as well as externally. From propositions 13, 14, 15, 16, and 17 of the XIIIth Book of Euclid we can see how highly suited are these bodies from their very natures for this process of inscription and circumscription. If now the five bodies be fitted into one another and if circles be described both inside and outside all of them, then we obtain precisely the number six of circles.

Now, if at any time the order of the world has been investigated on the basis of the fact that there exist six movable orbits about an immovable Sun, astronomy, at any rate, has omitted to do so. *Now, Copernicus has taken just six orbits of this kind, pairs of which are precisely related by the fact that those five bodies fit most perfectly into them, and this is the sum total of what follows.* Thus, we must heed Copernicus until someone else devises theories that will fit our philosophical conclusions even better, or until somebody will show us how that which could only be discovered by the best logic from the principles of nature could by mere chance have stolen into numbers or into the human mind. *For what could be more astonishing, what a more striking proof than the fact that what Copernicus concluded and interpreted,* a posteriori *from the phenomena, and from effects, (just like a blind man feeling his way with a staff, as he was wont to say to Rhaeticus, more through happy intuition than through reliable logical procedures) could all, I aver, have been best determined and understood with reasons which,* a priori, *stem from the causes, from the very idea of creation.*

J. Kepler: *Mysterium Cosmographicum*, Chapter 2, pp. 45–49.

2. Johannes Kepler (1571-1630)

Astronomia Nova (Heidelberg, 1609)

Translated by C. A. Russell from Kepler, *Gesammelte Werke,* ed. M. Caspar and F. Hammer, (Munich), Volume 3 (1937), pp. 29-33. Translation copyright © 1973 The Open University

In fact the sacred writings also speak to men concerning ordinary matters in which it is not their normal function to instruct men; they do this in a human manner so that they may be understood by men; they employ those terms which are in common usage for the purpose of introducing others more sublime and divine.

Why should it be extraordinary, therefore, if Scripture also speaks with senses that are human (when the true nature of things is at variance with the senses), either to scientific or ignorant men? Who does not know whether Psalm 19 contains a poetical allusion? Here, under the image of the sun, the Psalmist sings of the progress of the Gospel and indeed of the journey through this world of Christ our Lord, undertaken for our sake. The sun is said to emerge from the tabernacle of the horizon, as a bridegroom from his chamber, swift as a strong man ready to run a race. There is an imitation of this in Virgil—daybreak abandoning her golden couch to Tithonus. Certainly poetry amongst the Hebrews was earlier than that.

The Psalmist knew that the sun did not appear from the horizon just as from a tabernacle (though so it appears to our eyes). But he regarded the sun as truly moving because that is how it seems to the eye. And yet he makes *both* assertions because *both* have visual evidence. Neither in one case nor the other should he be thought to be speaking falsely. For the visual comprehension has its own truth appropriate to the deeper purpose of the Psalmist to foreshadowing the progress of the Gospel and indeed of the Son of God. Joshua further adds the valleys over against which the sun and the moon were moving; this is natural because that is the way it appeared to him at the Jordan. Nevertheless each of them attained his own objective. David did this (and with him Syracides), having revealed the splendour of God which determined that this was the way these visible things were presented to the eyes, ordered through the expression of the mystical sense. It was also true of Joshua. For him the sun had to be restrained in the middle of the sky for a whole day, according to the visual impression; but for other men it spent that same span of time lingering under the earth.

But the thoughtless reflect only on the verbal contrast—'the sun stood still' means 'the earth stood still'—not being careful to consider that this contradiction only arises within the confines of optics and astronomy. On that account it is not open to general human usage; nor are they willing to see that Joshua's sole object in his prayer was that the mountains should not steal the sun from him. That prayer was expressed in words consistent with visual impressions, since it would have been quite inappropriate for him at that time to consider astronomy or visual errors. Certainly if anyone had warned that the sun was not moving across the valley of Ajalon, but only seemed to do so, would not Joshua have replied that his prayer was that the day should be prolonged for him, by whatever means? It would have been just the same if anyone had proposed the view that the sun was for ever at rest but the earth was moving.

Moreover God readily perceived from Joshua's words what he wanted, and granted his prayer by checking the earth's motion so that the sun did seem to him to stand still. The main point of Joshua's petition certainly came to this, that is what might appear to him whatever might really be the case. Indeed there was nothing vain or invalid about this appearance but it was linked with the desired result.

Thus see Chapter 10 of my *Astronomy: the Optical Section* where you will find reasons why the sun in this way seems to all men to be moving, but not the earth: namely, because the sun seems small, but the earth truly appears to be large. Nor is the motion of the sun to be grasped by sight (since it gives the appearance of being slow) but by reason alone on account of the changed relationship to the mountains after some time. It is therefore impossible that reason not previously instructed should imagine anything other than that the earth is a kind of vast house with the vault of the sky placed on top of it; it is motionless and within it the sun being so small passes from one region to another, like a bird wandering through the air.

This universal image has produced the first line in the sacred page. *In the beginning*, said Moses, *God created the heaven and the earth;* this is a natural expression because these two aspects of the universe are those that chiefly meet the eye. It is as if Moses were saying to man 'all this architecture of the universe that you see, the brightness above, by which you are covered, the widespreading darkness below, upon which you stand—all this has been created by God'.

In other places man is questioned whether he has learned how to penetrate the height of the sky above or the depth of the earth beneath. This is natural because to the mass of men each of these appears equally to project into infinite space. Nevertheless, there never was a man who, listening rationally, would use these words to circumscribe the diligence of the astronomers, whether in demonstrating the most contemptible weakness of the earth by comparison with the sky, or through investigations of astronomical distance. These words do not speak about intellectualised dimensions, but about the dimension of reality—which, for a human body fixed on the earth and drinking in the free air, is totally impossible. Read the whole of Job Ch. 38 and compare with it the matters that are disputed in astronomy and physics.

If anyone alleges on the basis of Psalm 24 *The earth is founded upon the seas* (in order to establish some new philosophical dictum, however absurd to hear) that the earth is floating on the waters, may it not be rightly said to him that he ought to set free the Holy Spirit and should not drag Him in to the schools of physics to make a fool of Him. For in that place the Psalmist wishes to suggest nothing other than what men know beforehand and experience each day: the lands, uplifted after separation of the waters, have great rivers flowing through them and the seas around them on all sides. Doubtless the same is spoken of elsewhere, when the Israelites sing *By the waters of Babylon there we sat down*, i.e., by the side of the rivers, or on the banks of the Euphrates and Tigris.

If anyone receives the one freely, why not the other, so that in other places which are often quoted against the motion of the earth we should, in the same way, turn our eyes from physics to the tradition of scripture?

One generation passes away, says Ecclesiastes, *and another generation is born*, but the earth abides for ever. Is Solomon here, as it were, disputing with the astronomers? No, he is rather warning men of their changeableness whereas the earth, the home of the human race, always remains the same; the movement of the sun keeps returning it to its starting-point; the wind is driven in a circle, and returns to the same plan; rivers flow from their sources to the sea, and thence return to their sources. Finally, while some men perish others are born, and always the drama of life is the same; there is nothing new under the sun.

You are listening to no new principle of physics. It is a question of ethical instruction in a matter which is clear on its own, observed universally but receives scant consideration. That is why Solomon insists on the matter. Who does not know the earth to be always the same? Who does not see that the sun rising daily in the East, that the rivers run perpetually down to the sea, that the pattern of changes of the wind is fixed and recurring and that one generation succeeds another? Who in fact considers that the drama of life is being perpetually performed, with only a change of cast and that there is nothing new in human affairs? And so, by rehearsing things which everyone sees, Solomon warns of that which the majority wrongly neglect.

But some men think Psalm 104 to be wholly concerned with physics, since it is wholly concerned with physical matters. And there God is said to have *laid the foundations of the earth so that it should not be moved*, and that stability will remain from age to age. Nevertheless the Psalmist is a very long way from speculation about physical causes. He rests utterly in the greatness of God who made all these things and is unfolding a hymn to God the Creator, a hymn in which he runs in order through the whole world as it appears to our eyes.

But if you consider it carefully, it is a commentary on the Genesis account of creation in six days. For as in that account, the first three days are given for the separation of the regions; first light from the external darkness, secondly the waters from the waters (on the interposition of the firmament), and thirdly of the lands from the seas, when the earth became clothed with plants and trees: the three later days on the other hand, are for filling out the regions thus distinguished; day four for the sky, day five for seas and air, and day six for the earth. Thus in this Psalm there are six distinct parts corresponding to the work of the six days.

In the second verse he surrounds the Creator with light, the first of created things and the work of the first day, as with a garment.

The second part begins in the third verse and deals with the waters above the heavens by an extension of the sky, and atmospheric phenomena (which the Psalmist seems to associate with the waters above) namely clouds, winds, fiery whirlwinds and lightning.

The third part begins in verse 6, and celebrates the earth as the foundation of the things which he goes on to consider. He refers all things to the earth, and to its animal inhabitants. This is natural because according to visual appearances there are two primary parts of the world, the sky and the earth. Therefore this passage now goes on to contemplate the earth after so many ages, not to have subsided, not to have cracked open, not to be in a state of collapse, yet no one has ever discovered upon what foundations it has been laid.

He did not wish to teach those things about which men are ignorant but rather to recall to their minds those matters which they neglect, namely the greatness and power of God in the creation of so immense a mass, yet one so firm and stable. If an astronomer teaches that the earth is carried along through the stars, he neither destroys what the Psalmist says here nor tears apart the experience of men. Nevertheless it is true that the earth, the work of the divine Architect is not collapsing (as buildings that are consumed by age and decay habitually collapse); it is not swaying from side to side; the dwelling places of living creatures are not disturbed; rather is it true that the mountains and the coastlines remain firm, immovable before the force of the winds and floods, just as they had been from the beginning. But the Psalmist adds the most beautiful and vivid description of the separation of the seas from the continents, and adorns it with the addition of springs and of the advantages which fountains and rocks offer to birds and four-footed beasts. Nor does he pass over the adorning of the earth's surface as commemorated by Moses amongst the works of the third day; but he goes more deeply into this and takes it back to its origin, for example in the waters of the heavens; and embellishes it by mention of the advantages which flow from that embellishment for the support and cheerfulness of man as well as for the little dwellings of the beasts.

The fourth part begins in verse 20, celebrating the work of the fourth day, the sun and the moon, but especially the advantages which accrue, by the marking out of time, to animals and man; this really constitutes the subject matter with the result that it clearly appears that he is not here writing as an astronomer. Otherwise he would not have omitted reference to the five planets. Nothing is more admirable than their motion, nothing more beautiful, and there is nothing which testifies more evidently to the wisdom of their Creator amongst those who can understand.

The fifth part is in verse 26, concerning the work of the fifth day. The seas are filled with fish and adorned by navigation.

More obscurely, the sixth section is connected with verse 28 and treats of the animal inhabitants of the earth, created on the sixth day. And lastly he introduces the goodness of God in general in upholding all things and creating new ones. Therefore he refers everything which he had said about the world to living beings and he records nothing which is open to doubt. This is natural, not to enquire after unknown entities, but to invite men to consider the benefits which flow themselves from these works one day after another.

And I urge my reader also not to be forgetful of the divine goodness imparted to men, when the Psalmist invites him particularly to contemplate this, when having returned from the temple, he has again entered the school of astronomy. Let him join with me in praising and celebrating the wisdom and greatness of the Creator which I disclose to him from the deeper explanations of the form of the universe, from the enquiry into its causes, from the detection of errors of appearance. Thus not only let him recognise the well-being of living things throughout nature, in the firmness and stability of the world so that he reveres God's handiwork, but also let him recognise the wisdom of the Creator in its motion which is as mysterious as it is worthy of all admiration.

3. Galileo Galilei (1564-1642)

Letter to the Grand Duchess Christina (1615)
From *Discoveries and Opinions of Galileo,* translated with an introduction and notes by Stillman Drake (New York, 1957), pp. 175-216. Copyright © 1957 by Stillman Drake. Reprinted by permission of Doubleday & Company, Inc.

GALILEO GALILEI
TO
THE MOST SERENE
GRAND DUCHESS MOTHER:

Some years ago, as Your Serene Highness well knows, I discovered in the heavens many things that had not been seen before our own age. The novelty of these things, as well as some consequences which followed from them in contradiction to the physical notions commonly held among academic philosophers, stirred up against me no small number of professors—as if I had placed these things in the sky with my own hands in order to upset nature and overturn the sciences. They seemed to forget that the increase of known truths stimulates the investigation, establishment, and growth of the arts; not their diminution or destruction.

Showing a greater fondness for their own opinions than for truth, they sought to deny and disprove the new things which, if they had cared to look for themselves, their own senses would have demonstrated to them. To this end they hurled various charges and published numerous writings filled with vain arguments, and they made the grave mistake of sprinkling these with passages taken from places in the Bible which they had failed to understand properly, and which were ill suited to their purposes.

These men would perhaps not have fallen into such error had they but paid attention to a most useful doctrine of St. Augustine's, relative to our making positive statements about things which are obscure and hard to understand by means of reason alone. Speaking of a certain physical conclusion about the heavenly bodies, he wrote: "Now keeping always our respect for moderation in grave piety, we ought not to believe anything inadvisedly on a dubious point, lest in favor to our error we conceive a prejudice against something that truth hereafter may reveal to be not contrary in any way to the sacred books of either the Old or the New Testament."[1]

Well, the passage of time has revealed to everyone the truths that I previously set forth; and, together with the truth of the facts, there has come to light the great difference in attitude between those who simply and dispassionately refused to admit the discoveries to be true, and those who combined with their incredulity some reckless passion of their own. Men who were well grounded in astronomical and physical science were persuaded as soon as they received my first message. There were others who denied them or remained in doubt only because of their novel and unexpected character, and because they had not yet had the opportunity to see for themselves. These men have by degrees come to be satisfied. But some, besides allegiance to their original error, possess I know not what fanciful interest in remaining hostile not so much toward the things in question as toward their discoverer. No longer being able to deny them, these men now take refuge in obstinate silence, but being more than ever exasperated by that which has pacified and quieted other men, they divert their thoughts to other fancies and seek new ways to damage me.

I should pay no more attention to them than to those who previously contradicted me—at whom I always laugh, being assured of the eventual outcome—were it not that in their new calumnies and persecutions I perceive that they do not stop at proving themselves more learned than I am (a claim which I scarcely contest), but go so far as to cast against me imputations of crimes which must be, and are, more abhorrent to me than death itself. I cannot remain satisfied merely to know that the injustice of this is recognized by those who are acquainted with these men and with me, as perhaps it is not known to others.

[1] De Genesi ad literam, end of bk. ii. (Citations of theological works are taken from Galileo's marginal notes, without verification.)

Persisting in their original resolve to destroy me and everything mine by any means they can think of, these men are aware of my views in astronomy and philosophy. They know that as to the arrangement of the parts of the universe, I hold the sun to be situated motionless in the center of the revolution of the celestial orbs while the earth rotates on its axis and revolves about the sun. They know also that I support this position not only by refuting the arguments of Ptolemy and Aristotle, but by producing many counter-arguments; in particular, some which relate to physical effects whose causes can perhaps be assigned in no other way. In addition there are astronomical arguments derived from many things in my new celestial discoveries that plainly confute the Ptolemaic system while admirably agreeing with and confirming the contrary hypothesis. Possibly because they are disturbed by the known truth of other propositions of mine which differ from those commonly held, and therefore mistrusting their defense so long as they confine themselves to the field of philosophy, these men have resolved to fabricate a shield for their fallacies out of the mantle of pretended religion and the authority of the Bible. These they apply, with little judgment, to the refutation of arguments that they do not understand and have not even listened to.

First they have endeavored to spread the opinion that such propositions in general are contrary to the Bible and are consequently damnable and heretical. They know that it is human nature to take up causes whereby a man may oppress his neighbor, no matter how unjustly, rather than those from which a man may receive some just encouragement. Hence they have had no trouble in finding men who would preach the damnability and heresy of the new doctrine from their very pulpits with unwonted confidence, thus doing impious and inconsiderate injury not only to that doctrine and its followers but to all mathematics and mathematicians in general. Next, becoming bolder, and hoping (though vainly) that this seed which first took root in their hypocritical minds would send out branches and ascend to heaven, they began scattering rumors among the people

that before long this doctrine would be condemned by the supreme authority. They know, too, that official condemnation would not only suppress the two propositions which I have mentioned, but would render damnable all other astronomical and physical statements and observations that have any necessary relation or connection with these.

In order to facilitate their designs, they seek so far as possible (at least among the common people) to make this opinion seem new and to belong to me alone. They pretend not to know that its author, or rather its restorer and confirmer, was Nicholas Copernicus; and that he was not only a Catholic, but a priest and a canon. He was in fact so esteemed by the church that when the Lateran Council under Leo X took up the correction of the church calendar, Copernicus was called to Rome from the most remote parts of Germany to undertake its reform. At that time the calendar was defective because the true measures of the year and the lunar month were not exactly known. The Bishop of Culm,[2] then superintendent of this matter, assigned Copernicus to seek more light and greater certainty concerning the celestial motions by means of constant study and labor. With Herculean toil he set his admirable mind to this task, and he made such great progress in this science and brought our knowledge of the heavenly motions to such precision that he became celebrated as an astronomer. Since that time not only has the calendar been regulated by his teachings, but tables of all the motions of the planets have been calculated as well.

Having reduced his system into six books, he published these at the instance of the Cardinal of Capua[3] and the Bishop of Culm. And since he had assumed his laborious enterprise by order of the supreme pontiff, he dedicated this book *On the celestial revolutions* to Pope Paul III. When printed, the book was accepted by the holy Church, and it has been read and studied by everyone without the

[2] Tiedmann Giese, to whom Copernicus referred in his preface as "that scholar, my good friend."
[3] Nicholas Schoenberg, spoken of by Copernicus as "celebrated in all fields of scholarship."

faintest hint of any objection ever being conceived against its doctrines. Yet now that manifest experiences and necessary proofs have shown them to be well grounded, persons exist who would strip the author of his reward without so much as looking at his book, and add the shame of having him pronounced a heretic. All this they would do merely to satisfy their personal displeasure conceived without any cause against another man, who has no interest in Copernicus beyond approving his teachings.

Now as to the false aspersions which they so unjustly seek to cast upon me, I have thought it necessary to justify myself in the eyes of all men, whose judgment in matters of religion and of reputation I must hold in great esteem. I shall therefore discourse of the particulars which these men produce to make this opinion detested and to have it condemned not merely as false but as heretical. To this end they make a shield of their hypocritical zeal for religion. They go about invoking the Bible, which they would have minister to their deceitful purposes. Contrary to the sense of the Bible and the intention of the holy Fathers, if I am not mistaken, they would extend such authorities until even in purely physical matters—where faith is not involved—they would have us altogether abandon reason and the evidence of our senses in favor of some biblical passage, though under the surface meaning of its words this passage may contain a different sense.

I hope to show that I proceed with much greater piety than they do, when I argue not against condemning this book, but against condemning it in the way they suggest—that is, without understanding it, weighing it, or so much as reading it. For Copernicus never discusses matters of religion or faith, nor does he use arguments that depend in any way upon the authority of sacred writings which he might have interpreted erroneously. He stands always upon physical conclusions pertaining to the celestial motions, and deals with them by astronomical and geometrical demonstrations, founded primarily upon sense experiences and very exact observations. He did not ignore the Bible, but he knew very well that if his doctrine were proved, then it

could not contradict the Scriptures when they were rightly understood. And thus at the end of his letter of dedication, addressing the pope, he said:

"If there should chance to be any exegetes ignorant of mathematics who pretend to skill in that discipline, and dare to condemn and censure this hypothesis of mine upon the authority of some scriptural passage twisted to their purpose, I value them not, but disdain their unconsidered judgment. For it is known that Lactantius—a poor mathematician though in other respects a worthy author—writes very childishly about the shape of the earth when he scoffs at those who affirm it to be a globe. Hence it should not seem strange to the ingenious if people of that sort should in turn deride me. But mathematics is written for mathematicians, by whom, if I am not deceived, these labors of mine will be recognized as contributing something to their domain, as also to that of the Church over which Your Holiness now reigns."[4]

Such are the people who labor to persuade us that an author like Copernicus may be condemned without being read, and who produce various authorities from the Bible, from theologians, and from Church Councils to make us believe that this is not only lawful but commendable. Since I hold these to be of supreme authority, I consider it rank temerity for anyone to contradict them—when employed according to the usage of the holy Church. Yet I do not believe it is wrong to speak out when there is reason to suspect that other men wish, for some personal motive, to produce and employ such authorities for purposes quite different from the sacred intention of the holy Church.

Therefore I declare (and my sincerity will make itself manifest) not only that I mean to submit myself freely and renounce any errors into which I may fall in this discourse through ignorance of matters pertaining to religion, but that I do not desire in these matters to engage in disputes with anyone, even on points that are disputable. My goal is this alone; that if, among errors that may abound in these con-

[4] *De Revolutionibus* (Nuremberg, 1543), f. iiii.

siderations of a subject remote from my profession, there is anything that may be serviceable to the holy Church in making a decision concerning the Copernican system, it may be taken and utilized as seems best to the superiors. And if not, let my book be torn and burnt, as I neither intend nor pretend to gain from it any fruit that is not pious and Catholic. And though many of the things I shall reprove have been heard by my own ears, I shall freely grant to those who have spoken them that they never said them, if that is what they wish, and I shall confess myself to have been mistaken. Hence let whatever I reply be addressed not to them, but to whoever may have held such opinions.

The reason produced for condemning the opinion that the earth moves and the sun stands still is that in many places in the Bible one may read that the sun moves and the earth stands still. Since the Bible cannot err, it follows as a necessary consequence that anyone takes an erroneous and heretical position who maintains that the sun is inherently motionless and the earth movable.

With regard to this argument, I think in the first place that it is very pious to say and prudent to affirm that the holy Bible can never speak untruth—whenever its true meaning is understood. But I believe nobody will deny that it is often very abstruse, and may say things which are quite different from what its bare words signify. Hence in expounding the Bible if one were always to confine oneself to the unadorned grammatical meaning, one might fall into error. Not only contradictions and propositions far from true might thus be made to appear in the Bible, but even grave heresies and follies. Thus it would be necessary to assign to God feet, hands, and eyes, as well as corporeal and human affections, such as anger, repentance, hatred, and sometimes even the forgetting of things past and ignorance of those to come. These propositions uttered by the Holy Ghost were set down in that manner by the sacred scribes in order to accommodate them to the capacities of the common people, who are rude and unlearned. For the sake of those who deserve to be separated from the herd, it is necessary that wise expositors should produce the true senses

of such passages, together with the special reasons for which they were set down in these words. This doctrine is so widespread and so definite with all theologians that it would be superfluous to adduce evidence for it.

Hence I think that I may reasonably conclude that whenever the Bible has occasion to speak of any physical conclusion (especially those which are very abstruse and hard to understand), the rule has been observed of avoiding confusion in the minds of the common people which would render them contumacious toward the higher mysteries. Now the Bible, merely to condescend to popular capacity, has not hesitated to obscure some very important pronouncements, attributing to God himself some qualities extremely remote from (and even contrary to) His essence. Who, then, would positively declare that this principle has been set aside, and the Bible has confined itself rigorously to the bare and restricted sense of its words, when speaking but casually of the earth, of water, of the sun, or of any other created thing? Especially in view of the fact that these things in no way concern the primary purpose of the sacred writings, which is the service of God and the salvation of souls—matters infinitely beyond the comprehension of the common people.

This being granted, I think that in discussions of physical problems we ought to begin not from the authority of scriptural passages, but from sense-experiences and necessary demonstrations; for the holy Bible and the phenomena of nature proceed alike from the divine Word, the former as the dictate of the Holy Ghost and the latter as the observant executrix of God's commands. It is necessary for the Bible, in order to be accommodated to the understanding of every man, to speak many things which appear to differ from the absolute truth so far as the bare meaning of the words is concerned. But Nature, on the other hand, is inexorable and immutable; she never transgresses the laws imposed upon her, or cares a whit whether her abstruse reasons and methods of operation are understandable to men. For that reason it appears that nothing physical which sense-experience sets before our eyes, or which necessary demonstrations prove to us, ought to be called in question (much less condemned) upon the testimony of biblical passages which may have some different meaning beneath their words. For the Bible is not chained in every expression to conditions as strict as those which govern all physical effects; nor is God any less excellently revealed in Nature's actions than in the sacred statements of the Bible. Perhaps this is what Tertullian meant by these words:

"We conclude that God is known first through Nature, and then again, more particularly, by doctrine; by Nature in His works, and by doctrine in His revealed word."[5]

From this I do not mean to infer that we need not have an extraordinary esteem for the passages of holy Scripture. On the contrary, having arrived at any certainties in phys-ics, we ought to utilize these as the most appropriate aids in the true exposition of the Bible and in the investigation of those meanings which are necessarily contained therein, for these must be concordant with demonstrated truths. I should judge that the authority of the Bible was designed to persuade men of those articles and propositions which, surpassing all human reasoning, could not be made credible by science, or by any other means than through the very mouth of the Holy Spirit.

Yet even in those propositions which are not matters of faith, this authority ought to be preferred over that of all human writings which are supported only by bare asser-tions or probable arguments, and not set forth in a demon-strative way. This I hold to be necessary and proper to the same extent that divine wisdom surpasses all human judg-ment and conjecture.

But I do not feel obliged to believe that that same God who has endowed us with senses, reason, and intellect has intended to forgo their use and by some other means to give us knowledge which we can attain by them. He would not require us to deny sense and reason in physical matters which are set before our eyes and minds by direct experi-

[5] *Adversus Marcionem*, ii, 18.

ence or necessary demonstrations. This must be espe-cially true in those sciences of which but the faintest trace (and that consisting of conclusions) is to be found in the Bible. Of astronomy, for instance, so little is found that none of the planets except Venus are so much as mentioned, and this only once or twice under the name of "Lucifer." If the sacred scribes had had any intention of teaching people certain arrangements and motions of the heavenly bodies, or had they wished us to derive such knowledge from the Bible, then in my opinion they would not have spoken of these matters so sparingly in comparison with the infinite number of admirable conclusions which are demonstrated in that science. Far from pretending to teach us the con-stitution and motions of the heavens and the stars, with their shapes, magnitudes, and distances, the authors of the Bible intentionally forbore to speak of these things, though all were quite well known to them. Such is the opinion of the holiest and most learned Fathers, and in St. Augustine we find the following words:

"It is likewise commonly asked what we may believe about the form and shape of the heavens according to the Scriptures, for many contend much about these matters. But with superior prudence our authors have forborne to speak of this, as in no way furthering the student with re-spect to a blessed life—and, more important still, as taking up much of that time which should be spent in holy exer-cises. What is it to me whether heaven, like a sphere, sur-rounds the earth on all sides as a mass balanced in the center of the universe, or whether like a dish it merely covers and overcasts the earth? Belief in Scripture is urged rather for the reason we have often mentioned; that is, in order that no one, through ignorance of divine passages, finding any-thing in our Bibles or hearing anything cited from them of such a nature as may seem to oppose manifest conclusions, should be induced to suspect their truth when they teach, relate, and deliver more profitable matters. Hence let it be said briefly, touching the form of heaven, that our authors knew the truth but the Holy Spirit did not desire that men should learn things that are useful to no one for salvation."[6]

The same disregard of these sacred authors toward beliefs about the phenomena of the celestial bodies is repeated to us by St. Augustine in his next chapter. On the question whether we are to believe that the heaven moves or stands still, he writes thus:

"Some of the brethren raise a question concerning the motion of heaven, whether it is fixed or moved. If it is moved, they say, how is it a firmament? If it stands still, how do these stars which are held fixed in it go round from east to west, the more northerly performing shorter circuits near the pole, so that heaven (if there is another pole unknown to us) may seem to revolve upon some axis, or (if there is no other pole) may be thought to move as a discus? To these men I reply that it would require many subtle and profound reasonings to find out which of these things is actually so; but to undertake this and discuss it is consistent neither with my leisure nor with the duty of those whom I desire to instruct in essential matters more directly conducing to their salvation and to the benefit of the holy Church."[7]

From these things it follows as a necessary consequence that, since the Holy Ghost did not intend to teach us whether heaven moves or stands still, whether its shape is spherical or like a discus or extended in a plane, nor whether the earth is located at its center or off to one side, then so much the less was it intended to settle for us any other conclusion of the same kind. And the motion or rest of the earth and the sun is so closely linked with the things just named, that without a determination of the one, neither side can be taken in the other matters. Now if the Holy Spirit has purposely neglected to teach us propositions of this sort as irrelevant to the highest goal (that is, to our salvation), how can anyone affirm that it is obligatory to take sides on them, and that one belief is required by faith, while the other side is erroneous? Can an opinion be heretical and yet

[6] De Genesi ad literam ii, 9. Galileo has noted also: "The same is to be read in Peter the Lombard, master of opinions."

[7] Ibid., ii, 10.

have no concern with the salvation of souls? Can the Holy Ghost be asserted not to have intended teaching us something that does concern our salvation? I would say here something that was heard from an ecclesiastic of the most eminent degree: "That the intention of the Holy Ghost is to teach us how one goes to heaven, not how heaven goes."[8]

But let us again consider the degree to which necessary demonstrations and sense experiences ought to be respected in physical conclusions, and the authority they have enjoyed at the hands of holy and learned theologians. From among a hundred attestations I have selected the following:

"We must also take heed, in handling the doctrine of Moses, that we altogether avoid saying positively and confidently anything which contradicts manifest experiences and the reasoning of philosophy or the other sciences. For since every truth is in agreement with all other truth, the truth of Holy Writ cannot be contrary to the solid reasons and experiences of human knowledge."[9]

And in St. Augustine we read: "If anyone shall set the authority of Holy Writ against clear and manifest reason, he who does this knows not what he has undertaken; for he opposes to the truth not the meaning of the Bible, which is beyond his comprehension, but rather his own interpretation; not what is in the Bible, but what he has found in himself and imagines to be there."[10]

This granted, and it being true that two truths cannot contradict one another, it is the function of wise expositors to seek out the true senses of scriptural texts. These will unquestionably accord with the physical conclusions which manifest sense and necessary demonstrations have previously made certain to us. Now the Bible, as has been remarked, admits in many places expositions that are remote

[8] A marginal note by Galileo assigns this epigram to Cardinal Baronius (1538-1607). Baronius visited Padua with Cardinal Bellarmine in 1598, and Galileo probably met him at that time.

[9] Pererius on Genesis, near the beginning.

[10] In the seventh letter to Marcellinus.

LETTER TO THE GRAND DUCHESS CHRISTINA 187

from the signification of the words for reasons we have already given. Moreover, we are unable to affirm that all interpreters of the Bible speak by divine inspiration, for if that were so there would exist no differences between them about the sense of a given passage. Hence I should think it would be the part of prudence not to permit anyone to usurp scriptural texts and force them in some way to maintain any physical conclusion to be true, when at some future time the senses and demonstrative or necessary reasons may show the contrary. Who indeed will set bounds to human ingenuity? Who will assert that everything in the universe capable of being perceived is already discovered and known? Let us rather confess quite truly that "Those truths which we know are very few in comparison with those which we do not know."

We have it from the very mouth of the Holy Ghost that God delivered up the world to disputations, *so that man cannot find out the work that God hath done from the beginning even to the end.*[11] In my opinion no one, in contradiction to that dictum, should close the road to free philosophizing about mundane and physical things, as if everything had already been discovered and revealed with certainty. Nor should it be considered rash not to be satisfied with those opinions which have become common. No one should be scorned in physical disputes for not holding to the opinions which happen to please other people best, especially concerning problems which have been debated among the greatest philosophers for thousands of years. One of these is the stability of the sun and mobility of the earth, a doctrine believed by Pythagoras and all his followers, by Heracleides of Pontus[12] (who was one of them),

[11] Ecclesiastes 3:11.

[12] Heracleides was born about 390 B.C. and is said to have attended lectures by Aristotle at Athens. He believed that the earth rotated on its axis, but not that it moved around the sun. He also discovered that Mercury and Venus revolve around the sun, and may have developed a system similar to that of Tycho.

188 DISCOVERIES AND OPINIONS OF GALILEO

by Philolaus the teacher of Plato,[13] and by Plato himself according to Aristotle. Plutarch writes in his *Life of Numa* that Plato, when he had grown old, said it was most absurd to believe otherwise.[14] The same doctrine was held by Aristarchus of Samos,[15] as Archimedes tells us; by Seleucus[16] the mathematician, by Nicetas[17] the philosopher (on the testimony of Cicero), and by many others. Finally this opinion has been amplified and confirmed with many observations and demonstrations by Nicholas Copernicus. And Seneca,[18] a most eminent philosopher, advises us in his book on comets that we should more diligently seek to ascertain whether it is in the sky or in the earth that the diurnal rotation resides.

Hence it would probably be wise and useful counsel if, beyond articles which concern salvation and the establish-

[13] Philolaus, an early follower of Pythagoras, flourished at Thebes toward the end of the fifth century B.C. Although a contemporary of Socrates, the teacher of Plato, he had nothing to do with Plato's instruction. According to Philolaus the earth revolved around a central fire, but not about the sun (cf. note 7, p. 34).

[14] "Plato held opinion in that age, that the earth was in another place than in the very middest, and that the centre of the world, as the most honourable place, did appertain to some other of more worthy substance than the earth." (Trans. Sir Thomas North.) This tradition is no longer accepted.

[15] Aristarchus (ca. 310–230 B.C.) was the true forerunner of Copernicus in antiquity, and not the Pythagoreans as was generally believed in Galileo's time.

[16] Seleucus, who flourished about 150 B.C., is the only ancient astronomer known to have adopted the heliocentric system of Aristarchus. After his time this gave way entirely to the system founded by his contemporary Hipparchus.

[17] Nicetas is an incorrect form given by Copernicus to the name of Hicetas of Syracuse. Of this mathematician nothing is known beyond the fact that some of the ancients credited him instead of Philolaus with the astronomy which came to be associated with the Pythagoreans in general.

[18] Seneca (ca. 3–65 A.D.) was the tutor of Nero. He devoted the seventh book of his *Quaestiones Naturales* to comets. In the second chapter of this book he raised the question of the earth's rotation, and in the final chapters he appealed for patience and further investigation into such matters.

LETTER TO THE GRAND DUCHESS CHRISTINA   189

ment of our Faith, against the stability of which there is no danger whatever that any valid and effective doctrine can ever arise, men would not aggregate further articles unnecessarily. And it would certainly be preposterous to introduce them at the request of persons who, besides not being known to speak by inspiration of divine grace, are clearly seen to lack that understanding which is necessary in order to comprehend, let alone discuss, the demonstrations by which such conclusions are supported in the subtler sciences. If I may speak my opinion freely, I should say further that it would perhaps fit in better with the decorum and majesty of the sacred writings to take measures for preventing every shallow and vulgar writer from giving to his compositions (often grounded upon foolish fancies) an air of authority by inserting in them passages from the Bible, interpreted (or rather distorted) into senses as far from the right meaning of Scripture as those authors are near to absurdity who thus ostentatiously adorn their writings. Of such abuses many examples might be produced, but for the present I shall confine myself to two which are germane to these astronomical matters. The first concerns those writings which were published against the existence of the Medicean planets recently discovered by me, in which many passages of holy Scripture were cited.[19] Now that everyone has seen these planets, I should like to know what new interpretations those same antagonists employ in expounding the Scripture and excusing their own sim-

190   DISCOVERIES AND OPINIONS OF GALILEO

plicity. My other example is that of a man who has lately published, in defiance of astronomers and philosophers, the opinion that the moon does not receive its light from the sun but is brilliant by its own nature.[20] He supports this fancy (or rather thinks he does) by sundry texts of Scripture which he believes cannot be explained unless his theory is true; yet that the moon is inherently dark is surely as plain as daylight.

It is obvious that such authors, not having penetrated the true senses of Scripture, would impose upon others an obligation to subscribe to conclusions that are repugnant to manifest reason and sense, if they had any authority to do so. God forbid that this sort of abuse should gain countenance and authority, for then in a short time it would be necessary to proscribe all the contemplative sciences. People who are unable to understand perfectly both the Bible and the sciences far outnumber those who do understand. The former, glancing superficially through the Bible, would arrogate to themselves the authority to decree upon every question of physics on the strength of some word which they have misunderstood, and which was employed by the sacred authors for some different purpose. And the smaller number of understanding men could not dam up the furious torrent of such people, who would gain the majority of followers simply because it is much more pleasant to gain a reputation for wisdom without effort or study than to consume oneself tirelessly in the most laborious disciplines. Let us therefore render thanks to Almighty God, who in His beneficence protects us from this danger by depriving such persons of all authority, reposing the power of consultation, decision, and decree on such important matters in the high wisdom and benevolence of most prudent

[19] The principal book which had offended in this regard was the *Dianoia Astronomica . . .* of Francesco Sizzi (Venice, 1611). About the time Galileo arrived at Florence, Sizzi departed for France, where he came into association with some good mathematicians. In 1613 he wrote to a friend at Rome to express his admiration of Galileo's work on floating bodies and to deride its opponents. The letter was forwarded to Galileo. In it Sizzi had reported, though rather cryptically, upon some French observations concerning sunspots, and it was probably this which led Galileo to his knowledge of the tilt of the sun's axis (cf. note 14, p. 125). Sizzi was broken on the wheel in 1617 for writing a pamphlet against the king of France.

[20] This is frequently said to refer to J. C. Lagalla's *De phaenominis in orbe lunae . . .* (Venice, 1612), a wretched book which has the sole distinction of being the first to mention the word "telescope" in print. A more probable reference, however, seems to be to the *Dialogo di Fr. Ulisse Albergotti . . . nel quale si tiene . . . la Luna esser da sé luminosa . . .* (Viterbo, 1613).

Fathers, and in the supreme authority of those who cannot fail to order matters properly under the guidance of the Holy Ghost. Hence we need not concern ourselves with the shallowness of those men whom grave and holy authors rightly reproach, and of whom in particular St. Jerome said, in reference to the Bible:

"This is ventured upon, lacerated, and taught by the garrulous old woman, the doting old man, and the prattling sophist before they have learned it. Others, led on by pride, weigh heavy words and philosophize amongst women concerning holy Scripture. Others—oh, shame!—learn from women what they teach to men, and (as if that were not enough) glibly expound to others that which they themselves do not understand. I forbear to speak of those of my own profession who, attaining a knowledge of the holy Scriptures after mundane learning, tickle the ears of the people with affected and studied expressions, and declare that everything they say is to be taken as the law of God. Not bothering to learn what the prophets and the apostles have maintained, they wrest incongruous testimonies into their own senses—as if distorting passages and twisting the Bible to their individual and contradictory whims were the genuine way of teaching, and not a corrupt one."[21]

I do not wish to place in the number of such lay writers some theologians whom I consider men of profound learning and devout behavior, and who are therefore held by me in great esteem and veneration. Yet I cannot deny that I feel some discomfort which I should like to have removed, when I hear them pretend to the power of constraining others by scriptural authority to follow in a physical dispute that opinion which they think best agrees with the Bible, and then believe themselves not bound to answer the opposing reasons and experiences. In explanation and support of this opinion they say that since theology is queen of all the sciences, she need not bend in any way to accommodate herself to the teachings of less worthy sciences which are subordinate to her; these others must rather be referred to

[21] *Epistola ad Paulinum*, 103.

her as to their supreme empress, changing and altering their conclusions according to her statutes and decrees. They add further that if in the inferior sciences any conclusion should be taken as certain in virtue of demonstrations or experiences, while in the Bible another conclusion is found repugnant to this, then the professors of that science should themselves undertake to undo their proofs and discover the fallacies in their own experiences, without bothering the theologians and exegetes. For, they say, it does not become the dignity of theology to stoop to the investigation of fallacies in the subordinate sciences; it is sufficient for her merely to determine the truth of a given conclusion with absolute authority, secure in her inability to err.

Now the physical conclusions in which they say we ought to be satisfied by Scripture, without glossing or expounding it in senses different from the literal, are those concerning which the Bible always speaks in the same manner and which the holy Fathers all receive and expound in the same way. But with regard to these judgments I have had occasion to consider several things, and I shall set them forth in order that I may be corrected by those who understand more than I do in these matters—for to their decisions I submit at all times.

First, I question whether there is not some equivocation in failing to specify the virtues which entitle sacred theology to the title of "queen." It might deserve that name by reason of including everything that is learned from all the other sciences and establishing everything by better methods and with profounder learning. It is thus, for example, that the rules for measuring fields and keeping accounts are much more excellently contained in arithmetic and in the geometry of Euclid than in the practices of surveyors and accountants. Or theology might be queen because of being occupied with a subject which excels in dignity all the subjects which compose the other sciences, and because her teachings are divulged in more sublime ways.

That the title and authority of queen belongs to theology in the first sense, I think will not be affirmed by theologians who have any skill in the other sciences. None of these, I think, will say that geometry, astronomy, music, and medicine are much more excellently contained in the Bible than they are in the books of Archimedes, Ptolemy, Boethius, and Galen. Hence it seems likely that regal pre-eminence is given to theology in the second sense; that is, by reason of its subject and the miraculous communication of divine revelation of conclusions which could not be conceived by men in any other way, concerning chiefly the attainment of eternal blessedness.

Let us grant then that theology is conversant with the loftiest divine contemplation, and occupies the regal throne among sciences by dignity. But acquiring the highest authority in this way, if she does not descend to the lower and humbler speculations of the subordinate sciences and has no regard for them because they are not concerned with blessedness, then her professors should not arrogate to themselves the authority to decide on controversies in professions which they have neither studied nor practiced. Why, this would be as if an absolute despot, being neither a physician nor an architect but knowing himself free to command, should undertake to administer medicines and erect buildings according to his whim—at grave peril of his poor patients' lives, and the speedy collapse of his edifices.

Again, to command that the very professors of astronomy themselves see to the refutation of their own observations and proofs as mere fallacies and sophisms is to enjoin something that lies beyond any possibility of accomplishment. For this would amount to commanding that they must not see what they see and must not understand what they know, and that in searching they must find the opposite of what they actually encounter. Before this could be done they would have to be taught how to make one mental faculty command another, and the inferior powers the superior, so that the imagination and the will might be forced to believe the opposite of what the intellect understands. I am referring at all times to merely physical propositions, and not to supernatural things which are matters of faith.

I entreat those wise and prudent Fathers to consider with

great care the difference that exists between doctrines subject to proof and those subject to opinion. Considering the force exerted by logical deductions, they may ascertain that it is not in the power of the professors of demonstrative sciences to change their opinions at will and apply themselves first to one side and then to the other. There is a great difference between commanding a mathematician or a philosopher and influencing a lawyer or a merchant, for demonstrated conclusions about things in nature or in the heavens cannot be changed with the same facility as opinions about what is or is not lawful in a contract, bargain, or bill of exchange. This difference was well understood by the learned and holy Fathers, as proven by their having taken great pains in refuting philosophical fallacies. This may be found expressly in some of them; in particular, we find the following words of St. Augustine: "It is to be held as an unquestionable truth that whatever the sages of this world have demonstrated concerning physical matters is in no way contrary to our Bibles; hence whatever the sages teach in their books that is contrary to the holy Scriptures may be concluded without any hesitation to be quite false. And according to our ability let us make this evident, and let us keep the faith of our Lord, in whom are hidden all the treasures of wisdom, so that we neither become seduced by the verbiage of false philosophy nor frightened by the superstition of counterfeit religion."[22]

From the above words I conceive that I may deduce this doctrine: That in the books of the sages of this world there are contained some physical truths which are soundly demonstrated, and others that are merely stated; as to the former, it is the office of wise divines to show that they do not contradict the holy Scriptures. And as to the propositions which are stated but not rigorously demonstrated, anything contrary to the Bible involved by them must be held undoubtedly false and should be proved so by every possible means.

Now if truly demonstrated physical conclusions need not

[22] *De Genesi ad literam* i, 21.

LETTER TO THE GRAND DUCHESS CHRISTINA 195

be subordinated to biblical passages, but the latter must rather be shown not to interfere with the former, then before a physical proposition is condemned it must be shown to be not rigorously demonstrated—and this is to be done not by those who hold the proposition to be true, but by those who judge it to be false. This seems very reasonable and natural, for those who believe an argument to be false may much more easily find the fallacies in it than men who consider it to be true and conclusive. Indeed, in the latter case it will happen that the more the adherents of an opinion turn over their pages, examine the arguments, repeat the observations, and compare the experiences, the more they will be confirmed in that belief. And Your Highness knows what happened to the late mathematician of the University of Pisa[23] who undertook in his old age to look into the Copernican doctrine in the hope of shaking its foundations and refuting it, since he considered it false only because he had never studied it. As it fell out, no sooner had he understood its grounds, procedures, and demonstrations than he found himself persuaded, and from an opponent he became a very staunch defender of it. I might also name other mathematicians[24] who, moved by my latest discoveries, have confessed it necessary to alter the previously accepted system of the world, as this is simply unable to subsist any longer.

If in order to banish the opinion in question from the world it were sufficient to stop the mouth of a single man—as perhaps those men persuade themselves who, measuring the minds of others by their own, think it impossible that this doctrine should be able to continue to find adherents—then that would be very easily done. But things stand otherwise. To carry out such a decision it would be necessary not only to prohibit the book of Copernicus and the writings of other authors who follow the same opinion, but to ban the whole science of astronomy. Furthermore, it would be necessary to forbid men to look at the heavens, in order that

[23] Antonio Santucci (d. 1613).
[24] A marginal note by Galileo here mentions Father Clavius; cf. p. 153.

196 DISCOVERIES AND OPINIONS OF GALILEO

they might not see Mars and Venus sometimes quite near the earth and sometimes very distant, the variation being so great that Venus is forty times and Mars sixty times as large at one time as another. And it would be necessary to prevent Venus being seen round at one time and forked at another, with very thin horns; as well as many other sensory observations which can never be reconciled with the Ptolemaic system in any way, but are very strong arguments for the Copernican. And to ban Copernicus now that his doctrine is daily reinforced by many new observations and by the learned applying themselves to the reading of his book, after this opinion has been allowed and tolerated for those many years during which it was less followed and less confirmed, would seem in my judgment to be a contravention of truth, and an attempt to hide and supress her the more as she revealed herself the more clearly and plainly. Not to abolish and censure his whole book, but only to condemn as erroneous this particular proposition, would (if I am not mistaken) be a still greater detriment to the minds of men, since it would afford them occasion to see a proposition proved that it was heresy to believe. And to prohibit the whole science would be but to censure a hundred passages of holy Scripture which teach us that the glory and greatness of Almighty God are marvelously discerned in all his works and divinely read in the open book of heaven. For let no one believe that reading the lofty concepts written in that book leads to nothing further than the mere seeing of the splendor of the sun and the stars and their rising and setting, which is as far as the eyes of brutes and of the vulgar can penetrate. Within its pages are couched mysteries so profound and concepts so sublime that the vigils, labors, and studies of hundreds upon hundreds of the most acute minds have still not pierced them, even after continual investigations for thousands of years. The eyes of an idiot perceive little by beholding the external appearance of a human body, as compared with the wonderful contrivances which a careful and practiced anatomist or philosopher discovers in that same body when he seeks out the use of all those muscles, tendons, nerves, and bones; or when examining the functions of the heart and the other principal organs, he seeks the seat of the vital faculties, notes and observes the admirable structure of the sense organs, and (without ever ceasing in his amazement and delight) contemplates the receptacles of the imagination, the memory, and the understanding. Likewise, that which presents itself to mere sight is as nothing in comparison with the high marvels that the ingenuity of learned men discovers in the heavens by long and accurate observation. And that concludes what I have to say on this matter.

Next let us answer those who assert that those physical propositions of which the Bible speaks always in one way, and which the Fathers all harmoniously accept in the same sense, must be taken according to the literal sense of the words without glosses or interpretations, and held as most certain and true. The motion of the sun and stability of the earth, they say, is of this sort; hence it is a matter of faith to believe in them, and the contrary view is erroneous.

To this I wish first to remark that among physical propositions there are some with regard to which all human science and reason cannot supply more than a plausible opinion and a probable conjecture in place of a sure and demonstrated knowledge; for example, whether the stars are animate. Then there are other propositions of which we have (or may confidently expect) positive assurances through experiments, long observation, and rigorous demonstration; for example, whether or not the earth and the heavens move, and whether or not the heavens are spherical. As to the first sort of propositions, I have no doubt that where human reasoning cannot reach—and where consequently we can have no science but only opinion and faith—it is necessary in piety to comply absolutely with the strict sense of Scripture. But as to the other kind, I should think, as said before, that first we are to make certain of the fact, which will reveal to us the true senses of the Bible, and these will most certainly be found to agree with the proved fact (even though at first the words sounded otherwise), for two truths can never contradict each other. I take this to be an orthodox and indisputable doctrine, and I find it

specifically in St. Augustine when he speaks of the shape of heaven and what we may believe concerning that. Astronomers seem to declare what is contrary to Scripture, for they hold the heavens to be spherical, while the Scripture calls it "stretched out like a curtain."[25] St. Augustine opines that we are not to be concerned lest the Bible contradict astronomers; we are to believe its authority if what they say is false and is founded only on the conjectures of frail humanity. But if what they say is proved by unquestionable arguments, this holy Father does not say that the astronomers are to be ordered to dissolve their proofs and declare their own conclusions to be false. Rather, he says it must be demonstrated that what is meant in the Bible by "curtain" is not contrary to their proofs. Here are his words:

"But some raise the following objection. 'How is it that the passage in our Bibles, *Who stretcheth out the heavens as a curtain*, does not contradict those who maintain the heavens to have a spherical shape?' It does contradict them if what they affirm is false, for that is true which is spoken by divine authority rather than that which proceeds from human frailty. But if, peradventure, they should be able to prove their position by experiences which place it beyond question, then it is to be demonstrated that our speaking of a curtain in no way contradicts their manifest reasons."[26]

He then proceeds to admonish us that we must be no less careful and observant in reconciling a passage of the Bible with any demonstrated physical proposition than with some other biblical passage which might appear contrary to the first. The circumspection of this saint indeed deserves admiration and imitation, when even in obscure conclusions (of which we surely can have no knowledge through human proofs) he shows great reserve in determining what is to be believed. We see this from what he writes at the end of the second book of his commentary on Genesis, concerning the question whether the stars are to be believed animate:

[25] Psalms 103:2 (Douay); 104:2 (King James).
[26] *De Genesi ad literam* [ii 1 o].

"Although at present this matter cannot be settled, yet I suppose that in our further dealing with the Bible we may meet with other relevant passages, and then we may be permitted, if not to determine anything finally, at least to gain some hint concerning this matter according to the dictates of sacred authority. Now keeping always our respect for moderation in grave piety, we ought not to believe anything inadvisedly on a dubious point, lest in favor of our error we conceive a prejudice against something that truth hereafter may reveal to be not contrary in any way to the sacred books of either the Old or the New Testament."

From this and other passages the intention of the holy Fathers appears to be (if I am not mistaken) that in questions of nature which are not matters of faith it is first to be considered whether anything is demonstrated beyond doubt or known by sense-experience, or whether such knowledge or proof is possible; if it is, then, being the gift of God, it ought to be applied to find out the true senses of holy Scripture in those passages which superficially might seem to declare differently. These senses would unquestionably be discovered by wise theologians, together with the reasons for which the Holy Ghost sometimes wished to veil itself under words of different meaning, whether for our exercise, or for some purpose unknown to me.

As to the other point, if we consider the primary aim of the Bible, I do not think that its having always spoken in the same sense need disturb this rule. If the Bible, accommodating itself to the capacity of the common people, has on one occasion expressed a proposition in words of different sense from the essence of that proposition, then why might it not have done the same, and for the same reason, whenever the same thing happened to be spoken of? Nay, to me it seems that not to have done this would but have increased confusion and diminished belief among the people.

Regarding the state of rest or motion of the sun and earth, experience plainly proves that in order to accommodate the common people it was necessary to assert of these things precisely what the words of the Bible convey. Even in our own age, people far less primitive continue to maintain the same opinion for reasons which will be found extremely trivial if well weighed and examined, and upon the basis of experiences that are wholly false or altogether beside the point. Nor is it worth while to try to change their opinion, they being unable to understand the arguments on the opposite side, for these depend upon observations too precise and demonstrations too subtle, grounded on abstractions which require too strong an imagination to be comprehended by them. Hence even if the stability of heaven and the motion of the earth should be more than certain in the minds of the wise, it would still be necessary to assert the contrary for the preservation of belief among the all-too-numerous vulgar. Among a thousand ordinary men who might be questioned concerning these things, probably not a single one will be found to answer anything except that it looks to him as if the sun moves and the earth stands still, and therefore he believes this to be certain. But one need not on that account take the common popular assent as an argument for the truth of what is stated; for if we should examine these very men concerning their reasons for what they believe, and on the other hand listen to the experiences and proofs which induce a few others to believe the contrary, we should find the latter to be persuaded by very sound arguments, and the former by simple appearances and vain or ridiculous impressions.

It is sufficiently obvious that to attribute motion to the sun and rest to the earth was therefore necessary lest the shallow minds of the common people should become confused, obstinate, and contumacious in yielding assent to the principal articles that are absolutely matters of faith. And if this was necessary, there is no wonder at all that it was carried out with great prudence in the holy Bible. I shall say further that not only respect for the incapacity of the vulgar, but also current opinion in those times, made the sacred authors accommodate themselves (in matters unnecessary to salvation) more to accepted usage than to the true essence of things. Speaking of this, St. Jerome writes:

"As if many things were not spoken in the Holy Bible according to the judgment of those times in which they were acted, rather than according to the truth contained."27 And elsewhere the same saint says: "It is the custom for the biblical scribes to deliver their judgments in many things according to the commonly received opinion of their times."28 And on the words in the twenty-sixth chapter of Job, *He stretcheth out the north over the void, and hangeth the earth above nothing*,29 St. Thomas Aquinas notes that the Bible calls "void" or "nothing" that space which we know to be not empty, but filled with air. Nevertheless the Bible, he says, in order to accommodate itself to the beliefs of the common people (who think there is nothing in that space), calls it "void" and "nothing." Here are the words of St. Thomas: "What appears to us in the upper hemisphere of the heavens to be empty, and not a space filled with air, the common people regard as void; and it is usually spoken of in the holy Bible according to the ideas of the common people."30

Now from this passage I think one may very logically argue that for the same reason the Bible had still more cause to call the sun movable and the earth immovable. For if we were to test the capacity of the common people, we should find them even less apt to be persuaded of the stability of the sun and the motion of the earth than to believe that the space which environs the earth is filled with air. And if on this point it would not have been difficult to convince the common people, and yet the holy scribes forbore to attempt it, then it certainly must appear reasonable that in other and more abstruse propositions they have followed the same policy.

Copernicus himself knew the power over our ideas that is exerted by custom and by our inveterate way of conceiving things since infancy. Hence, in order not to increase for us the confusion and difficulty of abstraction, after he had

27 On Jeremiah, ch. 28.
28 On Matthew, ch. 13.
29 Job 26:7.
30 Aquinas on Job.

first demonstrated that the motions which appear to us to belong to the sun or to the firmament are really not there but in the firmament, he went on calling them motions of the sun and of the heavens when he later constructed his tables to apply them to use. He thus speaks of "sunrise" and "sunset," of the "rising and setting" of the stars, of changes in the obliquity of the ecliptic and of variations in the equinoctial points, of the mean motion and variations in motion of the sun, and so on. All these things really relate to the earth, but since we are fixed to the earth and consequently share in its every motion, we cannot discover them in the earth directly, and are obliged to refer them to the heavenly bodies in which they make their appearance to us. Hence we name them as if they took place where they appear to us to take place; and from this one may see how natural it is to accommodate things to our customary way of seeing them.

Next we come to the proposition that agreement on the part of the Fathers, when they all accept a physical proposition from the Bible in the same sense, must give that sense authority to such a degree that belief in it becomes a matter of faith. I think this should be granted at most only of those propositions which have actually been discussed by the Fathers with great diligence, and debated on both sides, with them all finally concurring in the censure of one side and the adoption of the other. But the motion of the earth and stability of the sun is not an opinion of that kind, inasmuch as it was completely hidden in those times and was far removed from the questions of the schools; it was not even considered, much less adhered to, by anyone. Hence we may believe that it never so much as entered the thoughts of the Fathers to debate this. Bible texts, their own opinions, and the agreement of all men concurred in one belief, without meeting contradiction from anyone. Hence it is not sufficient to say that because all the Fathers admitted the stability of the earth, this is a matter of faith; one would have to prove also that they had condemned the contrary opinion. And I may go on to say that they left this out because they had no occasion to reflect upon the matter and discuss it; their opinion was admitted only as current, and not as analyzed and determined. I think I have very good reason for saying this.

Either the Fathers reflected upon this conclusion as controversial, or they did not; if not, then they cannot have decided anything about it even in their own minds, and their incognizance of it does not oblige us to accept teaching which they never imposed, even in intention. But if they had reflected upon and considered it, and if they judged it to be erroneous, then they would long ago have condemned it; and this they are not found to have done. Indeed, some theologians have but now begun to consider it, and they are not seen to deem it erroneous. Thus in the *Commentaries on Job* of Didacus à Stunica, where the author comments upon the words *Who moveth the earth from its place . . .*,[31] he discourses at length upon the Copernican opinion and concludes that the mobility of the earth is not contrary to Scripture.

Besides, I question the truth of the statement that the church commands us to hold as matters of faith all physical conclusions bearing the stamp of harmonious interpretation by all the Fathers. I think this may be an arbitrary simplification of various council decrees by certain people to favor their own opinion. So far as I can find, all that is really prohibited is the "perverting into senses contrary to that of the holy Church or that of the concurrent agreement of the Fathers those passages, and those alone, which concern the edification of Christian doctrine." So said the Council of Trent in its fourth session. But the mobility or stability of the earth or sun is neither a matter of faith nor one contrary to ethics. Neither would anyone pervert passages of Scripture in opposition to the holy Church or to the Fathers, for those who have written on this matter have never employed scriptural passages. Hence it remains the office of grave and wise theologians to interpret the passages according to their true meaning.

[31] Job 9:6. The commentary was that of Didacus à Stunica, published at Toledo in 1584; cf. p. 219.

Council decrees are indeed in agreement with the holy Fathers in these matters, as may be seen from the fact that they abstain from enjoining us to receive physical conclusions as matters of faith, and from censuring the opposite opinions as erroneous. Attending to the primary and original intention of the holy Church, they judge it useless to be occupied in attempting to get to the bottom of such matters. Let me remind Your Highness again of St. Augustine's reply to those brethren who raised the question whether the heavens really move or stand still: "To these men I reply that it would require many subtle and profound reasonings to find out which of these things is actually so; but to undertake this and discuss it is consistent neither with my leisure nor with the duty of those whom I desire to instruct in essential matters more directly conducive to their salvation and to the benefit of the holy Church."[32]

Yet even if we resolved to condemn or admit physical propositions according to scriptural passages uniformly expounded in the same sense by all the Fathers, I still fail to see how that rule can apply in the present case, inasmuch as diverse expositions of the same passage occur among the Fathers. Dionysius the Areopagite says that it is the *primum mobile*[33] which stood still, not the sun.[34] St. Augustine is of the same opinion; that is, that all celestial bodies would be stopped; and the Bishop of Avila concurs.[35] What is

[32] Cf. note 6, p. 185.

[33] The outermost crystalline sphere was known as the *primum mobile*, or prime mover, and was supposed to complete each revolution in twenty-four hours, causing night and day. A part of its motion was imagined to be transmitted to each inner sphere, sweeping along the fixed stars and the planets (which included the sun and moon) at nearly its own speed. The inherent motion of the other spheres was supposed to be eastward at much slower rates. In the case of the sun, this speed would have the same proportion to that of the *primum mobile* as a day has to a year.

[34] In the *Epistola ad Polycarpum.*

[35] In the second book of St. Augustine's *De Mirabilius Sacrae Scripturae.* The Bishop of Avila referred to was Alfonso

more, among the Jewish authors endorsed by Josephus,[36] some held that the sun did not really stand still, but that it merely appeared to do so by reason of the shortness of the time during which the Israelites administered defeat to their enemies. (Similarly, with regard to the miracle in the time of Hezekiah, Paul of Burgos was of the opinion that this took place not in the sun but on the sundial.)[37] And as a matter of fact no matter what system of the universe we assume, it is still necessary to gloss and interpret the words in the text of Joshua, as I shall presently show.

But finally let us grant to these gentlemen even more than they demand; namely, let us admit that we must subscribe entirely to the opinion of wise theologians. Then, since this particular dispute does not occur among the ancient Fathers, it must be undertaken by the wise men of this age. After first hearing the experiences, observations, arguments, and proofs of philosophers and astronomers on both sides—for the controversy is over physical problems and logical dilemmas, and admits of no third alternative—they will be able to determine the matter positively, in accordance with the dictates of divine inspiration. But as to those men who do not scruple to hazard the majesty and dignity of holy Scripture to uphold the reputation of their own vain fancies, let them not hope that a decision such as this is to be made without minutely airing and discussing all the arguments on both sides. Nor need we fear this from men who will make it their whole business to examine most attentively the very foundations of this doctrine, and who will do so only in a holy zeal for the truth, the Bible, and the majesty, dignity, and authority in which every Christian wants to see these maintained.

Anyone can see that dignity is most desired and best secured by those who submit themselves absolutely to the

Tostado (1400–55), and the reference is to his twenty-second and twenty-fourth questions on the tenth chapter of Joshua.
[36] Flavius Josephus (ca. 37–95 A.D.), historian of the Jews.
[37] Isaiah 38:8. Paul of Burgos (ca. 1350–1435), also known as Paul de Santa Maria, was a Jewish convert to Christianity who became Bishop of Burgos.

holy Church and do not demand that one opinion or another be prohibited, but merely ask the right to propose things for consideration which may the better guarantee the soundest decision—not by those who, driven by personal interest or stimulated by malicious hints, preach that the Church should flash her sword without delay simply because she has the power to do so. Such men fail to realize that it is not always profitable to do everything that lies within one's power. The most holy Fathers did not share their views. They knew how prejudicial (and how contrary to the primary intention of the Catholic Church) it would be to use scriptural passages for deciding physical conclusions, when either experiments or logical proofs might in time show the contrary of what the literal sense of the words signifies. Hence they not only proceeded with great circumspection, but they left the following precepts for the guidance of others: "In points that are obscure, or far from clear, if we should read anything in the Bible that may allow of several constructions consistently with the faith to be taught, let us not commit ourselves to any one of these with such precipitous obstinacy that when, perhaps, the truth is more diligently searched into, this may fall to the ground, and we with it. Then we would indeed be seen to have contended not for the sense of divine Scripture, but for our own ideas by wanting something of ours to be the sense of Scripture when we should rather want the meaning of Scripture to be ours."[38] And later it is added, to teach us that no proposition can be contrary to the faith unless it has first been proven to be false: "A thing is not forever contrary to the faith until disproved by most certain truth. When that happens, it was not holy Scripture that ever affirmed it, but human ignorance that imagined it."

From this it is seen that the interpretation which we impose upon passages of Scripture would be false whenever it disagreed with demonstrated truths. And therefore we should seek the incontrovertible sense of the Bible with the

[38] This and the ensuing quotations from St. Augustine are referred to De Genesi ad litteram i, 18 and 19.

assistance of demonstrated truth, and not in any way try to force the hand of Nature or deny experiences and rigorous proofs in accordance with the mere sound of words that may appeal to our frailty. Let Your Highness note further how circumspectly this saint proceeds before affirming any interpretation of Scripture to be certain and secure from all disturbing difficulties. Not content that some given sense of the Bible agrees with some demonstration, he adds: "But when some truth is demonstrated to be certain by reason, it is still not certain whether in these words of holy Scripture the writer intended this idea, or some other that is no less true. And if the context of his words prove that he did not intend this truth, the one that he did intend will not thereby be false, but most true, and still more profitable for us to know." Our admiration of the circumspection of this pious author only grows when he adds the following words, being not completely convinced after seeing that logical proof, the literal words of the Bible, and all the context before and after them harmonize in the same thing: "But if the context supplies nothing to disprove this to be the author's sense, it yet remains for us to inquire whether he may not intend the other as well." Nor even yet does he resolve to accept this one interpretation and reject the other, appearing never to be able to employ sufficient caution, for he continues: "But if we find that the other also may be meant, it may be inquired which of them the writer would want to have stand, or which one he probably meant to aim at, when the true circumstances on both sides are weighed." And finally he supplies a reason for this rule of his, by showing us the perils to which those men expose the Bible and the Church, who, with more regard for the support of their own errors than for the dignity of the Bible, attempt to stretch its authority beyond the bounds which it prescribes to itself. The following words which he adds should alone be sufficient to repress or moderate the excessive license which some men arrogate to themselves: "It often falls out that a Christian may not fully understand some point about the earth, the sky, or the other elements of this world—the motion, rotation, magnitude,

and distances of the stars; the known vagaries of the sun and moon; the circuits of the years and epochs; the nature of animals, fruits, stones, and other things of that sort, and hence may not expound it rightly or make it clear by experiences. Now it is too absurd, yea, most pernicious and to be avoided at all costs, for an infidel to find a Christian so stupid as to argue these matters as if they were Christian doctrine; he will scarce be able to contain his laughter at seeing error written in the skies, as the proverb says. The worst of the matter is not that a person in error should be laughed at, but that our authors should be thought by outsiders to hold the same opinions, and should be censured and rejected as ignorant, to the great prejudice of those whose salvation we are seeking. For when infidels refute any Christian on a matter which they thoroughly understand, they thereby evince their slight esteem for our Bible. And why should the Bible be believed concerning the resurrection of the dead, the hope of eternal life, and the Kingdom of Heaven, when it is considered to be erroneously written as to points which admit of direct demonstration or unquestionable reasoning?"

There are men who, in defense of propositions which they do not understand, apply—and in a way commit—some text of the Bible, and then proceed to magnify their original error by adducing other passages that are even less understood than the first. The extent to which truly wise and prudent Fathers are offended by such men is declared by the same saint in the following terms: "Inexpressible trouble and sorrow are brought by rash and presumptuous men upon their more prudent brethren. When those who respect the authority of our Bible commence to reprove and refute their false and unfounded opinions, such men defend what they have put forth quite falsely and rashly by citing the Bible in their own support, repeating from memory biblical passages which they arbitrarily force to their purposes, without knowing either what they mean or to what they properly apply."

It seems to me that we may number among such men those who, being either unable or unwilling to comprehend the experiences and proofs used in support of the new doctrine by its author and his followers, nevertheless expect to bring the Scriptures to bear on it. They do not consider that the more they cite these, and the more they insist that they are perfectly clear and admit of no other interpretations than those which they put on them, the more they prejudice the dignity of the Bible—or would, if their opinion counted for anything—in the event that later truth shows the contrary and thus creates confusion among those outside the holy Church. And of these she is very solicitous, like a mother desiring to recover her children into her lap.

Your Highness may thus see how irregularly those persons proceed who in physical disputes arrange scriptural passages (and often those ill-understood by them) in the front rank of their arguments. If these men really believe themselves to have the true sense of a given passage, it necessarily follows that they believe they have in hand the absolute truth of the conclusion they intend to debate. Hence they must know that they enjoy a great advantage over their opponents, whose lot it is to defend the false position; and he who maintains the truth will have many sense-experiences and rigorous proofs on his side, whereas his antagonist cannot make use of anything but illusory appearances, quibbles, and fallacies. Now if these men know they have such advantages over the enemy even when they stay within proper bounds and produce no weapons other than those proper to philosophy, why do they, in the thick of battle, betake themselves to a dreadful weapon which cannot be turned aside, and seek to vanquish the opponent by merely exhibiting it? If I may speak frankly, I believe they have themselves been vanquished, and, feeling unable to stand up against the assaults of the adversary, they seek ways of holding him off. To that end they would forbid him the use of reason, divine gift of Providence, and would abuse the just authority of holy Scripture—which, in the general opinion of theologians, can never oppose manifest experiences and necessary demonstrations when rightly understood and applied. If I am correct, it will stand them in no stead to go running to the Bible to cover up

their inability to understand (let alone resolve) their opponents' arguments, for the opinion which they fight has never been condemned by the holy Church. If they wish to proceed in sincerity, they should by silence confess themselves unable to deal with such matters. Let them freely admit that although they may argue that a position is false, it is not in their power to censure a position as erroneous—or in the power of anyone except the Supreme Pontiff, or the Church Councils. Reflecting upon this, and knowing that a proposition cannot be both true and heretical, let them employ themselves in the business which is proper to them; namely, demonstrating its falsity. And when that is revealed, either there will no longer be any necessity to prohibit it (since it will have no followers), or else it may safely be prohibited without the risk of any scandal.

Therefore let these men begin to apply themselves to an examination of the arguments of Copernicus and others, leaving condemnation of the doctrine as erroneous and heretical to the proper authorities. Among the circumspect and most wise Fathers, and in the absolute wisdom of one who cannot err, they may never hope to find the rash decisions into which they allow themselves to be hurried by some particular passion or personal interest. With regard to this opinion, and others which are not directly matters of faith, certainly no one doubts that the Supreme Pontiff has always an absolute power to approve or condemn; but it is not in the power of any created being to make things true or false, for this belongs to their own nature and to the fact. Therefore in my judgment one should first be assured of the necessary and immutable truth of the fact, over which no man has power. This is wiser counsel than to condemn either side in the absence of such certainty, thus depriving oneself of continued authority and ability to choose by determining things which are now undetermined and open and still lodged in the will of supreme authority. And in brief, if it is impossible for a conclusion to be declared heretical while we remain in doubt as to its truth, then these men are wasting their time clamoring for condemnation of the motion of the earth and stability of the sun, which they have not yet demonstrated to be impossible or false.

Now let us consider the extent to which it is true that the famous passage in Joshua may be accepted without altering the literal meaning of its words, and under what conditions the day might be greatly lengthened by obedience of the sun to Joshua's command that it stand still.

If the celestial motions are taken according to the Ptolemaic system, this could never happen at all. For the movement of the sun through the ecliptic is from west to east, and hence it is opposite to the movement of the *primum mobile*, which in that system causes day and night. Therefore it is obvious that if the sun should cease its own proper motion, the day would become shorter, and not longer. The way to lengthen the day would be to speed up the sun's proper motion; and to cause the sun to remain above the horizon for some time in one place without declining towards the west, it would be necessary to hasten this motion until it was equal to that of the *primum mobile*. This would amount to accelerating the customary speed of the sun about three hundred sixty times. Therefore if Joshua had intended his words to be taken in their pure and proper sense, he would have ordered the sun to accelerate its own motion in such a way that the impulse from the *primum mobile* would not carry it westward. But since his words were to be heard by people who very likely knew nothing of any celestial motions beyond the great general movement from east to west, he stooped to their capacity and spoke according to their understanding, as he had no intention of teaching them the arrangement of the spheres, but merely of having them perceive the greatness of the miracle. Possibly it was this consideration that first moved Dionysius the Areopagite to say that in this miracle it was the *primum mobile* that stood still, and that when this halted, all the celestial spheres stopped as a consequence —an opinion held in detail by the Bishop of Avila. And indeed Joshua did intend the whole system of celestial spheres to stand still, as may be deduced from his simultaneous command to the

moon, which had nothing to do with lengthening the day. And under his command to the moon we are to understand the other planets as well, though they are passed over in silence here as elsewhere in the Bible, which was not written to teach us astronomy.

It therefore seems very clear to me that if we were to accept the Ptolemaic system it would be necessary to interpret the words in some sense different from their strict meaning. Admonished by the useful precepts of St. Augustine, I shall not affirm this to be necessarily the above sense, as someone else may think of another that is more proper and harmonious. But I wish to consider next whether this very event may not be understood more consistently with what we read in the Book of Joshua in terms of the Copernican system, adding a further observation recently pointed out by me in the body of the sun. Yet I speak always with caution and reserve, and not with such great affection for my own inventions as to prefer them above those of others, or in the belief that nothing can be brought forth that will be still more in conformity with the intention of the Bible.

Suppose, then, that in the miracle of Joshua the whole system of celestial rotations stood still, in accordance with the opinion of the authors named above. Now in order that all the arrangements should not be disturbed by stopping only a single celestial body, introducing great disorder throughout the whole of Nature, I shall next assume that the sun, though fixed in one place, nevertheless revolves upon its own axis, making a complete revolution in about a month, as I believe is conclusively proven in my *Letters on Sunspots*. With our own eyes we see this movement to be slanted toward the south in the more remote part of the sun's globe, and in the nearer part to tilt toward the north, in just the same manner as all the revolutions of the planets occur. Third, if we consider the nobility of the sun, and the fact that it is the font of light which (as I shall conclusively prove) illuminates not only the moon and the earth but all the other planets, which are inherently dark, then I believe that it will not be entirely unphilosophical to say that the sun, as the chief minister of Nature and in a

LETTER TO THE GRAND DUCHESS CHRISTINA   213

certain sense the heart and soul of the universe, infuses by its own rotation not only light but also motion into other bodies which surround it. And just as if the motion of the heart should cease in an animal, all other motions of its members would also cease, so if the rotation of the sun were to stop, the rotations of all the planets would stop too. And though I could produce the testimonies of many grave authors to prove the admirable power and energy of the sun, I shall content myself with a single passage from the blessed Dionysius the Areopagite in his book *Of the Divine Name*,[39] who writes thus of the sun: "His light gathers and converts to himself all things which are seen, moved, lighted, or heated; and in a word all things which are preserved by his splendor. For this reason the sun is called HELIOS, because he collects and gathers all dispersed things." And shortly thereafter he says: "This sun which we see remains one, and despite the variety of essences and qualities of things which fall under our senses, he bestows his light equally on them, and renews, nourishes, defends, perfects, divides, conjoins, cherishes, makes fruitful, increases, changes, fixes, produces, moves, and fashions all living creatures. Everything in this universe partakes of one and the same sun by His will, and the causes of many things which are shared from him are equally anticipated in him." And for so much the more reason," and so on.

The sun, then, being the font of light and the source of motion, when God willed that at Joshua's command the whole system of the world should rest and should remain for many hours in the same state, it sufficed to make the sun stand still. Upon its stopping all the other revolutions ceased; the earth, the moon, and the sun remained in the same arrangement as before, as did all the planets; nor in all that time did day decline towards night, for day was miraculously prolonged. And in this manner, by the stopping of the sun, without altering or in the least disturbing the other aspects and mutual positions of the stars, the day

[39] The book *Of the Divine Name*, then attributed to Dionysius the disciple of Paul, actually belongs to the late fifth or early sixth century.

214   DISCOVERIES AND OPINIONS OF GALILEO

could be lengthened on earth—which agrees exquisitely with the literal sense of the sacred text.

But if I am not mistaken, something of which we are to take no small account is that by the aid of this Copernican system we have the literal, open, and easy sense of another statement that we read in this same miracle, that the sun stood still *in the midst of the heavens.*[40] Grave theologians raise a question about this passage, for it seems very likely that when Joshua requested the lengthening of the day, the sun was near setting and not at the meridian. If the sun had been at the meridian, it seems improbable that it was necessary to pray for a lengthened day in order to pursue victory in battle, the miracle having occurred around the summer solstice when the days are longest, and the space of seven hours remaining before nightfall being sufficient. Thus grave divines have actually held that the sun was near setting, and indeed the words themselves seem to say so: *Sun, stand thou still, stand thou still.*[41] For if it had been near the meridian, either it would have been needless to request a miracle, or it would have been sufficient merely to have prayed for some retardation. Cajetan[42] is of this opinion, to which Magellan[43] subscribes, confirming it with the remark that Joshua had already done too many things that day before commanding the sun to stand still for him to have done them in half a day. Hence they are forced to interpret the words *in the midst of the heavens* a little knottily, saying that this means no more than that the sun stood still while it was in our hemisphere; that is, above our horizon. But unless I am mistaken we may avoid this and all other knots if, in agreement with the Copernican system, we place the sun in the "midst"—that is, in the center—of the celestial orbs and planetary rotations, as it is most necessary to do. Then take

[40] Joshua 10:13.
[41] Joshua 10:12.
[42] Thomas de Vio (1468–1534), Bishop of Gaeta, commenting on the *Summa Theologica* of Thomas Aquinas.
[43] Cosme Magalhaens (1553–1624), a Portuguese Jesuit who in 1612 had published a two-volume treatise on the Book of

LETTER TO THE GRAND DUCHESS CHRISTINA 215

any hour of the day, either noon, or any hour as close to evening as you please, and the day would be lengthened and all the celestial revolutions stopped by the sun's standing still *in the midst of the heavens*; that is, in the center, where it resides. This sense is much better accommodated to the words, quite apart from what has already been said; for if the desired statement was that the sun was stopped at midday, the proper expression would have been that it "stood still at noonday," or "in the meridian circle," and not "in the midst of the heavens." For the true and only "midst" of a spherical body such as the sky is its center.

As to other scriptural passages which seem to be contrary to this opinion, I have no doubt that if the opinion itself were known to be true and proven, those very theologians who, so long as they deem it false, hold these passages to be incapable of harmonious exposition with it, would find interpretations for them which would agree very well, and especially if they would add some knowledge of astronomical science to their knowledge of divinity. At present, while they consider it false, they think they find in Scripture only passages that contradict it; but if they once entertained a different view of the matter they would probably find as many more that would harmonize with it. And then they might judge that it is fitting for the holy Church to tell that God placed the sun in the center of heaven, and that by rotating it like a wheel gave to the moon and the other wandering stars their appointed courses, when she sings the hymn:

Most Holy God of Heaven
Who paints with fiery splendor
The brilliant center of the pole
Enriched with beauteous light;
Who, creating on the fourth day
The flaming disk of the sun
Gave order to the moon
And wandering courses to the stars . . .[44]

[44] From the hymn *God, Creator of All*, attributed to St. Ambrose.

216 DISCOVERIES AND OPINIONS OF GALILEO

And they could say that the name "firmament" agrees literally quite well with the starry sphere and all that lies beyond the revolutions of the planets, which according to this arrangement is quite firm and immovable. Again, with the earth turning, they might think of its poles when they read *He had not yet made the earth, the rivers, and the hinges of the terrestrial orb,*[45] for hinges would seem to be ascribed in vain to the earth unless it needed them to turn upon.

[45] Proverbs 8:26 (Douay). At present the word in question is translated "poles."

4. René Descartes (1596-1650)

Principia Philosophiae (Amsterdam, 1644)
From *Descartes: Philosophical Writings,* translated and edited by
Elizabeth Anscombe and Peter Thomas Geach (London,
1971), pp. 206-207, 215-219, 222-226, 235-238. Reprinted by
permission of Thomas Nelson & Sons Limited

[p. 206]   **II : PRINCIPLES OF MATERIAL THINGS**

XIX. We have thus seen that the nature of corporeal substance consists in its being something extended (*res extensa*), and that its extension is none other than is commonly ascribed to a space however ' empty '. From this we readily see that it is impossible for any part of matter to occupy more space at one time than at another; thus rarefaction is not possible except in the way already explained. And, again, there can be no more matter (corporeal substance) in a vessel filled with lead, gold, or some other such body, as heavy and solid (*duro*) as you will, than there is when it just contains air and is considered ' empty '. The quantity of a piece of matter depends not on its heaviness or solidity (*duritie*), but simply on its extension; and in a given vessel this is constant.

XX. We see also the impossibility of atoms—pieces of matter that are by their nature indivisible. If they exist, they must necessarily be extended, however small they are imagined to be; so we can still divide any one of them in thought (*cogitatione*) into two or more smaller ones, and thus we can recognise their divisibility. There is nothing we can divide in' thought but we can see to *be* divisible; if we were to judge that it was indivisible, our judgment would go against what we knew. Even if we imagined a Divine decree that some particle of matter could not be divided into smaller ones, it would not be properly speaking indivisible. Even if God made it not to be divisible by any creatures, he could not take away his own power of dividing it; for it is quite impossible for God to diminish his own power. . . . So, speaking absolutely, it will still be divisible, being such by its very nature.

★   ★   ★   ★

★   ★   ★   ★

[p. 215]

XXXVI. After considering the nature of motion, we must treat of its cause; in fact, of two sorts of cause. First, the universal and primary cause—the general cause of all the motions in the universe; secondly the particular cause that makes any given piece of matter assume a motion that it had not before.

As regards the general cause, it seems clear to me that it can be none other than God himself. He created matter along with motion and rest in the beginning; and now, merely by his ordinary co-operation, he preserves just the quantity of motion and rest in the material world that he put there in the beginning. Motion, indeed, is only a state (*modus*) of the moving body; but it has a certain definite quantity, and it is readily conceived that this quantity may be constant in the universe as a whole, while varying in any given part.   (We must reckon the quantity of motion in two pieces of matter as equal if one moves twice as fast as the other, and this in turn is twice as big as the first; again, if the motion of one piece of matter is retarded, we must assume an equal acceleration of some other body of the same size.)   Further, we conceive it as belonging to God's perfection, not only that he should in himself be unchangeable, but also that his operation should occur in a supremely constant and unchangeable manner. Therefore, apart from the changes of which we are assured by manifest experience or by divine revelation, and about which we can see, or believe [by faith], that they take place without any change in the Creator, we must not assume any others in the works of God, lest they should afford an argument for his being inconstant. Consequently it is most reasonable to hold that, from the mere fact that God gave pieces of matter various movements at their first

PRINCIPLES OF PHILOSOPHY

creation, and that he now preserves all this matter in being in the same way as he first created it, he must likewise always preserve in it the same quantity of motion.

XXXVII. From God's immutability we can also know certain rules or natural laws which are the secondary, particular causes of the various motions we see in different bodies. The *first* law is: *Every reality, in so far as it is simple and undivided, always remains in the same condition so far as it can, and never changes except through external causes.* Thus if a piece of matter is square, one readily convinces oneself that it will remain square for ever, unless something comes along from elsewhere to change its shape. If it is at rest, one thinks it will never begin to move, unless impelled by some cause. Now there is equally no reason to believe that if a body is moving its motion will ever stop, spontaneously that is, and apart from any obstacle. So our conclusion must be: *A moving body, so far as it can, goes on moving.*

We, however, live on the Earth, and the constitution of the Earth is such that all motions in her neighbourhood are soon arrested—often by insensible causes. Thus from our earliest years we have held the view that these motions (which in fact are brought to rest by causes unknown to us) come to an end spontaneously. And we tend to hold in all cases what we think we have observed in many cases— that motion ceases, or tends towards rest, by its very nature. Now this is in fact flatly opposed to the laws of nature; for rest is the opposite of motion, and nothing can by its own nature tend towards its opposite, towards its own destruction.

XXXVIII. Our everyday observation of projectiles completely confirms this rule. The reason why projectiles persist in motion for some time after leaving the hand that throws them is simply that when they once move they go on moving, until their motion is retarded by bodies that get in the way. Obviously the air, or other fluid in which

II : PRINCIPLES OF MATERIAL THINGS

they are moving, gradually retards their motion, so that it cannot last long. The resistance of air to the movement of other bodies may be verified by the sense of touch if we beat it with a fan; and the flight of birds confirms this. And the resistance of any fluid other than air to the motion of projectiles is even more obvious.

XXXIX. The *second* natural law is: *Any given piece of matter considered by itself tends to go on moving, not in any oblique path, but only in straight lines.* (Of course many pieces of matter are constantly being compelled to swerve by meeting with others; and, as I said, any motion involves a kind of circulation of matter all moving simultaneously.) The reason for this rule, like that for the last one, is the immutability and simplicity of the operation by which God preserves motion in matter. For he preserves the motion in the precise form in which it occurs at the moment when he preserves it, without regard to what it was a little while before. *In* the instant, of course, no motion can take place; but obviously the motion of any moving body is determined *at* any assigned instant of its duration as capable of being continued in a given direction; continued, that is, in a straight line, not some sort of curve. For example, a stone A is moving in a sling EA in a circle ABF. At the moment when it is at the point A, it has motion in a definite direction, viz. in a straight line towards C, where the straight line AC is a

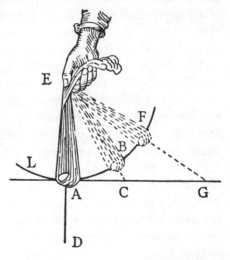

PRINCIPLES OF PHILOSOPHY

tangent to the circle.   It cannot be imagined that the stone
has any definite curvilinear motion; it is true that it
arrived at A from L along a curved path, but none of this
curvature can be conceived as inherent in its motion when
it is at the point A.   Observation confirms this; for if the
stone leaves the sling just then, it goes on towards C, not
towards B. . . .[1]

XL. The *third* natural law is this.   *When a moving body
collides with another, then if its own power of going on in a
straight line is less than the resistance of the other body, it
is reflected in another direction and retains the same amount of
motion, with only a change in its direction ; but if its power of
going on is greater than the resistance, it carries the other body along
with it, and loses a quantity of motion equal to what it imparts
to the other body.*   Thus we observe that hard projectiles,
when they strike some other hard body, do not stop moving
but are reflected in the opposite direction; on the other
hand, when they collide with a soft body, they readily
transfer all their motion to it, and are thus at once stopped.
This third law covers all the particular causes of corporeal
change—so far as they are themselves corporeal; I am
not now considering whether, or how, human or angelic
minds have the power to move bodies. . . .

XLI. To prove the first part of this law: there is a
difference between a motion as such and its determinate
direction; it is thus possible for the direction to change
while the motion remains unaltered.   Now, as I said, any
given reality which, like motion, is not complex but
simple, persists in being so long as it is not destroyed by any
external cause.   In a collision with a hard body, there is
an obvious reason why the motion of the other body that
collides with it should not continue in the same direction;
but there is no obvious reason why this motion should be

[1] [Descartes resumes this subject elsewhere, at *Principles* iii. lv-lvii,
lix.—Tr.]

II :   PRINCIPLES OF MATERIAL THINGS

stopped or lessened, for one motion is not the opposite of another motion; so the motion ought not to be diminished.

XLII. The second part is proved from the immutability of the divine operation; God preserving the world by the same activity by which he once created it. For all places are filled with body, and at the same time the motion of every body is rectilinear in tendency; so clearly, when God first created the world, he must not only have assigned various motions to its various parts, but also have caused their mutual impulses and the transference of motion from one to another; and since he now preserves motion by the same activity and according to the same laws, as when he created it, he does not preserve it as a constant inherent property of given pieces of matter, but as something passing from one piece to another as they collide. Thus the very fact that creatures are thus continually changing argues the immutability of God.

★   ★   ★   ★

[p. 222]

THE VISIBLE WORLD

A Selection from 'Principles of Philosophy' Part III

I. We have thus discovered certain principles as regards material objects, derived not from the prejudices of our senses but from the light of reason, so that their truth is indubitable; we must now consider whether they suffice to explain all natural phenomena. We must begin with the most general facts on which the rest depend—the construction of the visible universe as a whole. For correct theorising about this, two cautions are needed. First, we must consider the infinite power and goodness of God, and not be afraid that we are imagining his works to be too vast, too beautiful, too perfect; what we must beware of is, on the contrary, the supposition of any bounds to God's works that we do not certainly know, lest we may seem not to have a sufficiently grand conception of the power of the Creator.

II. Secondly, we must beware of thinking too proudly of ourselves. We should be doing this, not merely if we imagined any limits to the universe, when none are known to us either by reason or by divine revelation (as if our powers of thought could extend beyond what God has actually made); but also, and that in a special degree, if we imagined everything had been created by God for our sake; or even if we thought our minds had the power to comprehend the ends God set before himself in creating the world.

III. In ethics indeed it is an act of piety to say that God made everything for our sake, that we may be the more impelled to thank him, and the more on fire with love of

III : THE VISIBLE WORLD

him; and in a sense this is true; for we can make *some* use of all things—at least we can employ our mind in contemplating them, and in admiring God for his wonderful works.   But it is by no means probable that all things were made for our sake in the sense that they have no other use.   In physical theory this supposition would be wholly ridiculous and absurd; for undoubtedly many things exist (or did exist formerly and now do so no longer) that have never been seen or thought of by any man, and have never been any use to anybody.

IV. The principles we have discovered so far are so vast and so fertile, that their consequences are far more numerous than the observable contents of the visible universe; far too numerous, indeed, to be ever exhaustively considered. For an investigation of causes, I here present a brief account of the principal phenomena of nature.   Not that we should use these as grounds for proving anything; for our aim is to deduce an account of the effects from the causes, not to deduce an account of the causes from the effects.   It is just a matter of turning our mind to consider some effects rather than others out of an innumerable multitude; all producible, on our view, by a single set of causes.

XLII. . . . To discern the real nature of this visible universe, it is not enough to find causes in terms of which we may explain what we see far away in the heavens; we must also deduce from the same causes everything that we see close at hand on earth.   We need not indeed consider all of these phenomena in order to determine the causes of more general effects; but *ex postfacto* we shall know that we have determined these causes correctly only when we see that we can explain in terms of them, not merely the effects we had originally in mind, but also all other phenomena of which we did not previously think.

XLIII. But assuredly, if the only principles we use are such as we see to be self-evident; if we infer nothing from

PRINCIPLES OF PHILOSOPHY

them except by mathematical deduction; and if these inferences agree accurately with all natural phenomena: then we should, I think, be wronging God if we were to suspect this discovery of the causes of things to be delusive. God would, so to say, have made us so imperfectly that by using reason rightly we nevertheless went wrong.

XLIV. However, to avoid the apparent arrogance of asserting that the actual truth has been discovered in such an important subject of speculation, I prefer to waive this point; I will put forward everything that I am going to write just as a hypothesis. Even if this be thought to be false, I shall think my achievement is sufficiently worth while if all inferences from it agree with observation (*experimentis*); for in that case we shall get as much practical benefit from it as we should from the knowledge of the actual truth.

XLV. Moreover, in order to explain natural objects the better, I shall pursue my inquiry into their causes further back than I believe the causes ever in fact existed. There is no doubt that the world was first created in its full perfection; there were in it a Sun, an Earth, a Moon, and the stars; and on the Earth there were not only the seeds of plants, but also the plants themselves; and Adam and Eve were not born as babies, but made as full-grown human beings. This is the teaching of the Christian faith; and natural reason convinces us that it was so; for considering the infinite power of God, we cannot think he ever made anything that was not peerless. Nevertheless, in order to understand the stature of plants or man, it is far better to consider how they may now gradually develop from seed, rather than the way they were created by God at the beginning of the world; and in just the same way we may conceive certain elements, very simple and very easily understood, and from these seeds, so to say, we may prove that there could have arisen stars, and an Earth, and in fact

III : THE VISIBLE WORLD

everything we observe in this visible universe; and although we know perfectly well they never did arise in this way, yet by this method we shall give a far better account of their nature than if we merely describe what they now are. . . .

XLVI. From what has already been said it is established that all bodies in the universe consist of one and the same matter; that this is divisible arbitrarily into parts, and is actually divided into many pieces with various motions; that their motion is in a way circular, and that the same quantity of motion is constantly preserved in the universe. We cannot determine by reason how big these pieces of matter are, how quickly they move, or what circles they describe. God might have arranged these things in countless different ways; which way he in fact chose rather than the rest is a thing we must learn from observation. Therefore, we are free to make any assumption we like about them, so long as all the consequences agree with experience. So, by your leave, I shall suppose that all the matter constituting the visible world was originally divided by God into unsurpassably equal particles of medium size—that is, of the average size of those that now form the heavens and the stars; that they had collectively just the quantity of motion now found in the world; that . . . each turned round its own centre, so that they formed a fluid body, such as we take the heavens to be; and that many revolved together around various other points . . . and thus constituted as many different vortices as there now are stars in the world. XLVII. These few assumptions are, I think, enough to supply causes from which all effects observed in our universe would arise by the laws of nature previously stated; and I think one cannot imagine any first principles that are more simple, or easier to understand, or indeed more likely. The actual arrangement of things might perhaps be

PRINCIPLES OF PHILOSOPHY

inferable from an original Chaos, according to the laws of nature; and I once undertook to give such an explanation. But confusion seems less in accord with the supreme perfection of God the Creator of all things than proportion or order, and we can form a less distinct notion of it. . . . In any case, it matters very little what supposition we make; for change must subsequently take place according to the laws of nature; and it is hardly possible to make a supposition that does not allow of our inferring the same effects (perhaps with more labour) according to the same laws of nature. For according to these, matter must successively assume all the forms of which it admits; and if we consider these forms in order, we can at last come to that which is found in this universe. So no error is to be apprehended from a false supposition at this point.

★ ★ ★ ★

★   ★   ★   ★

[p. 235]

CCI. In considering every body as containing a multitude of particles that are not perceived by any sense,
I may not win the approval of those who take their senses as
the measure of what can be known.   But who can doubt
the existence of a multitude of bodies so small as to be
undetectable by sensation ?   One only has to consider the
question what it is that is added to a thing that is gradually
growing, or is taken away from a thing that is diminishing.
A tree grows day by day; its becoming bigger than it
was before is unintelligible, unless we conceive that some
body is being added to it.   Now who has ever detected by
his senses which particles are added to a growing tree in
a single day?   Again, at least those who recognise the
infinite divisibility of matter must admit that its parts may
be rendered so small as to be quite imperceptible to the
senses.   And it ought not to be surprising that we cannot
have sensations of very minute bodies; our nerves, which
have to be set in motion in order to produce sensation,
are not the smallest possible bodies; for they are like tiny
cords, consisting of many particles that are even smaller;
and thus they cannot be set in motion by the very smallest
bodies.

PRINCIPLES OF PHILOSOPHY

Again, I do not see how any reasonable man can deny the great advantage of forming ideas about microscopic events (*in minutis corpusculis*), which elude our senses by their mere minuteness, on the pattern of sensibly observed macro-scopic events (*in magnis corporibus*), instead of bringing into our explanation some new conception of things wholly dissimilar to sensible objects.   CCIII. But my assigning definite shapes, sizes and motions to insensible particles of bodies, just as if I had seen them, and this in spite of admitting that they are insensible, may make some people ask how I can tell what they are like.   My answer is this. Starting from the simplest and most familiar principles which our minds know by their innate constitution, I have considered in general the chief possible differences in size, shape, and position between bodies whose mere minuteness makes them insensible, and the sensible effects of their various interactions.   When I have observed similar effects among sensible objects, I have assumed that they arose from similar interactions of insensible bodies; especially as this seemed the only possible way of explaining them.   And I have been greatly helped by considering machines.   The only difference I can see between machines and natural objects is that the workings of machines are mostly carried out by apparatus large enough to be readily perceptible by the senses (as is required to make their manufacture humanly possible), whereas natural processes almost always depend on parts so small that they utterly elude our senses.   But mechanics, which is a part or species of physics, uses no concepts but belong also to physics; and it is just as 'natural' for a clock composed of such-and-such wheels to tell the time, as it is for a tree grown from such-and-such seed to produce a certain fruit. So, just as men with experience of machinery, when they know what a machine is for, and can see part of it, can readily form a conjecture about the way its unseen parts

IV : THE EARTH

are fashioned; in the same way, starting from sensible effects and sensible parts of bodies, I have tried to investigate the insensible causes ard particles underlying them.

CCIV. This may give us an idea of the possible constitution of Nature; but we must not conclude that this is the actual constitution.   There might be two clocks made by the same craftsman, equally good time-keepers, and with absolutely similar outsides; and yet the train of wheels inside might be completely different. Similarly, the supreme Craftsman might have produced all that we see in a variety of ways. I freely admit the truth of this; I shall think I have done enough if only what I have written is such as to accord accurately with all natural phenomena. This will suffice for practical application; for medicine, mechanics, and all other arts that may be brought to perfection by the aid of physics are concerned only with the sensible—with what can be reckoned as phenomena of nature. . . .

CCV. In fairness to the truth, however, it must be borne in mind that some things are considered as morally certain —certain for all practical purposes—although they are uncertain if we take into account God's absolute power. Suppose somebody is trying to read a letter written in Roman characters, but in cipher, and guesses that he must throughout substitute B for A, C for B, and in general replace any given letter by the one next following it; and suppose he finds that the result makes up Latin words; then he will have no doubt that the true meaning of the letter is contained in these words.   He knows this, of course, only by a guess; the writer of the letter may have put different letters, not the next following, in place of the real ones, so that the meaning of the cipher is quite different; but this could scarcely happen, and appears incredible. Now those who notice how many deductions are here made from a few principles . . . even if they thought my

PRINCIPLES OF PHILOSOPHY

assumption of these principles haphazard and groundless, would perhaps recognise that so many things could hardly hang together if they were false.

CCVI. Moreover, even as regards natural objects, there are some things that we regard as absolutely, not just morally, certain; relying on the metaphysical ground that, since God is supremely good and in no wise deceitful, the faculty he has given us for distinguishing truth from false-hood cannot err, so often as we use it properly, and perceive something distinctly by means of it. To this class belong mathematical proofs; the knowledge that material objects exist; and all self-evident reasonings about natural objects. And with these my own assertions may perhaps find a place, when it is considered how they have been inferred in an unbroken chain from the simplest primary principles of human knowledge. And the more so, if it is sufficiently realised that we can have no sensation of external objects unless they excite some local motion in our nerves, and that the fixed stars, being at a vast distance from us, can excite no such motion unless there is also some motion taking place in them and in the whole of the intermediate heavens; for once this is granted, then, at least as regards the general account I have given of the universe and the Earth, an alternative to the rest of my explanation seems hardly conceivable.

CCVII. Mindful, however, of my own weakness, I make no assertion. I submit everything to the authority of the Catholic Church, and to the judgment of wiser heads; and I would have no one believe anything without being persuaded by evident and invincible reasoning.

FINIS

5. René Descartes (1596-1650)

Letters to Mersenne (April 1634) and More (5 February 1649)

From *Descartes, Philosophical Letters*, translated and edited by Anthony Kenny (Oxford, 1970), pp. 25-27, 237-245. Reprinted by permission of The Clarendon Press

From the letter to Mersenne, April 1634

Reverend Father,

From your last I learn that my latest letters to you have been lost, though I thought I had addressed them very safely. In them I told you at length the reason why I did not send you my treatise. I am sure you will find it so. just that far from blaming me for resolving never to show it to anyone, you would be the first to exhort me to do so, if I were not already fully so resolved.

Doubtless you know that Galileo was recently censured by the Inquisitors of the Faith, and that his views about the movement of the earth were condemned as heretical. I must tell you that all the things I explained in my treatise, which

From the letter to Mersenne   *April 1634*

included the doctrine of the movement of the earth, were so interdependent that it is enough to discover that one of them is false to know that all the arguments I was using are unsound. Though I thought they were based on very certain and evident proofs, I would not wish, for anything in the world, to maintain them against the authority of the Church. I know that it might be said that not everything which the Roman Inquisitors decide is automatically an article of faith, before it is decided upon by a General Council. But I am not so fond of my own opinions as to want to use such quibbles to be able to maintain them. I desire to live in peace and to continue the life I have begun under the motto *to live well you must live unseen.* And so I am more happy to be delivered from the fear of my work's making unwanted acquaintances than I am unhappy at having lost the time and trouble which I spent on its composition.

*   *   *

As for the results you tell me of Galileo's experiments I deny them all; but I do not conclude the motion of the earth to be any less probable. I do indeed agree that the movement of a chariot, a boat, or a horse remains in some manner in a stone thrown from them, but there are other reasons which prevent it from remaining undiminished. As for a cannon ball shot off a high tower, it must take much longer descending than one allowed to fall vertically; for it meets a lot of air on its way, which resists its vertical motion as well as its horizontal motion.

I am astonished that an ecclesiastic should dare to write about the motion of the earth, whatever excuses he may give. For I have seen letters patent about Galileo's condemnation, printed at Liège on 20 September 1633, which contained the words '*though he pretended he put forward his view only hypothetically*' ; so that they seem to forbid even the use of this hypothesis in astronomy. For this reason I do not dare to tell him any of my thoughts on the topic. Moreover, I do not see that this censure has been endorsed by the Pope or

by any Council, but only by a single congregation of the
Cardinals of the Inquisition; so I do not altogether lose hope
that the case may turn out like that of the Antipodes, which
were similarly condemned long ago. So in time my World
may yet see the day; and in that case I shall need my own
arguments to use myself.

★ ★ ★ ★

Descartes to More, 5 February 1649

Sir,

The praises which you heap on me are proofs rather of
your kindness, than of any merit of mine, which could never
equal them. Such goodness, however, based on the mere
reading of my writings, displays so clearly the candour and
nobility of your mind, that though unacquainted with you
hitherto I have been completely captivated. So I will answer
very willingly the queries which you put to me.

1. The first question was why I defined body as extended
substance, rather than perceptible, tangible, or impenetrable substance. It is clear that if body is called perceptible
substance, it is defined by its relation to our senses, and thus
we explain only a certain property of it, rather than its whole
nature. This certainly does not depend upon our senses
since it could exist even though there were no men, and so I
do not see why you say that it is altogether necessary that all
matter should be perceptible by the senses. Just the opposite
is the case: all matter is completely imperceptible if it is
divided into parts much smaller than the particles of our

237

nerves and the individual parts are given a sufficiently rapid movement.

The argument of mine which you call cunning and almost sophistical I used only to refute the opinion of those who like you think that every body is perceptible by the senses. I think it does give a clear and definitive refutation of that view. For a body can retain its whole bodily nature without being soft or hard or cold or hot to the feeling, and without having any quality perceptible by the senses. You make a comparison with wax, which although it can be not square and not round cannot be completely without shape. But since according to my principles, all perceptible qualities consist solely in the fact that the particles of a body are in motion or at rest in a certain manner, in order to fall into the error which you seem to attribute to me here, I would have had to say that a body could exist without any of its particles being either at motion or at rest. But this is something which never entered my mind. Body, therefore, is not rightly defined as perceptible substance.

Let us see next whether body if more appropriately called impenetrable, or tangible substance, in the sense which you explained. Tangibility or impenetrability in a body is something like the ability to laugh in man; according to the common rules of logic it is a property of the fourth kind not a true and essential *differentia* such as I claim extension to be. Consequently, just as man is defined not as a risible animal, but as a rational animal, so body should be defined not by impenetrability but by extension. This is confirmed by the fact that tangibility and impenetrability involve a reference to parts and presuppose the concept of division or termination; whereas we can conceive a continuous body of indeterminate or indefinite size, in which there is nothing to consider except extension.

'But,' you say, 'God, or an angel, or any other self-subsistent thing is extended, and so your definition is too broad.' I never argue about words, and so if someone wants to say that God is in a sense extended, since He is everywhere, I have no objection. But I deny that true extension as

commonly conceived is to be found in God or in angels or in
our mind or in any substance which is not a body. Commonly
when people say that something is extended they mean that
it is imaginable—I leave on one side the question whether,
it is a fictional or real entity—and that it has various parts of
definite size and shape, each of which is non-identical with
the others. These parts can be distinguished in the imagination: some can be imagined as transferred to the place of
others, but no two can be imagined simultaneously in one and
the same place. Nothing of this kind can be said about
God or about our mind; they cannot be imagined, but only
grasped by the intellect; neither of them can be distinguished into parts, and certainly not into parts which have
definite sizes and shapes. Again, we easily understand that
the human mind and God, and several angels can all be at
the same time in one and the same place. So we clearly
conclude that no incorporeal substances are in any strict
sense extended. I conceive them as powers or forces, which
although they can act upon extended substances, are not
themselves extended; just as fire is in white hot iron without
itself being iron. Some people indeed do confuse the notion
of substance with that of extended matter. This is because
of the false prejudice which makes them believe that nothing
can exist or be intelligible without being also imaginable,
and because it is indeed true that nothing falls within the
scope of the imagination without being in some way
extended. Now just as we can say that health belongs only
to human beings, though by analogy medicine and a
temperate climate and many other things also are called
healthy; so too I call extended only what is imaginable and
has parts outside other parts of a determinate size and shape,
although other things also may be called extended by
analogy.

2. I pass to your second difficulty. If we examine what is
this extended being which I described, we will find that it
is no different from the space which is popularly regarded
sometimes as full and sometimes as empty, sometimes as
real and sometimes as imaginary. For everyone imagines in
space—even imaginary and empty space—various parts of
determinate size and shape, some of which can be transferred

in imagination to the place of others, but no two of which can be conceived as compenetrating each other at the same time in one and the same place, since it is contradictory for this to happen without any piece of space being removed. Now since I believe that such real properties can only exist in a real body, I dared to assert that there can be no completely empty space, and that whatever is extended is a genuine body. On this topic I did not hesitate to disagree with great men such as Epicurus, Democritus, and Lucretius, because I saw that they were guided by no solid reason, but only by the false prejudice with which we have all been imbued from our earliest years. As I warned in the third article of the second part, our senses do not always show us external bodies exactly as they are, but only in so far as they are related to us and can benefit or harm us. Despite this, we all decided when we were still children, that there is nothing in the world beside what the senses show us, and so there are no bodies which are imperceptible, and all places in which we perceive nothing are void. Since Epicurus, Democritus, and Lucretius never overcame this prejudice, I have no obligation to following their authority.

I am surprised that a man otherwise so perspicacious, having seen that he cannot deny that there is some substance in every space, since all the properties of extension are found in it, should none the less prefer to say that the divine extension fills up the space in which there are no bodies, rather than to admit that there can be no space without body. For as I said earlier, the alleged extension of God cannot be the subject of the true properties which we perceive very distinctly in all space. For God is not imaginable nor distinguishable into shaped and measurable parts.

But you are quite ready to admit that in the natural course of events there is no vacuum: you are concerned about God's power, which you think can take away the contents of a container while preventing its sides from meeting. For my part, I know that my intellect is finite and God's power is infinite, and so I set no bounds to it; I consider only what I can conceive and what I cannot conceive, and I take great pains that my judgement should accord with my under-

standing. And so I boldly assert that God can do everything
which I conceive to be possible, but I am not so bold as to
deny that He can do whatever conflicts with my understanding—I merely say that it involves a contradiction. And
so, since I see that it conflicts with my understanding for all
the body to be taken out of a container and for there to
remain extension, which I conceive in no way differently
from the body which was previously contained in it, I say
that it involves a contradiction that such extension should
remain there after the body has been taken away. I conclude
that the sides of the container must come together; and this
is altogether in accord with my other opinions. For I say
elsewhere that all motion is in a manner circular; from which
it follows that it cannot be clearly understood how God
could remove a body from a container without another body,
or the sides of the container, moving into its place by a
circular motion.

3. In the same way I say that it involves a contradiction
that there should be any atoms which are conceived as
extended and also indivisible. Though God might make
them such that they could not be divided by any creature,
we certainly cannot conceive Him able to deprive Himself
of the power of dividing them. Your comparison with
things which have been done and cannot be undone is not
to the point. For we do not take it as a mark of impotence
when someone cannot do something we do not understand
to be possible, but only when he cannot do something
which we distinctly perceive to be possible. Now we
certainly perceive it to be possible for an atom to be divided,
since we suppose it to be extended; and so, if we judge that
it cannot be divided by God, we shall judge that God cannot
do one of the things which we perceive to be possible. But
we do not in the same way perceive it to be possible for
what is done to be undone—on the contrary, we perceive
it to be altogether impossible, and so it is no defect of power
in God not to do it. The case is different with the divisibility
of matter; for though I cannot count all the parts into which
it is divisible, and therefore say that the number is indefinite,
I cannot assert that their division by God could never be
completed, because I know that God can do more things

241

than I can compass within my thought. Indeed I agreed in article 34, that this indefinite division of parts of matter sometimes actually takes place.

4. In my view it is not a matter of affected modesty, but of necessary caution to say that some things are indefinite rather than infinite. God is the only thing I positively conceive as infinite. As to other things like the extension of the world and the number of parts into which matter is divisible, I confess I do not know whether they are absolutely infinite; I merely know that I can see no end to them, and so, looking at them from my own point of view, I call them indefinite. True, our mind is not the measure of reality or of truth; but certainly it should be the measure of what we assert or deny. What is more absurd or more rash than to want to pass judgement on matters which we admit our mind cannot grasp? I am surprised that you seem to wish to do this when you say that if extension is only infinite in relation to us then it will in fact be finite. Not only this, you imagine some divine extension which goes further than the extension of bodies; and thus you suppose that God has parts side by side and is divisible, and attribute to Him all the essence of corporeal substance.

To remove all difficulty, I should explain that I call the extension of matter indefinite in the hope that this will prevent anyone imagining a place outside it into which the particles of my vortices might escape ; for on my view wherever such a place may be conceived there is some matter. When I say that matter is indefinitely extended, I am saying that it extends further than anything a human being can conceive. None the less, I think there is a very great difference between the vastness of this bodily extension and the vastness of God's extension, or rather not extension, since strictly He has none, but substance or essence; and so I call the latter simply infinite, and the former indefinite.

Moreover, I do not agree with what you very kindly concede, namely that the rest of my opinions could stand even if what I have written about the extension of matter were refuted. For it is one of the most important, and I

242

believe the most certain, foundations of my physics; and I
confess that no reasons satisfy me even in physics unless they
involve that necessity which you call logical or analytic,
provided you except things which can be known by experience alone, such as that there is only one sun and only one
moon around the earth and so on. Since in other matters
you are well disposed to my views, I hope that you will come
to agree with these too, if you reflect that it is a mere
prejudice which makes many people think that an extended
entity in which there is nothing to affect the senses is not a
true bodily substance but merely an empty space, and that
there are no bodies which are not perceptible to the senses,
and no substance which does not fall within the scope of
imagination and is consequently extended.

5. But there is no prejudice to which we are all more
accustomed from our earliest years than the belief that
dumb animals think. Our only reason for this belief is the
fact that we see that many of the organs of animals are not
very different from ours in shape and movement. Since we
believe that there is a single principle within us which
causes these motions—namely the soul, which both moves
the body and thinks—we do not doubt that some such soul
is to be found in animals also. I came to realize, however,
that there are two different principles causing our motions:
one is purely mechanical and corporeal and depends solely
on the force of the spirits and the construction of our organs,
and can be called the corporeal soul; the other is the incorporeal mind, the soul which I have defined as a thinking
substance. Thereupon I investigated more carefully whether
the motions of animals originated from both these principles
or from one only. I soon saw clearly that they could all
originate from the corporeal and mechanical principle, and I
thenceforward regarded it as certain and established that
we cannot at all prove the presence of a thinking soul in
animals. I am not disturbed by the astuteness and cunning
of dogs and foxes, or all the things which animals do for the
sake of food, sex, and fear; I claim that I can easily explain
the origin of all of them from the constitution of their
organs.

But though I regard it as established that we cannot prove there is any thought in animals, I do not think it is thereby proved that there is not, since the human mind does not reach into their hearts. But when I investigate what is most probable in this matter, I see no argument for animals having thoughts except the fact that since they have eyes, ears, tongues, and other sense-organs like ours, it seems likely that they have sensation like us; and since thought is included in our mode of sensation, similar thought seems to be attributable to them. This argument, which is very obvious, has taken possession of the minds of all men from their earliest age. But there are other arguments, stronger and more numerous, but not so obvious to everyone, which strongly urge the opposite. One is that it is more probable that worms and flies and caterpillars move mechanically than that they all have immortal souls.

It is certain that in the bodies of animals, as in ours, there are bones, nerves, muscles, animal spirits, and other organs so disposed that they can by themselves, without any thought, give rise to all the animal motions we observe. This is very clear in convulsive movements when the machine of the body moves despite the soul, and sometimes more violently and in a more varied manner than when it is moved by the will.

Second, it seems reasonable, since art copies nature, and men can make various automata which move without thought, that nature should produce its own automata, much more splendid than artificial ones. These natural automata are the animals. This is especially likely since we have no reason to believe that thought always accompanies the disposition of organs which we find in animals. It is much more wonderful that a mind should be found in every human body than that one should be lacking in every animal.

But in my opinion the main reason which suggests that the beasts lack thought is the following. Within a single species some of them are more perfect than others, as men are too. This can be seen in horses and dogs, some of whom learn what they are taught much better than others. Yet, although all animals easily communicate to us, by voice or bodily movement, their natural impulses of anger, fear, hunger and so on, it has never yet been observed that any brute animal reached the stage of using real speech, that is to say, of indicating by word or sign something pertaining to pure thought and not to natural impulse. Such speech is the only certain sign of thought hidden in a body. All men use it, however stupid and insane they may be, and though they may lack tongue and organs of voice; but no animals do. Consequently it can be taken as a real specific difference between men and dumb animals.

For brevity's sake I here omit the other reasons for denying thought to animals. Please note that I am speaking of thought, and not of life or sensation. I do not deny life to animals, since I regard it as consisting simply in the heat of the heart; and I do not deny sensation, in so far as it depends on a bodily organ. Thus my opinion is not so much cruel to animals as indulgent to men—at least to those who are not given to the superstitions of Pythagoras—since it absolves them from the suspicion of crime when they eat or kill animals.

Perhaps I have written at too great length for the sharpness of your intelligence; but I wished to show you that very few people have yet sent me objections which were as agreeable as yours. Your kindness and candour has made you a friend of that most respectful admirer of all who seek true wisdom,

Rene Descartes.

6. John Wilkins (1614-1672)

A Discourse Concerning a New Planet (London, 1640)
Title page, pp. 1-14, 16-28

A DISCOVRSE

concerning

A NEW PLANET

Tending to prove, That 'tis
probable our Earth is one of
the *Planets*.

The second Booke, now first
published.

*Digna res est Contemplatione, ut sciamus in
quo rerum statu scimus: pigerrimam sedem:
an velocissimam sedem: circa nos Deus omnia, an nos agat.* Sen. Nat. Quest. Lib. 7.
Cap. 2.

LONDON,
Printed by R.H. for *Iohn Maynard*, and
are to be sold at the *George* in
Fleetstreet, neer S. *Dunstans*
Church. 1640.

That the Earth

may be a Planet.

PROP. I.

*That the seeming Noveltie and Sin-
gularitie of this opinion, can be no
sufficient reason to prove it erro-
nious.*

IN the search of
Theologicall Truths, it
is the safest method, first
of all to looke unto Di-
vine Authority; because
that carryes with it as cleer an evidence
to our Faith, as any thing else can be to
our

B

That the Earth

our reason. But on the contrary, in the examination of Philosophicall points, it were a preposterous course to begin at the testimony and opinion of others, and then afterwards to descend unto the reasons that may bee drawne from the Nature and Essence of the things themselves: because these inartificiall Arguments (as the Logicians call them) doe not carry with them any cleere and convincing evidence; and therefore should come after those that are of more necessary dependance, as serving rather to confirme, than resolve the Iudgement.

But yet, so it is, that in those points which are besides the common opinion, men are carried away at the first by the generall cry, and seldome or never come so farre as to examine the reasons that may bee urged for them. And therefore, since it is the purpose of this discourse to remove those prejudices which may hinder our judgement in the like case, 'tis requisite that in the first place there bee some satisfaction given to those Arguments that may bee taken

may be a Planet.

ken from the Authoritie of others. Which Arguments are insisted on by our adversaries with much heate and violence.

What (say they) shall an upstart Noveltie thrust out our such a Truth as hath passed by successive tradition through all Ages of the World? and hath bin generally entertained, not onely in the opinion of the vulgar, but also of the greatest Philosophers and most learned men? * Shall wee thinke that amongst the multitude of those who in severall times have been eminent for new inventions and strange discoveries, there was noneable to finde out such a Secret as this, besides some fabulous Pithagorians, and of late *Copernicus*? Is it possible that the World should last for above five thousand yeares together, and yet the Inhabitants of it be so dull and stupid, as to be unacquainted with it's motion? Nay, shall wee thinke that those excellent men, whom the Holy Ghost made use of in the penning of Scripture, who were extraordinarily inspired with supernaturall Truths,
should

* *Alex. Roff. de Terrae motu, contra Lansb. lib.1.sect.1. cap.10.*

B 2

should notwithstanding be so grossely ignorant of so common a matter as this? Can wee beleeve, if there were any such thing, that *Iosuah*, and *Iob*, and *David*, and *Solomon*, &c. should know nothing of it? Certainly it must needs argue a strong affectation of Singulari-tie, for a man to take up any groundlesse fancy against such antient and generall Authority.

I answer : As wee should not bee so fondly conceited of our selves, and the extraordinary Abilities of these pre-sent ages, as to thinke every thing that is antient to be absolute : Or, as if it must needs bee with opinions, as it is with cloths, where the newest is for the most part best. So neither should we be so superstitiously devoted to Antiqui-tie, as for to take up every thing Cano-nicall, which drops from the pen of a Fa-ther, or was approved by the consent of the Antients. 'Tis an excellent saying, * δεῖ ἐλευθέριον εἶναι τῇ γνώμῃ τὸν μέλλοντα φιλοσοφεῖν. It behoves every one in the search of Truth, alwaies to preserve a Philosophi-call liberty : not to be so inslaved to the opinion

Alcinous.

opinion of any man, as to thinke what ever he sayes to be infallible. We must labour to find out what things are in themselves by our owne experience, and a through examination of their natures; not what another sayes of them. And it in such an impartiall enquiry, we chance to light upon a new way, and that which is besides the common rode, this is neither our fault, nor our unhappi-nesse.

Not our fault, because it did not arise from Singularity or Affectation. Not our unhappinesse, because it is rather a Priviledge to be the first in finding out such Truths, as are not discernable to every common eye. If Noveltie should alwaies be rejected, neither would Arts have arrived to that perfection wherein now wee enjoy them, nor could we ever hope for any future reformation: though all Truth be in it self Eternall; yet in re-spect of mens opinions, there is scarse any so antient, but had a beginning, and was once counted a Noveltie; and if for this reason it had been condemned as an errour, what a generall darknesse and

B 3

6   *That the Earth*

and ignorance would then have been in the World, in comparison of that light which now abounds; according to that of the Poet:

† Horat. lib.2. cp.1.

* *Quod si tam Antiquis Novitas invisa fuisset,*
Quam nobis, quid nunc esset vetus, aut quid habe-
Quod legeret tereretq; virtim publicus usus? (ret,

If our Forefathers had but hated thus,
All that were new, what had been old to us?
Or, how might any thing confirmed be,
For publicke use, by it's Antiquitie?

But for more full satisfaction of all those scruples that may arise from the seeming Novelty or Singularity of this opinion, I shall propose these following considerations.

Consid. 1.

Suppose it were a Noveltie : Yet 'tis in Philosophy, and that is made up of nothing else; but receives addition from every dayes experiment. True indeed, for Divinity wee have an infallible rule that do's plainly inform us of all necessary Truths; and therfore the Primitive Times are of greater Authority, because they were neerer to those holy Men who were

may be a Planet.   7

were the pen-men of Scripture. But now for Philosophy, there is no such reason: what ever the Schoole-men may talke; yet *Aristotles* works are not necessarily true, and hee himselfe hath by sufficient Arguments proved himselfe to be liable unto errour. Now in this case, if wee should speake properly, Antiquity do's consist in the old age of the World, not in the youth of it. In such Learning as may be increased by fresh experiments and new discoveries : 'tis wee are the Fathers, and of more Authority than former Ages ; because wee have the advantage of more time than they had, and Truth (wee say) is the Daughter of Time. However, there is nothing in this opinion so Magisterially propofed, but the Reader may use his owne liberty; and if all the reasons confid-red together, doe not seeme convincing unto him, he may freely reject it.

In those naturall points which carry with them any doubt or obscurity, it is the safest way to suspend our affents : and though we may dispute *pro* or *con* ; yet not to settle our opinion on either side.
B 4   In

That the Earth

In weighing the Authority of others, 'tis not their multitude that should prevaile, or their skill in some things that should make them of credit in every thing, but wee should examine what particular insight and experience they had in those times for which they are cited. Now 'tis plaine, that common people judge by their senses; and therefore, their voices are altogether unfit to decide any Philosophicall doubt, which cannot well be examined or explained without discourse and reason. And as for the antient Fathers, though they were men very eminent for their holy lives and extraordinary skill in Divinitie; yet they were most of them very ignorant in that part of Learning which concernes this opinion, as appeares by many of their grosse mistakes in this kinde, as that concerning the *Antipodes*, &c. and therefore it is not their opinion on neither, in this businesse, that to an indifferent seeker of Truth will bee of any strong Authority.

But against this it is * objected, That the instance of the *Antipodes* do's not argue

Things

* Alex.Roff. l.1.sect.c.8.

argue any speciall ignorance in these learned Men: Or, that they had lesse skil in such humane Arts than others; since *Aristotle* himself, and *Pliny*, did deny this as well as they.

I answer:

1 If they did, yet this do's make more to the present purpose: For if such great Schollers, who were so eminent for their knowledge in naturall things, might yet notwithstanding be grossely mistaken in such matters as are now evident and certaine: Why then wee have no reason to depend upon their assertions or Authorities, as if they were infallible.

2 Though these great Naturalists, for want of some experience were mistaken in that opinion, whilest they thought no place was habitable but the temperate *Zones*; yet it cannot be from hence inferred, that they denied the possibilitie of *Antipodes*: since these are such Inhabitants as live opposite unto us in the other temperate *Zone*; and 'twere an absurd thing to imagine that those who lived in different *Zones*, can be

That the Earth

be *Antipodes* to one another; and argues that a man did not understand, or else had forgotten that common distinction in *Geography*, wherein the relation of the Worlds Inhabitants unto one another, are reckoned up under these three heads; *Antæci, Periœci,* and *Antipodes.* But to let this passe: 'Tis certaine, that some of the Fathers did deny the being of any such, upon other more absurd grounds. Now if such as *Chrisostome, Lactantius,* &c. who were noted for great Schollers, and such too as flourished in these latter times, when all humane Learning was more generally profest, should notwithstanding be so much mistaken in so obvious a matter: Why then may wee not think that those Primitive Saints, who were the pen-men of Scripture, and eminent above others in their time for holinesse and knowledge, might yet be utterly ignorant of many Philosophicall Truths, which are commonly knowne in these dayes? 'Tis probable, that the Holy Ghost did informe them onely with the knowledge of those things whereof they were to be

may be a Planet.

be the pen-men, and that they were not better skilled in points of Philosophy than others. There were indeed some of them who were supernaturally indowed with humane Learning; yet this was, because they might thereby bee fitted for some particular ends, which all the rest were not appointed unto: thus *Solomon* was strangely gifted with all kinde of knowledge, in a great measure, because he was to teach us by his owne experience the extreme vanity of it, that we might not so settle our desires upon it, as if it were able to yeeld us contentment. So too the Apostles were extraordinarily inspired with the knowledge of Languages, because they were to preach unto all Nations. But it will not hence follow, that therfore the other holy pen-men were greater Schollers than others. 'Tis likely that *Iob* had as much humane Learning as most of them, because his Booke is more especially remarkable for lofty expressions, and discourses of Nature; and yet 'tis not likely that he was acquainted with all those mysteries which later Ages have discovered;

Eccl.1,18.

13 — may be a Planet.

LIB.2. Cap.1. †v. 28,29.

the † caufe of the Raine or Dewe, of Ice and Froft, and the like. By which queftions, it feemes *Iob* was fo utterly pufled, thathee is faine afterwards to humble himfelfe in this acknowledgement:

*Cap.42.3.

I have uttered that I underftood not, things too wonderfull for me, which I knew not: wherefore I abborre my felfe, and repent in duft and afhes.

So that 'tis likely thefe holy Men had not thefe humane Arts by any fpeciall infpiration, but by inftruction and ftudy, and other ordinary meanes; and therefore *Mofes* his skill in this kinde is called the Learning of the Egyptians. Now becaufe in thofe times all Sciences were taught onely in a rude and imperfect manner; therefore 'tis likely that they alfo had but a darke and confufe apprehenfion of things, and were liable

Act.7.22.

to the common errours. And for this reafon is it, why *Toftatus* (fpeaking of *Iofuahs* bidding the Moone ftand ftill as well as the Sun) faves, *Quod forte erat imperitus circa Aftrorum doctrinam, fentiens ut vulgares fentiunt*: That perhaps hee was unskilfull in Aftronomy, having

*Iob cap.10. Quæft. 19.

the

12 — That the Earth

LIB.2. Cap.1.

vered; becaufe when God would convince him of his owne folly and ignorance, he propofes to him fuch queftions, as being altogether unanfwerable; which notwithftanding, any ordinary Philofopher in thefe dayes might have refolued. As you may fee at large in the thirty eighth Chapter of that Booke.

The occafion was this: *Iob* having

*Cap.13.3.

before defired that he might difpute with the Almighty concerning the uprightneffe of his owne wayes, and the unreafonableneffe of thofe afflictions which he underwent, do's at length obtaine his defire in this kinde; and God vouchfafes in this thirty eighth chapter, to argue the cafe with him. Where hee do's fhew *Iob* how unfit he was to judge of the wayes of Providence, in difpofing of Bleffings and Afflictions, when as he was fo ignorant in ordinary matters, being not able to difcerne the reafon of naturall and common events. As *why the Sea fhould bee fo bounded from overflowing the land? What is the †bredth of the Earth? what is the *reafon of the Snow or Hayle? what was

†Ver.18. *Ver.22.

the

That the Earth

14

LIB. 2.
Cap. 1.

the same grosse conceit of the Heavens, as the vulgar had. From all which it may be inferred, that the ignorance of such good Men and great Schollers concerning these Philosophical points, can bee no sufficient reason, why after examination we should deny them, or doubt of their Truth.

Consid. 3.

'Tis considerable, that in the rudiments and first beginnings of *Astronomy*, and so in severall Ages after, this opinion hath found many Patrons, and those too Men of eminent note and learning. Such was more especially *Pythagoras*, who was generally and highly esteemed for his divine wit, and rare inventions; under whose mysterious sayings, there be many excellent Truths to bee discovered.

*　　*　　*　　*　　*

That the Earth

First, the Suns being in the centre of the World. Secondly, the earth's annuall motion about it, as being one of the planets: thirdly, it's diurnal revolution, wherby it caused day & night.

To his second reason I answer: First, that *Pythagoras* thought the Earth to be one of the Planets (as appeares by *Aristotles* testimony concerning him) and to move amongst them the rest. So that his opinion concerning the motion of the heavens, is not inconsistent with that of the earth. Secondly, but as for the coelestiall harmony, he might perhaps under this mysticall expression, according to his usuall custome, shadow forth unto us that mutuall proportion & harmonicall consent, which he did conceive in the severall bignes, distance, motions of the orbs. So that notwithstanding these objections, it is evident that *Pythagoras* was of this opinion, and that his Authority may adde somwhat for the confirmation of it. Vnto him assented *Aristarchus Samius*, who flourished about 280 yeares before the Birth of our Saviour, and was by reason of this opinion, arraigned for
pro-

* *Archimedes de arene numero.*

may be a Planet.

prophanes and sacriledge by the *Ariopagites*, because he had blasphemed the deity of *Vesta*, affirming the earth to move. To them agreed *Philaus, Heraclides, Pontius, Nicetas Syracusanus, Ecphantus, Lucippus,* and *Plato* himself (as some think.) So likewise *Numa Pompilius*, as *Plutarch* relates it in his life; who in reference to this opinion, built the temple of *Vesta* round, like the universe: in the middle of it was placed the perpetuall vestall fire; by which he did represent the Sunne in the centre of the world. All these men were in their severall times of speciall Note, as well for their extraordinarie learning, as for this opinion.

'Tis considerable, that since this Science of *Astronomy* hath bin raised to any perfection, there have been many of the best skill in it, that have assented unto that assertion which is here defended. Amongst whom was the Cardinall *Cusanus*; but more especially *Copernicus*, who was a man very exact and diligent in these studies for above 30 yeres together, from the yeare 1500 to 1530, and upwards: and since him, most of the best
C   Astro-

4. *Consid.*

De doct ignor.lib.2. cap.12.

18   LIB.2.   *That the Earth*

Astronomers have been of this side. So that now, there is scarce any of note and skil, who are not *Copernicus* his followers; and if we should goe to most voices, this opinion would carry it from any other.

It would be too tedious to reckon up the names of those that may be cited for it; I wil only mention some of the chief: Such were *Ioachinus Rheticus*, an elegant writer, *Christopherus Rothman*, *Mestlin*, a man very eminent for his singular skill in this Science; who though at the first he were a follower of *Ptolomy*, yet upon his second and more exact thoughts, he concluded *Copernicus* to be in the right, & that the usual *Hypothesis*, *prescriptione potius quàm ratione valet*, do's prevaile more by prescription then reason. So likewise *Erasmus Reinholdus*, who was the man that calculated the Prutenicall Tables from *Copernicus* his observations, and did intend to write a Commentarie upon his other Works, but that he was taken out of this life before hee could finish those resolutions. Vnto these also I might adde the Names of *Gilbert*, *Keplar*, *Galilæus*, with sundry others, who have

Præf. ad Narrat. Rbetici.

Ibid.

may be a Planet.   LIB.2.   19

have much beautified and confirmed this *Hypothesis*, with their new inventions. Nay I may safely affirme, that amongst the varietie of those opinions that are in *Astronomy*, there are more (of those which have skill in it) that are of this opinion, not only than any other side, but than all the rest put together. So that now it is a greater Argument of Singularitie to oppose it.

'Tis probable, that many other of the Antients would have assented unto this opinion, if they had been acquainted with those experiments which later times have found out for the confirmation of it: And therefore * *Rheticus* and † *Keplar* doe so often wish that *Aristotle* were now alive againe. Questionlesse he was so rational & ingenious a man (not halfe so obstinate as many of his followers) that upon such probabilities as these, he would quickly have renounced his owne Principles, and have come over to this side: for in one place, having proposed some questions about the heavens, which were not easie to bee resolved: He sets downe this rule, That in difficulties,

§ Confid.

* *in Narrationa.*

† *Præf. Cofmogr. cap.1. Item præf. ad 4.l. aftr. Copern.*

de cœl.l.2. c.12.

C 2

may be a Planet.

a frame of the cœlestiall bodies, from which wee might, in some measure, conceive of their different appearances; and according to which, wee might be able to calculate their motions. But now, 'tis *Copernicus* his endeavour, to propound unto us, the true naturall Causes of these severall Motions, and Appearances: It was the intent of the one, to settle the Imagination; and of the other, to satisfie the judgement. So, that wee have no reason to doubt of his assent unto this Opinion, if hee had but clearly understood all the grounds of it.

'Tis reported of *Clavius*, that when lying upon his Death-bed, he heard the first Newes of those Discoveries which were made by *Galileus* his Glasse, he brake forth into these words: *Videre Astronomos, quo pacto constituendi sunt orbes Cœlestes, ut hæc Phænomena salvari possint*: That it did behoove Astronomers, to consider of some other *Hypothesis*, beside that of *Ptolomy*, whereby they might salve all those new appearances.

C 3

That the Earth

ficulties, a man may take a liberty to speake that which seems most likely to him: and in such cases, an aptnesse to guesse at some resolution, for the satisfying of our Philosophicall thirst, do's deserve rather to be stiled by the name of Modestie, than Boldnes. And in another place, he referres the Reader to the different opinions of Astronomers, advising him to examine their severall rentents, as well *Eudoxus* as *Calippus*; and to entertaine that (not which is most antient, but) which is most exact and agreeable to reason. And as for *Ptolomy*, 'tis his counsell, that wee should endeavour to frame such suppositions of the Heavens, as might be more simple, being void of all superfluities: and he confesses, that his *Hypothesis* had many implications in it, together with sundry intricate and unlikely turnings, and therefore in the same place, hee seems to admonish us, that wee should not bee too confident the Heavens were really in the same Forme, wherein Astronomers did suppose them. So that 'tis likely, 'twas his chief intent to propose unto us such

Met.lib.12. cap.8.

Alm.lib.13. cap.2.

a

pearances. Intimating that this old one, which formerly he had defended, would not now ferve the turne: and doubtleffe, if it had been informed how congruous all thefe might have been unto the opinion of *Copernicus*, bee would quickly have turned on that fide. 'Tis confiderable, that amongft the followers of *Copernicus*, there are fcarce any, who were not formerly againft him; and fuch, as at firft, had been throughly feafoned with the Principles of *Ariftotle*; in which, for the moft part, they have no leffe fkil, than thofe who are fo violent in the defence of them. Whereas on the contrary, there are very few to bee found amongft the followers of *Ariftotle* and *Ptolomy*, that have read any thing in *Copernicus*, or doe fully underftand the Grounds of his opinion; and I thinke, not any, who having been once fetled with any ftrong affent on this fide, that have afterwards revolted from it. Now if we do but ferioufly weigh with our felves, that fo many ingenious, confidering men, fhould reject that opinion which they were nurfed up in, and which is generally approved

proved

proved as the truth; and that, for the embracing of such a *Paradox* as is condemned in Schooles, and commonly cryed downe, as being abfurd and ridiculous; I fay, if a man doe but well confider all this, he muft needs conclude, that there is fome ftrong evidence for it to bee found out by examination; and that in all probabilitie, this is the righter fide.

'Tis probable, that moft of thofe Authors who have oppofed this opinion, fince it hath bin confirmed by new difcoveries, were ftirred up thereunto by fome of thefe 3 infufficient grounds.

7 Confid.

1 An over-fond and partial conceit of their proper inventions. Every man is naturally more affected to his owne brood, than to that of which another is the Author; though perhaps, it may bee more agreeable to reafon. 'Tis very difficult for any one, in the fearch of Truth, to find in himfelfe fuch an indifferencie, as that his judgement is not at all fwayd by an overweening affection unto that which is proper unto himfelfe. And this perhaps might bee the firft reafon that moved the noble *Tycho* with fo much

C 4   heate

That the Earth

heat to oppose *Copernicus*, that so hee might make way for the spreading of that *Hypothesis*, which was of his owne invention. To this I might likewise refer that opinion of *Origanus* and Mr. *Carpenter*, who attribute to the earth only a diurnall revolution. It do's more especially concerne those men that are *Leaders* of severall sides, to beat downe any that should oppose them.

2   A servile and superstitious feare of derogating from the authoritie of the antients, or opposing that meaning of Scripture phrases; wherein the supposed infallible Church, hath for a long time understood them. 'Tis made part of the new Creed, set forth by *Pius* the fourth, 1564, That no man should assent unto any interpretation of Scripture, which is not approved of by the authoritie of the Fathers. And this is the reason why the *Iesuites*, who are otherwise the greatest affectors of those opinions, which seeme to be new and subtill, doe yet forbeare to say any thing in defence of this; but rather take all occasions to inveigh against it. * One of them do's expressely

* *Serrarius Commen. in Ios. cap.10. Quest. 14. So Lipsius Physiol.l.2.*

may be a Planet.

expressely condemn it for a heretic. And since him, it hath bin called in by † two Sessions of the *Cardinals*, as being an opinion both absurd and dangerous. And therefore likewise doe they punish it, by casting the Defenders of it into the Popes truest Purgatorie, the Inquisition: but yet neither these Councels, nor any (that I know of) since them, have proceeded to such a peremptorie censure of it, as to conclude it a heresie: fearing perhaps, lest a more exact examination, and the discoverie of future times, finding it to bee an undeniable Truth, it might redound to the prejudice of their Church, and it's infallibilitie. And therefore he that is most bitter against it, in the heat and violence of opposition, will not call it a heresie: the worst that he dares say of it, is, That it is *opinio temeraria quæ altero saltem pede intravit hæresios limen*; A rash opinion, and bordering upon heresie. Though unto this likewise he was incited, by the easinesse of disputation, and a desire of victorie, for it seemes many eminent men of that Church before him, were a great

Fromondus Anti-Arist. cap.6.

26   LIB. 2.

Tat the Earth

great deale more milde and moderate in their cenfures of it.

Paul the third, was not fo much offen-ded at *Copernicus*, when he dedicated his Worke unto him.

The Cardinall of *Cufa*, do's exprefly maintaine this opinion.

Scembergius, the Cardinall of *Capua*, did with much importunitie and great approbation, beg of *Copernicus* the com-mentaries that he writ in this kind. And it feems the Fathers of the Councell of *Trent*, were not fuch confident defenders of *Ptolomy's hypothefis* againft *Copernicus*, as many now are. For fpeaking of thofe intricate fubtilties, which the Fancies of men had framed, to maintaine the pra-ctice of the Church, they compared them to Aftronomers, who (fay they do faine *Excentricks* and *Epicycles*, and fuch engines of Orbes, to fave the *Phenomena*; though they know there are no fuch things. But now, becaufe this opinion of *Copernicus* in later times hath been fo ftrictly forbidden, and punifhed, it will concerne thofe of that Religion, to take heed of medling in the defence of it, but rather

27   LIB. 2.

may be a Planet.

rather to fubmit the liberty of their rea-fon, unto the command of their Superi-ors, and (which is very abfurd) even in naturall Queftions, not to affent unto any thing, but what authoritie fhall al-low of.

3 A iudging of things by fence, ra-ther than by difcourfe and reafon: a ty-ing of the meaning of Scripture, to the letter of it; and from thence concluding Philofophicall points, together with an ignorance of all thofe grounds and pro-babilities in Aftronomie, upon which this opinion is bottomed. And this in all likelihood, is the reafon why fome men, who in other things perhaps are able Schollers, doe write fo vehemently againft it: and why the common people in generall doe cry it downe, as being abfurd and ridiculous. Vnder this head I might referre the oppofition of 'r. *Fuller, Al. Rofs*, &c.

But now, no prejudice that may arife from the bare authoritie of fuch ene-mies as thefe, will be liable to fway the judgement of an indifferent confidering man; and I doubt not but that hee, who will

28	*That the Earth*
Lib.2.	will throughly weigh with himselfe thefe particulars that are here propoun-ded, may find fome fatisfaction for thefe Arguments, which are taken from the feeming Noveltie and Singularitie of this Opinion.

7. Robert Boyle (1627-1691)

A Disquisition about the Final Causes of Natural Things (1688)
From Boyle, *Works*, 5 vols. (London, 1744), vol. 4, 515-529,
551

A

DISQUISITION

ABOUT THE

FINAL CAUSES

O F

NATURAL THINGS:

Wherein it is inquired,

Whether, and (if at all) with what Cautions, a Naturalift fhould admit them ?

To which are fubjoined, by way of

APPENDIX,

SOME

UNCOMMON OBSERVATIONS

ABOUT

VITIATED SIGHT.

The PREFACE.

THERE are not many fubjects in the whole compafs of natural philo- fophy, that better deferve to be in- quired into by Chriftian philofophers, than that, which is difcourfed of in the following effay. For certainly it becomes fuch men to have curiofity enough to try at leaft, whether it can be difcovered, that there are any know- able final caufes to be confidered in the works of nature; fince, if we negleſt this inquiry, we live in danger of being ungrate- ful, in overlooking thofe ufes of things, that may give us juft caufe of admiring and thank- ing the author of them, and of lofing the be- nefits, relating as well to philofophy as piety, that the knowledge of them may afford us: and if there be no fuch things, we are more than in danger to mifpend our labour and in- duftry, in fruitlefs fearching for fuch things, as are not to be found. And an inquiry of this kind is now the more feafonable, becaufe two of the chief fects of the modern philofo- phizers do both of them, though upon dif- fering grounds, deny, that the naturalift ought at all to trouble or bufy himfelf about final caufes. For *Epicurus*, * and moft of his fol- lowers (for I except fome few late ones, ef- pecially the learned *Gaffendus*) banifh the confideration of the ends of things ; becaufe the world being, according to them, made by chance, no ends of any thing can be fup- pofed to have been intended. And on the contrary, † monfieur *des Cartes*, and moft of his followers, fuppofe all the ends of God in

* *Illud in his rebus vitium vehementer ineſto, Effugere illorumque errorem præmeditemus, Lumina qui faciunt oculorum clara creata profpicere ut poſſimus ——— Lucr. de rer. nat. lib.* IV. *ſeĉt.* 824.
† *Ita denique nullas unquam rationes circa res naturales, a fine, quem deus aut natura in iis faciendis ſibi propoſuit, deſumemus ; qui non tantum nobis debemus arrogare ut ejus conſiliorum participes eſſe putemus : Carteſius princip. philoſop. parte prima ar. ic.* 28.

things

516 *The* PREFACE.

things corporeal to be fo fublime, that it were prefumption in man to think his reafon can extend to difcover them. So that, according to thefe oppofite fects, it is either impertinent for us to feek after final caufes, or prefumptuous to think we may find them. Wherefore, I hope I fhall be excufed, if, having been engaged by fome folicitations, (wherewith it is needlefs to trouble the reader,) I did not decline to try, what the bare, but attentive, confideration of the fubject would fuggeft to my own thoughts. And though it was eafy to forefee, that by this means my friend might mifs of receiving in my effay divers things, that occurred not to me ; yet I confidered on the other fide, that fuch things would, notwithftanding my filence, be found in the authors that delivered them ; and it was very poffible, that, by the courfe I took, I might light upon fome thoughts, that I fhould have miffed, if I had prepoffeffed my mind with the opinions of others ; which I was the lefs tempted to do, becaufe an eafy profpect of my theme fufficed to let me fee I was like to have the Epicureans and Cartefians for my adverfaries, not my affiftants : and for the fchool-philofophers, the very flight account, that their mafter *Ariftotle* gives of one of my four queftions, (for of the reft, as far as I remember, he fays little or nothing,) gave me fmall hopes of being aided by them ; efpecially fince in this, as in many other queftions, they proceed upon grounds, that I cannot affent to. Anatomifts indeed, and fome phyficians, have done very laudably upon the ufes of the parts of the human body ; which I take this occafion to declare, that it may not be fufpected, that I do in the leaft undervalue their happy induftry, becaufe I tranfcribe not paffages out of their books : the reafons of which omiffion are, not only, that I had not any one book of anatomy at hand, when I was writing, but, that the ufes of the parts of man's body related but to a fmall part of my difcourfe ; to make which more comprehenfive, I took in the confideration of more general queftions, befides that, which was controverted between *Ariftotle* and the ancienter philofophers, who difputed how bodies, that were devoid of knowledge, could act for ends.

THOSE, that relifh no books in natural philofophy but fuch as abound in experiments, are feafonably advertifed, that I do not invite them to read this treatife ; wherein I thought it much more fuitable to the nature of my fubject and defign, to declare the works of God, than of men ; and confequently to deliver rather obfervations, than artificial experiments. And even of the former of thefe, though perhaps moft readers may find in the enfuing difcourfe feveral, that they have not met with in claffic authors, yet I fhall freely acknowledge, that, upon the review I made of what I writ, I find, though too late to repair the omiffion, that I have left feveral things unmentioned, that would have been very pertinent to my fubject ; which may, I hope, be more eafily excufed, becaufe, the body of the following difquifition having been written many years ago, and thrown by upon the death of the * gentleman, that preffed me for it, I could not then take notice of thofe many difcoveries in anatomy, and other parts of phyfiology, that have fince been happily made. But perhaps fome will think I may have more need to excufe the largenefs of fome parts of the following treatife, compared with the others. And I fhould rather grant than anfwer the objection, if I could not alledge, that the contagious boldnefs of fome baptized Epicureans engaged me to dwell much longer on the third propofition of the fourth fection, than I at firft intended. And on the other hand, the Cartefian opinion having of late made it requifite to handle the formerly difficult queftion, about the confideration of final caufes, after a new manner, I thought it unfit lightly to pafs over the paradox maintained by fo great a man, and judged it expedient in fome places (what I could not do without enlarging) to propofe thoughts adjufted to the prefent ftate of things in this affair ; in the management of which, I have had fo much more regard to fome other things, than to the fymmetry of the parts, whereof this tract confifts, that I will not fay, that I fear I have in it but thrown together materials for a juft difcourfe on my fubject ; fince to do fo was the main thing I intended. And if the materials be good and folid, they will eafily, in fo learned an age as this, find an architect, that will difpofe them in a more artful way, than I was either at leifure or follicitous to do.

* Mr. *Henry Oldenburg*, Secretary to the Royal Society.

AN

A N

E S S A Y,

INQUIRING

Whether, and how, a NATURALIST should consider FINAL CAUSES.

To my very learned Friend Mr. *F. O.*

SIR,

THOUGH in a book or two of mine, that you have already been pleased to peruse, there are some passages, whence you may easily enough gather, what I thought about your questions ; yet because the subject is of great moment, as well as difficulty, and you may suspect I have altered my opinion, I shall, without referring you to writings, which perhaps neither you nor I have at hand, set down succinctly, but yet as if I had said nothing of any of them before, my present thoughts about these four questions.

I. WHETHER, generally or indefinitely speaking, there be any final causes of things corporeal, knowable by naturalists ?

II. WHETHER, if the first question be resolved in the affirmative, we may consider final causes in all sorts of bodies, or only in some peculiarly qualified ones ?

III. WHETHER, or in what sense, the acting for ends may be ascribed to an unintelligent, and even inanimate body ?

IV. AND lastly, how far, and with what cautions, arguments may be framed upon the supposition of final causes ?

SECT. I.

TO begin with the first question ; those, that would exclude final causes from the consideration of the naturalist, are wont to do it (for aught I have observed) upon one of these two accounts: either that, with *Epicurus*, they think the world was the production of atoms and chance, without any intervention of a deity ; and that consequently it is improper and in vain to seek for final causes in the effects of chance : or, that they judge, with *Des Cartes*, that God being an omniscient agent, it is rash and presumptuous for men to think, that they know, or can investigate, what ends he proposed to himself in his actings about his creatures. The ground, on which the Epicureans have rejected final causes, has been disallowed by the philoso-

phers of almost all other sects ; and some have written sufficient confutations of it, which therefore I shall here forbear to insist on ; though some things I shall upon occasion observe, that may help, if not suffice, to discredit so unreasonable an opinion. But the Cartesian argument has been so prevalent among many learned and ingenious men, that it will be worth while (if it be but to excite better pens) to spend some time in the consideration of it.

PERHAPS one thing, that alienated that excellent philosopher, from allowing the consideration of final causes in physics, was, that the school-philosophers, and many other learned men, are wont to propose it too unwarily, as if there were no creature in the world, that was not solely, or at least chiefly, designed for the service or benefit of man ; insomuch, that I remember I have seen a body of divinity, published by a famous writer, wherein, to prove the opinion he favours, of those, that would have the world annihilated after the day of judgment, he urgeth this argument ; that since the world was made for the sake of man in his travelling condition (*hominis viatoris causa,*) when once man is possessed of his everlasting state of happiness or misery, there will be no further use of the world. The opinion, that gives rise to such presumptuous and unwarrantable expressions, did, as I guess by his objection, more shock *Des Cartes*, than I wonder, that it should displease him. But the indiscretion of men ought not to prejudice truth ; which must not be cast away, with the unwarrantable conceits, that some men have pinn'd upon it.

WHEREFORE, since I cannot entirely close, either with the opinion of the Epicureans, or of the Cartesians, I shall leave each party to maintain its own opinion, and proceed to propose mine ; for the clearing of which, and indeed of the disquisition of final causes, I shall beg leave to premise a distinction, which, though novel, I shall venture to employ, because it comprizes and distinguishes some things, which I think ought neither to be overlooked nor confounded.

518   *A* DISQUISITION *about the* FINAL CAUSES

I CONCEIVE then, that when we fpeak of the ends, which nature, or rather the author of nature, is faid to have in things corporeal, one of thefe four things may be fignified, or, if you like that expreffion better, the end defigned by nature may be fourfold :

FIRST, there may be fome grand and general ends of the whole world, fuch as the exercifing and difplaying the creator's immenfe power and admirable wifdom, the communication of his goodnefs, and the admiration and thanks due to him from his intelligent creatures, for thefe his divine excellencies, whofe productions manifeft his glory. And thefe ends, becaufe they regard the creation of the whole univerfe, I call the univerfal ends of God or nature.

SECONDLY, in a fomewhat more reftrained fenfe, there may be ends defigned in the number, fabric, placing, and ways of moving the great maffes of matter, that, for their bulks or qualities, are confiderable parts of the world ; fince it is very probable, that thefe bodies, fuch as the fun, moon, and fixed ftars, and the terraqueous globe, and perhaps each of its two chief parts, the earth and the fea, were fo framed and placed, as not only to be capable of perfevering in their own prefent ftate, but alfo as was moft conducive to the univerfal ends of the creation, and the good of the whole world, whereof they are notable parts. Upon which account thefe ends may, for diftinction's fake, be called cofmical or fyftematical, as regarding the fymmetry of the great fyftem of the world.

THERE is a third fort of ends, that do more peculiarly concern the parts of animals, (and probably plants too) which are thofe, that the particular parts of animals are deftinated to, and for the welfare of the whole animal himfelf, as he is an entire and diftinct fyftem of organized parts, deftinated to preferve himfelf and propagate his fpecies, upon fuch a theatre, (as the land, water, or air) as his ftructure and circumftances determine him to act his part on.   And thefe ends, to difcriminate them from others, may be called animal ends.

FOURTHLY, and laftly, there is another fort of ends, which, becaufe they relate particularly to man, may, for brevity's fake, be called human ends ; which are thofe, that are aimed at by nature, where fhe is faid to frame animals and vegetables, and other of her productions, for the ufe of man. And thefe ends themfelves may be diftinguifhed into mental, that relate to his mind, and corporeal, that relate to his body, not only as he is an animal framed like other animals, for his own prefervation, and the propagation of his fpecies (mankind ;) but alfo as he is framed for dominion over other animals and works of nature, and fitted to make them fubfervient to the deftinations, that one may fuppofe to have been made of them to his fervice and benefit.

THIS diftinction of final caufes, which, I hope, will not prove altogether ufelefs, being premifed, I fhall begin my intended difcourfe, by owning a diffent from both the oppofite opinions ; theirs, that, with the vulgar of learned men, will take no notice of final caufes but thofe we have ftiled human ones ; and theirs, that (as they think with *Des Cartes*) reject final caufes altogether ; fince, though I judge it erroneous to fay in the ftricteft fenfe, that every thing in the vifible world was made for the ufe of man, yet I think it is more erroneous to deny, that any thing was made for ends inveftigable by man.

IT is a known principle of the Cartefian philofophy, that there is always juft the fame quantity of motion in the world at one time, that there is at another : of which affertion this reafon is given, that there is no caufe, why God, who is immutable, fhould at the beginning of things, when he firft put matter into motion, have given it fuch a quantity of motion, as would need to be afterwards augmented or leffened. But I fee not, how by this negative way of arguing, thofe, that employ it, do not (implicitly at leaft) take upon them to judge of the ends, that God may have propofed to himfelf in natural things. For, without a fuppofition, that they know what God defigned in fetting matter a-moving, it is hard for them to fhew, that his defign could not be fuch, as might be beft accomplifhed by fometimes adding to, and fometimes taking from, the quantity of motion he communicated to matter at firft. And I think it may be worth confidering, whether, by this doctrine of theirs, the Cartefians do not more take upon them, than other philofophers, to judge of God's defigns.   For, if a man be known to be very wife, and have various ways of compaffing his feveral ends, he, that, feeing fome of thofe ways have a direct tendency to fome rational end, fhall conclude that end to be one of thofe, that is intended, does thereby lefs prefume, and exprefs more refpect to that wife man, than he, that fhould conclude, that thofe cannot be his ends, and that he can have no other defign knowable by us, except a certain general one named by the affertor.   And indeed, it feems more eafy to know, that this or that particular thing, for which an engine is proper, may be, among others, intended by the artificer, though never fo fkilful, than to know negatively, that he can have no other, than fuch or fuch an end.

AND how will a Cartefian affure me, that among the many ends, that he grants that God may have propofed to himfelf in the production of his mundane creatures, one may not be, that we, whom he has vouchfafed to make intelligent beings, and capable of admiring and praifing him, fhould find juft caufe to do fo, for the wifdom and goodnefs he has difplayed in the world? which attributes we could not well difcern or celebrate, unlefs we knew as well, that the creatures were made for fuch ufes, as that

they

of NATURAL THINGS. 519

they are exceedingly well fitted for them. I know God's immutability is alledged, to prove, that the quantity of motion is never varied ; but to me it is not evident, why God's having particular ends, though some of them seem to require a change in his way of acting in natural things, must be more inconsistent with his immutability, than his causing many things to be brought to pass, which though *ab æterno* he decreed to do, are yet not actually done, unless in process of time. And particularly it seems not clear, why God may not as well be immutable, though he should sometimes vary the quantity of motion, that he has put into the world, as he is, though, according to the opinion of most of the Cartesians themselves, he does daily create multitudes of rational souls, to unite them to human bodies ; especially considering, that these newly created substances are, according to *Des Cartes*, endowed with a power, to determine and regulate the motions of the spirits and the conarion, which are things clearly corporeal. I say not this, as if I absolutely rejected the Cartesian doctrine, about the continuance of the same quantity of motion in the whole mass of matter ; for, whether or no it be a truth, I think it no unuseful nor improbable hypothesis ; and I have not so much argued against it, as upon the grounds, on which they argue for it.

Wherefore, to come now to the thing itself, whereas monsieur *Des Cartes* objects, that it is a presumption for man to pretend to be able to investigate the ends, that the omniscient God proposed to himself in the making of his creatures ; I consider, by way of answer, that there are two very differing ways, wherein a man may pretend to know the ends of God in his visible works : for, he may either pretend to know only some of God's ends, in some of his works ; or he may pretend to know all his ends. He, that arrogates to himself to discover God's ends in this latter sense, will scarce be excused from a high presumption, and no less a folly, from the reason lately intimated in the Cartesian objection. But to pretend to know God's ends in the former sense, is not a presumption, but rather to take notice of them is a duty. For there are some things in nature so curiously contrived, and so exquisitely fitted for certain operations and uses, that it seems little less than blindness in him, that acknowledges, with the Cartesians, a most wise author of things, not to conclude, that, though they may have been designed for other, and perhaps higher uses, yet they were designed for this use. As he, that sees the admirable fabric of the coats, humors, and muscles of the eye, and how excellently all the parts are adapted to the making up of an organ of vision, can scarce forbear to believe, that the author of nature intended it should serve the animal, to which it belongs, to see with. The Epicureans indeed, that believe the world to have been produced but by the casual concourse of atoms, with-

out the intervention of any intelligent being, may have a kind of excuse, whereof other philosophers are destitute, that acknowledge a Deity, if not also a Providence. For the very supposition, for instance, that a man's eyes were made by chance, argues, that they need have no relation to a designing agent ; and the use, that a man makes of them, may be either casual too, or at least may be an effect of his knowledge, not of nature's. But when, upon the anatomical dissection, and the optical consideration, of a human eye, we see it is as exquisitely fitted to be an organ of sight, as the best artificer in the world could have framed a little engine, purposely and mainly designed for the use of seeing ; it is very harsh and incongruous to say, that an artificer, who is too intelligent either to do things by chance, or to make a curious piece of workmanship, without knowing what uses it is fit for, should not design it for an use, to which it is most fit.

It is not to be denied, that he may have more uses for it than one, and perhaps such uses, as we cannot divine : but this hinders not, but that, among its several uses, this, to which we see it so admirably adapted, should be thought one. And I see not, how it does magnify God's wisdom, or express our veneration of it, to exclude out of the number of his ends in framing human eyes, that most obvious and ready use, which we are sure is made of them, and which they could not be better fitted for. This may perhaps be not unfitly illustrated by the following comparison, whereof the application were superfluous. Suppose, that a country man, being in a clear day brought into the garden of some famous mathematician, should see there one of those curious gnomonic instruments, that shew at once the place of the sun in the zodiack, his declination from the æquator, the day of the month, the length of the day, &c. It would indeed be presumption in him, being unacquainted both with the mathematical disciplines, and the several intentions of the artist, to pretend or think himself able to discover all the ends, for which so curious and elaborate a piece was framed : but when he sees it furnished with a style, with horary lines and numbers, and in short, with all the requisites of a sun dial, and manifestly perceives the shadow to mark from time to time, the hour of the day, it would be no more a presumption than an error in him to conclude, that (whatever other uses the instrument is fit, or was designed for) it is a sun-dial, that was meant to shew the hour of the day.

AND here I shall demand of those, that will not allow us to think, that any natural things are directed to ends knowable by men ; whether, if the divine Author of them had really designed them for such ends, the things themselves are not so framed and directed, as in that case they should be? And whether the fabrick and management of natural things do really countenance or contradict our supposition?

I

FOR

520   A DISQUISITION *about the* FINAL CAUSES

FOR my part, after what has been already discoursed, I scruple not to confess, that I see not, why it should be reputed a disparagement to the wisdom of any agent whatsoever, to think, that his productions were designed for such ends, among others, as they are excellently framed and fitted for ; unless it did appear, that those ends were unworthy to be designed by the wise Agent. But that cannot be justly said in our present case ; since it is not injurious to the divine Author of things, to believe that some of the ends, to which he destinated divers of his corporeal works, were, to exert and communicate his exuberant goodness, and to receive from his intelligent creatures, such as men, an ardent love, a high admiration, and an obsequious gratitude, for having displayed so much wisdom and beneficence, in exquisitely qualifying his works to be wonderfully serviceable to one another, and a great number of them to be particularly subservient to the necessities and utilities of man.

AND indeed I can by no means assent to that assertion of *M. Des Cartes,* * That it cannot be said, that some of God's ends (in his corporeal works) are more manifest than others ; but that all of them lie equally hid in the abyss of the divine Wisdom ; since there are many of his creatures, some of whose uses are so manifest and obvious, that the generality of mankind, both philosophers and plebeians, have in all ages, and almost in all countries, taken notice of, and acknowledged them. And as to what he adds, (by which he seems to intimate the motive, that led him to make the forementioned assertion) that in physics, all things ought to be made out by certain and solid reasons ; to this I answer, first, that I see not, why the admitting, that the Author of things designed some of his works for these or those uses, amongst others, may not consist with the physical accounts of making of those things ; as a man may give a mechanical reason of the structure of every wheel and other part of a watch, and of their way of acting upon one another, when they are rightly put together, and in short, of the contrivance and phænomena of the little machine ; though he suppose, that the artificer designed it to shew the hours of the day, and though he have that intended use in his eye, whilst he explicates the fabric and operations of the watch. I answer, secondly, that I readily admit, that in physics we should indeed ground all things upon as solid reasons, as may be had ; but I see no necessity, that those reasons should be always precisely physical ; especially if we be treating, not of any particular phænomenon, that is pro-duced according to the course of nature established in the world, already constituted as this of ours is ; but of the first and general causes of the world itself ; from which causes, I see not, why the final causes, or uses, that appear manifestly enough to have been designed, should be excluded. And to me it is not very material, whether or no, in physics, or any other discipline, a thing be proved by the peculiar principles of that science or discipline, provided it be firmly proved by the common grounds of reason. And on this occasion let me observe, that the fundamental tenets of *M. Des Cartes*'s own philosophy are not by himself proved by arguments strictly physical, but either by metaphysical ones, or the more catholic dictates of reason, or the particular testimonies of experience. For when, for instance, he truly ascribes to God all the motion, that is found in matter, and consequently all the variety of phænomena, that occur in the world ; he proves not, by an argument precisely physical, that God, who is an immaterial agent, is the efficient cause of motion in matter ; but only by this, that since motion does not belong to the essence and nature of matter, matter must owe the motion it has to some other being : and then it is most agreeable to common reason to infer, that since matter cannot move itself, but it must be moved by some other being, that being must be immaterial, since otherwise some matter must be able to move itself contrary to the hypothesis. And when *Des Cartes* goes to demonstrate, that there is always in the universe the self-same quantity of motion, (that is, just as much at any one time, as at any other) and consequently, that as much motion as one body communicates to another, it loses itself ; he proves it by the immutability of God, which is not a physical argument strictly so called, but rather a metaphysical one ; as he formerly proved God's being the cause of all motion in matter, not by principles peculiar to physics, but by the common grounds of reason.

† THOUGH *Monsieur Des Cartes* does, as I have formerly shewn, speak very dogmatically and universally, against men's endeavouring or pretending to know any final causes in natural things ; for which reason I have, as well as the generality of his other readers, and even his disciples, looked upon the sense of those positive expressions, as containing his opinion ; yet, since I writ the foregoing part of this treatise, I lighted on a passage of his, wherein he seems to speak more cautiously or reservedly, opposing his reasoning to their opinion, who teach, that God hath no other

---

* *Nec fingi potest, aliquos Dei fines, magis quam alios, in propatulo esse ; omnes enim in imperscrutabili ejus sapientiæ abysso sunt eodem modo reconditi. Resp. Quart. ad object. Gassendi.*

† *C'est une chose, qui de soy est manifeste, que nous ne pouvons connoistre les fins de Dieu, si luy mesme ne nous les revele. Et encore qu'il soit vray en morale, eu egard a nous autres hommes, que toutes choses ont este faites pour la gloire de Dieu, a cause que les hommes sont obligez de louer Dieu pour tous ses ouvrages ; & qu'on puisse aussi dire, que le soleil a este fait pour nous eclairer, pour ce que nous experimentons, que le soleil en effet nous eclaire: ce seroit toutesfois une chose purrile & absurde, d'assurer en metaphysique, que Dieu, a la facon d'un homme superbe, n'auroit point eu d'autre fin en bastissant le monde, que celle d'estre loue par les hommes ; et qu'il n'auroit cree le soleil, qui est plusieurs fois plus grand que la terre; a autre dessein, que d'eclairer l'homme, qui n'en occupe qu'une tres petite partie.*

end

end in making the world, but that of being praifed by men. But in that fhort difcourfe, whereof this paffage is a part, there are two or three other things, wherein I cannot acquiefce. As firft, that it is felf-evident, that we cannot know the ends of God, unlefs he himfelf reveal them to us; (he muft mean in a fupernatural way, if he will not fpeak impertinently:) for what he fays to be evident of itfelf, is not at all fo to the generality of mankind, and even of philofophers; and therefore, I think, it ought not to be barely pronounced, but (if it can be) fhould be proved. And next, he does not fhew, how we are obliged to praife God for his works, if he had no intention to have us do fo, or that we fhould difcover any of the ends, for which he made them. If a judicious man fhould fee a great book, written in fome Indian language, which he is utterly a ftranger to, and fhould know nothing of it, but that it was made by a very intelligent phyfician; he might indeed conclude, that the work was not made by chance, but would have no means to be convinced by the infpection of the book itfelf, that it was compofed with great fkill and kindnefs, and deferved his praife and thanks; fince he could not know any of the particular ends, to which the feveral chapters of it were deftinated, nor confequently difcover how fkilfully they were fitted to reach fuch ends. What *Des Cartes* fays, that it is childifh and abfurd to think, that God had created the fun, which is many times bigger than the earth, only to afford light to man, who is but a fmall part of it, is fomewhat invidioufly propofed; there being few able writers, that confine the utility of the fun directly to the affording light to man; and the littlenefs of his bulk ought not to make it thought abfurd, that God may have had an efpecial eye to his welfare, in framing that bright globe; fince not only, for aught appears to us, that moft excellent engine of man's body is a more admirable thing than the fun, but the rational and immortal foul, that refides in it, is incomparably more noble than a thoufand maffes of brute matter, and that not fo much as organized, can be juftly reputed, (as will be hereafter more fully declared.) And fince, in this very difcourfe, the acute author of it confeffes, that we may know the ends of God's corporeal works, if he reveal them to us; a Chriftian philofopher may be allowed to think the fun was made, among other purpofes, to enlighten the earth, and for the ufe of man, fince the fcripture teaches us, that not only the fun and moon, but the ftars of the firmament, which *Des Cartes* not improbably thinks to be fo many funs, were made to give light to the earth, and were divided to all the nations that inhabit it. Perhaps it were not rafh to add, that I fee not, why the belief, that a man may know fome of God's ends in things corporeal, fhould more derogate from our veneration of his wifdom, than to think we know fome of his ends in other matters, of which the fcripture furnifhes us with a mul-

Deut. iv. 19.

titude of inftances, as (particularly) that of *Job* facrificing for his friends; and the declared ufes of the Urim and Thummim: fince God may, if he pleafes, declare truths to men, and inftruct them, by his creatures and his actions, as well as by his words: as when he taught *Noah* by the rain-bow, and *Jonah* by a gourd and a worm, and regulated the incampment of the Ifraelites by the guidance of a cloud and a fiery pillar. Laftly, whereas *Monfieur des Cartes* objects, that thofe he diffents from, talk, as if they looked upon God as a proud man, who defigned his works only to be praifed for them; I know not, whether in this place he fpeaks fo cautioufly and reverently of God, as he ought, and elfewhere is wont to do. For as humility, though it be a virtue in men, is extremely remote from being any of God's perfections; fo that may be pride in a man, who is but a creature, imperfect, dependent, and hath nothing, that he has not received, which would be none at all in God, who is uncapable of vice, and who may, if he pleafe, juftly propofe to himfelf his own glory for one of his ends, and both require and delight to be praifed by men for his works; fince he is moft worthy of all praife, and it is their duty and reafonable fervice, which he is gracioufly pleafed to approve of, to pay it him.

IT is not without trouble, that I find my felf obliged, by the exigency of my defign, fo much to oppofe, in feveral places of this prefent difcourfe, fome fentiments of *M. Des Cartes,* for whom otherwife I have a great efteem, and from whom I am not forward to diffent: and this I the rather declare to you, becaufe I am not at all of their mind, that think *M. Des Cartes* a favourer of atheifm, which, to my apprehenfion, would fubvert the very foundation of thofe tenets of mechanical philofophy, that are particularly his. But judging, that his doctrine (at leaft as it is underftood by feveral of his followers, as well as his adverfaries,) about the rejection of final caufes from the confideration of naturalifts, tends much to weaken, (as is elfewhere noted) if not quite to deprive us of one of the beft and moft fuccefsful arguments to convince men, that there is a God, and that they ought to admire, praife, and thank him; I think it my duty to prefer an important truth before my refpect to any man, how eminent foever, that oppofes it, and to confider more the glory of the great Author of nature, than the reputation of any one of her interpreters.

AND to ftrengthen what I have been faying, give me leave to mind you more exprefly here of what I have elfewhere intimated, *viz.* that the excellent contrivance of the great fyftem of the world, and efpecially the curious fabric of the bodies of animals, and the ufes of their fenfories, and other parts, have been made the great motives, that in all ages and nations induced philofophers to acknowledge a Deity, as the author of thefe admirable ftructures; and that the

522 *A* DISQUISITION *about the* FINAL CAUSES

nobleſt and moſt intelligent praiſes, that have been occaſioned and indited by the prieſts of nature, have been occaſioned and indited by the tranſcending admiration, which the attentive contemplation of the fabric of the univerſe, and of the curious ſtructures of living creatures, juſtly produced in them. And therefore it ſeems injurious to God, as well as unwarrantable in itſelf, to baniſh from natural philoſophy the conſideration of final cauſes ; from which chiefly, if not only, I cannot but think (though ſome learned men do otherwiſe) that God muſt reap the honour, that is due to thoſe glorious attributes, his wiſdom, and his goodneſs. And I confeſs I ſometimes wonder, that the Carteſians, who have generally, and ſome of them ſkilfully, maintained the exiſtence of a Deity, ſhould endeavour to make men throw away an argument, which the experience of all ages ſhews to have been the moſt ſucceſsful, (and in ſome caſes the only prevalent one) to eſtabliſh, among philoſophers, the belief and veneration of God. I know the *Carteſians* ſay, that their maſter has demonſtrated the exiſtence of a God, by the innate idea, that men have of a being infinitely perfect, who left it upon the mind of man, as the mark of an artiſt impreſt upon his work : and alſo, that they aſcribe to God the having made matter out of nothing, and alone put it into motion ; which ſufficiently argue the immenſity of his power. But though I would by no means weaken the argument drawn from the inbred notion of God, ſince I know, that divers learned men have acquieſced in it ; yet, on the other ſide, I ſee not, why we may not reaſonably think, that God, who, as themſelves confeſs, has been pleaſed to take care men ſhould acknowledge him, may alſo have provided for the ſecuring of a truth of ſo great conſequence, by ſtamping characters, or leaving impreſſes, that men may know his wiſdom and goodneſs by, as well without, upon the world, as within, upon the mind. The bare ſpeculation of the fabrick of the world, without conſidering any part of it, as deſtinated to certain (or determinate) uſes, may ſtill leave men unconvinced, that there is any intelligent, wiſe, and provident author and diſpoſer of things ; ſince we ſee generally the *Ariſtotelians* (before ſome of them were better inſtructed by the Chriſtian religion) did, notwithſtanding the extent, ſymmetry, and beauty of the world, believe it to have been eternal. And though they, whatever their maſter thought, did not believe it to have been created by God ; yet, becauſe they aſſerted, that animals, plants, &c. act for ends, they were obliged to acknowledge a provident and powerful being, that maintained and governed the univerſe, which they called nature ; though they too often dangerouſly miſtook, by ſometimes confounding this being with God himſelf, and at other times ſpeaking of it as co-ordinate with him, as in that famous axiom of *Ariſtotle, Deus & natura nihil faciunt fruſtra.* I acknowledge

therefore, that, as I ſet a juſt value upon the *Carteſian* proof of God's exiſtence, ſo I ſee no reaſon, why we ſhould disfurniſh ourſelves of any other ſtrong argument to prove ſo noble and important a truth ; eſpecially, ſince the *Carteſian* way of conſidering the world is very proper indeed to ſhew the greatneſs of God's power, but not, like the way I plead for, to manifeſt that of his wiſdom and beneficence. For, whereas a *Carteſian* does but ſhew, that God is admirably wiſe, upon the ſuppoſition of his exiſtence ; in our way the ſame thing is manifeſted by the effect of a wiſdom, as well as power, that cannot reaſonably be aſcribed to any other, than a moſt intelligent and potent being : ſo that by this way men may be brought, upon the ſame account, both to acknowledge God, to admire him, and to thank him.

SECT. II.

TO give you now my thoughts of the ſecond queſtion, viz. *Whether we may conſider final cauſes in all ſorts of bodies, or only in ſome peculiarly qualified ones* ; I muſt divide natural bodies into animate and inanimate. The former of which terms I here take in the larger ſenſe of thoſe, who under it comprehend, not only animals, but vegetables ; though I ſhall not diſdainfully reject the opinion of thoſe learned men, that are unwilling to allow plants a ſoul or life, at leaſt as properly ſo called, as that, which is confeſſedly granted to animals.

OF the inanimate bodies of the univerſe, the nobleſt, and thoſe, which, on this occaſion, deſerve chiefly to be conſidered, are the ſun, planets, and other cœleſtial bodies. For, when men ſaw thoſe vaſt and luminous globes, and eſpecially the ſun, move ſo conſtantly, and ſo regularly, about the earth, and diffuſe on it light and heat ; and by their various revolutions produce day and night, ſummer and winter, and the viciſſitudes of ſeaſons, that are ſo opportune for the inhabitants of the earth : the obſervers, I ſay, of all this concluded, both that theſe motions were guided by ſome divine being, and that they were deſigned for the benefit of man. Whether this be a demonſtrative collection, I ſhall not now debate ; but I ſee not, why it may not have thus much of probability in it, that in caſe a man ſhall think, that the fabrick of the cœleſtial parts of the world, was the curious production of an intelligent and divine agent, the regular phænomena of the heavens will not contradict him ; ſince there is nothing in that fabrick, that miſbecomes a divine author ; and the motions and operations of the ſun and ſtars are not ſuch, but that they will allow us to think, that, among other purpoſes, they were made to illuminate the terreſtrial globe, and bring heat and other benefits to the inhabitants of it : ſo that the contemplation of the heavens, which ſo manifeſtly *declare the glory of God,* Pſal. xix. may juſtly excite men, both to admire his 1.

power

power and wisdom in them, and to return him thanks and praises for the great benefits, that accrue to us by them.

But now, on the other side, it may be said, that in bodies inanimate, whether the portions of matter they confist of be greater or lesser, the contrivance is very rarely so exquisite, but that the various motions and occursions of the parts of matter may be, without much improbability, suspected to be capable, after many essays, to cast one another into divers of those circumvolutions of matter, that, I remember, *Epicurus* calls ουσροφας and *Des-Cartes vortices*; which being once made, may continue very long, by the means expressed by *Cartesius*, or by some other as probable ones. But, without allowing this hypothesis to be more than not very improbable, when I consider, what causes there may be to fear, that we are not yet sufficiently acquainted with the true system of the world, and are not usually sensible enough, how small a part we, and the terrestrial globe we inhabit, make of the universe; I am apt to fear too, that men are wont, with greater confidence than evidence, to assign the systematical ends and uses of the coelestial bodies, and to conclude them to be made and moved only for the service of the earth and its inhabitants. And though, even as a meer naturalist, I will not deny, that, as man actually receives benefits by the established order and motion of the stars, so one of the several uses intended by the author of nature in them, may particularly respect men; yet I am apt to think, that, by what we hitherto know, it will not be easy to be proved, that some, at least, of the coelestial bodies and motions may not be intended more for other purposes, than to cast their beams, or shed their influences (supposing they have some) upon the earth. And, at least, I cannot but think, that the situations of the coelestial bodies, do not afford by far so clear and cogent arguments of the wisdom and design of the author of the world, as do the bodies of animals and plants. And, for my part, I am apt to think, there is more of admirable contrivance in a man's muscles, than in (what we yet know of) the coelestial orbs; and that the eye of a fly is, (at least as far as appears to us,) a more curious piece of workmanship, than the body of the sun.

As for other inanimate bodies, as stones, metals &c, whose matter seems not organized, though there be no absurdity to think, that they also were made for distinct particular purposes, if not also for human uses; yet most of them are of such easy and unelaborate contextures, that it seems not absurd to think, that various occursions and justlings of the parts of the universal matter may at one time or other have produced them; since we see in some chymical sublimations, and christallizations of mineral and metalline solutions, and some other phænomena, where the motions appear not to be particularly guided and directed by an intelligent cause,

4

that bodies of as various contextures, as those are wont to be, may be produced; of which I have elsewhere given some instances.

If it be objected, that if we allow chance, or any thing else, without the particular guidance of a wise and all-disposing cause, to make a finely shaped stone, or a metalline substance, growing, as I have sometimes seen silver to do, in the form of a plant, it ought not to be denied, that chance may also make vegetables and animals; I can by no means allow the consequence. There are some effects, that are so easy, and so ready to be produced, that they do not infer any knowledge or intention in their causes; but there are others, that require such a number and concourse of conspiring causes, and such a continued series of motions or operations, that it is utterly improbable they should be produced without the superintendency of a rational agent, wise and powerful enough to range and dispose the several intervening agent's and instruments, after the manner requisite to the production of such a remote effect. And therefore it will not follow, that if chance could produce a slight contexture in a few parts of matter, we may safely conclude it able to produce so exquisit and admirable a contrivance, as that of the body of an animal. What then, if sometimes in sawing pieces of variegated marble, men happen, though rarely, to meet with the delineations or pictures (some of which I have beheld with pleasure) of towns, woods, and men? for, besides that the pleasingness and rarity of such spectacles inclines the imagination to favour them, and supply their defects; would any wise man therefore conclude, that a real town or wood, much less numbers of men, should be made by such a fortuitous concourse of matter? What comparison is there betwixt the workmanship, that seems to be expressed in a few irregular lines drawn upon a plane superficies, and perhaps two or three colours luckily placed, and the great multitude of nerves, veins, arteries, ligaments, tendons, membranes, bones, glandules, &c. that are required to the compleating of a human body; of which numerous parts (for the bones alone are reckoned to amount to three hundred) every one must have its determinate size, figure, consistence, situation, connexion, &c. and many, or all of them together, must conspire to such and such determinate functions or uses? And indeed, though I keep by me some curious ones, yet I never saw any inanimate production of nature, or, as they speak, of chance, whose contrivance was comparable to that of the meanest limb of the despicablest animal: and there is incomparably more art expressed in the structure of a dog's foot, then in that of the famous clock at Strasburg.

And though the paw of a dog will be confessed to be of a structure far inferior to that of the hand of a man; yet even this, however *Aristotle* prettily styles it the instrument of instruments, is a less considerable instance

524   *A* Disquisition *about the* FINAL CAUSES

instance to my present purpose, than another instance, which therefore, since my intended brevity permits me not to consider many, I shall pitch upon, as that, which I shall almost only insist on in the following part of this tract : and this instance is afforded me by the eye. For though the parts, that concur to make up that admirable organ of vision, are very numerous, yet how little any of them could have been spared or altered, unless for the worse, may appear by that great number of diseases, that have been observed in that little part of the body : since each of those diseases consist in this, that some of the coats, humours, or other parts of the eye, are brought into a state differing from that, whereto nature had designed it, and whereinto she had put it. It would be tedious so much as to enumerate the several distempers of the eye, whereunto physicians have given particular names ; wherefore I shall only mention two or three things, wherein one would scarce imagine, that a small recess from the natural state could bring any considerable, or perhaps sensible, inconvenience. That, which we call the pupil, is not (you know) a substantial part of the eye, but only a hole of the uvea ; which aperture is almost perpetually changing its bigness, according to the differing degrees of light, that the eye chances from time to time to be exposed to : and therefore one would not think, but that, whilst this hole remains open, it performs well enough its part, which is, to give admission to the incident beams of light, whether direct or reflected. And yet I lately saw and discoursed with a woman, who, after a fever, was not able to dilate the pupils of her eyes as formerly ; and though they were so very little narrower than ordinary, that I should scarce have taken any notice that it was at all so, if she had not told me of it, yet she complained she had thereby almost lost her sight, seeing objects in certain lights but very dimly and imperfectly. And though the præternatural constriction of the pupil be not a frequent distemper, yet it is not so rare, but that physicians have given it a place among the stated diseases of the eye. And on the other side though it appear by what hath been newly related, that a competent wideness of the pupil is requisite to clear and distinct vision, yet if its wideness exceed due limits, there is produced that distemper called *dilatatio pupillæ* ; which is worse than the former, because it oftentimes deprives the patient almost totally of his sight. And though it may seem but a slight circumstance, that the transparent coats of the eye should be devoid of colour, and of as little moment, that the *cornea* should be very smooth, provided it be transparent ; yet, when either of these circumstances is wanting, the sight may be much vitiated : as we see, that in the yellow-jaundice, when it is come to a high degree, the adventitious tincture, wherewith the eye is imbued, makes men think they see a yellowness in many ob-

jects, to which that colour does not belong. And I know an ingenious gentleman, who having had a small *pustula* excited and broken upon the *cornea*, though the eye have been long whole ; yet a very little inequality or depression, that still remains upon the surface of the transparent *cornea*, does so affect him, that though he can read well in a room, yet when he comes into the open fields or the streets, he for a pretty while (as himself has particularly complained to me) thinks many of the objects he looks on very glaring, and sees many others, as men do stones at the bottom of a brook or running water ; which I impute to the want of uniformity in the refraction of those reflected beams of light, that fall upon the *cornea*, whose surface is not so smooth and equal as it should be.

To give some further proof, that the eye was made with design, I shall here take notice of an observation or two, that do not occur in the dissection of a human eye, and therefore are not wont to be mentioned by anatomists.

I HAVE observed in frogs, (as I presume some others also may have done) that, besides those parts of the eye, which they have in common with men, dogs, cats, and the most part of other animals, they have a peculiar, whether membrane, or cartilage, or both, which ordinarily is not perceived, wherewith they can at pleasure cover the eye, without too much hindering the sight, because this membrane is as well transparent as strong ; so that it may pass for a kind of moveable *cornea*, and (if I may so call it) a kind of false-scabbard to the eye. In furnishing frogs with this strong membrane, the providence of nature seems to be conspicuous : for they being amphibious animals, designed to pass their lives in watery places, which for the most part abound with sedges, and other plants endowed with sharp edges or points, and the progressive motion of this animal being to be made, not by walking, but by leaping ; if his eyes were not provided of such a sheath as I have been mentioning, he must either shut his eyes, and so leap blindly, and by consequence dangerously, or, by leaving them open, must run a venture to have the *cornea* cut, prickt, or otherwise offended, by the edges or points of the plants, or what may fall from them upon the animal's eye : whereas this membrane, as was said, is like a kind of spectacle, that covers the eye without taking away the sight ; and as soon as the need of employing it is past, the animal at pleasure withdraws it into a little cell, where it rests out of the way, till there be occasion to use it again. This you may see, if you apply the point of a pin, or a pen, or any such sharp thing, to the eye of a frog, whilst you hold his head steady : for, to screen his eye, he will presently cover it (at least for the greatest part) with this membrane, which, when the danger is over, he will again withdraw. And because many, if not most sorts

4

of

of NATURAL THINGS.

of birds, are wont or deftinated to fly, (as more would do if not kept tame) among the branches of trees and bufhes; left the prickles, twigs, leaves, or other parts fhould wound or offend their eye, nature hath given them likewife fuch another kind of horny membrane, as we have been mentioning in frogs.

It is known, that men, and the generality of four-footed beafts, and of birds, have feveral mufcles belonging to their eyes; by the help of which mufcles they can turn them this way, or that way, at pleafure; and fo can obvert the organ of fenfe to the object, whether it be placed on the right hand or the left, or above or beneath the eye. But nature having not given that mobility to the eyes of flies, (the reafon whereof I fhall not now ftay to confider) fhe hath in recompence furnifhed them with a multitude of little protuberant parts finely ranged upon the convex of their large and protuberant eyes: fo that by the means of the number of thefe little ftuds (if I may fo call them) many beams of light, that rebound from objects placed on either hand, or above, or beneath, the level of the eye, fall conveniently enough upon that organ, to make the objects they come from vifible to the animal; which you will the more eafily believe, if you contemplate (as I have often done with great pleafure) even the eye of an ordinary flefh-fly, (for bees and other greater infects have immoveable eyes too, but I find them not fo pretty) in a good microfcope and a clear day; for you may reckon fome hundreds of thefe little round protuberances curioufly ranged on the convexity of a fingle eye.

But perhaps fome, whofe partiality for chance makes them willing to afcribe the ftructures of animals rather to that, than to a defigning caufe, will make them draw an objection, fit to be here obviated, againft our doctrine, from what we have obferved of the difference between human and other eyes; fince they will pretend, that all organs of fight ought to be conformed to thofe of men, as thofe, that are the beft and moft perfect. It is true, that man being juftly reputed the moft perfect of animals, it is not ftrange, that he fhould (as men generally do) prefume, that his eyes and other parts of his body are the beft contrived of any, that are to be found in nature. But yet I think we cannot from hence fafely conclude, that all eyes, which in other animals are of ftructures differing from thofe of man, are for that reafon defective. For I confider, firft, that the admirable wifdom difplayed by the author of things, in fitting the eyes and other organical parts of animals, for the ufes, that feem manifeftly to have been defigned in their fabrick, and for the refpective functions we actually fee them exercife, may juftly perfwade us, that the things, whofe reafons or ufes we do not alike difcern, are yet moft wifely conftituted; fuch an author as God having too much

knowledge to do any thing unfkilfully, and we having too much prefumption, if we think he can have in the framing of his creatures no ends, that are beyond our difcovery. And, fecondly, we may reprefent, that the eye is not to be confidered abftractedly as an inftrument of vifion, but as an inftrument belonging to an animal of this or that kind, and who is ordinarily to make ufe of it in fuch and fuch circumftances. And therefore I think it ought not at all to difparage, but rather highly recommend, the wifdom and providence of the great author of things, that he has furnifhed various fpecies of animals with organs of fight, that are very differingly framed and placed; fince this diverfity notably manifefts his great providence, and (if I may fo call it) forecaft, that has admirably fuited the eyes of the differing kinds of animals, both to the reft of their bodies, and (which I here mainly confider) to thofe parts of the great theatre of the world, on which he defigns, that they fhall live and act. Thus, though divers beafts, as horfes, oxen, and fome others, have their eyes furnifhed with a feventh mufcle, befides the fix they have in common with men; we muft not conclude, either that the organs of vifion are imperfect in men, or that thofe of thefe beafts have fomething fuperfluous. For horfes, &c. being to feed for the moft part on grafs and herbs of the field, and, that they may the better chufe their food, being obliged to make their eyes look very long downwards; the feventh mufcle does excellently ferve them to do fo, without that wearinefs, which, if they were not furnifhed with it, that durably conftrained pofture would be fure to give them; whereas man, who has no fuch neceffity of looking affiduoufly downwards, would be but incumbered by a feventh mufcle.

On the other fide, the defectivenefs obfervable in the eyes of fome animals, in comparifon of thofe of man, may be afcribed to the thriftinefs (if I may fo fpeak) of nature, that, on moft occafions, declines doing that, which is not neceffary to the particular ends fhe aims at in the fabrick of a part. Thus moles being defigned to live for the moft part under ground, the eyes, which nature hath given them, are fo little, in proportion to their bodies, that it is commonly believed, and even by fome learned men maintained, they have none at all. But though by anatomy, I, as well as fome others, that have tried, have found the contrary; yet their eyes are very differing from thofe of other four-footed beafts. Which is not to be wondered at, confidering, that the defign of nature was, that moles fhould live under ground, where a fight was needlefs and ufelefs, and where greater eyes would be more expofed to danger; and their fight, as dim as it is, is fufficient to make them perceive, that they are no longer under ground, (at leaft fo as they are wont to be) which feems to be the moft neceffary ufe they have of light and eyes.

526   A DISQUISITION *about the* FINAL CAUSES

ZOOGRAPHERS obferve, that the cameleon has a very uncommon ftructure of his vifive organs; fince, to omit leffer, though not inconfiderable, peculiarities, his eyes often move independantly from one another; fo that, for inftance, he may look directly forward with the right eye, and with the other at the fame time directly backwards towards his tail; or may turn the pupil of the former ftraight upwards, whilft he looks downwards with the other: which peculiar power feems to have been granted him by providence, that, being a very flow animal, and deftinated to live for the moft part in trees and bufhes, and there chiefly feed on flies; he may perceive them, which way foever they chance to come within the reach of his long tongue, by fuddenly darting out of which he catches his nimble prey.

WHEREAS it may be obferved, that many or moft, if not all, meer fifhes have the chryftalline humours of their eyes almoft fpherical, as to fenfe, and confequently far more round than that humour is wont to be found in man, and other terreftrial animals; this difference of figure, though it would be inconvenient in us, does very well accommodate fifhes; fince they living in the water, which, as a thicker medium, does much more refract the beams of light, than the air, through which they pafs to our eyes, it was fit, that the chryftalline humour of fifhes fhould be very globous, that, by the help of their figure, the beams already refracted by the water, fhould be yet fo much refracted and made convergent, as to paint the images fo near, as upon the bottom of the eye.

ONE, that being curious, had more opportunity, than I have, to furvey and reflect on the various ftructures of the organs of vifion in differing animals, may, if I miftake not, be able to find, by comparing them with the other parts of the fame animal, and the fcene he is defigned to act on, and the ufes he is to make of his eyes in his moft ordinary circumftances; fuch a perfon, I fay, may be able to offer a probable reafon of feveral differences in thofe organs, that, if commonly taken notice of, would feem to the cenforious to be aberrations of nature, or defects. To which purpofe I remember, that an ingenious cultivator of optics gives this reafon of what both he and I have taken notice of (though it be ufually overlooked) about the figure of the pupil; namely, that though it be oblong in horfes, oxen, and divers other quadrupeds, as well as in cats, yet in the former kinds of animals the pupil lies tranfverfly from the right fide of the eye to the left, but in cats its fituation is perpendicular; whereof he ingenioufly gueffes the reafon may be, that horfes and oxen being ufually to find their food growing on the ground, they can more conveniently receive the images of the laterally neighbouring grafs, &c. by having their pupils tranfverfly placed; whereas cats, being to live chiefly upon rats and mice, which are animals, that ufually climb up or run down walls and

other fteep places, the commodioufeft fituation of their pupil, for readily difcovering and following thefe objects, was to be perpendicular. But it is time we proceed in our difcourfe.

OTHER inftances to the fame purpofe with this are elfewhere delivered; and therefore I fhall now, to ftrengthen the apology for divine providence, take notice, that the differing ftructures and fituations of the eyes in feveral animals are very fit to fhew the fœcundity of the divine author's fkill, (if I may fo fpeak,) in being able to frame fo great a variety of exquifite inftruments of vifion. And indeed, if I may prefume to guefs at any of God's ends, that are not manifeft, (for other others of his ends feem confpicuous,) I fhould think, that this delightful and wonderful variety, that we may obferve, not only in animals themfelves confidered as entire fyftems, but in thofe parts of them, that appear deftinated for the fame function, as particularly that of feeing was defigned, at leaft among other ends, to difplay the multiplicity of the great creator's wifdom, and fhew his intelligent creatures, that his fkill is not confined to one fort of living engines, nor in the parts of the fame kind, (as eyes, ears, teeth, &c.) to the fame contrivances; but is able to make for the fame ufe, a multitude of furprifing organs or inftruments, though not perhaps all equally perfect, (fince, to do fo, we may think he muft make no animals but men,) yet all of them curious and exquifite in their kinds, and in order to their differing ends. To be able to frame both clocks, and watches, and fhips, and rockets, and granadoes, and pumps, and mills, &c. argues and manifefts a far greater fkill in an artificer, than he could difplay in making but one of thofe forts of engines, how artificially foever he contrived it. And the fame fuperiority of knowledge would be difplayed, by contriving engines of the fame kind, or for the fame purpofes, after very differing manners. As weights indeed are of great ufe and neceffity in the famous clock of *Strafburg*; and therefore it recommends the inventors of watches, not only that they can make clocks of a very little and eafily portable bulk, which the *Strafburg* machine is not, but can make a clock without weights, and by means of a fpring perform their office. And thus, though to fly it feems abfolutely neceffary, that an animal fhould be furnifhed with feathers, the wife creator hath fhewn, that he is not confined to make ufe of them for that purpofe; fince a flying fifh is able to move a great way in the air; and the Indies have lately furnifhed us with a fort of flying fquirrils, whereof I faw one alive at *Whitehall*. And though the flight of thefe is not long, yet there is another kind of animals without feathers, that can fly long enough, namely the batt; though fome of thefe, as I have feen, be little lefs than hens: and I have been affured by a credible eye-witnefs, that in the kingdom of Golconda he had feen much bigger.

3

BUT

of NATURAL THINGS. 527

But though this confideration may fuffice to juftify the wifdom of the creator, who being an agent moft free, as well as moft wife, men ought not to find fault, if he think fit to recommend his wifdom by difplaying it in very different manners ; yet this is not all that may be faid on this occafion. For there are many cafes, and perhaps far more than we imagine, wherein the peculiar, and in fome regards lefs perfect, fabric or fituation of an eye or other organical part, may be more convenient, than the correfpondent organ of man, to attain the ends, for which it was given to an animal, that was to act upon fuch a theatre, and live by fuch provifion. Befides that an organical part may, in fome animals, be intended for more ufes than in others, and therefore may require a differing ftructure, as in moles, the feet are otherwife framed or fituated, than in other quadrupeds, becaufe the chief ufe they were to make of them was not to walk upon the ground, but to dig themfelves ways under ground ; the provident δημιεργός wifely fuiting the fabric of the parts to the ufes, that were to be made of them : as a mechanic employs another contrivance of his wheels, pinions, &c. when he is to grind corn with a mill, that is to be driven by water, than when he is to do the fame thing by a mill, that is to be moved by the wind. And the cameleon has a tongue, both peculiarly fhaped, and of a length difproportionate to that of his body, becaufe he was to take his prey by fhooting out (if I may fo fpeak) his tongue at the flies he was to live upon, and could not often approach them very near without frighting them away. And in many cafes, in which this reflection does not fo properly take place, we may obferve, that there is a wonderful compenfation made for that, which feems a a defect in the parts of an animal of this or that particular fpecies, compared with the correfpondent ones of a man, or an animal of fome other fpecies.

Thus birds, that (except the batt, and and one or two more) want teeth to chew their food, are not only furnifhed with hard bills to break it ; and birds of prey, as hawks, &c. with crooked ones to tear it ; but, which is more confiderable, have crops to prepare and foften it, and very ftrong mufcular ftomachs to digeft and grind it : in which work they are ufually helped by gravel and little ftones, that they are led by inftinct to fwallow, and which are often found (and fometimes in amazing numbers,) in their ftomachs, where they may prove a vicarious kind of teeth.

I shall hereafter have occafion to fay fomewhat more againft their opinion, that find fault with thofe animated ftructures, that we think to be productions of the divine wifdom, under pretence, that the parts of fome living creatures are not fo curious and fymmetrical, as not to have been cafually producible. But, in the mean time, I fhall here note, for thofe, that afcribe fo much to chance, that chance is really no natural caufe or agent, but a creature of man's intellect. For the things, that are done in the corporeal world, are really done by the parts of the univerfal matter, acting and fuffering according to the laws of motion eftablifhed by the author of nature. But we men, looking upon fome of thefe parts as directed in their motions by God, or at leaft by nature, and difpofed to the attainment of certain ends ; if by the intervention of other caufes, that we are not aware of, an effect be produced very differing from that, which we fuppofed was intended, we fay, that fuch an effect was produced by chance. So that chance is indeed but a notion of ours, and fuch a thing, as a fchoolman might call an extrinfical denomination, and fignifies but this ; that in our apprehenfions the phyfical caufes of an effect did not intend the production of what they neverthelefs produced. And therefore I wonder not, that the philofophers, that preceded *Ariftotle*, fhould not treat of chance, among natural caufes ; as we may learn from *Ariftotle* himfelf, who is more juft to them in fufpecting they owned not fuch a caufe, than in taxing them of an omiffion for not having treated of it.

And on this occafion I fhall only add, before I proceed, that whereas fome of the moft curioufly fhaped kind of ftones, as the *Aftroites*, have emboldened many of the favourers of *Epicurus* to bring them into competition with thefe animals, or parts of animals, from their likenefs ro which they have received their names ; it is fit to be confidered, firft, that fome learned men have of late made it very probable, that fome of the curioufeft forts of thefe ftones were once really the animals, whofe fhapes they bear, or thofe parts of animals, which they refemble ; which animal fubftances were afterwards turned into ftones, by the fupervening of fome petrefcent matter, or petrifying caufe ; of which metamorphofis I have met with, and do elfewhere mention, more inftances, than are fit to be fo much as named in this place. Secondly, though fome of thofe forts of ftones were the production of the mineral kingdom, (for I will not be dogmatical in this point ;) yet, befides that it would not clearly follow, that they owe their fhapes to chance, fince there is no abfurdity to admit feminal principles in fome more elaborate forts of foffiles ; I think it would be very injurious to make thefe productions vie with the animals, to which they are compared. For the refemblance of fhapes, wherein alone they and the animals agree, being but the outward figure, is but a fuperficial thing, and not worthy to be mentioned, in comparifon of that, wherein they differ ; the rude and flight contexture of the beft fhaped ftones, being incomparably inferior to the internal contrivance of an animal, which muft confift of a multitude of parts, of fuch a figure, bulk, texture, fituation, &c. as cannot but be obvious to any, that have feen diffections fkilfully made. And it is not only in the ftable and quiefcent parts, that this great internal

528   *A* DISQUISITION *about the* FINAL CAUSES

ternal difference between stones, and the animals they resemble, is to be found; but there is in a living animal a greater difference, than any of the knives of anatomists can shew us in a dead one betwixt a stone, though never so curiously figured, and an animal. For there are, I know not how many, liquors, spirits, digestions, secretions, coagulations, and motions of the whole body, and of the limbs and other parts, which are lodged and performed in a living body, and not in a cadaver; and are perchance far more admirable, even than the structure of the stable and quiescent parts themselves. So that though a stone, outwardly very like a shell-fish, were made by chance; yet from thence to conclude, that chance may make a real living shell fish, would be to argue worse than he, that should contend, that because even an unskilful smith may make a hollow piece of metal like a watch case, though he can fill it but with filings of iron, or some other rude stuff, he must be able to make a watch; there being less difference betwixt the skill expressed in making the case of a watch and the movement, than in making a body like a shell, and the internal parts of a real fish: or to say, that because putrefaction and winds have sometimes made trees hollow, and blown them down into the water, where they swim like boats; therefore the like causes may make a galley built and contrived, as well within as without, according to the laws of naval architecture, and furnished with mariners to row it, steer it, and, in a word, to excite and guide all its motions to the best advantage, for the preservation and various uses of the vessel. In short, if chance sometimes does some strange things, it is in reference to what she herself, but not to what nature, uses to perform.

AND now, to give you the summary of my thoughts, about the second question; 1. I think, that from the ends and uses of the parts of living bodies the naturalist may draw arguments, provided he do it with due cautions, of which I shall speak under the fourth question. 2. That the inanimate bodies here below, that proceed not from seminal principles, have but a more parable texture, (if I may so speak) as earths, liquors, flints, pebbles, and will not easily warrant ratiocinations drawn from their supposed ends. 3. I think the cœlestial bodies do abundantly declare God's power and greatness, by the immensity of their bulk, and (if the earth stand still) the celerity of their motions, and also argue his wisdom and general providence as to them; because he has for so many ages kept so many vast vortices, or other masses of matter, in scarce conceivably rapid motions, without destroying one another, or losing their regularity. And I see no absurdity in supposing, that, among other uses of the sun, and of the stars, the service of man might be intended; but yet I doubt, whether, from the bare contemplation of the heavens and their motions, it may be cogently inferred, at least so strongly as final

causes may be from the structure of animals, that either the sole or the chief end of them all is to enlighten the earth, and bring benefits to the creatures, that live upon it.

IN what has been hitherto said on our second question, it is plain, that I suppose the naturalist to discourse meerly upon physical grounds. But if the revelations contained in the holy scriptures be admitted, we may rationally believe more, and speak less hesitantly, of the ends of God, than bare philosophy will warrant us to do. For if God is pleased to declare to us any thing concerning his intentions, in the making of his creatures, we ought to believe it, though the consideration of the things themselves did not give us the least suspicion of it; which yet in our case they do. And therefore a late ingenious author did causlessly reflect upon me, for having mentioned the enlightning of the earth, and the service of men, among the ends of God, which he thought undiscoverable by us. For whether or no we can discover them by meer reason, as divers of the heathen philosophers thought they did; yet sure we may know those, that God is pleased to reveal to us: and the persons I argued with were apparently such, as admitted the authority of the scriptures; which expressly teach us, that God made *the two great luminaries,* (for so I should render the Hebrew words אֶת־שְׁנֵי הַמְּאֹרֹת הַגְּדֹלִים) *the greater for the rule of the day, and the lesser for the rule of the night. And that he made the stars also,* and set them in the firmament, or rather expansum of the heaven, *to give light upon the earth.* And a little above, among the uses of the luminaries these are reckoned, *to divide the day from the night, and to be for signs, and for seasons, and for days and years.* And in another place, the prophet *Moses* dehorting the Israelites from worshipping the sun, the moon, and the stars, tells them, that the *Lord had imparted them unto all nations under the whole heaven.* And therefore those Cartesians, that, being divines, admit the authority of holy scripture, should not reject the consideration of such final causes, as revelation discovers to us; since it is certainly no presumption to think we know God's ends, when he himself acquaints us with them; nor to believe, that the sun, though it be generally esteemed to be a nobler body than the terrestrial globe, was made, among other purposes, to give light to its inhabitants. It is recorded in the book of *Genesis,* the design of God in making man was, that *men should subdue the earth* (as vast a globe as it is) *and have dominion over the fish of the sea, and over the fowl of the air, and over the cattle, and over all the earth,* and (to speak summarily) *over every living thing, that moveth upon the earth.* And the same book informs us, that after the deluge, God *delivered all terrestrial beasts, and fowl, and fishes, and every moving thing, that lives,* into the hands of men; and intended, that they should eat animals, as before the flood he had appointed them all the sorts of wholesome vegetables for their food.

Gen. i. 16.

Deut. iv. 19.

Gen. i. 26, 27, 28.

Gen. ix. 23.

And

of NATURAL THINGS.   529

And since God was pleased to appoint, that men should live on these creatures, it cannot be absurd to say, that, among other purposes, to which he destinated the sun, his shining upon the earth was one; since without his light and heat, men could not provide for, or enjoy themselves; and neither those plants, that men and cattle must live upon, could grow and ripen; nor (consequently) those animals, that were to be their principal food and serve them for many other uses, could be sustained and provided for. Many other texts, that shew, how much God was pleased to intend man's welfare, and dominion over many of his fellow-creatures, might be here alledged. But I shall content myself to mention, what the kingly prophet says in the 8th psalm, where speaking of man to his maker, he says; *Thou hast made him a little lower than the angels, and hast crowned him with glory and honour. Thou madest him to have dominion over the works of thine hands, and hast put all things under his feet.* Indeed if in man we consider only that visible part, his body; the smallness of it may make it thought improbable, that portions of the universe incomparably greater than he, should be at all intended to be serviceable to him. But Christians ought not to think this incredible, if they consider man, as he chiefly consists of a rational mind, which proceeds immediately from God, and is capable of knowing him, loving him, and being eternally happy with him. They, that despise man considered in this capacity, do very little know the worth of a rational soul; and estimate things like masons, and not like jewelers, who justly value a diamond no bigger than a bean, more than a whole quarry of ordinary stones. And particularly to those undervaluers of their own species, that are divines, it may be represented, that God, who will not be denied to be the best judge in this case, as in all others, was pleased to consider men so much, as to give *David* cause to admire it in the words lately cited; and not only to endow them with his image at their first creation, but when they had criminally lost and forfeited it, he vouchsafed to redeem them by no less than the sufferings and death of his own son, who is incomparably more excellent than the whole world. And it is not incredible, that God should have intended, that many of his other works should be serviceable to man; since by miraculous operations he hath sometimes suspended the laws of nature, and sometimes over-ruled them, upon the account of man: as may appear by *Noah*'s flood; by the passage of the *Israelites* on dry land through the Red Sea, and the river of *Jordan*; by the standing still of the sun and moon (or the terrestrial globe) at *Joshua*'s command; by the inefficacy of the burning fiery furnace on *Daniel*'s three companions; and (to be short) by the stupendous eclipse of the sun

Psalm viii. 5, 6.

at the full moon, at the crucifixion of the *Messias*. To which I might add, that the chief part of mankind, namely the children of God, will, by their most bountiful remunerator, be thought fit to inhabit the new world (for that, by an Hebraism, is meant by the *new heavens and the new earth* St. *Peter* speaks of) which shall succeed the renovation and refinement of the present world by the last fire, that will not only dissolve, but, if I may so speak, transfigure it. *2 Pet. iii. 10, 11, 12, 13.*

AND we shall the less scruple to admit, that such vast and bright bodies as the sun and moon may be designed (among other things) to be serviceable to men, if we consider, that it is so far from being a constant rule, that a thing more excellent cannot (by a wise agent) be employed for the good of one, that is less so, that not only the first angel, whose apparition we read of in the scripture, was sent to relieve *Hagar*, a slave wandring in a wilderness; another had regard to the life of a sooth-sayer's ass; and many others (and sometimes companies of them) were employed on earth to do good offices to particular persons: but of all the angels in general, the excellent epistle to the *Hebrews* informs us, That they *are ministring spirits, sent forth to minister unto them, who shall be heirs of salvation.* *Gen. xvi. 9, &c. Num. xxii. 23. Gen. xxxii. 1, 2. 2 Kings 16, 17. Heb. i. 14.*

★   ★   ★   ★

of NATURAL THINGS.

The CONCLUSION.

THE refult of what has been hitherto difcourfed, upon the four queftions propofed at the beginning of this fmall treatife, amounts in fhort to this :

THAT all confideration of final caufes is not to be banifhed from natural philofophy ; but that it is rather allowable, and in fome cafes commendable, to obferve and argue from the manifeft ufes of things, that the author of nature pre-ordained thofe ends and ufes.

THAT the fun, moon, and other cœleftial bodies, excellently declare the power and wifdom, and confequently the glory of God ; and were fome of them, among other purpofes, made to be ferviceable to man.

THAT from the fuppofed ends of inanimate bodies, whether cœleftial or fublunary, it is very unfafe to draw arguments to prove the particular nature of thofe bodies, or the true fyftem of the univerfe.

THAT as to animals, and the more perfect forts of vegetables, it is warrantable, not prefumptuous, to fay, that fuch and fuch parts were pre-ordained to fuch and fuch ufes, relating to the welfare of the animal (or plant) itfelf, or the fpecies it belongs to : but that fuch arguments may eafily deceive, if thofe, that frame them, are not very cautious, and careful to avoid miftaking, among the various ends, that nature may have in the contrivance of an animal's body, and the various ways, which fhe may fuccefsfully take to compafs the fame ends.   And,

THAT, however, a naturalift, who would deferve that name, muft not let the fearch or knowledge of final caufes make him neglect the induftrious indagation of efficients.

8. Robert Boyle (1627-1691)

The Christian Virtuoso (1690)
From Boyle, *Works*, 5 vols. (London, 1744), vol. 5, 37-44

THE
CHRISTIAN VIRTUOSO:
SHEWING,

That by being addicted to experimental philosophy, a man is rather assisted than indisposed to be a good Christian.

The FIRST PART.

To which are subjoined,

I. A discourse about the distinction, that represents some things as above reason, but but not contrary to reason.

II. The first chapters of a discourse, entitled, Greatness of mind promoted by Christianity.

The PREFACE.

WHEN many years ago I was induced to write something about the subject of the following treatise, I did it partly to give some satisfaction to a friend, and partly to impose upon myself an obligation, to consider the more attentively, upon what grounds it may be asserted, that there is no inconsistence between a man's being an industrious virtuoso, and a good Christian. How little fond I was of troubling the publick with a discourse of this nature, may be guessed by my having thrown it aside, among other neglected papers, for several years. And it had still continued in that obscurity, if the formerly unprevalent desires of those, that would have it appear in publick, had not been enforced by an observation or two, that I could not but make. For I could scarce avoid taking notice of the great and deplorable growth of irreligion, especially among those, that aspired to pass for wits, and several of them too for philosophers. And on the other side it was obvious, that divers learned men, as well as others, partly upon the score of their abhorrence of these infidels and libertines, and partly upon that of a well-meaning but ill-formed zeal, had brought many good men to think, that religion and philosophy were incompatible; both parties contributing to the vulgar error, but with this difference, that the libertines thought a virtuoso ought not to be a Christian, and the others, that he could not be a true one.

IT is like it may seem to some readers, that I have too much enlarged the notion of experience, and too much insisted on the proofs deducible from that topick : but it is not improbable, that others may approve the reasons, with which that ample notion of experience is, where it is proposed, accompanied. And the ingenious person, I was chiefly to please, being a lover and valuer of experience, and of arguments grounded on it, the desire of gratifying him enticed me to say so much, that when I took up the thoughts of making this treatise publick, I found the effects of my complaisance so interwoven with the other parts of the discourse, that I could not make any great alteration, (for some I did make) without almost spoiling the contexture of it.

I HOPE the equitable reader will not expect to find every subject, of which I have occasion to discourse, fully treated of : for I neither designed nor pretended to write a body of natural theology, nor a demonstration of the Christian religion, but thought it sufficient for me to consider the points I wrote of, as far forth as was necessary or very conducive to my purpose. And therefore I thought myself not only warranted, but obliged (in point of discretion) to decline the mention of several arguments and reflections, that would indeed have been very proper, if my design had been to shew, why one should be a Christian ; but impertinent to shew, that a virtuoso, while such, may be a true Christian. But as for this reason, I omitted many things, that would have enriched or adorned my discourse ; so I have endeavoured to make some amends, both by suggesting some new subjects, and

38 *The* PREFACE.

by adding, on thofe that have been already treated of by others, divers thoughts, into which I was led by the attentive confideration of the fubject itfelf ; on which fcore, they may probably not have yet occurred to the reader, and may appear to him, either to be new as to the fubftance, or if any of them be coincident with the more known ones, to have fomething peculiar as to the way of propounding or of applying them. And, I confefs, I was fomewhat encouraged to communicate my thoughts on thefe fubjects, by confidering, that (though it ought not to be fo, yet) it is notorious, that in the age we live in, there are too many perfons, that are like to be found more indifpofed to be impreffed on by arguments, in favour of religion, from profeffed divines, how worthy foever, than from fuch as I, who am a layman, and have been looked upon as no undiligent cultivator of experimental philofophy. And that the ftile might not be unfuitable to the writer, and the defign, I thought fit, in my arguments and illuftrations, both to employ comparifons drawn from telefcopes, microfcopes, &c. and to make frequent ufe of notions, hypothefes, and obfervations, in requeft among thofe, that are called the new philofophers. Which I the rather did, becaufe fome experience has taught me, that fuch a way of propofing and elucidating things, is either as moft clear, or, upon account of its novelty, wont to be more acceptable than any other to our modern virtuofi ; whom thus to gratify is a good ftep towards the perfuading of them. For it is eafy to obferve, that fome men are more acceffible to truth, and will be more prevailed upon by it, when it is prefented to them in one drefs, than when it appears in another ; as we daily fee, that fome perfons will be more eafily prevailed with to take a medicine, and that it will have a more kindly operation upon them, if it be exhibited in that form and confiftence, that is beft liked by the patients ; whereof fome love to have the ingredients the medicine is to confift of, offered them in a liquid, others in a foft, and others in a dry form.

Though I am wont, as well as inclinable, to fpare the prefent age ; and though my cenfures of fome reputed virtuofi, that live in it, are written with as harmlefs and friendly defigns, as was the feeming rudenefs of the angel to St. *Peter*, when he ftruck him on the fide, and haftily rouzed him, but to awake him, to take off his chains, and to free him from the danger that threatned him ; yet I fhall be more troubled and furprifed, if I fhall find the following treatife difliked by divers perfons, that would pafs for virtuofi, and by fome that are really fo. For fome men, that have but fuperficial, though confpicuous wits, are not fitted to penetrate fuch truths as require a lafting and attentive fpeculation ; and divers, that want not abilities, are fo taken up by their fecular affairs, and their fenfual pleafures, that they neither have difpofition, nor will have leifure to difcover thofe truths, that require both an attentive and penetrating

mind. And more than either of thefe forts of men there are, whom their prejudices do fo foreftal, or their intereft biafs, or their appetites blind, or their paffions difcompofe, too much to allow them a clear difcernment and right judgment of divine things. Upon which, and other accounts, I fhall not think it ftrange, if what I write fhall make no great impreffion on readers thus qualified, whom to convert, it is not enough to convince them : nor fhall I be greatly difcouraged, or think much the worfe of my arguments, if they do not make profelytes of thofe, whom finifter confiderations make fuch refolved adverfaries to the truth, that he alone, that can preach from heaven, is able to prevail upon them ; and they muft be converted almoft as *Saul* the perfecutor was, by an extraordinary light from heaven, and a power able to ftrike them to the ground. But though I am not fo little acquainted with the prefent age, as to expect to plead for religion with the approbation of atheifts, or of libertines ; yet I fhall not think my pains altogether mifpent, if what I have written, either ftartle any irreligious reader fo far, as to engage him to confult abler affertors of Chriftianity and virtue, than I pretend to be ; or elfe prove fo happy, as to confirm and ftrengthen, by new arguments and motives, thofe, that have heartily embraced the Chriftian faith and morals, though perhaps not upon the firmeft grounds. For it will be no fmall fatisfaction to me, if though I cannot convert the refolvedly irreligious, I fhall at leaft furnifh thofe, that are not fo, with prefervatives againft them, and hinder their impiety from being contagious.

But I fear, that thofe, that are enemies, both to the doctrines I propofe, and to the aims I purfue, will not be the only perfons, that will find fault with the following tract ; fince perhaps, there will not be wanting fome ingenious men, that expected, as well as defired, that I fhould never write but as a naturalift, becaufe they themfelves efteem nothing, fave the laws and phœnomena of nature, to be fubjects worthy of a philofophical pen : as if, becaufe rational fpirits are invifible and immaterial beings, all difquifitions about them muft be airy and uncertain fpeculations, and, like their objects, devoid of folidity and ufefulnefs. But though among thefe ingenious men there are feveral, whofe expectations from me I am much more difpofed to gratify, than appoint ; yet, on fuch an occafion as this, I muft take the liberty to own, that I do not think the corporeal world, nor the prefent ftate of things, the only or the principal fubjects, that an inquifitive man's pen may be worthily employed about ; and that there are fome things, that are grounded neither upon mechanical nor upon chemical notices or experiments, that are yet far from deferving to be neglected, and much lefs to be defpifed, or fo much as to be left uncultivated, efpecially by fuch writers, as being more concerned to act as Chriftians, than as virtuofi, muft alfo think, that fometimes they may ufefully bufy themfelves about the

ftudy

The PREFACE.

ftudy of divine things, as well as at other times employ their thoughts about the infpection of natural ones. There are fome objects, whofe noblenefs is fuch, that though we derive no advantage from them, but the contentment of knowing them, and that but very imperfectly too ; yet our virtuofi themfelves juftly think much pains and time, and perhaps coft too, well fpent in indeavouring to acquire fome conjectural knowledge of them : as may be inftanced in the affiduous and induftrious refearches they have made about the remote cœleftial part of the world, efpecially the ftars and comets, that our age has expofed to their curiofity. For moft of thefe, though they require chargeable telefcopes, and tedious, as well as unhealthy nocturnal obfervations, are objects, of which we can know very little with any certainty ; and which, for ought appears, we can make no ufeful experiments with. Since therefore we fo much prize a little knowledge of things, that are not only corporeal, but inanimate ; methinks we fhould not undervalue the ftudies of thofe men, that afpire to the knowledge of incorporeal and rational beings, which are incomparably more noble than all the ftars in the world, which are, as far as we know, but maffes of fenfelefs and ftupid matter. Since alfo the virtuofi defervedly applaud and cherifh the laborious induftry of anatomifts, in their enquiries into the ftructure of dead, ghaftly, and oftentimes unhealthfully as well as offenfively fœtid bodies ; can it be an employment improper for a Chriftian virtuofo, or unworthy of him, to endeavour the difcovery of the nature and faculties of the rational mind, which is that, that ennobles its manfion, and gives man the advantage he has of the beafts that perifh ?

I AM content, that merely natural philofophy fhould often employ my thoughts and my pen ; but I cannot confent it fhould engrofs them, and hinder me from being converfant with theological fubjects. And fince, among my friends, I have fome (and thofe not inconfiderable for their number, and much lefs for their merit) that prefs me to treat of religious matters, as well as others, that would have me addict myfelf to cultivate phyfical ones ; I, who think myfelf a debtor to both thefe forts, am willing to endeavour to gratify both ; and having already, on many occafions, prefented the latter fort with large, as well as publick, effects of my complaifance for them, I hope, they will not think it ftrange, that I fhould now and then have regard to the former fort, too ; efpecially fince I had higher motives than complaifance ought to be, to induce me to treat fometimes of things, that might be grateful to thofe friends, that are much fo to religious compofures.

I PRESUME it will be taken notice of, that, in the following treatife, as well as in divers of my other writings, efpecially about fubjects that are purely, or partly, philofophical, I make frequent ufe of fimilitudes, or comparifons : and therefore I think my felf here obliged to acknowledge once for all, that I

did it purpofely. And my reafons for this practice were, not only becaufe fit comparifons are wont to delight moft readers, and to make the notions they convey better kept in memory ; whence the beft orators and preachers have made great and fuccefsful ufe of metaphors, allegories, and other refemblances ; but I was induced to employ them chiefly for two other reafons : 1. That though I freely confefs, that arbitrary fimilitudes, and likewife thofe that are foreign to the fubject treated of, fuch as are moft of the vulgar ones, that are ufually borrowed from the fictions of the poets, and from the uncertain and often ill-applied relations of *Pliny*, *Ælian*, and other too frequently fabulous writers, are fcarce fit to be made ufe of but to vulgar readers, or popular auditories ; yet comparifons fitly chofen, and well applied, may, on many occafions, ufefully ferve to illuftrate the notions, for whofe fake they are brought, and, by placing them in a true light, help men to conceive them far better than otherwife they would do. And, 2. appofite comparifons do not only give light, but ftrength, to the paffages they belong to, fince they are not always bare pictures and refemblances, but a kind of arguments ; being oftentimes, if I may fo call them, analogous inftances, which do declare the nature, or way of operating, of the thing they relate to, and by that means do in a fort prove, that, as 'tis poffible, fo it is not improbable, that the thing may be fuch as it is reprefented : and therefore not only the illuftrious *Verulam*, though not more a florid, than a judicious writer, has, much to the fatisfaction of his readers, frequently made ufe of comparifons, in whofe choice and application he was very happy ; but that fevere philofopher, monfieur *Des Cartes* himfelf, fomewhere fays, that he fcarce thought, that he underftood any thing in phyficks, but what he could declare by fome apt fimilitude ; of which, in effect, he has many in his writings ; [as where he compares the particles of frefh water to little eels ; and the corpufcles of falt in the feawater to little rigid ftaves ; and where, after the Stoicks, he compares the fenfe of objects by the intervention of light to the fenfe, that a blind man hath of ftones, mud, &c. by the intervention of his ftaff.] To which I fhall add, that proper comparifons do the imagination almoft as much fervice, as microfcopes do the eye ; for, as this inftrument gives us a diftinct view of divers minute things, which our naked eyes cannot well difcern, becaufe thefe glaffes reprefent them far more large, than by the bare eye we judge them ; fo a fkilfully chofen and well applied comparifon much helps the imagination, by illuftrating things fcarce difcernible, fo as to reprefent them by things much more familiar and eafy to be apprehended.

I CONFESS I might, on fome occafions, have fpoken, not only more pofitively and boldly, but, as to many learned readers, more acceptably, if I would have difcourfed altogether like a Cartefian, or as a partizan of fome other modern fect of philofophizers. But, besides

40

The PREFACE.

befides that I am not minded to give myfelf up to any fect, I thought it convenient, that a difcourfe, defigned to work on perfons of differing perfuafions about philofophical matters, fhould not declare itfelf dogmatically, or unrefervedly, of a party; but employ rather the dictates of reafon, or principles either granted or little contefted, than proceed upon the peculiar principles of a diftinct party of philofophizers.

IF now and then I have infifted upon fome particular fubjects, more than appears abfolutely neceffary, I did it, becaufe that, though I wrote this treatife chiefly for my friends, yet I did not write it for them only, but was willing to lay hold on fome of the occafions, that the feries of my difcourfe offered me, to excite in my felf thofe difpofitions, that I endeavoured to produce in others, and, by infifting upon fome reflections, imprefs them more deeply upon my own mind; efpecially when I was treating of fome points, either fo important, or fo oppofed, or both, that they can fcarce be too much inculcated.

THE name of the perfon, to whom the following papers were addreffed, not being neceffary to be made publick, fome reafons made it thought convenient, that it fhould remain unmentioned.

POSTSCRIPT.

TO give an account of the prolixity, that fome might otherwife cenfure, of the foregoing preface, I muft advertife the reader, that it is of an ancient date; and that the firft part of the treatife, that it belongs to, was already written, and it was then defigned, that the fecond part fhould accompany it to the prefs: on which fcore it was prefumed, that, as the particulars, that make up the preamble, would not appear fuperfluous, in regard of the variety of fubjects to be treated of; fo its length would fcarce be found difproportionate to the bulk of the whole defigned book.

THE
CHRISTIAN VIRTUOSO:
SHEWING,

That by being addicted to experimental philofophy, a man is rather affifted than indifpofed to be a good Chriftian.

The FIRST PART.

SIR,

I PERCEIVE by what you intimate, that your friends Dr. *W.* and Mr. *N.* think it very ftrange, that I, whom they are pleafed to look upon as a diligent cultivater of experimental philofophy, fhould be a concerned embracer of the Chriftian religion; though divers of its articles are fo far from being objects of fenfe, that they are thought to be above the fphere of reafon. But though I prefume they may find many objects of the like wonder, among thofe with whom I am comprifed by them, under the name of the new virtuofi; and among thefe, they may meet with divers perfons more able than I, to eafe them of their wonder; yet fince they are pleafed by fingling me out, as it were to challenge me to do it, I fhall endeavour to make them think it at leaft lefs ftrange, that a great efteem of experience, and a high veneration for religion, fhould be compatible in the fame perfon. Wherefore I fhall not deny, that I am now and then bufied in devifing, and putting in practice, trials of feveral forts, and making reflections upon them: and I own too, that (about natural things) I have a great reverence for experience, in comparifon of authority. But withal, I declare, that to embrace Chriftianity, I do not think I need to recede from the value and kindnefs I have for experimental philofophy, any thing near fo far as your friends feem to imagine. And I hope it will appear, that if the experimental way of philofophifing I am addicted to have any things in it, that indifpofe a man to affent to the truth, and live according to the laws of the Chriftian religion; thofe few things are more than countervailed by the peculiar advantages, that it affords a man of a well-difpofed mind, towards the being a good Chriftian.

I SAID, a man of a well-difpofed mind, that is, one, that is both docile, and inclined to make pious applications of the truths he difcovers; becaufe fuch a qualification of mind, I hope, God, through his goodnefs, has vouchfafed me; and the occafion given by your friends to the following difcourfe relating peculiarly to me, a perfonal account of my opinions, and reafons of them, ought to fuffice. And it will be *ex abundanti,* (as they fpeak) if my difcourfe be found, as it often will be, to extend much further. Which re-

3

flection,

The CHRISTIAN VIRTUOSO.

flection I defire you would frequently have in your thoughts, to prevent miftaking the defign of the following epiftle.

I DOUBT not, but the popular prejudices, that I perceive your two friends, among many other more devout than well-informed perfons, have entertained, will make them think, that what I have now delivered needs good proof, and perhaps better than it is capable of. And therefore I hope you will eafily allow me the liberty, I am going to take, of briefly premifing fome things, to clear the way for the principal points defigned to be difcourfed of in this letter.

I KNOW you need not be told, that the philofophy, which is moft in requeft among the modern virtuofi, and which by fome is called the new, by others the corpufcularian, by others the real, by others (though not fo properly) the atomical, and by others again the Cartefian, or the mechanical philofophy, is built upon two foundations, reafon and experience. But it may not be impertinent to obferve to you, that although the peripatetick, and fome other philofophies, do alfo pretend to be grounded upon reafon and experience ; yet there is a great difference betwixt the ufe, that is made of thefe two principles, by the fchool-philofophers, and by the virtuofi. For thofe, in the framing of their fyftem, make but little ufe of experience ; contenting themfelves for the moft part to employ but few and obvious experiments, and vulgar traditions, ufually uncertain, and oftentimes falfe ; and fuperftructing almoft their whole phyficks upon abftracted reafon; by which I mean the rational faculty, endowed but with its own congenit or common notions and ideas, and with popular notices ; that is, fuch as are common among men, efpecially thofe that are any thing learned. But now, the virtuofi I fpeak of, and by whom, in this whole difcourfe, I mean thofe, that underftand and cultivate experimental philofophy, make a much greater and better ufe of experience in their philofophical refearches. For they confult experience both frequently and heedfully ; and, not content with the phænomena, that nature fpontaneoufly affords them, they are folicitous, when they find it needful, to enlarge their experience by trials purpofely devifed ; and ever and anon reflecting upon it, they are careful to conform their opinions to it ; or, if there be juft caufe, reform their opinions by it. So that our virtuofi have a peculiar right to the diftinguifhing title, that is often given them, of experimental philofophers.

I CAN fcarce doubt, but your friends have more than once obliged you to take notice of the profane difcourfes and licentious lives of fome virtuofi, that boaft much of the principles of the new philofophy. And I deny not, but that, if the knowledge of nature falls into the hands of a refolved atheift, or a fenfual libertine, he may mifemploy it to oppugn the grounds, or difcredit the practice of religion. But it will fare much otherwife, if a deep infight into nature be acquired by a man of probity and ingenuity, or at leaft free from prejudices and vices, that may indifpofe him to entertain and improve thofe truths of philofophy, that would naturally lead him to fentiments of religion. For, if a perfon thus qualified in his morals, and thereby difpofed to make ufe of the knowledge of the creatures to confirm his belief, and encreafe his veneration of the Creator (and fuch a perfon I here again advertife you, and defire you would not forget it, I fuppofe the virtuofo, this paper is concerned in, to be) fhall make a great progrefs in real philofophy ; I am perfuaded, that nature will be found very loyal to her author ; and inftead of alienating his mind from making religious acknowledgments, will furnifh him with weighty and uncommon motives, to conclude fuch fentiments to be highly rational and juft. On which occafion I muft not pretermit that judicious obfervation of one of the firft and greateft experimental philofophers of our age, Sir *Francis Bacon*, that God never wrought a miracle to convince atheifts ; becaufe in his vifible works he had placed enough to do it, if they were not wanting to themfelves. The reafon he gives for which remark, I fhall confirm, by obferving, that it is intimated in a paffage of St. *Paul*, afferting both " that the invifi- Rom.i.20. " ble things of God are clearly feen from the " creation of the world," as tokens and effects (as I remember the particle ἀπὸ in the Greek doth elfewhere fignify) and that his divinity and eternal power may be fo well underftood by the things that are made, that the Gentiles, who had but the light of nature to lead them to the acknowledgment of the true God, were excufelefs, for not being brought by that guide to that acknowledgment.

AND indeed, the experimental philofophy giving us a more clear difcovery, than ftrangers to it have, of the divine excellencies difplayed in the fabrick and conduct of the univerfe, and of the creatures it confifts of, very much indifpofeth the mind, to afcribe fuch admirable effects to fo incompetent and pitiful a caufe as blind chance, or the tumultuous juftlings of atomical portions of fenfelefs matter ; and leads it directly to the acknowledgment and adoration of a moft intelligent, powerful, and benign author of things, to whom alone fuch excellent productions may, with the greateft congruity, be afcribed. And therefore, if any of the cultivators of real philofophy pervert it to countenance atheifm, it is certainly the fault of the perfons, not the doctrine ; which is to be judged of by its own natural tendency, not by the ill ufe, that fome bad men may make of it ; efpecially if the prevaricating perfons are but pretenders to the philofophy they mifemploy ; which character will perhaps be found to belong to moft, if not all, the atheiftical and profane men, the objection means. For moft of thefe do as little underftand the myfteries of nature, as believe thofe of Chriftianity ; and of divers of them it may be truly faid, that their fenfuality, and lufts, and paffions, darkened and feduced

M

duced

duced their intellects: their immorality was the original cause of their infidelity; nor were they led by philosophy to irreligion, but got and perverted some smattering of philosophy, to countenance the irreligious principles, they brought with them to the study of it.

BUT all this notwithstanding, I fear, if not foresee, that you will surmise, that the study of natural philosophy, how innocent soever it may be in it self, will, in this libertine city, engage me to converse with many, who, though they pass for virtuosi, are indeed atheists; whose contagious company must endanger, if not infect me.

THIS obliges me to tell you, that though I have no reason to take it at all unkindly, that you are jealous of me on the score of being solicitous for my safety; yet I hope my danger is not so great as you may apprehend it. For first, I must own to you, that I do not think there are so many speculative atheists, as men are wont to imagine. And though my conversation has been pretty free and general among naturalists, yet I have met with so few true atheists, that I am very apt to think, that mens want of due information, or their uncharitable zeal, has made them mistake or misrepresent many for deniers of God, that are thought such, chiefly because they take uncommon methods in studying his works, and have other sentiments of them, than those of vulgar philosophers. And in the next place I must tell you, that having, through the goodness of God, chosen my religion, not inconsiderately, but upon mature deliberation, I do not find those virtuosi, you call atheists, such formidable adversaries, as those that are afraid to hear them, do, by that apprehension, appear to think them. And indeed, I have observed the physical arguments of the atheists to be but very few, and those far enough from being unanswerable. And as for the very chief of them, though they are wont to puzzle such as are not versed in nice speculations, because they represent the assertion of a deity as a doctrine encumbered with inextricable difficulties; yet I do not think the objections solidly grounded, since the same difficulties, or others not inferior, may be urged against those hypotheses and principles, that the deniers of God do or must admit. And indeed, most of the perplexing difficulties the atheists lay so much stress on, do not proceed from any absurdity contained in the tenent of the theists, but from the nature of things; that is, partly from the dimness and other imperfections of our human understandings, and partly from the abstruse nature, that, to such bounded intellects, all objects must appear to have, in whose conception infinity is involved; whether that object be God, or atoms, or duration, or some other thing, that is uncausable. For, however we may flatter our selves, I fear we shall find, upon strict and impartial trial, that finite understandings are not able clearly to resolve such difficulties, as exact a clear comprehension of what is really infinite.

BUT to pursue this discourse would lead us too far. And it is more fit, after so much has been said concerning not only the design of this tract, but the new philosophy, the virtuosi, and my self, to proceed to those more particular things, that directly tend to the main scope of our epistle.

THE first advantage, that our experimental philosopher, as such, hath towards being a Christian, is, that his course of studies conduceth much to settle in his mind a firm belief of the existence, and divers of the chief attributes, of God: which belief is, in the order of things, the first principle of that natural religion, which it self is pre-required to revealed religion in general, and consequently to that in particular, which is embraced by Christians.

THAT the consideration of the vastness, beauty, and regular motions, of the heavenly bodies; the excellent structure of animals and plants; besides a multitude of other phænomena of nature, and the subserviency of most of these to man; may justly induce him, as a rational creature, to conclude, that this vast, beautiful, orderly, and (in a word) many ways admirable system of things, that we call the world, was framed by an author supremely powerful, wise, and good, can scarce be denied by an intelligent and unprejudiced considerer. And this is strongly confirmed by experience, which witnesseth, that in almost all ages and countries, the generality of philosophers, and contemplative men, were persuaded of the existence of a deity, by the consideration of the phænomena of the universe; whose fabrick and conduct they rationally concluded could not be deservedly ascribed, either to blind chance, or to any other cause than a divine being.

BUT though it be true, that " God hath " not left himself without witness," even to perfunctory considerers, by stamping upon divers of the more obvious parts of his workmanship such conspicuous impressions of his attributes, that a moderate degree of understanding, and attention, may suffice to make men acknowledge his being: yet I scruple not to think that assent very much inferior to the belief, that the same objects are fitted to produce in an heedful and intelligent contemplator of them. For the works of God are so worthy of their author, that besides the impresses of his wisdom and goodness, that are left as it were upon their surfaces, there are a great many more curious and excellent tokens and effects of divine artifice, in the hidden and innermost recesses of them; and these are not to be discovered by the perfunctory looks of oscitant or unskilful beholders; but require, as well as deserve, the most attentive and prying inspection of inquisitive and well-instructed considerers. And sometimes in one creature there may be I know not how many admirable things, that escape a vulgar eye, and yet may be clearly discerned by that of a true naturalist; who brings with him, besides a more than common curiosity and attention, a competent knowledge of anatomy, opticks, cosmography, mechanicks, and chemistry. But treating elsewhere purposely of this

The CHRISTIAN VIRTUOSO. 43

this subject, it may here suffice to say, that God has couched so many things in his visible works, that the clearer light a man has, the more he may discover of their unobvious exquisiteness, and the more clearly and distinctly he may discern those qualities, that lie more obvious. And the more wonderful things he discovers in the works of nature, the more auxiliary proofs he meets with to establish and enforce the argument, drawn from the universe and its parts, to evince that there is a God : which is a proposition of that vast weight and importance, that it ought to endear every thing to us, that is able to confirm it, and afford us new motives to acknowledge and adore the divine author of things.

In reference to this matter, we may confidently say, that the experimental philosophy has a great advantage of the scholastick. For in the peripatetick schools, where things are wont to be ascribed to certain substantial forms and real qualities ; (the former of which are acknowledged to be very abstruse and mysterious things, and the latter are many of them confessedly occult ;) the accounts of nature's works may be easily given in a few words, that are general enough to be applicable to almost all occasions. But these uninstructive terms do neither oblige nor conduct a man to deeper searches into the structure of things, nor the manner of being produced, and of operating upon one another. And consequently are very insufficient to disclose the exquisite wisdom, which the omniscient maker has expressed in the peculiar fabricks of bodies, and the skilfully regulated motions of them, or of their constituent parts : from the discernment of which things nevertheless it is, that there is, by way of result, produced in the mind of an intelligent contemplator a strong conviction of the being of a divine opificer, and a just acknowledgment of his admirable wisdom. To be told, that an eye is the organ of sight, and that this is performed by that faculty of the mind, which from its function is called visive, will give a man but a sorry account of the instruments and manner of vision itself, or of the knowledge of that opificer, who, as the Scripture Psal. xciv. speaks, "formed the eye." And he that can 9. take up with this easy theory of vision, will not think it necessary to take the pains to dissect the eyes of animals, nor study the books of mathematicians, to understand vision ; and accordingly will have but mean thoughts of the contrivance of the organ, and the skill of the artificer, in comparison of the ideas, that will be suggested of both of them to him, that being profoundly skilled in anatomy and opticks, by their help takes asunder the several coats, humours, and muscles, of which that exquisite dioptrical instrument consists : and having separately considered the figure, size, consistence, texture, diaphaneity, or opacity, situation, and connexions of each of them, and their coaptation in the whole eye, shall discover, by the help of the laws of opticks, how admirably this little organ is fitted to receive the incident

beams of light, and dispose them in the best manner possible for completing the lively representation of the almost infinitely various objects of sight.

It is easy for men to say in general terms, that the word is wisely framed ; but I doubt it often happens, that men confess, that the creatures are wisely made, rather because upon other grounds they believe God to be a wise agent, than because so slight an account, as the school philosophy gives of particular creatures, convinces them of any divine wisdom in the Creator. And though I am willing to grant, that some impressions of God's wisdom are so conspicuous, that (as I lately intimated) even a superficial philosopher may thence infer, that the author of such works must be a wise agent ; yet how wise an agent he has in those works expressed himself to be, none but an experimental philosopher can well discern. And it is not by a slight survey, but by a diligent and skilful scrutiny of the works of God, that a man must be, by a rational and affective conviction, engaged to acknowledge with the prophet, that the author of nature is " wonderful in counsel, and excellent in Isa. xxviii. " working," 29.

II. After the existence of the deity, the next grand principle of natural religion, is the immortality of the rational soul ; whose genuine consequence is, the belief and expectation of a future and everlasting state. For this important truth, divers arguments may be alledged, that may persuade a sober and well-disposed man to embrace it : but to convince a learned adversary, the strongest argument, that the light of nature supplies us with, seems to be that, which is afforded by the real philosophy. For this teacheth us to form true and distinct notions of the body, and the mind ; and thereby manifests so great a difference in their essential attributes, that the same thing cannot be both. This it makes out more distinctly, by enumerating several faculties and functions of the rational soul ; such as to understand, and that so, as to form conceptions of abstracted things, of universals, of immaterial spirits, and even of that infinitely perfect one, God himself : and also to conceive, and demonstrate, that there are incommensurable lines, and surd numbers ; to make ratiocinations, and both cogent and concatenated inferences, about these things ; to express their intellectual notions, *pro re natâ*, by words or instituted signs to other men ; to exercise free-will about many things ; and to make reflections on its own acts, both of intellect and will. For these and the like prerogatives, that are peculiar to the human mind, and superior to any thing, that belongs to the outward senses, or to the imagination itself, manifest, that the rational soul is a being of an higher order than corporeal ; and consequently, that the seat of these spiritual faculties, and the source of these operations, is a substance, that being in its own nature distinct from the body, is not naturally subject to die or perish with it.

I

44   *The* CHRISTIAN VIRTUOSO.

AND in reference to this truth, our virtuoso hath an advantage of a mere school-philosopher. For being acquainted with the true and real causes of putrefaction, and other physical kinds of corruption ; and thereby discerning, that the things, that destroy bodies, are the avolation, or other recess of some necessary parts, and such a depraving transposition of the component portions of matter, as is altogether incongruous to the structure and mechanical modification, that is essential to a body of that species or kind it belongs to : our naturalist, I say, knowing this, plainly perceives, that these causes of destruction can have no place in the rational soul ; which being an immaterial spirit, and consequently a substance not really divisible, can have no parts expelled or transposed, and so being exempted from the physical causes of corruption that destroys bodies, she ought to last always. And being a rational creature, endowed with internal principles of acting, as appears in free-will, she ought to live for ever, unless it please God to annihilate her ; which we have no reason to suppose he will do.   But on the other side, the modern peripateticks (for I question, whether *Aristotle* himself were of the same opinion) maintain substantial forms, by some of them stiled *semi substantiæ*, to which in apes, elephants, and others, that pass for ingenious animals, they ascribe some such faculties and functions, as seem to differ but gradually from those of the rational soul ; and (how innocent soever I grant their intentions to be) their doctrine tends much to enervate, if not quite to disable the chief physical way of probation, whence the immortality of man's mind is justly inferred.   For since according to the peripateticks, substantial forms are, as they speak, enduced out of the power or potentiality of the matter ; and do so depend upon it, not only as to action, but as to being, that they cannot at all subsist without it ; but when the particular body (as an herb, a stone, or a bird) is destroyed, they perish with it, or (as some of them scarce intelligibly express the same thing) fall back into the bosom of the matter : I think they give great advantage to atheists and cavillers, to impugn the mind's immortality.

FOR if to an ape, or other brute animal, there belongs a being more noble than matter, that can actuate and inform it, and make itself the architect of its own mansion, though so admirable as that of an ape, or an elephant ; if this being can in the body it hath framed, perform all the functions of a vegetable soul ; and besides those, see, hear, taste, smell, imagine, infer, remember, love, hate, fear, hope, expect, &c. and yet be a mortal thing, and perish with the body ; it will not be difficult for those enemies of religion, who are willing to think the soul mortal, because their brutish lives make them wish she were, to fancy, that human minds are but a somewhat more noble, but not for that less mortal kind of substantial forms, as amongst sensitive souls themselves, which they acknowledge to be equally mortal, there is a great disparity in degrees, that of a monkey, for instance, being very far superior to that of an oister.

9. Isaac Newton (1642-1727)

Four Letters from Sir Isaac Newton to Doctor Bentley containing some Arguments in Proof of a Deity
(London, 1756)
Letter 1 (written 10 December 1692)
Title page, pp. 1-11

FOUR LETTERS

FROM

SIR ISAAC NEWTON

TO

DOCTOR BENTLEY.

CONTAINING

SOME ARGUMENTS

IN

PROOF of a DEITY.

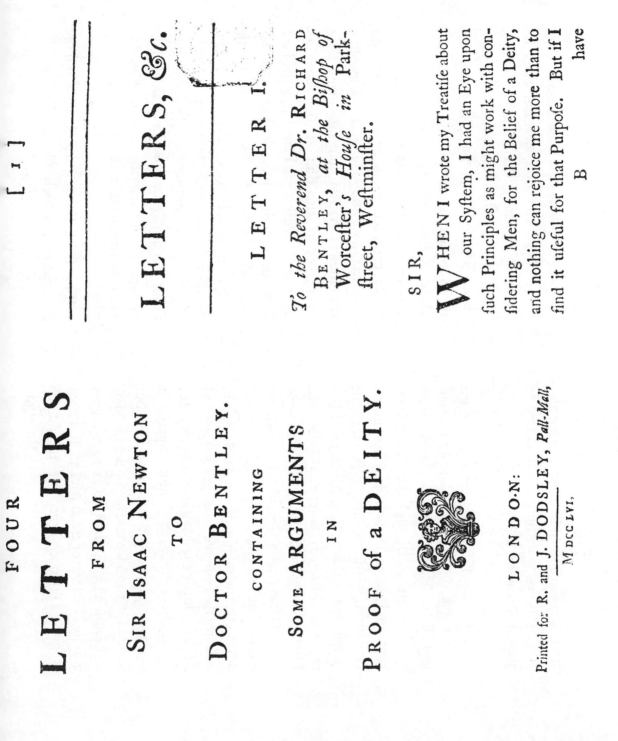

LONDON:

Printed for R. and J. DODSLEY, *Pall-Mall,*

MDCCLVI.

[1]

LETTERS, &c.

LETTER I.

To the Reverend Dr. RICHARD BENTLEY, *at the Bishop of Worcester's House in Park-street, Westminster.*

SIR,

WHEN I wrote my Treatise about our System, I had an Eye upon such Principles as might work with considering Men, for the Belief of a Deity, and nothing can rejoice me more than to find it useful for that Purpose. But if I have

B

[2]

have done the Public any Service this way, it is due to nothing but Industry and patient Thought.

As to your first Query, it seems to me that if the Matter of our Sun and Planets, and all the Matter of the Universe, were evenly scattered throughout all the Heavens, and every Particle had an innate Gravity towards all the rest, and the whole Space, throughout which this Matter was scattered, was but finite; the Matter on the outside of this Space would by its Gravity tend towards all the Matter on the inside, and by consequence fall down into the middle of the whole Space, and there compose one great spherical Mass. But if the Matter was evenly posed throughout an infinite Space, it could never convene into one Mass, but some of it would convene into one Mass and some into another, so as to make an infinite Number of great Masses, scattered at great Distances from one to another through-

[3]

throughout all that infinite Space. And thus might the Sun and fixt Stars be formed, supposing the Matter were of a lucid Nature. But how the Matter should divide itself into two sorts, and that Part of it, which is fit to compose a shining Body, should fall down into one Mass and make a Sun, and the rest, which is fit to compose an opaque Body, should coalesce, not into one great Body, like the shining Matter, but into many little ones; or if the Sun at first were an opaque Body like the Planets, or the Planets' lucid Bodies like the Sun, how he alone should be changed into a shining Body, whilst all they continue opaque, or all they be changed into opaque ones, whilst he remains unchanged, I do not think explicable by meer natural Causes, but am forced to ascribe it to the Counsel and Contrivance of a voluntary Agent.

The same Power, whether natural or supernatural, which placed the Sun in
B 2   the

[4]

the Center of the fix primary Planets, placed *Saturn* in the Center of the Orbs of his five secondary Planets, and *Jupiter* in the Center of his four secondary Planets, and the Earth in the Center of the Moon's Orb; and therefore had this Cause been a blind one, without Contrivance or Design, the Sun would have been a Body of the same kind with *Saturn, Jupiter,* and the Earth, that is, without Light and Heat. Why there is one Body in our System qualified to give Light and Heat to all the rest, I know no Reason, but because the Author of the System thought it convenient; and why there is but one Body of this kind I know no Reason, but because one was sufficient to warm and enlighten all the rest. For the *Cartesian* Hypothesis of Suns losing their Light, and then turning into Comets, and Comets into Planets, can have no Place in my System, and is plainly erroneous; because it is certain that as often as they appear to us, they descend into the System

of

[5]

of our Planets, lower than the Orb of *Jupiter,* and sometimes lower than the Orbs of *Venus* and *Mercury,* and yet never stay here, but always return from the Sun with the same Degrees of Motion by which they approached him.

To your second Query, I answer, that the Motions which the Planets now have could not spring from any natural Cause alone, but were impressed by an intelligent Agent. For since Comets descend into the Region of our Planets, and here move all manner of ways, going sometimes the same way with the Planets, sometimes the contrary way, and sometimes in cross ways, in Planes inclined to the Plane of the Ecliptick, and at all kinds of Angles, 'tis plain that there is no natural Cause which could determine all the Planets, both primary and secondary, to move the same way and in the same Plane, without any considerable Variation: This must have been the Effect

[6]

fect of Counsel. Nor is there any natural Cause which could give the Planets those just Degrees of Velocity, in Proportion to their Distances from the Sun, and other central Bodies, which were requisite to make them move in such concentrick Orbs about those Bodies. Had the Planets been as swift as Comets, in Proportion to their Distances from the Sun (as they would have been, had their Motion been caused by their Gravity, whereby the Matter, at the first Formation of the Planets, might fall from the remotest Regions towards the Sun) they would not move in concentrick Orbs, but in such eccentrick ones as the Comets move in. Were all the Planets as swift as *Mercury*, or as slow as *Saturn* or his Satellites; or were their several Velocities otherwise much greater or less than they are, as they might have been had they arose from any other Cause than their Gravities; or had the Distances from the Centers about which they move, been greater or

less

[7]

less than they are with the same Velocities; or had the Quantity of Matter in the Sun, or in *Saturn, Jupiter,* and the Earth, and by consequence their gravitating Power been greater or less than it is; the primary Planets could not have revolved about the Sun, nor the secondary ones about *Saturn, Jupiter,* and the Earth, in concentrick Circles as they do, but would have moved in Hyperbolas, or Parabolas, or in Ellipses very eccentrick. To make this System therefore, with all its Motions, required a Cause which understood, and compared together, the Quantities of Matter in the several Bodies of the Sun and Planets, and the gravitating Powers resulting from thence; the several Distances of the primary Planets from the Sun, and of the secondary ones from *Saturn, Jupiter,* and the Earth; and the Velocities with which these Planets could revolve about those Quantities of Matter in the central Bodies; and to compare and adjust all these

Things

[8]

Things together, in so great a Variety of Bodies, argues that Cause to be not blind and fortuitous, but very well skilled in Mechanicks and Geometry.

To your third Query, I answer, that it may be represented that the Sun may, by heating those Planets most which are nearest to him, cause them to be better concocted, and more condensed by that Concoction. But when I consider that our Earth is much more heated in its Bowels below the upper Crust by subterraneous Fermentations of mineral Bodies than by the Sun, I see not why the interior Parts of *Jupiter* and *Saturn* might not be as much heated, concocted, and coagulated by those Fermentations as our Earth is; and therefore this various Density should have some other Cause than the various Distances of the Planets from the Sun. And I am confirmed in this Opinion by considering, that the Planets of *Jupiter* and *Saturn*, as they are rarer than

[9]

than the rest, so they are vastly greater, and contain a far greater Quantity of Matter, and have many Satellites about them; which Qualifications surely arose not from their being placed at so great a Distance from the Sun, but were rather the Cause why the Creator placed them at great Distance. For by their gravitating Powers they disturb one another's Motions very sensibly, as I find by some late Observations of Mr. *Flamsteed*, and had they been placed much nearer to the Sun and to one another, they would by the same Powers have caused a considerable Disturbance in the whole System.

To your fourth Query, I answer, that in the Hypothesis of Vortices, the Inclination of the Axis of the Earth might, in my Opinion, be ascribed to the Situation of the Earth's Vortex before it was absorbed by the neighbouring Vortices, and the Earth turned from a Sun to a

C   Comet;

[10]

Comet; but this Inclination ought to de-
creafe conftantly in Compliance with the
Motion of the Earth's Vortex, whofe
Motion of the Earth's Vortex, whofe
Axis is much lefs inclined to the Ecliptick, as appears by the Motion of the
Moon carried about therein. If the Sun
by his Rays could carry about the Planets, yet I do not fee how he could
thereby effect their diurnal Motions.

Laftly, I fee nothing extraordinary in
the Inclination of the Earth's Axis for
proving a Deity, unlefs you will urge it
as a Contrivance for Winter and Summer, and for making the Earth habitable towards the Poles ; and that the
diurnal Rotations of the Sun and Planets,
as they could hardly arife from any Caufe
purely mechanical, fo by being determined all the fame way with the annual
and menftrual Motions, they feem to
make up that Harmony in the Syftem,
which, as I explaind above, was the
Effect of Choice rather than Chance.

There

[11]

There is yet another Argument for a
Deity, which I take to be a very ftrong
one, but till the Principles on which it
is grounded are better received, I think
it more advifable to let it fleep.

I am,

to command,

Your moſt humble Servant,

IS. NEWTON.

Cambridge,
Decemb. 10, 1692.

C 2

LET-

10. Richard Bentley (1662-1742)

A Confutation of Atheism from the Origin and Frame of the World
(London, 1693)
Part 3

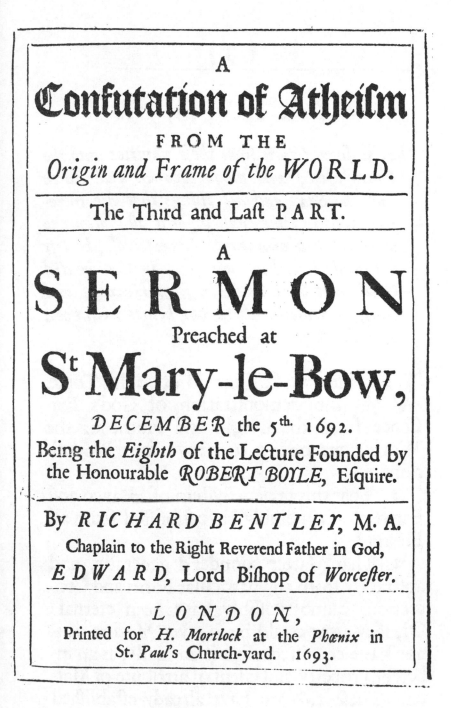

A

Confutation of Atheism

FROM THE

Origin and Frame of the WORLD.

The Third and Laſt PART.

A

SERMON

Preached at

St Mary-le-Bow,

DECEMBER the 5ᵗʰ. 1692.

Being the *Eighth* of the Lecture Founded by
the Honourable *ROBERT BOYLE*, Eſquire.

By *RICHARD BENTLEY*, M. A.

Chaplain to the Right Reverend Father in God,

EDWARD, Lord Biſhop of *Worceſter*.

LONDON,
Printed for *H. Mortlock* at the *Phœnix* in
St. *Paul's* Church-yard.   1693.

(3)

Acts XIV. 15, &c.

That ye should turn from these vanities unto the living God, who made Heaven and Earth and the Sea, and all things that are therein: Who in times past suffer'd all Nations to walk in their own ways. Nevertheless, he left not himself without witness, in that he did Good, and gave us Rain from Heaven, and fruitfull Seasons, filling our hearts with Food and Gladness.

WHen we first enter'd upon this Topic, the demonstration of God's Existence from the Origin and Frame of the World, we offer'd to prove four Propositions.

1. That this present System of Heaven and Earth cannot possibly have subsisted from all Eternity.

2. That Matter consider'd generally, and abstractly from any particular Form and Concretion, cannot possibly have been eternal: Or, if Matter could be so; yet Motion cannot have coexisted with it eternally, as an inherent property and essential attribute of Matter. These two we have already established

A 2   in

in the preceding Difcourfe; we fhall now
fhew in the third place,

3. That, though we fhould allow the Atheifts, that Matter and Motion may have been
from everlafting; yet if (as they now fuppofe)
there were once no Sun nor Starrs nor Earth
nor Planets; but the Particles, that now conftitute them, were diffufed in the mundane
Space in manner of a Chaos without any concretion and coalition; thofe difperfed Particles
could never of themfelves by any kind of Natural motion, whether call'd Fortuitous or Mechanical, have conven'd into this prefent or any
other like Frame of Heaven and Earth.

I. And firft as to that ordinary Cant of il-
literate and puny Atheifts, the *fortuitous or cafual concourfe of Atoms*, that compendious and
eafy Difpatch of the moft important and difficult affair, the Formation of a World; (befides
that in our next undertaking it will be refuted
all along) I fhall now briefly difpatch it, from
what hath been formerly faid concerning the
true notions of Fortune and Chance. Whereby it is evident, that in the Atheiftical Hypothefis of the World's production, Fortuitous
and Mechanical muft be the felf-fame thing.
Becaufe *Fortune* is no real entity nor phyfical
effence, but a mere relative fignification, de-
noting

Serm. V.
p. 6, 7.

noting only this; That such a thing said to fall out by Fortune, was really effected by material and neceſſary Cauſes; but the Perſon, with regard to whom it is called Fortuitous, was ignorant of thoſe Cauſes or their tendencies, and did not deſign nor foreſee ſuch an effect. This is the only allowable and genuine notion of the word Fortune. But thus to affirm, that the World was made *fortuitouſly*, is as much as to ſay, That before the World was made, there was ſome Intelligent Agent or Spectator; who deſigning to do ſomething elſe, or expecting that ſomething elſe would be done with the Materials of the World, there were ſome occult and unknown motions and tendencies in Matter, which mechanically formed the World beſide his deſign or expectation. Now the Atheiſts, we may preſume, will be loth to aſſert a fortuitous Formation in this proper ſenſe and meaning; whereby they will make Underſtanding to be older than Heaven and Earth. Or if they ſhould ſo aſſert it; yet, unleſs they will affirm that the Intelligent Agent did diſpoſe and direct the inanimate Matter, (which is what we would bring them to) they muſt ſtill leave their Atoms to their mechanical Affections; not able to make one ſtep toward the production

6   *A Confutation of Atheism from the*

duction of a World beyond the neceſſary
Laws of Motion. It is plain then, that *Fortune*,
as to the matter before us, is but a ſynony-
mous word with Nature and Neceſſity.   It
remains that we examin the adequate mean-
Serm. V. ing of *Chance* ; which properly ſignifies, That
p. 12, 13. all events called Caſual, among inanimate Bodies, are mechanically and naturally produced
according to the determinate figures and textures and motions of thoſe Bodies ; with this
negation only, That thoſe inanimate Bodies
are not conſcious of their own operations,
nor contrive and caſt about how to bring ſuch
events to paſs. So that thus to ſay, that the
World was made *caſually* by the concourſe of
Atoms, is no more than to affirm, that the
Atoms compoſed the World mechanically
and fatally ; only they were not ſenſible of
it, nor ſtudied and conſider'd about ſo noble
an undertaking. For if Atoms formed the
World according to the eſſential properties
of Bulk, Figure and Motion, they formed it
mechanically ; and if they formed it mechanically without perception and deſign, they
formed it *caſually*. So that this negation of
Conſciouſneſs being all that the notion of
Chance can add to that of Mechaniſm ; We,
that do not diſpute this matter with the Atheists,

ifts, nor believe that Atoms ever acted by Counfel and Thought, may have leave to confider the feveral names of *Fortune* and *Chance* and *Nature* and *Mechanifm*, as one and the fame Hypothefis. Wherefore once for all to overthrow all poffible Explications which Atheifts have or may affign for the formation of the World, we will undertake to evince this following Propofition :

II. That the Atoms or Particles which now conftitute Heaven and Earth, being once fe-parate and diffufed in the Mundane Space, like the fuppofed *Chaos*, could never *without a God by their Mechanical affections* have con-vened into this prefent Frame of Things or any other like it.

Which that we may perform with the greater clearnefs and conviction; it will be neceffary, in a difcourfe about the Formation of the World, to give you a brief account of fome of the moft principal and fyftematical *Phænomena*, that occurr in the World now that it is formed.

(1.) The moft confiderable *Phænomenon* belonging to Terreftrial Bodies is the general action of *Gravitation*, whereby All known Bo-dies in the vicinity of the Earth do tend and prefs toward its Center ; not only fuch as are

senfibly

fenfibly and evidently Heavy, but even thofe that are comparatively the Lighteft, and even in their proper place, and natural Elements, (as they ufually fpeak) as Air gravitates even in Air and Water in Water. This hath been demonftrated and experimentally proved beyond contradiction, by feveral ingenious Perfons of the prefent Age, but by none fo perfpicuoufly and copioufly and accurately, as by the Honourable Founder of this Lecture in his incomparable Treatifes of the *Air* and *Hydroftaticks.*

Mr. *Boyle's* Phyfi-com-Exp. of Air. Hydro-ftat.Para-doxes.

(2.) Now this is the conftant Property of *Gravitation* ; That the weight of all Bodies around the Earth is ever proportional to the Quantity of their Matter : As for inftance, a Pound weight (examin'd Hydroftatically) of all kinds of Bodies, though of the moft different forms and textures, doth always contain an equal quantity of folid Mafs or corporeal Subftance. This is the ancient Doctrine of the *Epicurean* Phyfiology, then and fince very probably indeed, but yet precarioufly afferted : But it is lately demonftrated and put beyond controverfy by that very excellent and divine Theorift Mr. *Ifaac Newton*, to whofe moft admirable fagacity and induftry we fhall frequently be obliged in this and the following Difcourfe.

Lucret. lib. 1.

Newton Philof. Natur. Princ. Math. lib. 3. prop.6.

I

Origin and Frame of the World. 9

I will not entertain this Auditory with an account of the Demonstration; but referring the Curious to the Book it self for full satisfaction, I shall now proceed and build upon it as a Truth solidly established, *That all Bodies weigh according to their Matter*; provided only that the compared Bodies be at equal distances from the Center toward which they weigh. Because the further they are removed from the Center, the lighter they are: decreasing gradually and uniformly in weight, in a duplicate proportion to the Increase of the Distance.

(3.) Now since Gravity is found proportional to the Quantity of Matter, there is a manifest Necessity of admitting a *Vacuum*, another principal Doctrine of the *Atomical* Philosophy. Because if there were every-where an absolute plenitude and density without any empty pores and interstices between the Particles of Bodies, then all Bodies of equal dimensions would contain an equal Quantity of Matter; and consequently, as we have shewed before, would be equally ponderous: so that Gold, Copper, Stone, Wood, &c. would have all the same specifick weight; which Experience assures us they have not: neither would any of them descend in the Air, as we all see they do; because, if all Space was Full, even the Air would be as dense and specifically as

B   heavy

heavy as they. If it be said, that, though the difference of specifick Gravity may proceed from variety of Texture, the lighter Bodies being of a more loose and porous compositi-on, and the heavier more dense and compact; yet an æthereal subtile Matter, which is in a perpetual motion, may penetrate and pervade the minutest and inmost Cavities of the closest Bodies, and adapting it self to the figure of e-very Pore, may adequately fill them; and so prevent all Vacuity, without increasing the weight: To this we answer; That that subtile Matter it self must be of the same Substance and Nature with all other Matter, and there-fore It also must weigh proportionally to its Bulk; and as much of it as at any time is com-prehended within the Pores of a particular Bo-dy must gravitate jointly with that Body: so that if the Presence of this æthereal Matter made an absolute Fullness, all Bodies of equal dimensions would be equally heavy: which being refuted by experience, it necessarily fol-lows, that there is a Vacuity; and that (not-withstanding some little objections full of ca-vil and sophistry) mere and simple Extension or Space hath a quite different nature and no-tion from real Body and impenetrable Sub-stance.

(4.) This

Origin and Frame of the World. 11

(4.) This therefore being eftablifhed ; in the next place it's of great confequence to our prefent enquiry, if we can make a computation, How great is the whole Summ of the Void fpaces in our fyftem, and what proportion it bears to the corporeal fubftance. By many and accurate Trials it manifeftly appears, that Refined Gold, the moft ponderous of known Bodies, (though even that muft be allowed to be porous too, being diffoluble in *Mercury* and *Aqua Regis* and other Chymical Liquors ; and being naturally a thing impoffible, that the Figures and Sizes of its conftituent Particles fhould be fo juftly adapted, as to touch one another in every Point,) I fay, Gold is in fpecifick weight to common Water as 19 to 1 ; and Water to common Air as 850 to 1 : fo that Gold is to Air as 16150 to 1. Whence it clearly appears, feeing Matter and Gravity are always commenfurate, that (though we fhould allow the texture of Gold to be intirely clofe without any vacuity) the ordinary Air in which we live and refpire is of fo thin a compofition, that 16149 parts of its dimenfions are mere emptinefs and Nothing ; and the remaining One only material and real fubftance. But if Gold it felf be admitted, as it muft be, for a porous Concrete, the proportion of Void to Body in the texture of common Air will be fo much the greater.

Mr. Boyle of Air and Porofity of Bodies.

And

And thus it is in the lowest and denfeſt region of the Air near the furface of the Earth, where the whole Maſs of Air is in a ſtate of violent compreſſion, the inferior being preſs'd and conſtipated by the weight of all the incumbent. But, ſince the Air is now certainly known Mr. *Boyle* ibid. to conſiſt of elaſtick or ſpringy Particles, that have a continual tendency and endeavour to expand and diſplay themſelves ; and the dimenſions, to which they expand themſelves, to be reciprocally as the Compreſſion; it follows, that the higher you aſcend in it, where it is leſs and leſs compreſs'd by the ſuperior Air, the more and more it is rarefied.   So that at the hight of a few miles from the furface of the Earth, it is computed to have ſome million parts of empty ſpace in its texture for one of ſolid Matter.   And at the hight of one Terre-

Newton Philoſ. Nat.Prin-cipia. Math. p. 503.

ſtrial Semid. (not above 4000 miles) the Æther is of that wonderfull tenuity, that by an exact calculation, if a ſmall Sphere of common Air of one Inch Diameter (already 16149 parts Nothing) ſhould be further expanded to the thinneſs of that Æther, it would more than take up the Vaſt Orb of *Saturn*, which is many million-million times bigger than the whole Globe of the Earth.   And yet the higher you aſcend above that region, the Rarefaction ſtill gradually increaſes without ſtop or limit: ſo that,

that, in a word, the whole Concave of the Firmament, except the Sun and Planets and their Atmofpheres, may be confider'd as a mere Void.   Let us allow then, that all the Matter of the Syftem of our Sun may be 50000 times as much as the whole Mafs of the Earth; and we appeal to Aftronomy, if we are not liberal enough and even prodigal in this conceffion. And let us fuppofe further, that the whole Globe of the Earth is intirely folid and compact without any void interftices; notwithftanding what hath been fhewed before, as to the texture of Gold it felf. Now though we have made fuch ample allowances ; we fhall find, notwithftanding, that the void Space of our Syftem is immenfly bigger than all its corporeal Mafs. For, to proceed upon our fuppofition, that all the Matter within the Firmament is 50000 times bigger than the folid Globe of the Earth ; if we affume the Diameter of the *Orbis Magnus* (wherein the Earth moves about the Sun) to be only 7000 times as big as the Diameter of the Earth (though the lateft and moft accurate Obfervations make it thrice 7000) and the Diameter of the Firmament to be only 100000 times as long as the Diameter of the *Orbis Magnus* (though it cannot poffibly be lefs than that, but may be vaftly and unfpeakably bigger) we muft pronounce, after fuch large conceffions

on

14   *A Confutation of Atheiſm from the*

on that ſide and ſuch great abatements on ours, That the Summ of Empty Spaces within the Concave of the Firmament is 6860 million million million times bigger than All the Matter contain'd in it.

Now from hence we are enabled to form a right conception and imagination of the ſuppoſed Chaos; and then we may proceed to determin the controverſy with more certainty and ſatisfaction; whether a World like the Preſent could poſſibly without a Divine Influence be formed in it or no?

(1.) And *firſt*, becauſe every Fixt Star is ſuppoſed by Aſtronomers to be of the ſame Nature with our Sun; and each may very poſſibly have Planets about them, though by reaſon of their vaſt diſtance they be inviſible to Us: we will aſſume this reaſonable ſuppoſition, That the ſame proportion of Void Space to Matter, which is found in our Sun's Region within the Sphere of the Fixt Starrs, may competently well hold in the whole Mundane Space. I am aware, that in this computation we muſt not aſſign the whole Capacity of that Sphere for the Region of our Sun; but allow half of its Diameter for the *Radii* of the ſeveral Regions of the next Fixt Starrs. So that diminiſhing our former number, as this laſt conſideration requires; we may ſafely affirm from certain

tain

tain and demonſtrated Principles, That the empty Space of our Solar Region (comprehending half of the Diameter of the Firmament) is 8575 hundred thouſand million million times more ample than all the corporeal ſubſtance in it. And we may fairly ſuppoſe, that the ſame proportion may hold through the whole Extent of the Univerſe.

(2.) And *ſecondly* as to the ſtate or condition of Matter before the World was a-making, which is compendiouſly expreſt by the word *Chaos*; they muſt ſuppoſe, that either All the Matter of our Syſtem was *evenly* or well-nigh evenly diffuſed through the Region of the Sun, this would repreſent a particular Chaos: or All Matter univerſally ſo ſpread through the whole Mundane Space; which would truly exhibit a General Chaos; no part of the Univerſe being rarer or denſer than another. Which is agreeable to the ancient Deſcription of it, That * *the Heavens and Earth had* μίαν ἰδέαν, μίαν μορφὴν, *one form*, one texture and conſtitution: which could not be, unleſs all the Mundane Matter were *uniformly* and evenly diffuſed. 'Tis indifferent to our Diſpute, whether they ſuppoſe it to have continued a long time or very little in the ſtate of Diffuſion. For if

there

* Diod. Sicul. lib. 1. Καla τὴν ἐξ ἀρχῆς τῶν ὅλων ϲύϲαϲιν μίαν ἔχειν ἰ Nαν ἰϵανόντε κỳ γῆν, μεμιγμένης αὐτῶν τῆς φύϲεως. Apoll. Rhodius lib. 1. Ἡϲϑεν δ᾿ ὡς γαῖα κỳ ἐρανὸς ἠδὲ ϑάλαϲϲα, τὸ πϵρὶν ἐπ᾿ ἀλλήλοιϲι μῇ ϲυναρηϵϑτα μορφῇ.

there was but one fingle Moment in all paft Eternity, when Matter was fo diffufed: we fhall plainly and fully prove, that it could never have convened afterwards into the prefent Frame and Order of Things.

(3.) It is evident from what we have newly proved, that in the Suppofition of fuch a Chaos or fuch an even diffufion either of the whole Mundane Matter or that of our Syftem (for it matters not which they affume) every fingle Particle would have a Sphere of Void Space around it 8575 hundred thoufand million million times bigger than the dimenfions of that Particle. Nay further, though the proportion already appear fo immenfe; yet every fingle Particle would really be furrounded with a Void fphere Eight times as capacious as that newly mention'd; its Diameter being compounded of the Diameter of the Proper fphere, and the Semi-diameters of the contiguous Spheres of the neighbouring Particles. From whence it appears, that every Particle (fuppofing them globular or not very oblong) would be above Nine Million times their own length from any other Particle. And moreover in the whole Surface of this Void fphere there can only Twelve Particles be *evenly* placed (as the Hypothefis requires) that is, at equal Diftances from the Central one and each other. So that
if

Origin and Frame of the World. 17

if the Matter of our Syſtem or of the Univerſe was equally diſperſed, like the ſuppoſed Chaos ; the reſult and iſſue would be, not only that every Atom would be many Million times its own length diſtant from any other : but if any One ſhould be moved Mechanically (without direction or attraction) to the limit of that diſtance ; 'tis above a hundred million millions Odds to an unit, that it would not ſtrike upon any other Atom, but glide through an empty interval without any contact.

(4.) 'Tis true, that while I calculate theſe Meaſures, I ſuppoſe all the Particles of Matter to be at abſolute reſt among themſelves, and ſituated in an exact and mathematical evenneſs ; neither of which is likely to be allowed by our Adverſaries, who not admitting the former, but aſſerting the eternity of Motion, will conſequently deny the latter alſo : becauſe in the very moment that Motion is admitted in the Chaos, ſuch an exact evenneſs cannot poſſibly be preſerved. But this I do, not to draw any argument againſt them from the Univerſal Reſt or accurately equal diffuſion of Matter ; but only that I may better demonſtrate the great Rarity and Tenuity of their imaginary Chaos, and reduce it to computation. Which computation will hold with exactneſs enough, though we allow the Parti-

C   cles

18   *A Confutation of Atheism from the*

cles of the Chaos to be varioufly moved, and to differ fomething in fize and figure and fituation. For if fome Particles fhould approach nearer each other than in the former Proportion ; with refpect to fome other Particles they would be as much remoter. So that notwithftanding a fmall diverfity of their Pofitions and Diftances, the whole Aggregate of Matter, as long as it retain'd the name and nature of Chaos, would retain well-nigh an uniform tenuity of Texture, and may be confider'd as an homogeneous Fluid. As feveral Portions of the fame fort of Water are reckon'd to be of the fame fpecifick gravity ; though it be naturally impoffible that every Particle and Pore of it, confider'd Geometrically, fhould have equal fizes and dimenfions.

We have now reprefented the true fcheme and condition of the Chaos ; how all the Particles would be difunited ; and what vaft intervals of empty Space would lye between each. To form a Syftem therefore, 'tis neceffary that thefe fquander'd Atoms fhould convene and unite into great and compact Maffes, like the Bodies of the Earth and Planets. Without fuch a coalition the diffufed Chaos muft have continued and reign'd to all eternity. But how could Particles fo widely difperfed combine into that clofenefs of Texture? Our Adverfaries

ries can have only thefe two ways of accounting for it. *Either* by the Common Motion of Matter, proceeding from external Impulfe and Conflict (without attraction) by which every Body moves uniformly in a direct line according to the determination of the impelling force. For, they may fay, the Atoms of the Chaos being varioufly moved according to this catholic Law, muft needs knock and interfere; by which means fome that have convenient figures for mutual coherence might chance to ftick together, and others might join to thofe, and fo by degrees fuch huge Maffes might be formed, as afterwards became Suns and Planets: or there might arife fome vertiginous Motions or Whirlpools in the Matter of the Chaos; whereby the Atoms might be thruft and crowded to the middle of thofe Whirlpools, and there conftipate one another into great folid Globes, fuch as now appear in the World. + Or *fecondly* by mutual Gravitation or Attraction. For they may affert, that Matter hath inherently and effentially fuch an intrinfeck energy, whereby it inceffantly tends to unite it felf to all other Matter: fo that feveral Particles placed in a Void fpace at any diftance whatfoever would without any external impulfe fpontaneoufly convene and unite together. And thus the Atoms of the Chaos,

C 2 though

though never fo widely diffufed, might by this innate property of Attraction foon affemble themfelves into great fphærical Maffes, and conftitute Syftems like the prefent Heaven and Earth.   This is all that can be propofed by Atheifts, as an efficient caufe of a World.   For as to the *Epicurean* Theory, of Atoms defcending down an infinite fpace by an inherent principle of Gravitation, which tends not toward other Matter, but toward a *Vacuum* or Nothing; *Lucret.* and verging from the Perpendicular ✱ *no body* *Nec regi-* *knows why nor when nor where* ; 'tis fuch mifera- *one loci* *certa,nec* ble abfurd ftuff, fo repugnant to it felf, and fo *tempore* contrary to the known Phænomena of Nature *certo.* (yet it contented fupine unthinking Atheifts for a thoufand years together) that we will not now honour it with a fpecial refutation.   But what it hath common with the other Explications, we will fully confute together with Them in thefe three Propofitions. ✝

(1.) That by Common Motion (without attraction) the diffever'd Particles of the Chaos could never make the World; could never convene into fuch great compact Maffes, as the Planets now are ; nor either acquire or continue fuch Motions, as the Planets now have. ✝

(2.) That fuch a mutual Gravitation or fpontaneous Attraction can neither be inherent and effential to Matter ; nor ever fupervene to it,

unlefs

unlefs imprefs'd and infufed into it by a Divine Power.

(3.) That though we fhould allow fuch Attraction to be natural and effential to all Matter ; yet the Atoms of a Chaos could never fo convene by it, as to form the prefent Syftem : or if they could form it, it could neither acquire fuch Motions, nor continue permanent in this ftate, without the Power and Providence of a Divine Being.

I. And firft, that by Common Motion the Matter of Chaos could never convene into fuch Maffes, as the Planets now are. Any man, that confiders the fpacious void Intervals of the Chaos, how immenfe they are in proportion to the bulk of the Atoms, will hardly induce himfelf to believe, that Particles fo widely diffeminated could ever throng and crowd one another into a clofe and compact texture. He will rather conclude, that thofe few that fhould happen to clafh, might rebound after the collifion ; or if they cohered, yet by the next conflict with other Atoms might be feparated again, and fo on in an eternal viciffitude of Faft and Loofe, without ever confociating into the huge condenfe Bodies of Planets ; fome of whofe Particles upon this fuppofition muft have travell'd many millions of Leagues through the gloomy regions of Chaos, os, to place themfelves where they now are. But then how rarely would there be any clafhing at all? how very rarely in comparifon to the number of Atoms? The whole multitude of them, generally fpeaking, might freely move and rove for ever with very little occurring or interfering. Let us conceive two of the neareft Particles according to our former Calculation; or rather let us try the fame proportions in another Example, that will come eafier to the Imagination.   Let us fuppofe two Ships, fitted with durable Timber and Rigging, but without Pilot or Mariners, to be placed in the vaft *Atlantick* or the *Pacifique* Ocean, as far afunder as may be. How many thoufand years might expire,before thofe folitary Veffels fhould happen to ftrike one againft the other? But let us imagin the Space yet more ample, even the whole face of the Earth to be covered with Sea, and the two Ships to be placed in the oppofite Poles: might not they now move long enough without any danger of clafhing? And yet I find, that the two neareft Atoms in our evenly diffufed Chaos have ten thoufand times lefs proportion to the two Void circular Planes around them, than our two Ships would have to the whole Surface of the Deluge.   Let us affume then another Deluge ten thoufand times larger than Noah's.   Is it not now utterly incredible,

credible, that our two Veſſels, placed there Antipodes to each other, ſhould ever happen to concur? And yet let me add, that the Ships would move in one and the ſame Surface; and conſequently muſt needs encounter, when they either advance towards one another in direct lines, or meet in the interſection of croſs ones; but the Atoms may not only fly ſide-ways, but over likewiſe and under each other: which makes it many million times more improbable, that they ſhould interfere than the Ships, even in the laſt and unlikelieſt inſtance. But they may ſay, Though the Odds indeed be unſpeakable that the Atoms do not convene in any ſet number of Trials, yet in an infinite Succeſſion of them may not ſuch a Combination poſſibly happen? But let them conſider, that the improbability of Caſual Hits is never diminiſhed by repetition of Trials; they are as unlikely to fall out at the Thouſandth as at the Firſt. So that in a matter of mere Chance, when there is ſo many Millions odds againſt any aſſign- Serm. V. able Experiment; 'tis in vain to expect it ſhould P. 32. ever ſucceed, even in endleſs Duration.

But though we ſhould concede it to be ſimply poſſible, that the Matter of Chaos might convene into great Maſſes, like Planets: yet it's abſolutely impoſſible, that thoſe Maſſes ſhould *acquire* ſuch revolutions about the Sun. Let

us fuppofe any one of thofe Maffes to be the
Prefent Earth. Now the annual Revolution of
the Earth muft proceed (in this Hypothefis) *either* from the Summ and Refult of the feveral
motions of all the Particles that formed the
Earth, *or* from a new Impulfe from fome external Matter, after it was formed. The *former*
is apparently abfurd, becaufe the Particles that
form'd the round Earth muft needs convene
from all points and quarters toward the middle, and would generally tend toward its Center; which would make the whole Compound
to reft in a Poife: or at leaft that overplus of
Motion, which the Particles of one Hemifphere
could have above the other, would be very
fmall and inconfiderable; too feeble and lan-
guid to propell fo vaft and ponderous a Body
with that prodigious velocity. And *fecondly*,
'tis impoffible, that any external Matter fhould
impell that compound Mafs, after it was formed. 'Tis manifeft, that nothing elfe could impell it, unlefs the Æthereal Matter be fuppofed
to be carried about the Sun like a *Vortex* or
Whirlpool, as a Vehicle to convey It and the
reft of the Planets. ✢ But this is refuted from
what we have fhewn above, that thofe Spaces of
the Æther may be reckon'd a mere Void, the
whole Quantity of their Matter fcarce amount-
ing to the weight of a Grain. 'Tis refuted alfo
from

from Matter of Fact in the Motion of Comets; which, as often as they are vifible to Us, are in the Region of our Planets; and there are obferved to move, fome in quite contrary courfes to Theirs, and fome in crofs and oblique ones, in Planes inclined to the Plane of the Ecliptick in all kinds of Angles: which firmly evinces, that the Regions of the Æther are empty and free, and neither refift nor affift the Revolutions of Planets.   But moreover there could not poffibly arife in the Chaos any *Vortices* or Whirlpools at all; either to form the Globes of the Planets, or to revolve them when formed.   'Tis acknowledged by all, that inanimate unactive Matter moves always in a ftreight Line, nor ever reflects in an Angle, nor bends in a Circle (which is a continual reflexion) unlefs *either* by fome external Impulfe, that may divert it from the direct motion, *or* by an intrinfec Principle of Gravity or Attraction, that may make it defcribe a curve line about the attracting Body.   But this latter Caufe is not now fuppofed: and the former could never beget Whirlpools in a Chaos of fo great a Laxity and Thinnefs. For 'tis matter of certain experience and univerfally allowed, that all Bodies moved circularly have a perpetual endeavour to recede from the Center, and every moment would fly out in right Lines, if they were

D   not

Newton
ibidem
p. 480.

not violently reſtrain'd and kept in by contiguous Matter. But there is no ſuch reſtraint in a Chaos, no want of empty room there; no poſſibility of effecting one ſingle Revolution in way of a *Vortex*, which neceſſarily requires either an abſolute Fulneſs of Matter, or a pretty cloſe Conſtipation and mutual Contact of its Particles.

And for the ſame reaſon 'tis evident, that the Planets could not *continue* their Revolutions about the Sun; though they could poſſibly acquire them. For to drive and carry the Planets in ſuch Orbs as they now deſcribe, that Æthereal Matter muſt be compact and denſe, as denſe as the very Planets themſelves: otherwiſe they would certainly fly out in Spiral Lines to the very circumference of the *Vortex*. But we have often inculcated, that the wide Tracts of the Æther may be reputed as a mere extended Void. So that there is nothing (in this Hypotheſis) that can retain and bind the Planets in their Orbs for one ſingle moment; but they would immediately deſert them and the neighbourhood of the Sun, and vaniſh away in Tangents to their ſeveral Circles into the Abyſs of Mundane Space.

II. Secondly we affirm, that mutual Gravitation or ſpontaneous Attraction cannot poſſibly be innate and eſſential to Matter. By Attraction

traction we do not here underſtand what is improperly, though vulgarly, called ſo, in the operations of drawing, ſucking, pumping, &c. which is really Pulſion and Truſion; and belongs to that Common Motion, which we have already ſhewn to be inſufficient for the formation of a World.   But we now mean (as we have explain'd it before) ſuch a power and quality, whereby all parcels of Matter would mutually attract or mutually tend and preſs to all others; ſo that (for inſtance) two diſtant Atoms *in vacuo* would ſpontaneouſly convene together without the impulſe of external Bodies.   Now we ſay, if our Atheiſts ſuppoſe this power to be inherent and eſſential to Matter; they overthrow their own Hypotheſis: there could never be a Chaos at all upon theſe terms, but the preſent form of our Syſtem muſt have continued from all Eternity; againſt their own Suppoſition, and what we have proved in our Laſt. *Vide* Serm. VI. & Serm. VIII. For if they affirm, that there might be a Chaos notwithſtanding innate Gravity; then let them aſſign any Period though never ſo remote, when the diffuſed Matter might convene. They muſt confeſs, that before that aſſigned Period Matter had exiſted eternally, inſeparably endued with this principle of Attraction; and yet had never attracted nor convened before, during that infinite duration: which is

D 2   ſo

28   *A Confutation of Atheism from the*

fo monſtrous an abſurdity, as even They will bluſh to be charged with.   But ſome perhaps may imagin, that a former Syſtem might be diſſolved and reduced to a Chaos, from which the preſent Syſtem might have its Original, as that Former had from another, and ſo on: new Syſtems having grown out of old ones in infinite Viciſſitudes from all paſt eternity.   But we ſay, that in the Suppoſition of innate Gravity no Syſtem at all could be diſſolved. For how is it poſſible, that the Matter of ſolid Maſſes like Earth and Planets and Starrs ſhould fly up from their Centers againſt its inherent principle of mutual Attraction, and diffuſe it ſelf in a Chaos? This is abſurder than the other: That only ſuppoſed innate Gravity not to be exerted; This makes it to be defeated, and to act contrary to its own Nature. So that upon all accounts this eſſential power of Gravitation or Attraction is irreconcilable with the Atheiſt's own Doctrine of a Chaos.   And ſecondly 'tis repugnant to Common Senſe and Reaſon. 'Tis utterly unconceivable, that inanimate brute Matter (without the mediation of ſome Immaterial Being) ſhould operate upon and affect other Matter without mutual Contact; that diſtant Bodies ſhould act upon each other through a *Vacuum* without the intervention of ſomething elſe by and through which
the

the action may be conveyed from one to the other. We will not obscure and perplex with multitude of words, what is so clear and evident by its own light, and must needs be allowed by all, that have any competent use of Thinking, and are initiated into, I do not say the Mysteries, but the plainest Principles of Philosophy. Now mutual Gravitation or Attraction (in our present acception of the Words) is the same thing with This; 'tis an operation or vertue or influence of distant Bodies upon each other through an empty Interval, without any *Effluvia* or Exhalations or other corporeal Medium to convey and transmit it. This Power therefore cannot be innate and essential to Matter. And if it be not essential; it is consequently most manifest (seeing it doth not depend upon Motion or Rest or Figure or Position of Parts, which are all the ways that Matter can diversify it self) that it could never *supervene* to it, unless imprefs'd and infused into it by an immaterial and divine Power. ┼

We have proved, that a Power of mutual Gravitation, without contact or impulse, can in no-wise be attributed to mere Matter: or if it could; we shall presently shew, that it would be wholly unable to form the World out of *Chaos*. But by the way; what if it be made appear, that there is really such a Power of
Gravity

30   *A Confutation of Atheism from the*

Gravity perpetually acting in the conftitution
of the prefent Syftem? This would be a new
and invincible Argument for the Being of God:
being a direct and pofitive proof, that an immaterial living Mind doth inform and actuate
the dead Matter, and fupport the Frame of the
World.   I will lay before you fome certain
Phænomena of Nature; and leave it to your
confideration from what Principle they can
proceed. 'Tis demonftrated, That the Sun,
Moon and all the Planets do reciprocally gravitate one toward another: that the Gravitating power of each of Thefe is exactly proportional to their Matter, and arifes from the feveral Gravitations or Attractions of every individual Particle that compofe the whole Mafs:
that all Matter near the Surface of the Earth,
for example, doth not only gravitate downwards, but upwards alfo and fide-ways and toward all imaginable Points; though the Tendency downwards be prædominant and alone
difcernible, becaufe of the Greatnefs and Near-
nefs of the attracting Body, the Earth: that e-
very Particle of the whole Syftem doth attract
and is attracted by all the reft, All operating
upon All: that this *Univerfal Attraction or Gravitation* is an inceffant, regular and uniform
Action by certain and eftablifhed Laws according to Quantity of Matter and Longitude of
Diftance:

Origin and Frame of the World. 31

Diſtance: that it cannot be deſtroyed nor impair'd nor augmented by any thing, neither by Motion nor Reſt, nor Situation nor Poſture, nor alteration of Form, nor diverſity of Medium: that it is not a Magnetical Power, nor the effect of a Vortical Motion; thoſe common attempts toward the Explication of Gravity: Theſe things, I ſay, are fully demonſtrated, as matters of Fact, by that very ingenious Author, whom we cited before. Now how is it poſſible that theſe things ſhould be effected by any Material and Mechanical Agent? We have evinced, that mere Matter cannot operate upon Matter without mutual Contact. It remains then, that theſe Phænomena are produced *either* by the intervention of Air or Æther or other ſuch medium, that communicates the Impulſe from one Body to another; *or* by Effluvia and Spirits that are emitted from the one, and pervene to the other. We can conceive no other way of performing them Mechanically. But what impulſe or agitation can be propagated through the Æther from one Particle entombed and wedged in the very Center of the Earth to another in the Center of *Saturn?* Yet even thoſe two Particles do reciprocally affect each other with the ſame force and vigour, as they would do at the ſame diſtance in any other Situation imaginable. And becauſe the

Newton Philoſophiæ Naturalis Princ. Math. lib. III.

the Impulfe from this Particle is not directed to That only; but to all the reft in the Univerfe, to all quatters and regions, at once invariably and inceffantly: to do this mechanically; the fame phyfical Point of Matter muft move all manner of ways equally and conftantly in the fame inftant and moment; which is flatly impoffible. But if this Particle cannot propagate Motion; much lefs can it fend out Effluvia to all points without intermiffion or variation; fuch multitudes of Effluvia as to lay hold on every Atom in the Univerfe without miffing of one. Nay every fingle Particle of the very Effluvia (feeing they alfo attract and gravitate) muft in this Suppofition emit other fecondary Effluvia all the World over; and thofe others ftill emit more, and fo *in infinitum.* Now if thefe things be repugnant to human reafon; we have great reafon to affirm, That Univerfal Gravitation, a thing certainly exiftent in Nature, is above all Mechanifm and material Caufes, and proceeds from a higher principle, a Divine energy and impreffion.

III. Thirdly we affirm; That, though we fhould allow, that reciprocal Attraction is effential to Matter; yet the Atoms of a Chaos could never fo convene by it, as to form the prefent Syftem; or if they could form it, yet it could neither acquire thefe Revolutions, nor fubfift

in

in the prefent condition, without the Confer-
vation and Providence of a Divine Being.

(1.) For firft, if the Matter of the Univerfe, and
confequently the Space through which it's diffufed, be fuppofed to be *Finite* (and I think it might
be demonftrated to be fo; but that we have already exceeded the juft meafures of a Sermon)
then, fince every fingle Particle hath an innate
Gravitation toward all others, proportionated by
Matter and Diftance: it evidently appears, that
the outward Atoms of the Chaos would neceffarily tend inwards and defcend from all quarters
toward the Middle of the whole Space (for in refpect to every Atom there would lie through the
Middle the greateft quantity of Matter and the
moft vigorous Attraction) and would there form
and conftitute one huge fphærical Mafs; which
would be the only Body in the Univerfe. It is
plain therefore, that upon this Suppofition the
Matter of the Chaos could never compofe fuch
divided and different Maffes, as the Starrs and
Planets of the prefent World.

But allowing our Adverfaries, that The Planets might be compofed: yet however they could
not poffibly acquire fuch Revolutions in Circular Orbs, or (which is all one to our prefent purpofe) in Ellipfes very little Eccentric. For let them
affign any place where the Planets were formed.
Was it nearer to the Sun, than the prefent diftances are? But that is notoriously abfurd: for then

E

their

they muſt have aſcended from the place of their Formation, againſt the eſſential property of mutual Attraction. Or were each formed in the ſame Orbs, in which they now move? But then they muſt have moved from the Point of Reſt, in an horizontal Line without any inclination or deſcent. Now there is no natural Cauſe, neither Innate Gravity nor Impulſe of external Matter, that could beget ſuch a Motion. For Gravity alone muſt have carried them downwards to the Vicinity of the Sun. And that the ambient Æther is too liquid and empty, to impell them horizontally with that prodigious celerity, we have ſufficiently proved before. Or were they made in ſome higher regions of the Heavens; and from thence deſcended by their eſſential Gravity, till they all arrived at their reſpective Orbs; each with its preſent degree of Velocity, acquired by the fall? But then why did they not continue their deſcent, till they were contiguous to the Sun; whither both Mutual Attraction and Impetus carried them? What natural Agent could turn them aſide, could impell them ſo ſtrongly with a tranſverſe Side-blow againſt that tremendous Weight and Rapidity, when whole Worlds are a falling? But though we ſhould ſuppoſe, that by ſome croſs attraction or other they might acquire an obliquity of deſcent, ſo as to miſs the body of the Sun, and to fall on one ſide of it: then indeed the force of their Fall would carry them quite
beyond

beyond it ; and fo they might fetch a compafs about it, and then return and afcend by
the fame fteps and degrees of Motion and Velocity, with which they defcended before.　Such
an eccentric Motion as this,　much after the
manner that Comets revolve about the Sun, they
might poffibly acquire by their innate principle
of Gravity : but circular Revolutions in concentric Orbs about the Sun or other central Body
could in no-wife be attain'd without the power
of the Divine Arm.　For the Cafe of the Planetary Motions is this.　Let us conceive all the Planets to be formed or conftituted with their Centers in their feveral Orbs ;　and at once to be imprefs'd on them this Gravitating Energy toward
all other Matter, and a tranfverfe Impulfe of a
juft quantity in each,　projecting them directly
in Tangents to thofe Orbs.　The Compound
Motion, which arifes from this Gravitation and
Projection together, defcribes the prefent Revolutions of the Primary Planets about the Sun, and
of the Secondary about Thofe : the Gravity prohibiting, that they cannot recede from the Centers of their Motions ; and the tranfverfe Impulfe
with-holding, that they cannot approach to them.
Now although Gravity could be innate(which we
have proved that it cannot be) yet certainly this
projected, this tranfverfe and violent Motion can
only be afcribed to the Right hand of the *moft high*
God, Creator of Heaven and Earth.

E 2

But

But finally, though we grant, that these Circular Revolutions could be naturally attained; or, if they will, that this very individual World in its present posture and motion was actually formed out of Chaos by Mechanical Causes: yet it requires a Divine Power and Providence to have conserved it so long in the present state and condition. We have shewed, that there is a Transverse Impulse impress'd upon the Planets, which retains them in their several Orbs, that they be not drawn down by their gravitating Powers toward the Sun or other central Bodies. Gravity we understand to be a constant Energy or Faculty (which God hath infused into Matter) perpetually acting by certain Measures and (naturally) inviolable Laws; I say, a *Faculty* and Power: for we cannot conceive that the *Act* of Gravitation of this present Moment can propagate it self or produce that of the next. But 'tis otherwise as to the Transverse Motion; which (by reason of the Inactivity of Matter and its inability to change its present State either of Moving or Resting) would from one single Impulse continue for ever equal and uniform, unless changed by the resistence of occurring Bodies or by a Gravitating Power; so that the Planets, since they move Horizontally (whereby Gravity doth not affect their swiftness) and through the liquid and unresisting Spaces of the Heavens (where either no Bodies at all or inconsiderable ones do occur) may

pre-

preserve the same Velocity which the first Impulse imprest upon them, not only for five or six thousand years, but many Millions of Millions. It appears then, that if there was but One Vast Sun in the Universe, and all the rest were Planets, revolving around him in Concentric Orbs, at convenient Distances: such a System as that would very long endure; could it but naturally have a Principle of Mutual Attraction, and be once actually put into Circular Motions. But the Frame of the present World hath a quite different structure: here's an innumerable multitude of Fixt Starrs or Suns; all of which are demonstrated (and supposed also by our Adversaries) to have Mutual Attraction: or if they have not; even Not to have it is an equal Proof of a Divine Being, that hath so arbitrarily indued Matter with a Power of Gravity not essential to it, and hath confined its action to the Matter of its own Solar System: I say, all the Fixt Starrs have a principle of mutual Gravitation; and yet they are neither revolved about a common Center, nor have any Transverse Impulse nor any thing else to restrain them from approaching toward each other, as their Gravitating Powers incite them. Now what Natural Cause can overcome Nature it self? What is it that holds and keeps them in fixed Stations and Intervals against an incessant and inherent Tendency to desert them? Nothing could hinder, but that the Outward Starrs with
their

their Syftems of Planets muft neceffarily have
defcended toward the middlemoft Syftem of the
Univerfe, whither all would be the moft ftrongly
attracted from all parts of a Finite Space. It is
evident therefore that the prefent Frame of Sun
and Fixt Starrs could not poffibly fubfift without
the Providence of that almighty Deity, *who fpake*
Pfal. 148. *the word and they were made, who commanded and
they were created ; who hath made them Faft for
ever and ever, and hath given them a Law, which
fhall not be broken.*

(2.) And fecondly in the Suppofition of an *infinite* Chaos, 'tis hard indeed to determin, what
would follow in this imaginary Cafe from an innate Principle of Gravity. But to haften to a
conclufion, we will grant for the prefent, that the
diffufed Matter might convene into an infinite
Number of great Maffes at great diftances from
one another, like the Starrs and Planets of this
vifible part of the World. But then it is impoffible, that the Planets fhould naturally attain thefe
circular Revolutions, either by intrinfec Gravitation or the impulfe of ambient Bodies. It is plain,
here is no difference as to this ; whether the
World be Infinite or Finite : fo that the fame Arguments that we have ufed before, may be equally urged in this Suppofition. And though we
fhould concede, that thefe Revolutions might be
acquired, and that all were fettled and conftituted in the prefent State and Pofture of Things ;

yet,

yet, we fay, the continuance of this Frame and Order for fo long a duration as the known ages of the World mult neceffarily infer the Exiftence of God. For though the Univerfe was Infinite, the Fixt Starrs could not be fixed, but would naturally convene together, and confound Syftem with Syftem: for, all mutually attracting, every one would move whither it was moft powerfully drawn. This, they may fay, is indubitable in the cafe of a Finite World, where fome Syftems muft needs be Outmoft, and therefore be drawn toward the Middle: but when Infinite Syftems fucceed one another through an Infinite Space, and none is either inward or outward; may not all the Syftems be fituated in an accurate Poife; and, becaufe equally attracted on all fides, remain fixed and unmoved? But to this we reply; That unlefs the very mathematical Center of Gravity of every Syftem be placed and fixed in the very mathematical Center of the Attractive Power of all the reft; they cannot be evenly attracted on all fides, but muft preponderate fome way or other. Now he that confiders, what a mathematical Center is, and that Quantity is infinitly divifible; will never be perfuaded, that fuch an Univerfal Equilibrium arifing from the coincidence of Infinite Centers can naturally be acquired or maintain'd. If they fay; that upon the Suppofition of Infinite Matter, every Syftem would be infinitly, and therefore equally attracted on all fides; and confequently sequently would rest in an exact Equilibrium, be the Center of its Gravity in what Position soever: This will overthrow their very Hypothesis; at this rate in an *infinite Chaos* nothing at all could be formed; no Particles could convene by mutual Attraction; for every one there must have Infinite Matter around it, and therefore must rest for ever being evenly balanced between Infinite Attractions. Even the Planets upon this principle must gravitate no more toward the Sun, than any other way: so that they would not revolve in curve Lines, but fly away in direct Tangents, till they struck against other Planets or Starrs in some remote regions of the Infinite Space. An equal Attraction on all sides of all Matter is just equal to no Attraction at all: and by this means all the Motion in the Universe must proceed from external Impulse alone ; which we have proved before to be an incompetent Cause for the Formation of a World.

And now, O thou almighty and eternal Creator, *having consider'd the Heavens the work of thy* **Psal. 8.** *fingers, the Moon and the Starrs which thou hast ordained,* with all the company of Heaven we laud and magnify thy glorious Name, evermore praising thee and saying ; Holy, Holy, Holy, Lord God of Hosts, Heaven and Earth are full of thy Glory: Glory be to thee, O Lord most High.

FINIS.

11. John Ray (1627-1705)

The Wisdom of God Manifested in the Works of the Creation
(London, 1691)
From the 9th edition (London, 1727), title page, pp. 114-142,
343-344, 368-375

THE
WISDOM of GOD

Manifested in the

WORKS

OF THE

CREATION.

In TWO PARTS.

V I Z.

The Heavenly Bodies, Elements, Meteors, Foſſils, Vegetables, Animals, (Beaſts, Birds, Fiſhes, and Inſects); more particularly in the Body of the Earth, its Figure, Motion, and Conſiſtency; and in the admirable Structure of the Bodies of Man, and other Animals; as alſo in their Generation, &c. With Anſwers to ſome Objections.

By *JOHN RAY,* late Fellow of the *Royal Society.*

The NINTH EDITION, Corrected.

L O N D O N:

Printed by WILLIAM and JOHN INNYS, Printers to the *Royal Society*, at the Weſt-End of St. *Paul's.*
M DCC XXVII.

[p. 114]

Of Bodies endued with a sensitive Soul, or Animals.

I proceed now to the Consideration of Animate Bodies endu'd with a sensitive Soul, call'd *Animals*. Of these I shall only make some general Observations, not curiously consider the Parts of each particular *Species*, save only as they serve for Instances or Examples.

First of all, because it is the great Design of Provi-

Part I. *in the* CREATION: 115

Providence to maintain and continue every Species, I fhall take Notice of the great Care and
abundant Provifion that is made for the fecuring
this End. *Quanta ad eam rem vis, ut in fuo
quæque genere permaneat? Cic.* Why can we
imagine all Creatures fhould be made Male and
Female but to this Purpofe? Why fhould there
be implanted in each Sex fuch a vehement and
inexpugnable Appetite of Copulation? Why in
viviparous Animals, in the Time of Geftation,
fhould the Nourifhment be carried to the *Em-
bryon* in the Womb, which at other Times goeth
not that Way? When the Young is brought
forth, how comes all the Nourifhment then to
be transferr'd from the Womb to the Breaft or
Paps, leaving its former Chanel, the Dam at
fuch Time being for the moft Part lean and ill-
favour'd? To all this I might add, as a great
Proof and Inftance of the Care that is taken,
and Provifion made for the Prefervation and Continuance of the Species, the lafting Fœcundity
of the Animal Seed or Egg in the Females of
Man, Beafts and Birds. I fay, the Animal Seed,
becaufe it is to me highly probable, that the
Females, as well of Beafts as Birds, have in them
from their firft Formation the Seeds of all the
Young they will afterwards bring forth, which
when they are all fpent and exhaufted by what
Means foever, the Animal becomes barren and
effete. Thefe Seeds in fome Species of Animals continue Fruitful, and apt to take Life by
the Admixture of the Male-feed fifty Years or
more, and in fome Birds fourfcore or an hun-

dred,

116   *The* WISDOM *of* GOD Part I.

dred.   Here I cannot omit one very remarkable Obfervation I find in *Cicero: Atque ut in-
telligamus* (faith he) *nihil horum effe fortuitum,
fed hæc omnia providæ folertifque naturæ, quæ
multiplices fœtus procreant, ut fues, ut canes,
his mammarum data eft multitudo, quas eafdem
paucas habent eæ beftiæ quæ pauca gignunt.   That
we may underftand that none of thefe Things* (he
had been fpeaking of) *is fortuitous, but that all
are the Effects of provident and fagacious Nature;
multiparous Quadrupeds, as Swine, as Dogs, are
furnifhed with a Multitude of Paps: Whereas
thofe Beafts which bring forth few, have but a
few.*

That flying Creatures of the greater Sort,
that is, *Birds,* fhould all lay Eggs, and none
bring forth live Young, is a manifeft Argument of Divine Providence, defigning thereby
their Prefervation and Security, that there might
be the more Plenty of them; and that neither
the Birds of Prey, the Serpent, nor the Fowler,
fhould ftraiten their Generations too much:
For if they had been viviparous, the Burden of
their Womb, if they had brought forth any
competent Number at a time, had been fo great
and heavy, that their Wings would have fail'd
them, and they become an eafy Prey to their
Enemies : Or, if they had brought but one or
two at a time, they would have been troubled
all the Year long with feeding their Young, or
bearing them in their Womb.   *Dr.* More *Antid.
Atheifm, l. 2. c. 9.*

This Mention of feeding their Young puts
me

me in mind of two or three confiderable Obfervations referring thereto.

First, feeing it would be for many Reafons
inconvenient for Birds to give Suck, and yet
no lefs inconvenient, if not deftructive, to the
Chicken upon Exclufion, all of a fudden, to
make fo great a Change in its Diet, as to pafs
from liquid to hard Food, before the Stomach be
gradually confolidated, and by Ufe ftrengthen'd
and habituated to grind and concoct it, and its
tender and pappy Flefh fitted to be nourifh'd by
fuch ftrong and folid Diet, and before the Bird
be by little and little accuftom'd to ufe its Bill,
and gather it up, which at firft it doth but very flowly and imperfectly; therefore Nature
hath provided a large Yolk in every Egg, a
great Part whereof remaineth after the Chicken
is hatch'd, and is taken up and enclos'd in
its Belly, and by a Chanel made on purpofe,
receiv'd by degrees into the Guts, and ferves
inftead of Milk to nourifh the Chick for a confiderable time; which neverthelefs mean while
feeds itfelf by the Mouth a little at a time,
and gradually more and more, as it gets a per-
fecter Ability and Habit of gathering up its
Meat, and its Stomach is ftrengthen'd to ma-
cerate and concoct it, and its Flefh harden'd
and fitted to be nourifh'd by it.

Secondly, That Birds which feed their Young
in the Neft, tho' in all likelihood they have
no Ability of counting the Number of them,
fhould yet (tho' they bring but one Morfel of
Meat at a time, and have not fewer (it may be)
I 3 than

than feven or eight Young in the Neft together, which at the Return of their Dams, do
all at once with equal Greedinefs, hold up their
Heads and gape) not omit or forget one of them,
but feed them all; which, unlefs they did carefully obferve and retain in Memory which they
had fed, which not, were impoffible to be done:
This, I fay, feems to me moft ftrange and admirable, and beyond the Poffibility of a mere Machine to perform.

Another Experiment I fhall add, to prove,
that tho' Birds have not an exact Power of num-
bring, yet have they of diftinguifhing many
from few, and knowing when they come near
to a certain Number: And that is, that when
they have laid fuch a Number of *Eggs*, as they
can conveniently cover and hatch, they give
over and begin to fit; not becaufe they are
neceffarily determined to fuch a Number; for
that they are not, as is clear, becaufe they are
in Ability to go on and lay more at their Pleafure. Hens, for Example, if you let their *Eggs*
alone, when they have laid fourteen or fifteen,
will give over and begin to fit; whereas, if you
daily withdraw their *Eggs*, they will go on to
lay five Times that Number: [Yet fome of
them are fo cunning, that if you leave them
but one *Egg*, they will not lay to it, but for-
fake their Neft.] This holds not only in do-
meftick and manfuete Birds, for then it might
be thought the Effect of Cicuration or Inftitu-
tion, but alfo in the wild; for my honour'd
Freind Dr. *Martin Lifter* inform'd me, that of
his

Part I.   *in the* CREATION.   119

his own Knowledge one and the fame *Swallow,*
by the fubftracting daily of her *Eggs,* proceeded to lay nineteen fucceffively, and then gave
over; as I have *elfewhere noted.

Now that I am upon this Subject   *Preface to
of the Number of *Eggs,* give me   Mr. *Willough-*
Leave to add a remarkable Obferva- *by's* Ornithol.
tion referring thereto, *viz.* That Birds, and fuch
oviparous Creatures, as are long-liv'd, have *Eggs*
enough at firft conceiv'd in them to ferve them
for many Years laying, probably for as many
as they are to live, allowing fuch a Proportion
for every Year, as will ferve for one or two In-
cubations; whereas Infects, which are to breed
but once, lay all their *Eggs* at once, have they
never fo many. Now, had thefe Things been
govern'd by Chance, I fee no Reafon why it
fhould conftantly fall out fo.

Thirdly, The marvellous fpeedy Growth of
Birds that are hatch'd in Nefts, and fed by the
Old ones there, 'till they be fledg'd, and come
almoft to their full Bignefs, at which Perfection
they arrive within the fhort Term of about one
Fortnight, feems to me an Argument of Providence, defigning thereby their Prefervation, that
they might not lie long in a Condition expos'd
to the Ravine of any Vermine that may find
them, being utterly unable to efcape or fhift for
themfelves.

Another and no lefs effectual Argument may
be taken from the Care and Providence us'd for
the Hatching and Rearing their Young: And
firft, they fearch out a fecret and quiet Place

I 4   where

120   *The* WISDOM *of* GOD Part I.

where they may be fecure and undifturb'd in
their Incubation; then they make themfelves
Nefts every one after his Kind, that fo their
Eggs and *Young* may lie foft and warm, and
their Exclufion and Growth be promoted. Thefe
Nefts are fome of them fo elegant and artificial,
that it is hard for Man to imitate them and
make the like.   I have feen Nefts of an *Indian*
Bird fo artificially compos'd of the Fibres, I
think, of fome Roots, fo curioufly interwoven
and platted together, as is admirable to behold :
Which Nefts they hang on the End of the Twigs
of Trees over the Water, to fecure their *Eggs*
and *Young* from the Ravage of *Apes* and *Mon-
keys*, and other Beafts, that might elfe prey upon
them.   After they have laid their *Eggs*, how
diligently and patiently do they fit upon them
'till they be hatch'd, fcarce affording themfelves
time to go off to get them Meat ? Nay, with
fuch an ardent and impetuous Defire of fitting
are they infpired, that if you take away all their
Eggs, they will fit upon an empty Neft : And
yet one would think that fitting were none of
the moft pleafant Works.   After their Young
are hatch'd, for fome time they do almoft conftantly brood them under their Wings, left the
Cold and fometimes perhaps the Heat fhould
harm them.   All this while alfo they labour
hard to get them Food, fparing it out of their
own Bellies, and pining themfelves almoft to
Death rather than they fhould want. Moreover,
it is admirable to obferve with what Courage
they are at that time infpir'd, that they will
even

Part I. *in the* CREATION. 121

even venture their own Lives in Defence of them. The moſt timorous, as *Hens* and *Geeſe*, become then ſo couragious, as to dare to fly in the Face of a Man that ſhall moleſt or diſ-quiet their Young, which would never do ſo much in their own Defence. Theſe things be-ing contrary to any Motions of Senſe, or In-ſtinct of Self-preſervation, and ſo eminent pie-ces of Self-denial, muſt needs be the Works of Providence, for the Continuation of the Spe-cies, and upholding of the World : Eſpecially if we conſider that all theſe Pains is beſtow'd upon a Thing which takes no Notice of it, will render them no thanks for it, nor make them any Requital, or Amends ; as alſo, that after the *Young* is come to ſome growth, and able to ſhift for itſelf, the old One retains no ſuch ϛοργὴ to it, take no further Care of it, but will fall upon it, and beat it indifferently with others. To theſe I ſhall add three Obſervations more relating to this Head. The firſt borrow'd of Dr. *Cudworth*, Syſtem, *pag. 69.* One thing ne-ceſſary to the Conſervation of the *Species* of Animals; that is, the keeping up conſtantly in the World a due numerical Proportion be-tween the Sexes of *Male* and *Female*, doth ne-ceſſarily infer a ſuperintending Providence. For did this depend only upon Mechaniſm, it cannot well be conceiv'd, but that in ſome Ages or other there ſhou'd happen to be all *Males*, or all *Females*, and ſo the Species fail. Nay, it cannot well be thought otherwiſe, but that there is in this a Providence, ſuperior to that

of

122   *The* WISDOM *of* GOD Part I.

of the *Plaſtick* or *Spermatick Nature*, which hath
not ſo much of Knowledge and Diſcretion allow'd to it, as whereby to be able to govern
this Affair.

The Second of Mr. *Boyle* in his Treatiſe
of the *high Veneration Man's Intellect owes to*
God. p. 32. that is, the Conveniency of the
Seaſon (or Time of Year) of the Production of
Animals, when there is proper Food and En-
tertainment ready for them. *So we ſee, that,*
according to the uſual Courſe of Nature, Lambs,
Kids, and many other living Creatures, are
brought into the World at the Spring of the Year;
when tender Graſs, and other Nutritive Plants,
are provided for their Food. And the like may
be obſerv'd in the Production of Silk-worms, (yea,
all other *Eruca's,* and many Inſects more) *whoſe*
Eggs, according to Nature's Inſtitution, are
hatch'd when Mulberry-Trees begin to bud, and
put forth thoſe Leaves, whereon thoſe precious
Inſects are to feed; the Aliments being tender,
whilſt the Worms themſelves are ſo, and grow-
ing more ſtrong and ſubſtantial, as the Inſects
encreaſe in Vigour and Bulk. To theſe I ſhall
add another Inſtance, that is of the *Waſp,* whoſe
Breeding is deferr'd till after the Summer-Solſtice, few of them appearing before *July:* Whereas one would be apt to think the vigorous and
quickning Heat of the Sun in the Youth of the
Year ſhould provoke them to generate much
ſooner: [Provoke them, I ſay, becauſe every
Waſp's-Neſt is begun by one great Mother-
Waſp, which over-lives the Winter, lying hid
in

Part I. *in the* CREATION. 123

in fome hollow Tree or other *Latibulum*;] becaufe then, and not till then, Pears, Plumbs, and
other Fruit, defign'd principally for their Food
begin to ripen.

The Third is mine own, That all Infects
which do not themfelves feed their Young,
nor treafure up Provifion in Store for their Suftenance, lay their *Eggs* in fuch Places as are
moft convenient for their Exclufion, and where,
when hatch'd, their proper Food is ready for
them: So, for Example, we fee two Sorts of white
Butterflies faftening their *Eggs* to Cabbage-
Leaves, becaufe they are fit Aliment for the
Catterpillers that come of them; whereas
fhould they affix them to the Leaves of a Plant
improper for their Food, fuch Catterpillers muft
needs be loft, they chufing rather to die than
to tafte of fuch Plants; for that Kind of Infect
(I mean Catterpillers) hath a nice and delicate Palate, fome of them feeding only upon
one particular *Species* of Plant, others on divers
indeed, but thofe of the fame Nature and
Quality; utterly refufing them of a contrary.
Like Inftances might be produc'd in the other
Tribes of Infects; it being perpetual in all, if
not hinder'd or imprifon'd, electively to lay
their *Eggs* in Places where they are feldom loft
or mifcarry, and where they have a Supply of
Nourifhment for their Young fo foon as they
are hatch'd, and need it: Whereas fhould they
fcatter them carelefly and indifferently in any
Place, the greateft Part of the Young would in
all Likelihood perifh foon after their Exclufion
for

124 *The* WISDOM *of* GOD Part I.

for want of Food, and ſo their Numbers continually decreaſing, the whole Species in a few
Years would be in Danger to be loſt : Whereas
no ſuch thing, I dare ſay, hath happened ſince
the firſt Creation.

It is here very remarkable, that thoſe Inſects, for whoſe Young Nature hath not made
Proviſion of ſufficient Suſtenance, do themſelves
gather and lay up in ſtore for them. So for
Example : The *Bee*, the proper Food of whoſe
* *Eulæ* is Honey, or perchance *Eri-*
* Bee-mag- *thace*, (which we engliſh *Bee-Bread*)
got.   neither of which Viands being any
where to be found amaſs'd by Nature in Quantities ſufficient for their Maintenance, doth herſelf
with unwearied Diligence and Induſtry, flying
from Flower to Flower, collect and treaſure
them up.

To theſe I ſhall now add an Obſervation of
Mr. *Lewenhoeck*'s, concerning the ſudden Growth
of ſome ſorts of Inſects, and the Reaſon of it.

It is (ſaith he) a wonderful Thing, and worthy the Obſervation, in Fleſh-Flies, that a Fly-
Maggot, in five Days ſpace after it is hatch'd,
arrives at its full Growth and perfect Magnitude. For if to the perfecting of it there were
requir'd, ſuppoſe a Month's time or more, (as
in ſome other Maggots is needful) it is impoſſible that about the Summer-Solſtice any ſuch
Flies ſhou'd be produc'd, becauſe the Fly-Maggots have no Ability to ſearch out any other
Food than that wherein they are placed by their
Dams. Now this Food, ſuppoſe it be Fleſh, Fiſh,

or

or the Entrails of Beasts, lying in the Fields, expos'd to the hot Sun-beams, can last but a few Days in Case and Condition to be a fit Aliment for these Creatures, but will soon be quite parch'd and dry'd up. And therefore the most wise Creator hath given such a Nature and Temperament to them, that within a very few Days they attain to their just Growth and Magnitude. Whereas, on the contrary, other Maggots, who are in no such Danger of being straitned for Food, continue a whole Month or more before they give over to eat, and cease to grow. He proceeds further to tell us, that some of these *Fly-Maggots* which he fed daily with fresh Meat, he brought to Perfection in four Days time; so that he conceives that in the Heat of Summer the *Eggs* of a *Fly*, or the *Maggots* contain'd in them, may in less than a Month's space run thro' all their Changes, and come to perfect Flies, which may themselves lay *Eggs* again.

Secondly, I shall take notice of the various strange Instincts of Animals, which will necessarily demonstrate, that they are directed to Ends unknown to them, by a wise Superintendent: As, 1. That all Creatures should know how to defend themselves, and offend their Enemies; where their natural Weapons are situate, and how to make use of them. A *Calf* will so manage his Head as tho' he would push with his Horns even before they shoot. A *Boar* knows the use of his Tushes; a *Dog* of his Teeth; a *Horse* of his Hoofs; a *Cock* of his Spurs; a *Bee* of her Sting; a Ram will butt
with

126 *The* WISDOM *of* GOD Part I.

with his Head, yea tho' he be brought up tame, and never faw that manner of Fighting. Now, why another Animal which hath no Horns fhould not make a Shew of pufhing, or no Spurs, of ftriking with his Legs, and the like, I know not, but that every Kind is providentially directed to the Ufe of its proper and natural Weapons. 2. That thofe Animals that are weak, and have neither Weapons nor Courage to fight, are for the moft part created fwift of Foot or Wing, and fo being naturally timorous, are both willing and able to fave themfelves by Flight. 3. That Poultry, Partridge, and other Birds, fhould at the firft Sight know Birds of Prey, and make Sign of it by a peculiar Note of their Voice to their Young, who prefently thereupon hide themfelves: That the Lamb fhould acknowledge the Wolf its Enemy, though it had never feen one before, as is taken for granted by moft Naturalifts, and may, for ought I know, be true, argues the Providence of Nature, or more truly the God of Nature, who, for their Prefervation, hath put fuch an Inftinct into them. 4. That Young Animals, as foon as they are brought forth, fhould know their Food: As for Example; fuch as are nourifhed with Milk prefently find their way to the Paps, and fuck at them; whereas none of thofe that are not defign'd for that Nourifhment ever offer to fuck, or feek out any fuch Food. Again, 5. That fuch Creatures as are whole-footed, or Fin-toed *viz.* fome Birds, and Quadrupeds, are naturally directed to go into the Water, and fwim there,

Part I. *in the* CREATION. 127

there, as we fee *Duclings*, tho' hatch'd and
led by a Hen, if fhe brings them to the Brink
of a River or Pond of Water, they prefently
leave her, and in they go, tho' they never
faw any fuch Thing done before; and tho' the
Hen clucks and calls, and doth what fhe can
to keep them out. This *Pliny* takes Notice of,
Hift. Nat. lib. 10. *cap.* 55. in thefe Words,
fpeaking of Hens: *Super omnia eft Anatum Ovis
fubditis atque exclufis admiratio, primo non
planè agnofcentis fœtum: mox incertos incubitus
follicitè convocantis: Poftremo lamenta circa
pifcinæ ftagna, mergentibus fe pullis naturâ duce.*
So that we fee every Part in Animals is fitted
to its Ufe, and the Knowledge of this Ufe
put into them: For neither do any Sort of
Web-footed Fowls live conftantly upon the
Land, or fear to enter the Water, nor any
Land-Fowl fo much as attempt to fwim there.
6. Birds of the fame Kind make their Nefts
of the fame Material, laid in the fame Order,
and exactly of the fame Figure; fo that by
the Sight of the Neft one may certainly know
what Bird it belongs to. And this they do,
tho' living in diftant Countries. and tho' they
never faw, nor could fee any Neft made, that
is, tho' taken out of the Neft and brought
up by Hand; neither were any of the fame
Kind ever obferv'd to make a different Neft,
either for Matter or Fafhion. This, together
with the curious and artificial Contexture of
fuch Nefts, and their Fitnefs and Convenience
for the Reception, Hatching, and Cherifhing the
Eggs

128 *The* WISDOM *of* GOD Part I.

Eggs and *Young* of their respective Builders,
(which we have before taken notice of) is a
great Argument of a superior Author of their
and other Natures, who hath endu'd them with
these Instincts, whereby they are as it were
acted and driven to bring about Ends which
themselves aim not at, (so far as we can difcern) but are directed to; for (as *Aristotle* observes) οὖτε τέχνη, οὖτε ζητήσαντα, οὖτε βουλευσάμενα
ποιεῖ, *They act not by Art, neither do they enquire, nei-*
ther do they deliberate about what they do. And
therefore, as Dr. *Cudworth* saith well, they
are not Masters of that Wisdom according to
which they act, but only passive to the Instincts and Impresses thereof upon them. And
indeed to affirm, that brute Animals do all
these Things by a Knowledge of their own,
and which themselves are Masters of, and that
without Deliberation and Consultation, were
to make them to be endued with a most perfect Intellect, far transcending that of human
Reason : Whereas it is plain enough, that
Brutes are not above Consultation, but below
it ; and that these Instincts of Nature in them,
are nothing but a kind of Fate upon them.

The Migration of Birds from an hotter to a
colder Country, or a colder to an hotter, according to the Seasons of the Year, as their Nature
is, I know not how to give an Account of, it is
so strange and admirable. What moves them to
shift their Quarters ? You will say, the Disagreeableness of the Temper of the Air to the Constitution of their Bodies, or Want of Food.
But

But how come they to be directed to the same Place yearly, though sometimes but a little Island, as the *Soland-Goose* to the *Basse* of *Edinburgh-Frith*, which they could not possibly see, and so it could have no Influence upon them that Way? The Cold or the Heat might possibly drive them in a right Line from either, but that they shou'd impel Land-Birds to venture over a wide Ocean, of which they can see no End, is strange and unaccountable: One would think that the Sight of so much Water, and present Fear of Drowning, shou'd overcome the Sense of Hunger, or Disagreeableness of the Temper of the Air. Besides, how come they to steer their Course aright to their several Quarters, which before the Compass was invented was hard for a Man himself to do, they being not able, as I noted before, to see them at that Distance? Think we that the *Quails*, for instance, could see quite cross the *Mediterranean-Sea*? And yet, it's clear, they fly out of *Italy* into *Africk*, lighting many times on Ships in the midst of the Sea, to rest themselves when tired and spent with Flying. That they shou'd thus shift Places, is very convenient for them, and accordingly we see they do it; which seems to be impossible they should, unless themselves were endued with Reason, or directed and acted by a superior intelligent Cause.

The like may be said of the Migration of divers Sorts of Fishes: As for Example; the *Salmon*, which from the Sea yearly ascends up

K 2

130 *The* WISDOM *of* GOD Part I.

a River fometimes 400 or 500 Miles, only to caft their Spawn, and fecure it in Banks of Sand, for the Prefervation of it 'till the Young be hatch'd or excluded, and then return to Sea again. How thefe Creatures when they have been wandring a long time in the wide Ocean, fhould again find out and repair to the Mouths of the fame Rivers, feem to me very ftrange, and hardly accountable, without Recourfe to Inftinct, and the Direction of a fuperior Caufe. That Birds, feeing they have no Teeth for the Maftication and Preparation of their Food, fhould for the more convenient Comminution of it in their Stomachs or Gizzards, fwallow down little Pebble-ftones, or other hard Bodies, and becaufe all are not fit or proper for that Ufe, fhould firft try them in their Bills, to feel whether they be rough or angular, for their Turns; which if they find them not to be, they reject them. When thefe by the working of the Stomach are worn fmooth, or too fmall for their Ufe, they avoid them by Siege, and pick up others. That thefe are of great Ufe to them for the grinding of their Meat, there is no doubt. And I have obferv'd in Birds that have been kept up in Houfes, where they could get no Pebbles, the very Yolks of their Eggs have changed Colour, and become a great deal paler, than theirs who have their Liberty to go abroad.

Befides, I have obferved in many Birds, the Gullet, before its Entrance into the Gizzard, to be much dilated, and thick fet, or as it

were

Part I. *in the* CREATION. 131

were granulated, with a Multitude of Glandules, each whereof was provided with its excretory Veffel, out of which, by an eafy Preffure, you might fqueeze a Juice or Pap, which ferved for the fame Ufe which the *Saliva* doth in Quadrupeds; that is, for the Macerating and Diffolution of the Meat into a Chyle. For that the *Saliva*, notwithftanding its Infipidnefs, hath a notable Virtue of macerating and diffolving Bodies, appears by the Effects it hath in killing of Quickfilver, fermenting of Dough like Leaven or Yeaft, taking away Warts, and curing other cutaneous Diftempers; fometimes exulcerating the Jaws, and rotting the Teeth.

Give me leave to add one Particular more concerning Birds, which fome may perchance think too homely and indecent to be mentioned in fuch a Difcourfe as this; yet becaufe it is not below the Providence of Nature, and de-figned for Cleanlinefs, and fome great Men have thought it worth the obferving, I need not to be afham'd to take notice of it; that is, that in young Birds that are fed in the Neft, the Excrement that is avoided at one time is fo vifcid, that it hangs together in a great Lump, as if it were inclofed in a Film, fo that it may eafily be taken up, and carried away, by the old Bird in her Bill. Befides, by a ftrange Inftinct, the young Bird elevates her hinder Parts fo high, for the moft part, that fhe feldom fails to caft what comes from her clear over the Side of the Neft. So we fee here is a double Provifion made to keep the

K 2   Neft

132   *The* WISDOM *of* GOD Part I.

Neſt clean, which, if it were defiled with Ordure, the young Ones muſt neceſſarily be utterly marred and ruined.   7. The *Bee*, a Creature of the loweſt Forms of Animals, ſo that no Man can ſuſpect it to have any conſiderable Meaſure of Underſtanding, or to have Knowledge of, much leſs to aim at, any End, yet makes her Combs and Cells with that Geometrical Accuracy, that ſhe muſt needs be acted by an Inſtinct implanted in her by the wiſe Author of Nature : For firſt, ſhe plants them in a perpendicular Poſture, and ſo cloſe together, as with Conveniency they may, beginning at the Top, and working downwards, that ſo no Room may be loſt in the Hive, and that ſhe may have eaſy Acceſs to all the Combs and Cells.   Beſides, the Combs being wrought double, that is, with Cells on each Side, a common Bottom, or Partition-Wall, could not in any other Site have ſo conveniently, if at all, received or contained the Honey.   Then ſhe makes the particular Cells moſt Geometrically and Artificially, as the famous Mathematician *Pappus* demonſtrates in the Preface to his third Book of *Mathematical Collections.*   Firſt of all, (ſaith he, ſpeaking of the Cells) it is convenient that they be of ſuch Figures as may cohere one to another, and have common Sides, elſe there would be empty Spaces left between them to no Uſe, but to be weakening and ſpoiling of the Work, if any Thing ſhould get in there.   And therefore, though a round Figure be moſt capacious for the Honey,
and

and moſt convenient for the *Bee* to creep into, yet did ſhe not make choice of that, becauſe then there muſt have been triangular Spaces left void. Now there are only three rectilineous and ordinate Figures which can ſerve to this Purpoſe ; and inordinate, or unlike ones, muſt have been not only leſs elegant and beautiful, but unequal. [Ordinate Figures are ſuch as have all their Sides, and all their Angles equal.] The three ordinate Figures are, *Triangles, Squares,* and *Hexagons* ; for the Space about any Point may be fill'd up either by ſix equilateral *Triangles,* or four *Squares,* or three *Hexagons* ; whereas three *Pentagons* are too little, and three *Heptagons* too much. Of theſe three, the *Bee* makes uſe of the *Hexagon,* both becauſe it is more capacious than either of the other, provided they be of equal Compaſs, and ſo equal Matter ſpent in the Conſtruction of each : And Secondly, Becauſe it is moſt commodious for the Bee to creep into : And Laſtly, Becauſe in the other Figures, more Angles and Sides muſt have met together at the ſame Point, and ſo the Work could not have been ſo firm and ſtrong. Moreover, the Combs being double, the Cells on each Side the Partition are ſo order'd, that the Angles on one Side inſiſt upon the Centers of the Bottoms of the Cells on the other Side, and not Angle upon or againſt Angle; which alſo muſt needs contribute to the Strength and Firmneſs of the Work. Theſe Cells ſhe fills with Honey for her Winter-Proviſion, and curiouſly cloſes them up with Covers of

K 3   Wax,

134 *The* WISDOM *of* GOD Part I.

Wax, that keep the included Liquor from ſpilling, and from external Injuries; as Mr. *Boyle* truly obſerves, *Treatiſe of Final Cauſes, p. 169.* Another ſort of *Bee,* I have obſerved, may be called the *Tree-Bee,* whoſe Induſtry is admirable in making Proviſion for her Young. Firſt, ſhe digs round Vaults or Burrows [*Cuniculos*] in a rotten or decay'd Tree, of a great Length; in them ſhe builds or forms her cylindrical Neſts or Caſes reſembling Cartrages, or a very narrow Thimble only in Proportion longer, of Pieces of Roſe or other Leaves, which ſhe ſhares off with her Mouth, and plats and joins cloſe together by ſome glutinous Subſtance. Theſe Caſes ſhe fills with a red Pap, of a thinner Conſiſtence than an Electuary, of no pleaſant Taſte, which where ſhe gathers, I know not: And which is moſt remarkable, ſhe forms theſe Caſes, and ſtores them with this Proviſion, before ſhe hath any young One hatch'd, or ſo much as an Egg laid: For on the Top of the Pap ſhe lays one Egg, and then cloſes up the Veſſel with a Cover of Leaves. The encloſ'd Egg ſoon becomes an *Eula,* or Maggot, which feeding upon the Pap till it comes to its full Growth, changes to a *Nympha,* and after comes out a Bee. Another Inſect noted for her ſeeming Prudence, in making Proviſion for the Winter, propoſed by *Solomon* to the Sluggard for his Imitation, is the *Ant,* which (as all Naturaliſts agree) hoard up Grains of Corn againſt the Winter for her Suſtenance:

And

Part I.   *in the* CREATION.   135

And is reported by fome to * bite off the *Ger-men* of them, left they fhould fprout by the Moifture of the Earth; which I look upon as a mere Fiction : Nei-   * Plin. l. 11. c. 30.

ther fhou'd I be forward to credit the former Relation, were it not for the Authority of the *Scripture*, becaufe I could never obferve any fuch ftoring of Grain by our Countrey-Ants.

Yet there is a Quadruped taken notice of even by the Vulgar, for laying up in ftore Provifion for the Winter; that is, the *Squirrel*, whofe Hoards of Nuts are frequently found, and pillaged by them,

The *Beaver* is by credible Perfons, Eye-witneffes, affirm'd to build him Houfes for Shelter and Security in Winter-time.   See Mr. *Boyle* of *Final Caufes*, p. 173.

Befides thefe I have mentioned, an hundred others may be found in Books relating efpecially to Phyfick, as, that *Dogs*, when they are fick, fhould vomit themfelves by eating Grafs : That *Swine* fhould refufe Meat fo foon as they feel themfelves ill, and fo recover by Abftinence : That the Bird *Ibis* fhould teach Men the Way of adminiftring Clyfters, *Plin. lib. 8. cap. 27.* The wild *Goats* of *Dictamus* for drawing out of Darts, and healing Wounds : The *Swallow* the Ufe of *Celandine* for repairing the Sight, &c. *ibid.* Of the Truth of which, becaufe I am not fully fatisfied, I fhall make no Inference from them.

Thirdly, I fhall remark the Care that is taken for the Prefervation of the Weak, and fuch as

K 4   are

136 *The* WISDOM *of* GOD Part I.

are expofed to the Injuries, and preventing the
Encreafe of fuch as are noifome and hurtful :
For as it is a Demonftration of the Divine Power and Magnificence to create fuch Variety of
Animals, not only great but fmall, not only
ftrong and couragious, but alfo weak and timorous; fo is it no lefs Argument of his Wifdom to give to thefe Means, and the Power
and Skill of ufing them, to preferve themfelves
from the Violence and Injuries of thofe.   That
of the Weak fome fhou'd dig Vaults and Holes
in the Earth, as *Rabbets*, to fecure themfelves
and their Young ; others fhou'd be arm'd with
hard Shells ; others with Prickles, the reft that
have no fuch Armature, fhou'd be endued with
great Swiftnefs or Pernicity : And not only fo,
but fome alfo have their Eyes ftand fo prominent, as the *Hare*, that they can fee as well behind as before them, that fo they may have their
Enemy alway in their Eye ; and long, hollow,
moveable Ears, to receive and convey the leaft
Sound, or that which comes from far, that they
be not fuddenly furprized or taken (as they fay)
Napping.   Moreover, it is remarkable, that in
this Animal, and in the *Rabbet*, the Mufcles
of the Loyns and Hind-legs are extraordinarily large in Proportion to the reft of the Body, or thofe of other Animals, as if made
on Purpofe for Swiftnefs, that they may be able
to efcape the Teeth of fo many Enemies as
continually purfue and chafe them.   Add here-
to the Length of their Hind-legs, which is no
fmall

Part I.   *in the* CREATION.   137

small Advantage to them, as is noted by Dame *Julan Barns*, in an antient Dialogue in Verse between the Huntsman and his Man: The Man there asks his Master, What is the Reason, why the Hare when she is near spent makes up a Hill? The Master answers, That Nature hath made the Hinder-legs of the Hare longer than the Fore-legs; by which Means she climbs the Hill with much more Ease than the Dogs, whose Legs are of equal Length, and so leaves the Dogs behind her, and many Times escapes away clear, and saves her Life.   This last Observation, I must confess myself to have borrowed out of the Papers of my honoured Friend Mr. *John Aubrey*, which he was pleased to give me a Sight of.

I might here add much concerning the Wiles and Ruses, which these timid Creatures make use of to save themselves, and escape their Persecutors, but that I am somewhat diffident of the Truth of those Stories and Relations, I shall only aver what myself have sometimes observ'd of a Duck, when closely pursued by a Water-Dog; she not only dives to save herself, (which yet she never does but when driven to an exigent, and just ready to be caught, because it is painful and difficult to her) but when she comes up again, brings not her whole Body above Water, but only her Bill, and Part of her Head, holding the rest underneath, that so the Dog, who the mean time turns round and looks about him, may not espy her, 'till she have recover'd Breath.

As

138 *The* WISDOM *of* GOD Part I.

As for *Sheep*, which have no natural Weapons or Means to defend or secure themselves, neither Heels to run, nor Claws to dig; they are deliver'd into the Hand, and committed to the Care and Tuition of Man; and serving him for divers Uses, are nourished and protected by him; and so enjoying their Beings for a Time, by this Means propagate and continue their Species: So that there are none destitute of some Means to preserve themselves, and their Kind; and these Means so effectual, that notwithstanding all the Endeavours and Contrivances of Man and Beast to destroy them, there is not to this Day one *Species* lost of such as are mention'd in Histories, and consequently and undoubtedly neither of such as were at first created.

Then for Birds of Prey, and rapacious Animals, it is remarkable what *Aristotle* observes, That they are all solitary, and go not in Flocks, Γαμψωνύχων οὐδὲν ἀγελαῖον, no Birds of Prey are gregarious. Again, that such Creatures do not greatly multiply, τῶν γαμψωνύχων ὀλιγοτόκα πάντα. They for the most Part breeding and bringing forth but one or two, or at least, a few Young Ones at once: Whereas they that are feeble and timorous are generally multiparous; or, if they bring forth but a few at once, as *Pigeons*, they compensate that by their often breeding, *viz.* every Month but two throughout the Year; by this Means providing for the Continuation of their Kind. But for the Security of these rapacious Birds, it is worthy the noting, that because

Part I.   *in the* CREATION.   139

caufe a Prey is not always ready, but perhaps they may fail of one fome Days, Nature hath made them patient of a long *inedia*, and befides, when they light upon one, they gorge themfelves fo therewith, as to fuffice for their Nourifhment for a confiderable Time.

Fourthly, I fhall note the exact Fitnefs of the Parts of the Bodies of Animals to every one's Nature and Manner of Living. A notable Inftance of which we have in the *Swine*, a Creature well known, and therefore what I fhall obferve of it is obvious to every Man. His proper and natural Food being chiefly the Roots of Plants, he is provided with a long and ftrong Snout ; long, that he might thruft it to a fufficient Depth into the Ground, without Offence to his Eyes ; ftrong and conveniently formed for the rooting and turning up the Ground. And befides, he is endued with a notable Sagacity of Scent, for the finding out fuch Roots as are fit for his Food. Hence in *Italy*, the ufual Method for finding and gathering of *Trufles*, or fubterraneous Mufhromes, (called by the *Italians Tartufali*, and in *Latin Tubera terræ*) is, by tying a Cord to the Hind-leg of a Pig, and driving him before them into fuch Paftures as ufually produce that Kind of Mufhrome, and obferving where he ftops and begins to root, and there digging, they are fure to find a *Trufle* ; which when they have taken up, they drive away the Pig to fearch for more. So I have myfelf obferved, that in Paftures where there are *Earth-nuts* to be found up and down

in

140 *The* WISDOM *of* GOD Part I.

in feveral Patches, tho' the Roots lie deep in the Ground, and the Stalks be dead long before and quite gone, the Swine will by their Scent eafily find them out, and root only in thofe Places where they grow.

This rooting of the Hog in the Earth, calls to mind another Inftance of like Nature, that is the *Porpeffe*, which, as his *Englifh* Name *Porpeffe*, i. e. * *Porc pefce*, imports, re-
* Swine-fifh.   fembles the Hog, both in the Strength of his Snout, and alfo in the Manner of getting his Food by rooting,   For we found the Stomach of one we deffected, full of *Sand-Eels*, or *Launces*, which for the moft Part lie deep in the Sand, and cannot be gotten but by rooting or digging there.   We have feen the Country-People in *Cornwall*, when the Tide was out, to fetch them out of the Sand with Iron-Hooks thruft down under them, made for that Purpofe.

Furthermore, that very Action for which the Swine is abominated, and look'd upon as an unclean and impure Creature, namely wallowing in the Mire, is defign'd by Nature for a very good End and Ufe, *viz.* not only to cool his Body, for the fair Water would have done that as well, nay, better, for commonly the Mud and Mire in Summer-time is warm; but alfo to fuffocate and deftroy Lice, Fleas, and other noifom and importunate Infects, that are troublefome and noxious to him. For the fame Reafon do all the Poultry-kind, and divers other Birds, bask themfelves in the Duft in Summer-time

Part I.   *in the* CREATION.   141

time and hot Weather, as is obvious to every one to obferve.

2. A fecond and no lefs remarkable Inftance, I fhall produce, out of Dr. *More's Antidote againft Atheifm,* lib. 2. cap. 10. in a poor and contemptible Quadruped, the *Mole.*

Firft of all (faith he) her Dwelling being under Ground, where nothing is to be feen, Nature hath fo obfcurely fitted her with Eyes, that Naturalifts can fcarcely agree, whether fhe hath any Sight at all or no. [In our Obfervation, *Moles* have perfect Eyes, and Holes for them through the Skin, fo that they are outwardly to be feen by any that fhall diligently fearch for them; tho' indeed they are exceeding fmall, not much bigger than a great Pin's Head.] But for Amends, what fhe is capable of for her Defence and Warning of Danger, fhe has very eminently conferr'd upon her; for fhe is very quick of hearing, [doubtlefs her fubterraneous Vaults are like Trunks to convey any Sound a great Way.] And then her fhort Tail and fhort Legs, but broad Fore-feet armed with fharp Claws, we fee by the Event to what purpofe they are, fhe fo fwiftly working herfelf under Ground, and making her Way fo faft in the Earth, as they that behold it cannot but admire it. Her Legs therefore are fhort, that fhe need dig no more than will ferve the mere Thicknefs of her Body: And her Fore-feet are broad, that fhe may fcoup away much Earth at a Time: And fhe has little or no Tail, becaufe fhe courfes it not on the Ground like a *Rat* or *Moufe,* but lives under the

Earth,

142   *The* WISDOM *of* GOD Part I.

Earth, and is fain to dig herself a Dwelling there; and she making her Way thro' so thick an Element, which will not easily yield as the Water and Air do; it had been dangerous to draw so long a Train behind her; for her Ene-my might fall upon her Rear, and fetch her out before she had perfected and got full Pos-session of her Works: Which being so, what more palpable Argument of Providence than she?

★   ★   ★   ★

[P. 343]

The Providence of Nature is wonderful in a *Camel,* or *Dromadary,* both in the Structure of his Body, and in the Provision that is made for the Sustenance of it. Concerning the first, I shall instance only in the Make of his Foot, the Sole whereof, as the *Parisian Academists* do ob-serve, is flat and broad, being very fleshy, and covered only with a thick, soft, and somewhat callous Skin, but very fit and proper to travel in sandy Places; such as are the Desarts of *Africk* and *Asia.* We thought (say they) that this Skin was like a living Sole, which wore not with the Swiftness and the Continuance of the March, for which this *Animal* is almost indefatigable. And it may be this Softness of the Foot, which yields and fits itself to the Ruggedness and Un-eavenness of the Roads, does render the Feet less capable of being worn, than if they were more solid.

Z 4   As

344 *The* WISDOM *of* GOD Part II.

As to the Second, the Provifion that is made for their Suftenance in their continued Travels over fandy Defarts, the fame Academifts obferve, That at the Top of the fecond Ventricle (for they are ruminant Creatures, and have four Sto-machs) there were feveral fquare Holes, which were the Orifices of about twenty Cavities, made like Sacks placed between the two Membranes, which do compofe the Subftance of this Ventri-cle. The View of thefe Sacks made us to think, that they might well be the Refervatories, where *Pliny* fays, That Camels do a long time keep the Water, which they drink in great Abundance when they meet with it, to fupply the Wants which they may have thereof in the dry De-farts, wherein they are ufed to travel; and where it is faid, that thofe that do guide them, are fometimes forced, by Extremity of Thirft, to open their Bellies, in which they do find Water.

That fuch an Animal as this, fo patient of long Thirft, fhould be bred in fuch droughty and parched Countries, where it is of fuch eminent Ufe for travelling over thofe dry and fandy De-farts, where no Water is to be had fometimes in two or three Days Journey, no candid and confiderable Perfon but muft needs acknowledge to be an Effect of Providence and Defign.

★ ★ ★ ★

[p. 368]

I fhould now proceed to anfwer fome Objections which might be made againft the Wifdom and Goodnefs of God in the Contrivance and Governance of the World, and all Creatures therein contained. But that is too great and difficult a Task for my Weaknefs, and would take up more time than I have at prefent to fpare, were I qualified for it; and befides, fwell this Volume to too great a Bulk. Only I fhall fay fomething to one Particular, which was fuggefted to me by a Learned and Pious * Friend.

* Mr. *Rob. Burfcough* of *Totnefs,* in *Devon.*

Objeᶜt. A wife Agent aᶜts for Ends. Now what End can there be of creating fuch a vaft Multitude of Infeᶜts, as the World is filled with ; moft of which feems to be ufelefs, and fome alfo noxious and pernicious to Man, and other Creatures ?

Anfw. To this I fhall Anfwer; 1. As to the Multitude of *Species,* or Kinds. 2. As to the Number of *Individuals,* in each Kind.

Firft, As to the Multitude of *Species,* (which we muft needs acknowledge to be exceeding great, they being not fewer, perchance more

Part II. *in the* CREATION? 369

more than Twenty Thoufand.) I anfwer there were fo many made.

1. To manifeft and difplay the Riches of the Power and Wifdom of God, *Pfalm* civ. 24. *The Earth is full of thy Riches; fo is this great and wide Sea, wherein are Things creeping innumerable,* &c. We fhould be apt to think too meanly of thofe Attributes of our Creator, fhould we be able to come to an End of all his Works, even in this Sublunary World. And therefore, I believe, never any Man yet did, never any Man fhall, fo long as the World endures, by his utmoft Induftry, attain to the Knowledge of all the *Species* of Nature. Hitherto we have been fo far from it, that in Vegetables, the Number of thofe which have been difcovered this laft Age, hath far exceeded that of all thofe which were known before. So true is that we quoted before out of *Seneca, Pufilla res eft mundus, nifi in eo quod quærat omnis, mundus habeat.* The World is fo richly furnifhed and provided, that Man need not fear Want of Employment, fhould he live to the Age of *Methufelah,* or ten times as long. But of this, having touched it already, I fhall add no more.

2. Another Reafon why fo many Kinds of Creatures were made, might be to exercife the contemplative Faculty of Man; which is in nothing fo much pleas'd, as in Variety of Objects. We foon grow weary of one Study; and if all the Objects of the World could be comprehended by us, we fhould, with *Alex-*

B b *ander*

370 *The* WISDOM *of* GOD Part II.

ander, think the World too little for us, and grow weary of running in a Round of feeing the fame Things. New Objects afford us great Delight, efpecially if found out by our own Induftry. I remember *Clufius* faith of himfelf, " That upon the Difcovery of a new " Plant, he did not lefs rejoice, than if he had " found a rich Treafure." Thus God is pleafed, by referving Things to be found out by our Pains and Induftry, to provide us Employment moft delightful and agreable to our Natures and Inclinations.

3. Many of thefe Creatures may be ufeful to us, whofe Ufes are not yet difcovered, but referved for the Generations to come, as the Ufes of fome we now know are but of late Invention, and were unknown to our Forefathers. And this muft needs be fo, becaufe, as I faid before, the World is too great for any Man, or Generation of Men, by his, or their utmoft Endeavours, to difcover and find out all its Store and Furniture, all its Riches and Treafures.

Secondly, As to the Multitude of Individuals in each Kind of *Infect*. I Anfwer,

1. It is defigned to fecure the Continuance and Perpetuity of the feveral Species; which, if they did not multiply exceedingly, fcarce any of them could efcape the Ravine of fo many Enemies as continually affault and prey upon them, but would endanger to be quite deftroyed and loft out of the World.

2. This

Part II.   On the CREATION.   371

2. This vast Multitude of Insects is useful
to Mankind, if not immediately, yet mediate-
ly.   It cannot be denied, that Birds are of great
Use to us; their Flesh affording us a good Part
of our Food, and that the most delicate too,
and their other Parts Physick, not excepting
their very Excrements.   Their Feathers serve
to stuff our Beds and Pillows, yielding us soft
and warm Lodging, which is no small Convenience and Comfort to us, especially in these
Northern Parts of the World.   Some of them
have also been always employed by Military
Men in Plumes, to adorn their Crests, and
render them formidable to their Enemies.   Their
Wings and Quills are made use of for Writing-
Pens, and to brush and cleanse our Rooms, and
their Furniture.   Besides, by their melodious
Accents they gratify our Ears; by their beautiful Shapes and Colours, they delight our Eyes,
being very ornamental to the World, and rendring the Country where the Hedges and Woods
are full of them, very pleasant and chearly,
which without them wou'd be no less lonely
and melancholy.   Not to mention the Exercise, Diversion, and Recreation, which some of
them give us.

Now Insects supply Land-Birds the chiefest
Part of their Sustenance: Some, as the entire
Genus of *Swallows*, live wholly upon them,
as I could easily make out, did any Man deny
or doubt of it: And not *Swallows* alone, but
also *Wood-peckers*, if not wholly, yet chiefly;
and all other Sorts of Birds partly, especial-

372 *The* WISDOM *of* GOD Part II.

ly in Winter-time, when Infects are their main
Support, as appears by diffecting their Sto-
machs.

As for young Birds, which are brought up
in the Neft by the old, they are fed chiefly, if
not folely, by Infects.   And therefore for the
Time when Birds for the moft Part breed in
the Spring, when there are Multitudes of Caterpillars to be found on all Trees and Hedges.
Moreover, it is very remarkable, that of many fuch Birds, as when grown up, feed almoft
wholly upon Grain, the young ones are nourifh'd by Infects.   For Example, *Pheafants* and
Partridges, which are well known to be gra-
nivorous Birds, the Young live only, or moftly,
upon Ants Eggs.   Now Birds, being of a hot
Nature, are very voracious Creatures, and eat
abundantly, and therefore there had need be
an infinite Number of Infects produced for
their Suftenance.   Neither do Birds alone, but
many Sorts of Fifhes, feed upon Infects, as
is well known to Anglers, who bait their
Hooks with them.   Nay, which is more ftrange,
divers Quadrupeds feed upon Infects, and
fome live wholly upon them, as two Sorts of
Tamunduus upon Ants, which therefore are
called in *Englifh* Ant-Bears ; the *Camelion* upon
Flies ; the Mole upon Earth-Worms : The
Badger alfo lives chiefly upon Beetles, Worms,
and other Infects.

Here we may take Notice by the way, That
becaufe fo many Creatures live upon Ants and
their Eggs, Providence hath fo order'd it, that
they

Part II. *in the* CREATION. 373

they fhould be the moft numerous of any Tribe
of Infects that we know.

Conformable to this Particular, is the Reafon
my ingenious and inquifitive Friend Mr. *Derham*,
before remember'd, hath given of the Production
of fuch innumerable Multitudes of fome Aqua-
tick Infects.

I have often thought (*faith he*) that there
was fome more than ordinary Ufe in the Creation for fuch Infects as are vaftly numerous ;
fuch as the *Pulices Aquatici*, which are in fuch
Swarms, as to difcolour the Waters, and many others : And therefore I have bent my Enquiries to find out the Ufes of fuch Creatures;
wherein I have fo far fucceeded, as to difcover,
that thofe vaftly fmall *Animalcula*, not to be
feen without a Microfcope, with which the
Waters are replete, ferve for Food to fome
others of the fmall Infects of the Water, particularly to the *Nympha Culicaria* [*Hirfuta* it may
be called] figured in *Swammerdam*. For view-
ing that *Nympha* one Day, to obferve the Motion of its Mouth, and for what Purpofe it is
in fuch continual Motion; whether as Fifh to
get Air, or to fuck in Food, or both, I could
plainly perceive the Creature to fuck in many
of thefe moft minute *Animalcula*, that were
fwimming briskly about in the Water. Neither yet do thefe Animalcules ferve only for
Food to fuch *Nymphæ*, but alfo to another to
me anonymous Infect of the Waters, of a
dark Colour, cleft as it were in funder, and
fcarce fo big as the fmalleft Pin's Head. Thefe

B b 3   Infects

374 *The* WISDOM *of* GOD Part II.

Infects hunt these *Animalcules*, and other small
Creatures that occur in the Water, and devour
them : And I am apt to think, although I have
not yet seen it, that the *Pulex aquaticus arboref-
cens* liveth upon these, or more minute and tender Animalcules, and that it is to catch them
that it so leaps in the Water.

This to me seems a wonderful Work of
God, to provide for the minuteft Creatures of
the Waters Food proper for them, that is, minute and tender, and fit for their Organs of
Swallowing.

As for noxious Infects, why there should
be so many of them produced, if it be de-
manded,

I answer, 1. That many that are noxious
to us, are falutary to other Creatures; and
some that are Poison to us, are Food to them.
So we see the Poultry-kind feed upon *Spiders:*
Nay, there is scarce any noxious Infect, but
one Bird or other eats it, either for Food or
Physick. For many, nay, moft of those Creatures, whose Bite, or Sting, is poisonous, may
safely be taken entire into the Stomach. And
therefore it is no wonder, that not only the
Ibis of *Egypt*, but even *Storks* and *Peacocks*, prey
upon and deftroy all Sorts of *Serpents*, as well
as *Locufts* and *Caterpillars*.

2. Some of the moft venomous and pernicious of Infects afford us noble Medicines, as
Scorpions, *Spiders*, and *Cantharides*.

3. These Infects seldom make use of their
offensive Weapons, unless affaulted or pro-
voked

voked in their own Defence, or to revenge an Injury. Let them but alone, and annoy them not, nor diſturb their Young, and, unleſs accidentally, you ſhall ſeldom ſuffer by them.

Laſtly, God is pleaſed ſometimes to make uſe of them as Scourges, to chaſtize or puniſh wicked Perſons, or Nations, as he did *Herod* and the *Egyptians*. No Creature ſo mean and contemptible, but God can, when he pleaſes, produce ſuch Armies of them, as no humane Force is able to conquer, or deſtroy; but they ſhall of a ſudden conſume and devour up all the Fruits of the Earth, and whatever might ſerve for the Suſtenance of Man, as *Locuſts* have often been obſerved to do.

Did theſe Creatures ſerve for no other Uſe, as they do many; yet thoſe that make them an Objection againſt the Wiſdom of God, may (as Dr. *Cockburn* well notes) as well upbraid the Prudence and Policy of a State for keeping Forces, which generally are made up of very rude and inſolent People, which yet are neceſſary, either to ſuppreſs Rebellions, or puniſh Rebels, and other diſorderly and vicious Perſons, and keep the World in quiet.

12. John Ray (1627-1705)

Three Physico-Theological Discourses (London, 1693)
Inset between pp. 132 and 133 and plates II, III, IV

place this Half-sheet next after p. 132. before the 3 Plates.

Reflecting upon the length of this Discourse, concerning the Original of these Bodies, I am suspicious that the vulgar and inconsiderate Reader will be ready to demand, What needs all this ado? To what purpose so many words about so trivial a Subject? What reference hath the consideration of Shells and Bones of Fishes petrified to Divinity? Wherefore I shall in a few words shew the great importance of this Disquisition concerning formed Stones, and the Determination of their Original.

For, 1st, If we adhere to their Opinion: who hold them to have been original Productions of Nature, in imitation only of the Shells and Bones of Fishes: We put a Weapon into the Atheist's hands, affording him a strong Argument to prove that even Animals themselves are casual Productions, and not the effects of Counsel or Design. For to what end are these Bodies curiously figured and adorned? if for no other but to exhibit such a Form, for the Ornament of the Universe, or to gratifie the Curiosity of Man; these are but general ends, whereas the parts of every Species of Body are formed and fitted to the particular Uses and Conveniences of that Body. And if Nature would delineate or imprint Figures upon Bodies, only to be Spectacles to Man, one would think it should not have made choice of those

of

of the Shells and Bones of Fishes, but rather of such as were absolutely new and different from any frequently seen or belonging to Animals; which serve rather to amuse than delight him. But 2ly, we find in the Earth not only Stones formed in imitation of Shells; but real Shells, Teeth and Bones of Fishes, or Bodies so like them, that they are not to be distinguished by Figure, Texture, Colour, Weight, or any other Accident. Now what greater Argument can the Atheist desire to prove, that the Shells of Fishes were never designed by any provident Efficient for their Defence, or their Bones for the sustaining of their Bodies, but that the Fish and Shell containing it, and the Bones sustaining it, did casually concur; than that there should be real Shells produced without any Fish in them, and that in dry places where no Fish ever did or could breed, or indeed live, and real Fish-bones, where there never was nor could be any Fish.

Doth it not than concern a Divine to be acquainted with this Objection against the Bodies of Animals being the effects of Counsel and Design, and provided with an answer to it. For my part I must needs confess that this Argument weighs so with me, whether from that innate Prolepsis my self, and I think most other Men have of the Prudence of Nature in all its Operations, or from mine own observing that in all other things, it acts for ends, that it is alone

sufficient

ed, and fhall here omit, repeating only two that refer to Divinity.

1. Thefe Bodies being found difperfed all over the Earth, they of the contrary Opinion demand how they come there? If it be anfwered, That they were brought in by the general Deluge; in contradiction thereto, they argue thus. If thefe Stones were found fcattered fingly and indifferently all the Earth over, there might be indeed fome reafon to imagine that they were brought in by the Floud; but being found in fome particular places only, either lying thick in great Beds of Sand and Gravel, or amaffed together in huge Lumps, by a ftony Cement fuch Beds muft in all likelihood have been the effect of thofe Animals breeding there for a confiderable time, whereas the Floud continued upon the Earth but ten Months, during half which time it's not likely that the Mountains were covered; and yet there are found of thefe Bodies upon very high Mountains, not excepting the Appenine and Alps themfelves. Whence they conclude, that they were neither brought in by the Floud, nor bred during the Floud, but fome other way produced. For if they were the Shells of Fifhes, or their Bones, the Water muft needs have covered the whole Earth, even the Mountains themfelves for a much longer time than is confiftent with the Scripture-Hiftory of the Floud, and therefore we muft feek fome other original of thefe Bodies. If

fufficient to preponderate all the Arguments againft the contrary Opinions, though I acknowledge them to be of great force and hard to be anfwered, and to incline or rather conftrain me to allow that thefe Bodies were either real Bones and Shells of Fifhes, or owe their Figure to them. I cannot (to ufe the Words of F. Columna) prevail with my felf to believe, that Nature ever made Teeth without a Jaw, or Shells without an Animal Inhabitant, or fingle Bones, no not in their own proper Element, much lefs in a ftrange one. Who even of the Vulgar beholding any confiderable part of an Animal which he fees not the ufe of, is not apt prefently to ask what it ferves for, as by that innate Prolepfis I mentioned before, prefuming it was not made in vain, but for fome end and ufe. Suppofe any of us fhould find in the Earth the compleat Skeleton of a Man, he muft be as credulous as the Atheift, if he could believe that it grew there of it felf, and never had relation to any Man's Body. Why then fhould we think that the entire Skeletons of Fifhes found fometimes in the Earth, had no other Original? nor ever were any part of living Fifhes.

* *

2ly, If we chufe and embrace the contrary Opinion, viz. That thefe Bodies were the real Shells and Bones of Fifhes, or owe their Figures to them, we fhall find that this alfo is urged with many and almoft unfuperable Difficulties, the principal of which I have already produced

If we stick to the Letter of the Scripture-History of the Creation, that the Creation of Fishes succeeded the Separation of Land and Sea, and that the six days wherein the World was created, were six natural Days and no more, it is very difficult to return a satisfactory Answer to this Objection: I shall therefore only add a conjecture of my own, and that is, That possibly at the first Creation, the whole Earth was not all at once uncovered, but only those parts whereabout Adam and the other Animals were created, and the rest gradually afterwards, perchance not in many Years; during which time these Shell-fish might breed abundantly all the Sea over, the bottom whereof being elevated and made dry Land, the Beds of Shell-fish, must necessarily be raised together with it.

2. It will hence follow that many Species of Animals have been lost out of the World, which Philosophers and Divines are unwilling to admit, esteeming the Destruction of any one Species a dismembring of the Universe, and rendring the World imperfect. Whereas they think the Divine Providence is especially concerned and solicitous to secure and preserve the Works of the Creation. And truly so it is, as appears, in that it was so careful to lodge all Land-Animals in the Ark at the time of the general Deluge, and in that of all Animals recorded in Natural Histories, we cannot say that there hath

hath been any one Species lost, no not of the most infirm and most exposed to injury and ravine. Moreover it is likely, that as there neither is nor can be any new Species of Animal produced, all proceeding from Seeds at first created; so Providence without which one individual Sparrow falls not to the Ground, doth in that manner watch over all that are created, that an entire Species shall not be lost or destroyed by any Accident. Now I say, if these Bodies were sometimes the Shells and Bones of Fish, it will thence follow, that many Species have been lost out of the World, as for example, those Ophiomorphous ones, whose Shells are now called Cornua Ammonis, of which there are many Species, none whereof at this day, appear in our or other Seas, so far as I have hitherto seen, heard or read. To which I have nothing to reply, but that there may be some of them remaining some where or other in the Seas, though as yet they have not come to my Knowledge. For though they may have perished, or by some Accident been destroyed out of our Seas, yet the Race of them may be preserved and continued still in others. So though Wolves and Bevers, which we are well assured were sometimes native of England, have been here utterly destroyed and extirpated out of this Island, yet there remain plenty of them still in other Countrys.

By what hath been said concerning the nature and

T A B. II.   Pag. 162.

FIG. 1, 2. Several Fragments and Lumps of petrify'd Shells, as they lie in Quarries and ...ds under ground ; on many of these Petrifactions there still remain some *Laminæ*, or Plates of the Original Shells, which prove them not to be Stones primarily so figur'd.

Fig. 3. The *Cornu Ammoni.*   ng in Rocks with other petrify'd Bodies.

T A B. III.   ag. 162.

FIG. 1, 2. Two petrify'd Fishes lying in Stone, with their Scales and Bones.

Fig. 3. A Sea-Urchin petrify'd with its Prickles broken off, which are a sort of *Lapis Judaicus*, or *Jew-Stones* ; their Insertions on the Studs or Protuberances of the Shell are here shewn. See their History and Manner of Lying in Stone and Beds, in *Agostino Scilla.* ... *Napoli.*

T A B. IV.   Pag. 162.

FIG. 1, 2, 3, 4, 5, 6, 7, 8, 9, 10, 11, 12, 13, 14. Several petrify'd Teeth of Dog-Fishes, Sharks, and other Fishes.

Fig. 15, 16. The same lying in a Tophaceous Bed, and also in a Jaw-Bone.

Fig. 17. The petrify'd Teeth of a Wolf-Fish, in a piece of the Jaw; the Round Ones, or Grinders, are sold in *Maltæ* for petrified Eyes of Serpents ; and by our Jewellers and Goldsmiths for Toad-stones, commonly put in Rings.

Fig. 18, 19, 20. Other petrify'd Bones of Fishes, especially Joynts, or Vertebres of Back-bones, one with two stony Spines, issuing out, f. 20. See them more at large in the Draughts of that curious Sicilian Painter, *Agostino Scilla.*

Place this before Tab. II. p. 162.

---

and original of Stones, I hope it may appear, that this is no idle and unnecessary Discourse, but very momentous and important ; and this Subject, as mean as it seems, worthy the most serious consideration of Christian Philosophers and Divines ; concerning which, though I have spent many thoughts, yet can I not fully satisfie my self, much less then am I likely to satisfie others.

But I promise my self and them more full satisfaction shortly from the Labours of those who are more conversant and better acquainted with these Bodies than I, who have been more industrious in searching them out, and happy in discovering them, who have been more curious and diligent in considering and comparing them, more critical and exact in observing and noting their nature, texture, figure, parts, places, differences, and other accidents, than my self, and particularly that learned and ingenious Person before remembred.

The following Tables, containing some Species of the most different Genera of these Bodies, viz. Shark's Teeth, Wolf-fish's Teeth, Cockles or Concha, Periwinkles or Turbens, Cornua Ammonis or Serpent stones, Sea-urchins and their Prickles, Vertebres and other Bones of Fishes, entire Fishes Petrifi'd, and of those some singly, some represented as they lye in Beds and Quarries under Ground, for the information of those who are less acquainted with such Bodie, were thought fit to be added to this Edition.

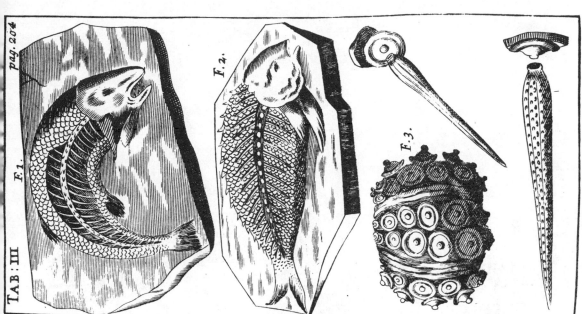

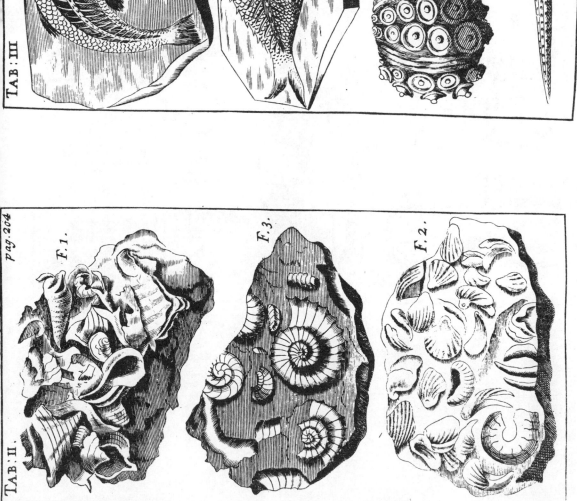

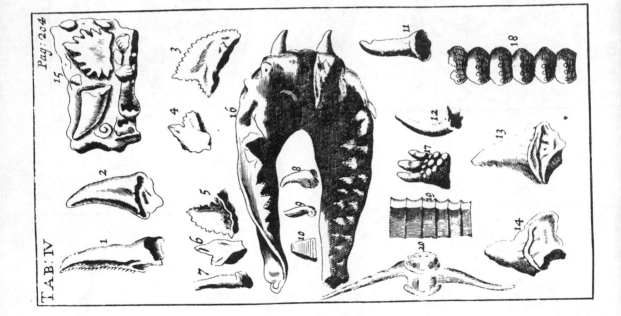

13. William Derham (1657-1735)

Physico-Theology: or, a Demonstration of the Being and Attributes of
God, from His Works of Creation (London, 1713)
From the new edition (London, 1798), vol. 1, 257-270; vol. 2,
394-400

[Vol. 1]

CHAP. X.

Of the Balance of Animals, or the due Proportion in which the World is stocked with them.

THE whole surface of our globe can afford room and support only to such a number of all sorts of creatures. And if by their doubling, trebling, or any other multiplication of their kind, they should increase to double or treble that number, they must starve, or devour one another. The keeping therefore the balance even, is manifestly a work of the Divine wisdom and providence. To which end, the great author of life hath determined the life of all creatures to such a length, and their increase to such a number, proportional to their use in the world. The life of some creatures is long, and their increase but small, and by that means they do not over-stock the world. And the same benefit is effected, where the increase is great, by the brevity of such creatures lives, by their great use, and the frequent occasions there are of them for food to man or other animals. It is a very remarkable act of the Divine providence, that useful creatures are produced in great plenty (*a*), and

(*a*) *Benigna circa hoc Natura, innocua & esculenta animalia fœcunda generavit.*—" Nature in her bounty hath rendered those animals

s

VOL. I.

and others in lefs. The prodigious and frequent increafe of infects*, both in and out of the waters, may exemplify the one; and it is obfervable in the other, that creatures lefs ufeful, or by their voracity pernicious, have commonly fewer young, or do feldomer bring forth: of which many inftances might be given in the voracious beafts and birds. But there is one fo peculiar an animal, as if made for a particular inftance in our prefent cafe, and that is the condor of *Peru* (b), a fowl of that magnitude,

animals very prolific, which are wholefome and fit for the food of man."—*Plin. Nat. Hift.* l. 8. c. 55.

(b) *Captain J. Strong, gave me this account, together with a quill-feather of the condor of Peru. On the coaft of Chili, they met with this bird in about 33° f. lat. not far from Mocha, an Ifland in the fouth fea,—they fhoot it fiting on a cliff, by the fea-fide; that it was 16 feet from wing to wing extended; that the Spanifh inhabitants told them they were afraid of thefe birds, left they fhould prey upon their children. And the feather he gave me (faith the Doctor) is two feet four inches long; the quill-part five inches three quarters*

tude, ftrength, and appetite, as to feize not only on the fheep, and leffer cattle, but even the larger beafts, yea, the very children too. Now thefe, as they are the moft pernicious of birds, fo are they the moft rare, being feldom feen, or only one, or a few in large countries; enough to keep up the fpecies; but not to overcharge the world.

Thus the balance of the animal world, is, throughout all ages, kept even; and by a curious harmony and juft proportion between the increafe of all animals and the length of their lives, the world is through all ages well, but not over ftored: *One generation paffeth away, and another generation*

quarters long, and one inch and half about in the largeft part. It weighed 3 dr. 17 gr. and half, and is of a dark brown colour.—Dr. Sloane in Philof. Tranf. No. 208.

To this account, the Doctor (in a letter to Mr. Ray, March 31, 1694, with other papers of Mr. Ray's, in my hands) adds the teftimony of Jof. Acofta, l. 4. c. 7. and Garcilaff. de la Vega, who, l. 8. c. 19. faith, *There are other fowls called by the Spaniards Condor. Many of thefe fowls, having been killed by the Spaniards, had their proportion taken, and from end to end of their wings meafured 15 or 16 feet.*—Nature, to temper and allay their fiercenefs, denied them the talons which are given to the eagle; their feet being tipped with claws like a hen: however, their beak is ftrong enough to tear off the hide, and rip up the bowels of an ox. Two of them will attempt a cow or bull, and devour him: and it hath often happened, that one of them alone hath affaulted boys of ten or twelve years of age, and eaten them. Their colour is black and white, like a magpie. It is well there are but few of them; for if they were many, they would very much deftroy the cattle. They have on the fore-part of their heads a comb, not pointed like that

s 2

* Linnæus was the firft who obferved one ufe of infects which his own hypothefis refpecting the generation of plants had led him to remark. This is, that by fhifting from one plant to another of the fame fpecies, they convey the pollen of the male plant to the ftigma of the female. " In this way," fays he, " it is reafonable to think that many diœcious plants are impregnated. Nay even the hermaphrodites themfelves are greatly obliged to the different tribes of infects, which by fluttering and treading in the corolla, are conftantly fcattering the pollen about the ftigma."
EDITOR.

tion cometh (c); fo equally in its room, to balance the flock of the terraqueous globe in all ages, and places, and among all creatures; that it is an actual demonftration of our Saviour's affertion, *Mat.* x. 29. that the moft inconfiderable, common creature, *even a sparrow,* (*two of which are fold for a farthing,*) *doth not fall on the ground without our heavenly Father.*

This providence of God is remarkable in every fpecies of living creatures: but that efpecial management of the recruits and decays of mankind, fo equally all the world over, deferves our efpecial obfervation. In the beginning of the world, and fo after *Noah's* flood, the longevity of men, as it was of abfolute neceffity to the more fpeedy peopling of the new world; fo is it a fpecial inftance of the Divine Providence in this matter (d). And the fame

that of a cock; but rather even, in the form of a razor. When they come to alight from the air, they make fuch a humming noife, with the fluttering of their wings, as is enough to aftonifh, or make a man deaf.

(c) *Ecclef.* i. 4.

(d) The divine providence doth not only appear in the longevity of man, immediately after the creation and flood; but also in their different longevity at thofe two times. Immediately after the creation, when the world was to be peopled by one man, and one woman, the age of the greateft part of thofe on record, was 900 years, and upwards. But after the flood, when there were three perfons by whom the world was to be peopled, none of thofe patriarchs, except *Shem,* arrived to the age of 500; and only the three firft of *Shem's* line, viz. *Arphaxad, Salah,* and *Eber,*

fame Providence appears in the following ages, when the world was pretty well peopled, in reducing the common age of man then to 120 years, (*Gen.* vi. 3.) in proportion to the occafions of the world at that time. And laftly, when the world was fully peopled after the flood, (as it was in the age of *Mofes,* and fo down to our prefent time,) the leffening the common age of man to 70 or 80 years (e), (the age mentioned by *Mofes, Pfal.* xc. 10. this

Eber, came near that age; which was in the firft century after the flood. But in the fecond century, we do not find any reached the age of 240. And in the third century, (about the latter end of which *Abraham* was born,) none, except *Terah,* arrived to 200 years: by which time the world was fo well peopled, (that part of it, at leaft, where *Abraham* dwelt,) that they had built cities, and began to be cantoned into diftinct nations and focieties, under their refpective kings; fo that they were able to wage war, four kings againft five. *Gen.* xiv. Nay, if the accounts of *Anian, Berobhus, Manetho,* and others, yea *Africanus,* be to be credited; the world was fo well peopled, even before the times we fpeak of, as to afford fufficient numbers for the great kingdoms of *Affyria, Egypt, Perfia,* &c. But learned men generally, with great reafon, rejeci thefe as legendary accounts.

If the reader hath a mind to fee a computation of the increafe of mankind, in the three firft centuries after the flood, he may find two different ones of the moft learned archbifhop *Ufher,* and *Petavius;* together with a refutation of the fo early beginning of the *Affyrian* monarchy; as alfo reafons for placing *Abraham* near 1000 years after the flood, in our moft learned bifhop *Stillingfleet's Orig. Sacr. Book* iii. *chap.* 4. *fect.* 9.

(e) That the common age of man hath been the fame in all ages fince the world was peopled, is manifeft from profane as well

s 3

262   OF THE NUMBER   B. IV.

this, I say,) is manifestly an appointment of the same infinite Lord that ruleth the world: for, by this

well as sacred history. To pass by others: *Plato* lived to the age of 81, and was accounted an old man. And those which *Pliny* reckons up, *l. 7. c. 48*, as rare examples of long life, may for the most part be matched by our modern histories; especially such as *Pliny* himself gave credit unto. Dr. *Plot* hath given us divers instances in his history of *Oxfordshire*, c. 2. sect. 3. and c. 8. sect. 54. and History of *Staffordshire*, c. 8. sect. 91, &c. Among others, one is of twelve tenants of Mr. *Bidulph*'s, that together made 1000 years of age. But the most considerable examples of aged persons among us, is of old *Parr* of *Shropshire*, who lived 152 years nine months, according to the learned Dr. *Harvey*'s account; and *Henry Jenkins* of *Yorkshire*, who lived 169 years, according to the account of my learned and ingenious friend Dr. *Tancred Robinson*; of both which, with others, see *Lowth. Abridg. Phil. Transf. v. iii.* p. 306. The great age of *Parr* of *Shropshire* minds me of an observation of the reverend Mr. *Plaxton*, that in his two parishes of *Kinardsey* and *Donington* in *Shropshire*, every sixth soul was 60 years of age, or upwards. *Phil. Transf. No.* 310.

And if we step farther north into *Scotland*, we shall find divers recorded for their great age: of which I shall present the reader with only one modern example of one *Laurence*, who married a wife after he was 100 years of age, and would go out to sea a fishing in his little boat, when he was 140 years old; and is lately dead of no other distemper but mere old age, saith Sir *Rob. Sibbald, Prodr. Hist. Nat. Scot.* P. 44. and l. 3. P. 4.

As for foreigners, the examples would be endless; and therefore that of *Job. Ottele* shall suffice, who was as famous for his beard, as for being 115 years of age. He was but two *Brabant* ells $\frac{2}{5}$ high; and his long grey beard was one ell $\frac{1}{4}$ long. His picture and account may be seen in *Ephem. Germ. T. 3. Obs.* 163. As for the story *Roger Bacon* tells, of one that lived 900 years by the help of a certain medicine, and many other such stories,

CH. X.   OF ANIMALS.   263

this means, the peopled world is kept at a convenient stay; neither too full, nor too empty. For if men (the generality of them, I mean) were to live now to *Methuselah*'s age of 969 years, or only to *Abraham*'s, long after the flood, of 175 years, the world would be too much over-run; or if the age of man was limited to that of divers other animals, to ten, twenty, or thirty years only; the decays then of mankind would be too fast: but at the middle rate mentioned, the balance is nearly even, and life and death keep an equal pace. Which equality is so great and harmonious, and so manifest an instance of the divine management, that I shall spend some remarks upon it.

stories, I look upon them as fabulous. And no better is that of the *wandering Jew*, named *Job. Buttadeus*, said to have been present at our Saviour's crucifixion: although very serious stories are told of his being seen at *Antwerp*, and in *France*, about the middle of the last century but one; and before in *ann.* 1542, conversed with by *Paul of Eitsen*, bishop of *Sleswick*; and before that, viz. in 1228, seen and conversed with by an *Armenian archbishop's gentleman*; and by others at other times.

If the reader hath a mind to see more examples, he may meet with some of all ages, in the learned *Hakewill's Apol.* p. 181. where he will also find that learned author's opinion of the causes of the brevity and length of human life. The brevity thereof he attributeth to a too tender education, sucking strange nurses, too hasty marriages; but above all, to luxury, high sauces, strong liquors, &c. The longevity of the antients he ascribes to temperance in meat and drink, anointing the body, the use of saffron and honey, warm clothes, lesser doors and windows, less physic and more exercise.

S 4   It

264   OF THE NUMBERS   B. IV.

It appears from our best accounts of these matters, that in our *European* parts (*f*), and I believe the same is throughout the world; that, I say, there is a certain rate and proportion in the propagation

(*f*) The proportions which *marriages* bear to *births*, and *births* to *burials*, in divers parts of *Europe*, may be seen at an easy view in this TABLE:

NAMES OF THE PLACES.	Marriages to Births: as	Births to Burials: as
England in general.		
London.	1 to 4·63	1·12 to 1
Hampshire, from 1569, to 1658.	1 to 4·	1 to 1·1
Tiverton in *Devon.* 1560, to 1649.	1 to 4·	1·2 to 1
Cranbrook in *Kent*, 1560, to 1649.	1 to 3·7	1·26 to 1
Aynho in *Northamptonsh.* for 118 years.	1 to 3·9	1·6 to 1
Leeds in *Yorkshire* for 122 years.	1 to 5	1·6 to 1
Harwood in *Yorkshire* 57 years.	1 to 3·7	1·07 to 1
Upminster in *Essex* 100 years.	1 to 3·4	1·23 to 1
Frankfort on the *Main* in 1695.	1 to 4·6	1·08 to 1
Old middle and lower *Marck* in 1698.	1 to 3·7	1·2 to 1
Domin. of the K. of *Prussia* in 1698.	1 to 3·7	1·9 to 1
Breslaw in *Silesia* from 1687, to 1691.	1 to 3·7	1·5 to 1
Paris in 1670, 1671, 1672.	1 to 4·7	1·6 to 1

Which table I made from major *Graunt's* observations on the bills of mortality; Mr. *King's* observations in the first of Dr. *Davenant's* essays; and what I find put together by my ingenious friend Mr. *Lowthorp*, in his Abridgment, vol. 3. p. 668, and my own register of *Upminster*. That from *Aynho* register in *Northamptonshire*, I had from the present rector, the learned and ingenious Mr. *Wasse*: and I was promised some accounts from the north, and divers other parts of this kingdom; but have not yet received them: only those of *Leeds* and *Harwood* in *Yorkshire*, from my curious and ingenious friend Mr. *Thoresby.*

Of

CH. X.   OF ANIMALS.   265

of mankind: such a number marry (*g*), so many are born, such a number die; in proportion to the number of persons in every nation, county, or parish. And as to births, two things are very considerable: one is the proportion of males and females (*b*), not in a wide proportion, not an uncertain,

(*g*) The preceding table shews, that marriages, one with another, do each of them produce about four births; not only in *England*, but in other parts of *Europe* also.

And by Mr. *King's* estimate, (the best computations I imagine of any, being derived from the best accounts; such as the marriage, birth, burial-act, the poll-books, &c. by his estimate, I say,) about one in 104 marry. For he judgeth the number of the people in *England*, to be about five millions and a half; of which about 41,000 annually marry. As to what might be farther remarked concerning marriages, in regard of the rights and customs of several nations, the age to which divers nations limited marriages, &c. it would be endless, and too much out of the way to mention them: I shall only therefore, for the reader's diversion, take notice of the jeer of *Lactantius, quare apud poetas salacissimus Jupiter desiit liberos tollere? Utrum sexagenarius factus, & ei lex Papia fibulam imposuit?*—" Why has Jupiter, the most salacious of all the gods, ceased to have progeny? Is it that, being now above sixty years old, he is padlocked by the Papian law."—Lactant. Instit. l. 1. c. 16. By which *lex Papia*, men were prohibited to marry after 60, and women after 50 years of age.

(*b*) Major *Graunt* (whose conclusions seem to be well-grounded) and Mr. *King* disagree in the proportions they assign to males and females. This latter makes in *London* 10 males to be to 13 females; in other cities and market-towns, 8 to 9; and in the villages and hamlets, 100 males to 99 females. But major *Graunt*, both from the *London* and country bills, faith, there are 14 males to 13 females: from whence he justly infers, *That the Christian religion, prohibiting polygamy, is more agreeable to the law of Nature than Mahometism, and others that allow it,* c. 8. This

13

tain, accidental number at all adventures; but nearly equal. Another thing is, that a few more are born than appear to die, in any certain place(*i*); which

This proportion of 14 to 13, I imagine, is nearly juſt, it being agreeable to the bills I have met with, as well as thoſe in Mr. *Graunt.* In the 100 years, for example, of my own pariſh-regiſter, although the burials of males and females were nearly equal, being 636 males, and 623 females, in all that time; yet there were baptiſed 709 males, and but 675 females, which is 13 females to 13·7 males. Which inequality ſhews, not only, that one man ought to have but one wife; but alſo that every woman may, without polygamy, have an huſband, if ſhe doth not bar herſelf by the want of virtue, by denial, &c. Alſo this ſurpluſage of males is very uſeful for the ſupplies of war, the ſeas, and other ſuch expences of the men above the women.

That this is a work of the Divine Providence, and not a matter of chance, is well made out by the very laws of chance, by a perſon able to do it, the ingenious and learned Dr. *Arbuthnot.* He ſuppoſeth *Thomas* to lay againſt *John,* that for 82 years running, more males ſhall be born than females; and giving all allowances in the computation to *Thomas's* ſide, he makes the odds againſt *Thomas,* that it doth not happen ſo, to be near five millions of millions, of millions to one; but for ages of ages (according to the world's age) to be near an infinite number to one againſt *Thomas. Vide Phil. Tranſ.* No. 328.

(*i*) The foregoing table ſhews, that in *England* in general, fewer die than are born, there being but one death to 1 $\frac{12}{100}$ births. But in *London* more die than are born. So by Dr. *Davenant's* table, the cities likewiſe and market-towns bury 1 $\frac{66}{100}$ to one birth. But in *Paris* they out-do *London,* their deaths being 1 $\frac{1}{4}$ to one birth: the reaſon of which I conceive is, becauſe their houſes are more crowded than in *London.* But in the villages of *England,* there are fewer die than are born, there being but 1 death to 1 $\frac{17}{10}$ births. And yet major *Graunt,* and Dr. *Da-*

which is an admirable proviſion for the extraordinary emergencies and occaſions of the world; to ſupply unhealthful places, where death out-runs life; to make up the ravages of great plagues and diſeaſes, and the depredations of war and the ſeas; and to afford a ſufficient number for colonies in the unpeopled parts of the earth. Or on the other hand, we may ſay, that ſometimes thoſe extraordinary expences of mankind may be not only a juſt puniſhment of the ſins of men; but alſo a wiſe means to keep the balance of mankind even; as one would be ready to conclude, by conſidering the *Aſiatic* and other the more fertile countries, where prodigious multitudes are yearly ſwept away with great plagues, and ſometimes war; and yet thoſe countries are ſo far from being waſted, that they remain full of people.

And now upon the whole matter, What is all this but admirable and plain management? What can the maintaining, throughout all ages and places, theſe proportions of mankind, and all other creatures; this harmony in the generations of men be, but the work of One that ruleth the world?

cities and market-towns, than are in the country, notwithſtanding the *London* births are fewer than the country; the reaſon of which ſee in *Graunt,* c. 7. and *Davenant, ubi ſupra,* p. 21.

The laſt remark I ſhall make from the foregoing table ſhall be, that we may from thence judge of the healthfulneſs of the places there mentioned. If the year 1658 was the mean account of the three *Marks,* theſe places bid the faireſt for being moſt health-

Is it possible that every species of animals should so evenly be preserved, proportionate to the occasions of the world? That they should be so well balanced in all ages and places, without the help of Almighty wisdom and power? How is it possible by the bare rules and blind acts of Nature, that there should be any tolerable proportion; for instance, between males and females, either of mankind, or of any other creature (k); especially such as are of a ferine, not of a domestic nature, and consequently out of the command and management of man? How could life and death keep such an even pace through all the animal world? If we should take it for granted, that, according to the scripture history, the world had a beginning, (as who can deny it (l)? or if we should suppose the destruction

(k) *Quid loquar, quanta ratio in bestiis ad perpetuam conservationem earum generis apparet? Nam primùm aliæ mares, aliæ fæminæ sunt, quod perpetuitatis causâ machinata Natura est.*— "What is more admirable than the proportion observed by Nature between the numbers of males and females in the different tribes of animals, so wisely ordered for the preservation of the species?"— *Cic. de Nat. Deor. l. 2. c. 51.*

(l) Although *Aristotle* held the eternity of the world, yet he seems to have retracted that opinion, or to have had a different opinion when he wrote his *Metaphysics*; for in his first book he affirms, that *God is the cause and beginning of all things*; and in his book *de Mundo* he saith, *There is no doubt but God is the maker and conservator of all things in the world.* And the *Stoic*'s opinion is well known, who strenuously contended, That the contrivance and beauty of the heavens and earth, and all creatures, was owing to a wife, intelligent Agent. Of which *Tully*, gives a large account in his second book *de Nat. Deor.* in the person of *Balbus.*

thereof

thereof by *Noah*'s flood : how is it possible, after the world was replenished,) that in a certain number of years, by the greater increase and doublings of each species of animals ; that, I say, this rate of doubling (m) should cease ; or that it should be compensated

(m) I have before, in *note* (g), observed, That the ordinary rate of the doubling or increase of mankind is, that every marriage, one with another, produces about four births ; but some have much exceeded that. *Babo*, earl of *Abensberg*, had 32 sons and eight daughters ; and being invited to hunt with the emperor *Henry* II. and bring but few servants, brought only one servant, and his 32 sons. To these many others might be added ; but one of the most remarkable instances I have any where met with, is that of Mrs. *Honywood*, mentioned by *Hakewill*, *Camden*, and other authors ; but having now before me the names, with some remarks, (which I received from a pious neighbouring descendant of the fame Mrs. *Honywood*,) I shall give a more particular account than they. Mrs. *Mary Honywood* was daughter and one of the co-heiresses of *Robert Atwaters*, Esq; of *Lenham* in *Kent*. She was born in 1527, married in *February* 1543, at 16 years of age, to her only husband *Robert Honywood*, of *Charing* in *Kent*, Esq. She died in the 93d year of her age, in *May* 1620. She had 16 children of her own body, seven sons and nine daughters : of which one had no issue, three died young, and the youngest was slain at *Newport*-battle, *June* 20, 1600. Her grand-children in the second generation, were 114 ; in the third, 228 ; and nine in the fourth generation. So that she could say the same that the distich doth, made of one of the *Dalburg*'s family of *Basil*:

1   2   3   4
Mater ait Natæ, dic Natæ, filia Natam
5   6
Ut moneat, Natæ, plangere Filiolam.

1   2   3   4
Rise up Daughter, and go to thy Daughter, for her Daughter;
5   6
Daughter hath a Daughter. Mrs. *Honywood* was a very pious woman,

pensated by some other means? That the world should be as well, or better stocked than now it is, in 1656 years, (the time between the creation and the flood; this,) we will suppose may be done by the natural methods of each species doubling or increase: but in double that number of years, or at this distance from the flood, of 4000 years, that the world should not be over-stocked, can never be made out, without allowing an infinite Providence.

I conclude then this observation with the Psalmist's words, *Psal.* civ. 29, 30, *Thou hidest thy face, all creatures are troubled; thou takest away their breath, they die, and return to their dust. Thou sendest forth thy Spirit, they are created; and thou renewest the face of the earth.*

woman, afflicted, in her declining age, with despair, in some measure; concerning which, some divines once discoursing with her, she in a passion said, *She was as certainly damned as this glass is broken* (throwing a *Venice* glass against the ground, which she had then in her hand). But the glass escaped breaking, as credible witnesses attested.

END OF THE FIRST VOLUME.

CHAP. II.

That God's Works ought to be inquired into, and that such Inquiries are commendable.

THE *Creator* doubtless did not bestow so much curiosity, and exquisite workmanship and skill upon his creatures, to be looked upon with a careless, incurious eye, especially to have them slighted or contemned; but to be admired by the rational part of the world, to magnify his own power, wisdom, and goodness throughout all the world, and the ages thereof: and therefore we may look upon it as a great error not to answer those ends of the infinite *Creator*, but rather to oppose and affront them. On the contrary, my text commends God's works, not only for being great, but also approves of those curious and ingenious inquirers, that *seek them out, or pry into them.* And the more we pry into and discover of them, the greater and more glorious we find them to be, the more worthy of, and the more expresly to proclaim their great *Creator*.

Commendable then are the researches, which many amongst us have, of late years, made into the works of Nature, more than hath been done in some ages before. And therefore when we are asked, *Cui bono?* To what purpose such inquiries, such pains, such expence? the answer is easy, it is is to anfwer the ends for which God beftowed fo much art, wifdom, and power about them, as well as given us fenfes to view and furvey them, and an underftanding and curiofity to fearch into them: It is to follow and trace him, when and whither he leads us, that we may fee and admire his handy-work ourfelves, and fet it forth to others, that they may fee, admire, and praife it alfo. I fhall then conclude this inference with what *Elihu* recommends, *Job.* xxxvi. 24, 25. *Remember that thou magnify his work, which men behold. Every man may fee it, men may behold it afar off.*

C H A P. III.

That God's Works are manifeft to all: whence the Unreafonablenefs of Infidelity.

THE concluding words of the preceding chapter fuggefts a third inference, that the works of God are fo vifible to all the world, and withal fuch manifeft indications of the being, and attributes of the infinite Creator, that they plainly argue the vilenefs and perverfenefs of the atheift, and leave him inexcufable. For it is a fign a man is a wilful, perverfe atheift, that will impute fo glorious a work, as the creation is, to any thing, yea, a mere *nothing*, (as chance is,) rather than to God (a). It

(a) *Galen* having taken notice of the neat diftribution of the nerves to the mufcles, and other parts of the face, cries out, [partibus] *Hæc enim fortunæ funt opera? Cæterùm tum omnibus inermiti, tantofque effe fingulos [nervos] magnitudine, quanta particulæ erat neceffe; haud fcio an hominum fit fobriorum ad fortunam opificem id revocare. Alioqui quid tandem erit, quod cum providentiâ & arte efficitur? Omnino enim hoc ei contrarium effe debet, quod cafu ac fortuito fit.*—" Are thefe forfooth the operations of chance? When we obferve the infertion of the nerves in the feveral parts of the body, and their proportionate magnitude to the part in which they are inferted, can any man in his fober judgment refer that to the operation of chance? If fo, what is there elfe that is the refult of forefight and of art? For it muft be in its nature contrary to that which is effected by chance." —And afterwards,

It is a fign the man is wilfully blind, that he is under the power of the devil, under the government of prejudice, luft, and paffion, not right reafon, that will not difcern what every one can fee, *what every man may behold afar off,* even the exiftence and attributes of the Creator from his works. For *as there is no fpeech or language where their voice is not heard, their line is gone out through all the earth, and their words to the end of the world:* fo all, even the barbarous nations, that never heard of God, have from thefe his works inferred the exiftence of a Deity, and paid their homages to fome deity, although they have been under great miftakes in their notions and concluftions about him. But however, this fhews how naturally and univerfally all mankind agree, in deducing their belief of a God from the contemplation of his works, or as even *Epicurus* himfelf, in *Tully* (b), faith, from *a notion*

afterwards, *Hæc quidem atque ejufmodi artis fcil. ac fapientie opera effe dicemus, fi modò fortune tribuenda funt que funt contraria; fetgue jam quod in proverbiis—Fluvii furfum fluent; fi opera que mallum habent neque ornamentum, neque rationem, neque modum artis effe; contraria verò fortune duxerimus, &c.—* "For every thing that is wild and irregular we muft then attribute to art and wifdom, if we efteem its contrary to be the refult of chance; and thus in the words of the Proverbs, the rivers will run backwards to their fource, if we hold every thing in which we perceive neither reafon nor beauty to be the refult of fkill, and every thing poffeffed of thofe qualities to be the effect of chance."—*Galen ubi fupra,* l. 11. c. 7.

(b) *Primum effe Deo, quod in omnium animis,* &c. And a little after, *Cùm enim non inftituto aliquo, aut more, aut lege fit opinio com-*

notion that Nature itfelf hath imprinted upon the minds of men. For, faith he, *what nation is there, or what kind of men, that without any teaching or inftructions, have not a kind of anticipation or preconceived notion of a deity?*

An atheift therefore (if ever there was any fuch) may juftly be efteemed a monfter among rational beings; a thing hard to be met with in the whole tribe of mankind; an oppofer of all the world (c); a rebel againft human nature and reafon, as well as againft his God.

But above all monftrous is this, or would be in fuch as have heard of God, who have had the benefit of the clear gofpel revelation. And ftill more monftrous this would be, in one born and baptized in the Chriftian church, that hath ftudied Nature, and

ftituta, maneatque ad unum omnium firma confenfo, intelligi necefle eft, effe Deos, quoniam infitas eorum vel potiùs innatas cognitiones habemus. De quo autem omnium natura confeniti, id verum effe necefle eft. Effe igitur Deos confitendum eft.— "For as that opinion is neither the effect of education, of cuftom, nor of human laws, but is firmly rooted in the confent of all mankind, we muft thence of neceffity conclude that there is a God, from that innate opinion of the mind. That in which all mankind confents muft be a truth. We muft then confefs there is a God."—*Cicer. de Nat. Deor.* l 1. c. 16, 17.

(c) The atheift in denying a God, doth, as *Plutarch* faith, endeavour—*immobilia movere, & bellum inferre non tantùm longo tempori, fed & multis hominibus, gentibus, & familiis, quas religiofus Deorum cultus, quafi divino furore correptas, tenuit.—* "To move what is immoveable, and to wage war, not only with time, but with all nations, kindreds, and families, who with fervent zeal have paid religious worfhip to the Divinity."—*Plutar. de*

CH. III. GOD'S WORKS ARE MANIFEST. 399

and pried farther than others into God's works. For such an one (if it be poffible for fuch to be) to deny the exiftence or any of the attributes of God, would be a great argument of the infinite inconvenience of thofe fins of intemperance, luft, and riot, that have made the man abandon his reafon, his fenfes, yea, I had almoft faid his very human nature (*d*), to engage him thus to deny the being of God.

So alfo it is much the fame monftrous infidelity, at leaft it betrays the fame atheiftical mind, to deny God's providence, care, and government of the world, or (which is a fpawn of the fame *Epicurean principles*) to deny *Final Caufes* (*e*) in God's works of creation; or with the profane, in *Pfal.* lxxiii. 11. to fay, *How doth God know? and is there knowledge in the moft High?* For as the witty and eloquent Salvian faith (*f*), *They that affirm nothing is feen by God, will, in all probability, take away the fubftance*

(*d*) See before, *note* (*b*).

(*e*) *Galen,* having fubftantially refuted the *Epicurean* principles of *Afclepiades,* by fhewing his ignorance in anatomy and philofophy, and by demonftrating all the *caufes* to be evidently in the works of nature, viz. *final, efficient, inftrumental, material, and formal caufes,* concludes thus againft his fortuitous atoms, *ex quibus intelligi poteft : conditiorem noftrum in formandis particulis unum bunc fequi fcopum, nempe ut quod melius eft eligat.*—" Whence we may conclude that our great Creator, in the formation of bodies, has invariably followed this one rule, always to choofe what is beft."—*Galen de Uf. Part.* l. 6. c. 13.

(*f*) *De Gubern. Dei,* l. 4. p. 124. *meo Libro;* alfo *l.* 7. *c.* 14.

400 GOD'S WORKS ARE MANIFEST. B. XI.

*ftance as well as fight of God.—But what fo great madnefs, faith he, as that when a man doth not deny God to be the creator of all things, he fhould deny him to be the governor of them? or when be confeffeth him to be the maker, he fhould fay, God neglefteth what he hath fo made * ?*

* See a difcuffion of the utility of the refearch into *Final Caufes,* in the Preliminary Account of the Life and Writings of Mr. Derham, p. xl.

14. Edmond Halley (1656-1742)

'Some Considerations about the Cause of the Universal Deluge', *Philosophical Transactions of the Royal Society*, *33* (1724-1725), 118-123

VII. *Some Confiderations about the Caufe of the uni-*
verfal Deluge, laid before the Royal Society, on
the 12th of December 1694. By Dr. Ed-
mond Halley, *R. S. S.*

THE Account we have of the univerfal Deluge is
no where fo exprefs as in the Holy Scriptures ;
and the exact Circumftances as to point of Time, do
fhew that fome Records had been kept thereof more
particularly than is wont in thofe things derived
from remote Tradition, wherein the Hiftorical *Minu-*
tiæ are loft by length of Time. But the fame feem
much too imperfect to be the Refult of a full Revelation from the Author of this dreadful Execution upon Mankind, who would have fpoke more amply as
to the Manner thereof, had He thought fit to lay open
the Secrets of Nature to the fucceeding Race of Men ;
and I doubt not but to all that confider the 7th Chapter of *Genefis* impartially, it will pafs for the Remains
of a much fuller Account of the *Flood* left by the Patriarchs to their Pofterity, and derived from the Revelation of *Noah* and his Sons. It muft be granted,
that there are fome Difficulties as to the Conftruction
of the *Ark,* the Reception and Agreement of the
Animals among themfelves, and Prefervation of it in
fo immenfe and boundlefs an Ocean, during that *Wind*
which

(119)

which God fent to dry the Waters away, efpecially
when it firft came on Ground : But it muft alfo be allowed, that length of Time may have added, as well
as taken away many notable Circumftances, as in moft
other Cafes of the Story of remote Times and Actions.

This we may, however, be fully affured of, that
fuch a Deluge has been ; and by the many Signs of
marine Bodies found far from and above the Sea, 'tis
evident, that thofe Parts have been once under Water:
or, either that the Sea has rifen to them, or they have
been raifed from the Sea ; to explicate either of which
is a Matter of no fmall Difficulty, nor does the facred
Scripture afford any Light thereto.   All that it fays
to help us is, that all the Fountains of the great Deep,
תְהוֹם רַבָּה, were burft, or broken up;   that the
Windows, or Cataracts of Heaven were opened, and
that it rained inceffantly forty Days and Nights.   Now
the Rain of forty Days and Nights will be found to be
a very fmall Part of the Caufe of fuch a Deluge ; for
fuppofing it to rain all over the Globe as much in each
Day, as it is now found to do in one of the rainieft
Counties of *England* in the whole Year, *viz.* about
forty Inches of Water *per Diem*, forty fuch Days
could cover the whole Earth with but about twenty two Fathom Water, which would only drown the
low Lands next the Sea, but the much greater Part
would efcape.   What is meant by the Fountains of
the *Abyffe* being broken up, and the opening of the
Windows of Heaven, feems not fo eafy to be underftood, but is intended to indicate the *Modus* of the
Deluge, which was, according to the *Mofaic Philofophy*, from the letting in of the Waters above the
Firmament, mentioned *Genefis* 1. 7. by the Windows

VOL. XXXIII.   T   of

(120)

of Heaven ; and the rifing up out of the Ground of the Waters under the Earth, fpoken of in the fecond Commandment : Or, (if you will underftand that by the תְהוֹם רַבָּה is meant the great Ocean) by the overflowing of the Sea, rifing upon the Land, which is exprefs'd by the breaking up of the Fountains of the great Deep. So that we may reafonably conclude, that by the one of thofe Expreffions is meant an extraordinary fall of Waters from the Heavens, not as Rain, but in one great Body ; as if the Firmament, fuppofed by *Mofes* to fuftain a *Supra-aerial Sea*, had been broken in, and at the fame Time the Ocean did flow in upon the Land, fo as to cover all with Water.

By an extraordinary Encreafe of the Waters this could not be effected, for that at this Time there is not Water fufficient of itfelf to cover any more of the Earth than now it doth ; and to fuppofe a Creation and Annihilation of Water on purpofe to deftroy the Earth, is by much the moft difficult Hypothefis that can be thought of to effect it. A change of the *Center* of *Gravity*, about which Center the Sea is formed, feemed not an improbable Conjecture, till it appeared that this Center of Gravity was the neceffary Refult of the Materials of which our Globe confifts, and not alterable whilft the Parts thereof remained in the fame Pofition : And befides this Suppofition could not drown the whole Globe, but only that Part thereof towards which the Center of Gravity was tranflated, leaving the other Hemifphere all dry:

I fhall fay nothing of Dr. *Burnet*'s Hypothefis, nor of the many Infufficiencies thereof, as jarring as much with the Phyfical Principles of Nature, as with the Holy Scriptures, which he has undertaken to reconcile.

(121)

cile. Dr. *Hook*'s Solution of this Problem, as he has not fully difcovered himfelf, I cannot undertake to judge of; but his Compreffion of a Shell of Earth into a *prolate Spheroide*, thereby preffing out the Waters of an Abyfs under the Earth, may very well account for drowning two extream oppofite Zones of the Globe; but the middle Zone, being by much the greater Part of the Earth's Surface, muft by this means be raifed higher from the Center, and confequently arife more out of the Water than before; and befides, fuch a Suppofition cannot well be accounted for from Phyfical Caufes, but require a preternatural *digitus Dei*, both to comprefs, and afterwards reftore the Figure of the Globe.

But the Almighty generally making ufe of Natural Means to bring about his Will, I thought it not amifs to give this Honourable Society an Account of fome Thoughts that occurr'd to me on this Subject; wherein, if I err, I fhall find my felf in very good Company.

In Num· 190. of thefe Tranfactions, I have propofed the cafual *Choc* of a *Comet*, or other tranfient Body, as an Expedient to change inftantly the Poles and Diurnal Rotation of the Globe; at that Time only aiming to fhew how the *Axis* of the *Earth* being chang'd, would occafion the Sea to recede from thofe Parts towards which the Poles did approach, and to encreafe upon and overflow thofe Parts wherefrom the Poles were departed; but at that Time I did not confider the great Agitation fuch a *Choc* muft neceffarily occafion in the Sea, fufficient to anfwer for all thofe ftrange Appearances of heaping vaft Quantities of Earth and high Cliffs upon Beds of Shells, which once were the Bottom of the Sea; and raifing up Mountains where none were before, mixing the Elements into

T 2 fuch

(122)

such a Heap as the Poets defcribe the *old Chaos* ; for such a *Choc* impelling the folid Parts would occafion the Waters, and all fluid Subftances that were unconfined, as the Sea is, with one *Impetus* to run violently towards that Part of the Globe where the Blow was received ; and that with Force fufficient to rake with it the whole Bottom of the Ocean, and to carry it upon the Land ; heaping up into Mountains thofe earthy Parts it had born away with it, in thofe Places where the oppofite Waves balance each other, *mifcens ima fummis*, which may account for thofe long continued Ridges of Mountains. And again, the Recoil of this Heap of Waters would return towards the oppofite Parts of the Earth, with a leffer *Impetus* than the firft, and fo reciprocating many times, would at laft come to fettle in fuch a Manner as we now obferve in the Structure of the fuperficial Parts of the Globe.

In this Cafe it will be much more difficult to fhew how *Noah* and the *Animals* fhould be preferved, than that all things in which was the Breath of Life, fhould hereby be deftroyed. Such a *Choc* would alfo occafion a differing Length of the Day and Year, and change the Axis of the Globe, according to the Obliquity of the Incidence of the Stroak, and the Direction thereof, in relation to the former Axis. That fome fuch thing has happened, may be guefs'd, for that the Earth feems as if it were new made out of the Ruins of an old World, wherein appear fuch Animal Bodies as were before the Deluge, but by their own Nature and Defences from the Weather, have endured ever fince, either petrified, or elfe entire in *ftatu naturali*. Such a *Choc* may have occafioned that vaft Depreffion of the *Cafpian Sea*, and other great Lakes in the World ; and 'tis not unlikely, but that extream Cold felt in the

I   North

(123)

North-Weſt of *America*, about *Hudſon's-Bay*, may be occaſioned by thoſe Parts of the World having once been much more Northerly, or nearer the Pole than now they are ; whereby there are immenſe Quantities of Ice yet unthaw'd in thoſe Parts, which chill the Air to that degree, that the Sun's warmth ſeems hardly to be felt there, and of which the Poet might juſtly ſay, *Frigus iners illic habitat pallorque tremorque — Ac jejuna fames.*

If this Speculation ſeem worthy to be cultivated, I ſhall not be wanting farther to inſiſt on the Conſequences thereof, and to ſhew how it may render a probable Account of the ſtrange Cataſtrophe we may be ſure has at leaſt once happened to the Earth.

15. Colin Maclaurin (1698-1746)

An Account of Sir Isaac Newton's Philosophical Discoveries
(London, 1748)
From the 3rd edition (London, 1775): pp. 396-412

C H A P. IX.

Of the Supreme Author and Governor of the universe, the True and Living God.

1. *ARISTOTLE* concludes his treatise *de mundo*, with obferving, that " to treat of the world without faying any thing of its Author would be impious ;" as there is nothing we meet with more frequently and conftantly in nature, than the traces of an All-governing Deity. And the philofopher who overlooks thefe, contenting himfelf with the appearances of the material univerfe only, and the mechanical laws of motion, neglects what is moft excellent ; and prefers what is imperfect to what is fupremely perfect, finitude to infinity, what is narrow and weak to what is unlimited and almighty, and what is perifhing to what endures for ever. Such

8   who

who attend not to so manifest indications of supreme wisdom and goodness, perpetually appearing before them wherever they turn their views or enquiries, too much resemble those antient philosophers who made night, matter, and chaos, the original of all things.

2. As we have neither ideas nor words sufficient to describe the first cause, so *Aristotle*, in the conclusion of the above-mentioned treatise, is obliged to content himself with comparing him with what is chief and most excellent, in every kind *. Thus we say he is the king or lord of all things, the parent of all his creatures, the soul of the world, or great spirit that animates the whole. Such expressions, though well meant at first, were sometimes abused afterwards; particularly, that of his being the *anima mundi*, which was apt to represent him not only as the active and self-moving principle, but likewise as passive and suffering from the actions and motions of bodies. The abstruse nature of the subject gave occasion to the latter *Platonists*, particularly to *Plotinus*, to introduce the most mystical and unintelligible notions concerning the Deity and the worship we owe to him; as when he tells us that intellect or understanding is not to be ascribed to the Deity, and that our most perfect worship of him consists, not in acts of veneration, reverence, gratitude or love; but in a certain mysterious self-annihilation, or total extinction of all our faculties. These doctrines, however absurd, have had follow-

---

* Καθόλυ δὲ, ὅπερ ἐν νἠι κυβερνήτης, ἐν ἅρμαῖι δὲ ἡνίοχος, ἐν χορῷ δὲ κορυφαῖος, ἐν πόλει δὲ νόμος, ἐν ρατοπέδῳ δὲ ἡγεμὼν τῦτο θεὸς ἐν κόσμῳ· πλὴν καθ᾽ ὅσον, τοῖς μὲν χαμαῖηρὸν τὸ ἄρχειν, πολυκίνητὸν τε κ᾽ πολυμέριμνον· τῷ δὲ, ἄλυπον, ἄπονόν τε κ᾽ πάσης κεχωρισμένον σωματικῆς ἀσθενείας· ἐν ἀκινήτῳ γὰρ ἱδρυμέρῳ πάνΙα κινεῖ, κ᾽ περιάγει ὅπου βάλεΙαι, κ᾽ ὅπως, ἐν διαφόροις ἰδέαις τε κ᾽ φύσεσιν. Cap. 6.

ers,

ers, who, in this, as in other cafes, by aiming too high, far beyond their reach, overftrain their faculties, and fall into folly or madnefs ; contributing, as much as lies in them, to bring true piety and devotion into contempt.

3. Neither are they to be commended, who, under the pretence of magnifying the effential power of the fupreme caufe, make truth and falfhood entirely to depend on his will ; as we obferved of *Des Cartes*, Book I. Chap. 4. Such tenets have a direct tendency to introduce the abfurd opinion, that intellectual faculties may be fo made, as clearly and diftinctly to perceive that to be true, which is really falfe. They judge much better, who, without fcruple, meafure the divine omnipotence itfelf, and the poffibility of things, by their own clear ideas concerning them ; affirming that God himfelf cannot make contradictions to be true at the fame time ; and reprefent the certain part of our knowledge, in fome degree, as the knowledge and wifdom of the Deity imparted to us, in the views of nature which he has laid before us.

4. The fublimity of the fubject is apt to exalt and tranfport the minds of men, beyond what their faculties can always bear : therefore, to fupport them, allegorical and enigmatical reprefentations have been invented, which, in procefs of time, have produced the greateft abufes. When metaphorical figures and names came to be confidered as realities, in place of the true God, falfe deities were fubftituted without number, and, under the pretence of devotion, a worfhip was paid to the moft deteftable characters, that tended to extinguifh the notions of true worth and virtue amongft men.

3

5. As

5. As there are no enquiries of a more arduous nature than thofe that relate to the Deity, or of near fo great importance to intellectual beings, that difcern betwixt truth and falfhood, betwixt right and wrong ; fo it is manifeft, that there are none in which the utmoft caution and fobernefs of thought is more requifite. Hence it is a very unpleafant profpect to obferve with how great freedom, or rather licentioufnefs, philofophers have advanced their rafh and crude notions concerning his nature and effence, his liberty and other attributes. What freedoms were taken by *Des Cartes* in defcribing the formation of the univerfe without his interpofition, and in pretending to deduce from his attributes confequences that are now known to be falfe, we explained in the firft book, almoft in his own words. A manner of proceeding fo unjuftifiable, in fo ferious and important a fubject, ought, one would think, to have difgufted the fober and wife part of mankind. *Spinoza*, while he carried the doctrine of abfolute neceffity to the moft monftrous height, and furpaffed all others in the weaknefs of his proofs as well as the impiety of his doctrines, yet affects to fpeak, on feveral occafions, in the higheft terms of veneration for the Deity. Mr. *Leibnitz* and many of his difciples have likewife maintained the fame doctrine of abfolute neceffity, extending it to the Deity himfelf, of whom our ideas are fo inadequate, and whom it fo much concerns us not to mifreprefent. But Sir *Ifaac Newton* was eminently diftinguifhed for his caution and circumfpection, in fpeaking or treating of this fubject, in difcourfe as well as in his writings ; tho' he has not efcaped the reproaches of his adverfaries, even in this refpect. As the Deity is the fupreme and firft caufe, from whom all other caufes derive their whole force and energy, fo he
thought

400   Sir Isaac Newton's   Book IV.

thought it moft unaccountable to exclude *Him only*
out of the univerfe.   It appeared to him much more
juft and reafonable, to fuppofe that the whole chain
of caufes, or the feveral *feries* of them, fhould centre in him as their fource and fountain; and the
whole fyftem appear depending upon him the only
independent caufe.

6. The plain argument for the exiftence of the
Deity, obvious to all and carrying irrefiftible conviction with it, is from the evident contrivance and
fitnefs of things for one another, which we meet
with throughout all parts of the univerfe.   There is
no need of nice or fubtle reafonings in this matter :
a manifeft contrivance immediately fuggefts a contriver.   It ftrikes us like a fenfation; and artful
reafonings againft it may puzzle us, but it is without fhaking our belief.   No perfon, for example,
that knows the principles of optics and the ftructure
of the eye, can believe that it was formed without
fkill in that fcience ; or that the ear was formed without the knowledge of founds ; or that the male and
female in animals were not formed for each other,
and for continuing the fpecies.   All our accounts
of nature are full of inftances of this kind.   The admirable and beautiful ftructure of things for final
caufes, exalt our idea of the *Contriver :* the unity of
defign fhews him to be *One.*   The great motions in
the fyftem, performed with the fame facility as the
leaft, fuggeft his *Almighty Power,* which gave motion to the earth and the celeftial bodies, with equal
eafe as to the minuteft particles.   The fubtility of
the motions and actions in the internal parts of bodies, fhews that his influence penetrates the inmoft
receffes of things, and that He is equally *active* and
prefent every where.   The fimplicity of the laws
that prevail in the world, the excellent difpofition
                                                    of

of things, in order to obtain the beſt ends, and the beauty which adorns the works of nature, far ſuperior to any thing in art, ſuggeſt his conſummate *Wiſdom.* The uſefulneſs of the whole ſcheme, ſo well contrived for the intelligent beings that enjoy it, with the internal diſpoſition and moral ſtructure of thoſe beings themſelves, ſhew his unbounded *Goodneſs.* Theſe are the arguments which are ſufficiently open to the views and capacities of the unlearned, while at the ſame time they acquire new ſtrength and luſtre from the diſcoveries of the learned. The Deity's acting and interpoſing in the univerſe, ſhew that he *governs* it as well as formed it, and the depth of his counſels, even in conducting the material univerſe, of which a great part ſurpaſſes our knowledge, keep up an inward veneration and awe of this great Being, and diſpoſe us to receive what may be otherwiſe revealed to us concerning him. It has been juſtly obſerved, that ſome of the laws of nature now known to us, muſt have eſcaped us if we had wanted the ſenſe of ſeeing. It may be in his power to beſtow upon us other ſenſes of which we have at preſent no idea; without which it may be impoſſible for us to know all his works, or to have more adequate ideas of himſelf. In our preſent ſtate, we know enough to be ſatisfied of our dependency upon him, and of the duty we owe to him the lord and diſpoſer of all things. He is not the object of ſenſe; his eſſence, and indeed that of all other ſubſtances, is beyond the reach of all our diſcoveries; but his attributes clearly appear in his admirable works. We know that the higheſt conceptions we are able to form of them are ſtill beneath his real perfections; but his power and dominion over us, and our duty towards him, are manifeſt.

7. Sir *Iſaac Newton* is particularly careful, always to repreſent him as a free agent; being juſtly apprehenſive

D d

henfive of the dangerous confequences of that doctrine which introduces a fatal or abfolute neceffity
prefiding over all things.   He made the world, not
from any neceffity determining him, but when he
thought fit: matter is not infinite or neceffary, but
he created as much of it as he thought proper: he
placed the fyftems of the fixed ftars at various diftances from each other, at his pleafure: in the folar
fyftem, he formed the planets of fuch a number, and
difpofed them at various diftances from the fun, as
he pleafed: he has made them all move from weft to
eaft, though it is evident from the motions of the
comets, that he might have made them move from
eaft to weft. In thefe and other inftances, we plainly
perceive the veftiges of a wife agent, but acting freely
and with perfect liberty.

As caution was a diftinguifhing part of Sir *Ifaac
Newton*'s character, but no way derogatory from his
penetration and the acutenefs and fublimity of his
genius ; fo we have particular reafon on this occafion
to applaud it, and to own that his philofophy has
proved always fubfervient to the moft valuable purpofes, without ever tending to hurt them.

8. As in treating of this unfathomable fubject we
are at a lofs for ideas and words, in any tolerable degree, adequate to it, and, in order to convey our
notions with any ftrength, are obliged to have recourfe to figurative expreffions, as was obferved already ; fo it is hardly poffible for the moft cautious
to make ufe of fuch as may not be liable to excep-
tions, from angry and captious men. Sir *Ifaac Newton*, to exprefs his idea of the divine *Omniprefence*, had
faid that the Deity perceived whatever paffed in fpace
fully and intimately, as it were in his *Senforium*. A
clamour was raifed by his adverfaries, as if he meant
that

that space was to the Deity what the *Senforium* is to our minds.   But whoever confiders this expreffion without prejudice, will allow that it conveys a very ftrong idea of the intimate prefence of the Deity every where, and of his perceiving whatever happens in the completeft manner, without the ufe of any intermediate agents or inftruments, and that Sir *Ifaac* made ufe of it with this view only; for he very carefully guards againft our imagining that external objects act upon the Deity, or that he fuffers any paffion or reaction from them.   It is commonly fuppofed that the mind is intimately confcious of the impreffions upon the fenforium, and that it is immediately prefent there, and there only; and as we muft derive our ideas of the attributes of God from what we know of our minds, or of thofe of others, in the beft manner we can, by leaving out all imperfection and limitation; fo it was hardly poffible to have reprefented to us the divine *Omniprefence* and *Omnifcience* in a ftronger light, than by this comparifon. But the fondnefs of philofophers for their favourite fyftems, often irritates them againft thofe, who, in the purfuit of truth, innocently overturn their doctrines, and provokes them to catch at any occafion of finding fault.

9. But the greateft clamour has been raifed againft Sir *Ifaac Newton*, by thofe who have imagined that he reprefented *infinite fpace* as an attribute of the Deity, and that He is prefent in all parts of fpace by diffufion.   The truth is, no fuch expreffions appear in his writings: he always thought and fpoke with more veneration of the divinity than to allow himfelf fuch liberties.   On the contrary, he tells * us that
" the

* Æternus eft & infinitus, omnipotens & omnifciens ,id eft, durat ab æterno in æternum, & adeft ab infinito in infinitum: om- nia

D d 2

" the Deity endures from eternity to eternity, and is present from infinity to infinity; but that he is not eternity or infinity, space or duration." He adds indeed, that as the Deity exifts neceffarily, and by the fame neceffity exifts every where and always, he conftitutes space and duration : but it does not appear that this expreffion can give any juft ground of complaint; for it is faying no more than that fince he is effentially and neceffarily prefent in all parts of space and duration, thefe of confequence, muft alfo neceffarily exift.

10. This idea is fo far from giving any juft ground of complaint, that it accounts for the neceffary exift-ence of space, in a way worthy of the Deity, and fuggefts the noble improvement we may make of this doctrine, which lies fo plain and open before us. Sir *Ifaac Newton* is fo far from reprefenting the Deity as prefent in space by diffufion (as fome have advanced very unjuftly) that he exprefly tells us * there are fucceffive parts in duration, and co-exiftent parts in space. But that neither are found in the foul or principle of thought which is in man; and that far lefs can they be found in the divine fubftance. As man is one and the fame in all the periods of his life, and thro' all the variety of fenfations and paffions to which he is fubject; much more muft we allow the fupreme Deity to be one and the fame in all time, and

nia regit, & omnia cognofcit, quæ fiunt aut fieri poffunt. Non eft æternitas & infinitas, fed æternus & infinitas; non eft duratio & fpatium, fed durat & adeft. Durat femper, & adeft ubique, & exiftendo femper & ubique, durationem & fpatium conftituit. *Neut. Princip Scholium Generale*, pag. 528.

* Partes dantur fucceffivæ in duratione, coexiftentes in fpatio, neutræ in perfona hominis feu principio ejus cogitante; & multo minus in fubftantia cogitante Dei. Omnis homo quatenus res fentiens, eft unus & idem homo durante vitâ fuâ in omnibus & fingulis fenfuum organis. Deus eft unus & idem Deus femper & ubique, *ibid.*

in all fpace, free from change and external influence. He adds, that the Deity is prefent every where, *non per virtutem folam fed etiam per fubftantiam, fed modo prorfus incorporeo, modo nobis penitus ignoto.* It is plain therefore, that he was far from meaning that the Deity was prefent every where by the diffufion of his fubftance, as a body is prefent in fpace by having its parts diffufed in it. Nor is it furprizing that we fhould be at a lofs to give a fatisfactory account of the manner of God's omniprefence. Our knowledge of things penetrates not into their fubftance : we perceive only their figure, colour, external furface, and the effects they have upon us, but no fenfe, or act of reflection, difcovers to us their fubftance ; and much lefs is the divine fubftance known to us. As a blind man knows not colours, and has no idea of the fenfation of thofe who fee, fo we have no notion how the Deity knows and acts.

11. His exiftence and his attributes are, in a fenfible and fatisfactory manner, difplayed to us in his works ; but his effence is unfathomable. From our exiftence and that of other contingent beings around us, we conclude that there is a *firft caufe*, whofe exiftence muft be neceffary, and independent of any other being ; but it is only *a pofteriori* that we thus infer the neceffity of his exiftence, and not in the fame manner that we deduce the neceffity of an eternal truth in geometry, or the property of a figure from its effence : nor is it even with that direct felf-evidence which we have for the neceffary exiftence of fpace. We mention this only to do juftice to Sir *Ifaac Newton*'s notion, when he fuggefts that the neceffary exiftence of fpace is relative to the neceffary exiftence of the Deity. Philofophers have had always difputes about infinite fpace and duration ; and probably their contefts on thefe fubjects will never

D d 3   have

406   Sir Isaac Newton's   Book IV.

have an end : all we want to reprefent is only, that
what is fo briefly and modeftly advanced by this great
man on thofe fubjects, is, at leaft, as rational and
worthy of the Deity, and as well founded in true
philofophy, as any of their fchemes ; though it muft
be expected that the beft account we can form of
matters of fo arduous a nature, will be liable to difficulties and objections. As for thofe who will not allow fpace to be any thing real, we obferved above that
the reality of motion, which is known by experience,
argues the reality of abfolute fpace ; without admitting which, we fhould have nothing but confufion
and contradictions in natural philofophy. Many
other arguments, particularly thofe drawn from the
axiom, *non entis nulla funt attributa*, for the reality of
fpace, whofe parts are fubject to menfuration and various relations, have been treated of largely by others.

12. We obferved above, that as the Deity is the
firft and fupreme caufe of all things, fo it is moft unaccountable to exclude him out of nature, and reprefent him as an *intelligentia extramundana*. On the
contrary, it is moft natural to fuppofe him to be the
chief mover throughout the whole univerfe, and
that all other caufes are dependent upon him ; and
conformable to this is the refult of all our enquiries
into nature ; where we are always meeting with
powers that furpafs mere mechanifm, or the effects of
matter and motion. The laws of nature are conftant and regular, and, for ought we know, all of
them may be refolved into one general and extenfive
power ; but this power itfelf derives its properties
and efficacy, not from mechanifm, but, in a great
meafure, from the immediate influences of the firft
mover. It appears, however, not to have been his
intention, that the prefent ftate of things fhould
continue for ever without alteration ; not only from
                                        what

Chap. 9.   PHILOSOPHICAL DISCOVERIES.   407

what paſſes in the moral world, but from the phænomena of the material world likewiſe ; as it is evident
that it could not have continued in its preſent ſtate
from eternity.

13. The power of gravity, by which the celeſtial
bodies perſevere in their revolutions, penetrates to
the centres of the ſun and planets without any diminution of virtue, and is extended to immenſe diſtances, decreaſing in a regular courſe.   Its action is
proportional to the quantity of ſolid matter in bodies,
and not to their ſurfaces, as is uſual in mechanical
cauſes : this power therefore, ſeems to ſurpaſs mere
mechaniſm.   But, whatever we ſay of this power, it
could not poſſibly have produced, at the beginning,
the regular ſituation of the orbs and the preſent diſpoſition of things.   Gravity could not have determined the planets to move from weſt to eaſt in orbits
nearly circular, almoſt in the ſame plane ; nor could
this power have projected the comets with all variety
of directions.   If we ſuppoſe the matter of the
ſyſtem to be accumulated in the centre by its gravity, no mechanical principles, with the aſſiſtance
of this power of gravity, could ſeparate the vaſt
maſs into ſuch parts as the ſun and planets, and, after carrying them into their different diſtances, project them in their ſeveral directions, preſerving ſtill
the equality of action and reaction, or the ſtate of
the centre of gravity of the ſyſtem.   Such an exqui-
ſite ſtructure of things could only ariſe from the contrivance and powerful influences of an intelligent,
free, and moſt potent agent.   The ſame powers,
therefore, which at preſent govern the material univerſe, and conduct its various motions, are very different from thoſe which were neceſſary to have produced it from nothing, or to have diſpoſed it in the
admirable form in which it now proceeds.

14. As

14. As we cannot but conceive the univerfe, as depending on the firft caufe and chief mover, whom it would be abfurd, not to fay impious, to exclude from acting in it ; fo we have fome hints of the manner in which he operates in nature, from the laws which we find eftablifhed in it. Though he is the fource of all efficacy, yet we find that place is left for fecond caufes to act in fubordination to him ; and mechanifm has its fhare in carrying on the great fcheme of nature *. The eftablifhing the equality of action and reaction, even in thofe powers which feem to furpafs mechanifm, and to be more immediately derived from him, feems to be an indication that thofe powers, while they derive their efficacy from him, are however, in a certain degree, circumfcribed and regulated in their operations by mechanical principles ; and that they are not to be confidered as mere immediate volitions of his (as they are often reprefented) but rather as inftruments made by him, to perform the purpofes for which he intended them. If, for example, the moft noble phænomena in nature be produced by a rare elaftic *ætherial medium*, as Sir *Ifaac Newton* conjectured, the whole efficacy of this medium muft be refolved into his power and will, who is the fupreme caufe. This, however, does not hinder, but that the fame medium may he fubject to the like laws as other elaftic fluids, in its actions and vibrations ; and that, if its nature was better known to us, we might make curious and ufeful difcoveries concerning its effects, from thofe laws. It is eafy to fee that this conjecture no way derogates from the government and influences of

---

* Ἀλλὰ τοῦτο ἦν τὸ θειότατον, τὸ μετὰ ῥαςώνης ᾗ ἁπλῆς κινήσεως παντοδατὰς ἀποτελεῖν ἰδέας, ὥσπέρ ἀμελει δρῶσιν οἱ μηχανοποιοί διὰ μιᾶς ὀργάνκ σχαςηρίας, πολλὰς ᾗ ποικίλας ἐνεργείας ἀποτελεῦντες. *Ariftot.* ubi fupra.

the

the Deity; while it leaves us at liberty to purfue our enquiries concerning the nature and operations of fuch a medium. Whereas they who haftily refolve thofe powers into immediate volitions of the fupreme caufe, without admitting any intermediate inftruments, put an end to our enquiries at once; and deprive us of what is probably the moft fublime part of philofophy, by reprefenting it as imaginary and fictitious: by which means, as we obferved above *, they hurt thofe very interefts which they appear fo fanguine to promote; for the higher we rife in the fcale of nature, towards the fupreme caufe, the views we have from philofophy appear more beautiful and extenfive. Nor is there any thing extraordinary in what is here reprefented concerning the manner in which the Supreme Caufe acts in the univerfe, by employing fubordinate inftruments and agents, which are allowed to have their proper force and efficacy; for this we know is the cafe in the common courfe of nature; where we find gravity, attraction, repulfion, &c. conftantly combined and compounded with the principles of mechanifm: and we fee no reafon why it fhould not likewife take place in the more fubtile and abftrufe phænomena and motions of the fyftem.

15. It has been demonftrated by ingenious men, that great revolutions have happened in former times on the furface of the earth, particularly from the phænomena of the *Strata*; which fometimes are found to lie in a very regular manner, and fometimes to be broken and feparated from each other to very confiderable diftances, where they are found again in the fame order; from the impreffions of plants left upon the hardeft bodies dug deep out of

* Book I. Chap. 5. Sect. 2.

the

the earth, and in places where fuch plants are not now found to grow; and from bones of animals both of the land and fea, difcovered fome hundreds of yards beneath the prefent furface of the earth, and at very great diftances from the fea. Some philofophers explain thefe changes by the revolutions of comets, or other natural means: but as the Deity has formed the univerfe dependent upon himfelf, fo as to require to be altered by him, though at very diftant periods of time; it does not appear to be a very important queftion to enquire whether thefe great changes are produced by the intervention of inftruments, or by the fame immediate influences which firft gave things their form.

16. We cannot but take notice of one thing, that appears to have been defigned by the author of nature: he has made it impoffible for us to have any communication from this earth with the other great bodies of the univerfe, in our prefent ftate; and it is highly probable, that he has likewife cut off all communication betwixt the other planets, and betwixt the different fyftems. We are able, by telefcopes, to difcover very plainly mountains, precipices and cavities in the moon: but who tread thofe precipices, or for what purpofes thofe great cavities (many of which have a little elevation in the middle) ferve, we know not; and are at a lofs to conceive how this planet, without any atmofphere, vapours, or feas, (as is now the common opinion of aftronomers) can ferve for like purpofes as our earth. We obferve fudden and furprizing revolutions on the furface of the great planet *Jupiter*, which would be fatal to the inhabitants of the earth. We obferve, in them all, enough to raife our curiofity, but not to fatisfy it. From hence, as well as from the ftate of the moral world, and many other consi-

confiderations, we are induced to believe, that our
prefent ftate would be very imperfect without a fub-
fequent one; wherein our views of nature, and of
its great author, may be more clear and fatisfactory.
It does not appear to be fuitable to the wifdom that
fhines throughout all nature, to fuppofe that we
fhould fee fo far, and have our curiofity fo much
raifed concerning the works of God, only to be dif-
appointed at the end. As man is undoubtedly the
chief being upon this globe, and this globe may be
no lefs confiderable, in the moft valuable refpects,
than any other in the folar fyftem, and this fyftem,
for ought we know, not inferior to any in the univerfal fyftem; fo, if we fhould fuppofe man to perifh, without ever arriving at a more complete knowledge of nature, than the very imperfect one he attains in his prefent ftate; by analogy, or parity of
reafon, we might conclude, that the like defires
would be fruftrated in the inhabitants of all the other
planets and fyftems; and that the beautiful fcheme
of nature would never be unfolded, but in an exceedingly imperfect manner, to any of them. This,
therefore, naturally leads us to confider our prefent
ftate as only the dawn or beginning of our exiftence,
and as a ftate of preparation or probation for farther
advancement: which appears to have been the opinion of the moft judicious philofophers of old. And
whoever attentively confiders the conftitution of
human nature, particularly the defires and paffions
of men, which appear greatly fuperior to their prefent objects, will eafily be perfuaded that man was
defigned for higher views than of this life. Thefe
the author of nature may have in referve to be
opened up to us, at proper periods of time, and after due preparation. Surely it is in his power to
grant us a far greater improvement of the faculties
we already poffefs, or even to endow us with new

10   faculties,

412   Sir Isaac Newton's, &c.   Book IV.

faculties, of which, at this time, we have no idea, for penetrating farther into the fcheme of nature, and approaching nearer to himfelf, the firft and fupreme caufe. We know not how far it was proper or neceffary that we fhould not be let into knowledge at once, but fhould advance gradually, that, by comparing new objects, or new difcoveries, with what was known to us before, our improvements might be more complete and regular; or how far it may be neceffary or advantageous, that intelligent beings fhould pafs through a kind of infancy of knowledge. For new knowledge does not confift fo much in our having accefs to a new object, as in comparing it with others already known, obferving its relations to them, or difcerning what it has in common with them, and wherein their difparity confifts. Thus our knowledge is vaftly greater than the fum of what all its objects feparately could afford; and when a new object comes within our reach, the addition to our knowledge is the greater, the more we already know; fo that it increafes not as the new objects increafe, but in a much higher proportion. * * *

F I N I S.

16. Baron Paul Heinrich Dietrich von Holbach (1723-1789)

Système de la Nature (London, 1770)
From *The System of Nature,* translated by Samuel Wilkinson,
3 vols. (London, 1820-1821), vol. 1, 20-31, 34-35, 46-47; vol.
2, 100-108

20   §YSTEM OF NATURE.

Every thing in the universe is in motion : the es-
sense of matter is to act: if we consider its parts,
attentively, we shall discover there is not a particle that enjoys absolute repose. Those which appear
to us to be without motion, are, in fact, only in relative or apparent rest; they experience such an imperceptible motion, and expose it so little on their
surfaces, that we cannot perceive the changes they
undergo. All that appears to us to be at rest, does
not, however, remain one instant in the same state.
All beings are continually breeding, increasing, decreasing, or dispersing, with more or less dullness or
rapidity. The insect called EPHEMERON, is produced and perishes in the same day ; of consequence,
it experiences the greatest changes of its being very
rapidly, in our eyes. Those combinations which
form the most solid bodies, which appear to enjoy
the most perfect repose, are nevertheless decomposed,
and dissolved in the course of time. The hardest
stones, by degrees, give way to the contact of air.
A mass of iron, which time, and the action of the
atmosphere, has gnawed into rust, must have been in
motion, from the moment of its formation, in the
bowels of the earth, until the instant we behold it in
this state of dissolution.
Natural philosophers, for the most part, seem not
to have sufficiently reflected on what they call the
nisus ; that is to say, the incessant efforts one body
is making on another, but which, notwithstanding
appear, to our superficial observation, to enjoy the
most perfect repose. A stone of five hundred weight
seems to rest quiet on the earth, nevertheless, it never
ceases for an instant, to press with force upon the
earth, which resists or repulses it in its turn. Will

the assertion be ventured, that the stone and earth do not act? Do they wish to be undeceived? They have nothing to do but interpose their hand betwixt the earth and the stone; it will then be discovered, that notwithstanding its seeming repose, the stone has power adequate to bruise it; because the hand has not energies sufficient, within itself, to resist effectually both the stone and earth.—Action cannot exist in bodies without re-action. A body that experiences an impulse, an attraction, or a pressure of any kind, if it resists, clearly demonstrates by such resistance that it re-acts; from whence it follows, there is a concealed force, called by these philosophers *vis inertia*, that displays itself against another force; and this clearly demonstrates, that this inert force is capable of both acting and re-acting. In short, it will be found, on close investigation, that those powers which are called *dead*, and those which are termed *live* or *moving*, are powers of the same kind; which only display themselves after a different manner. Permit us to go a greater distance yet. May we not say, that in those bodies, or masses, of which their whole become evident from appearances to us to be at rest, there is notwithstanding, a continual action, and counter-action, constant efforts, uninterrupted or communicated force, and continued opposition? In short, a *nisus*, by which the constituting portions of these bodies press one upon another, mutually resisting each other, acting and re-acting incessantly? that this reciprocity of action, this simultaneous re-action, keeps them united, causes their particles to form a mass, a body, and a combination, which, viewed in its whole, has the appearance of complete rest, notwithstanding no one of its particles really

22   SYSTEM OF NATURE.

ceases to be in motion for a single instant? These collective masses appear to be at rest, simply by the equality of the motion—by the responsory impulse of the powers acting in them.

Thus it appears that bodies enjoying perfect repose, really receive, whether upon their surface, or in their interior, a continual communicated force, from those bodies by which they are either surrounded or penetrated, dilated or contracted, rarified or condensed: in fact, from those which compose them; whereby their particles are incessantly acting and re-acting, or in continual motion, the effects of which are displayed by extraordinary changes. Thus heat rarifies and dilates metals, which is evidence deducible that a bar of iron, from the change of the atmosphere alone, must be in continual motion; that there is not a single particle in it that can be said to enjoy rest even for a single moment. In those hard bodies, indeed, the particles of which are in actual contact, and which are closely united, how is it possible to conceive, that air, cold, or heat, can act upon one of these particles, even exteriorly, without the motion being communicated to those which are most intimate and minute in their union? Without motion, how should we be able to comprehend the manner in which our sense of smelling is affected, by emanations escaping from the most solid bodies, of which all the particles appear to be at perfect rest? How could we, even by the assistance of a telescope, see the most distant stars, if there was not a progressive motion of light from these stars to the retina of our eye?

Observation and reflection ought to convince us, that every thing in Nature is in continual motion—

that there is not a single part, however small, that enjoys repose—that Nature acts in all—that she would cease to be Nature if she did not act. Practical knowledge teaches us, that without unceasing motion, nothing could be preserved—nothing could be produced—nothing could act in this Nature. Thus the idea of Nature necessarily includes that of motion. But it will be asked, and not a little triumphantly, from whence did she derive her motion? Our reply is, we know not, neither do they—that *we* never shall, that *they* never will. It is a secret hidden from us, concealed from them, by the most impenetrable veil. We also reply, that it is fair to infer, unless they can logically prove to the contrary, that it is in herself, since she is the great whole, out of which nothing can exist. We say this motion is a manner of existence, that flows, necessarily, out of the nature of matter; that matter moves by its own peculiar energies; that its motion is to be attributed to the force which is inherent in itself; that the variety of motion, and the phenomena which result, proceed from the diversity of the properties—of the qualities—of the combinations, which are originally found in the primitive matter, of which Nature is the assemblage.

Natural philosophers, for the most part, have regarded as inanimate, or as deprived of the faculty of motion, those bodies which are only moved by the intervention of some agent or exterior cause; they have considered themselves justified in concluding, that the matter which forms these bodies is perfectly inert in its nature. They have not forsaken this error, although they must have observed, that whenever a body is left to itself, or disengaged from those

24   SYSTEM OF NATURE.

obstructions which oppose themselves to its descent, it has a tendency to fall or to approach the centre of the earth, by a motion uniformly accelerated ; they have rather chosen to suppose a visionary exterior cause, of which they themselves had but an imperfect idea, than admit that these bodies held their motion from their own peculiar nature.

These philosophers, also, notwithstanding they saw above them an infinite number of globes that moved with great rapidity round a common centre, still adhered to their favourite opinions ; and never ceased to suppose some whimsical causes for these movements, until the immortal Newton clearly demonstrated that it was the effect of the gravitation of these celestial bodies towards each other. Experimental philosophers, however, and amongst them the great Newton himself, have held the cause of gravitation as inexplicable. Notwithstanding the great weight of this authority, it appears manifest that it may be deduced from the motion of matter, by which bodies are diversely determined. Gravitation is nothing more than a mode of moving—a tendency towards a centre : to speak strictly, all motion is relative gravitation ; since that which falls relatively to us, rises, with relation to other bodies. From this it follows, that every motion in our microcosm is the effect of gravitation ; seeing that there is not in the universe either top or bottom, nor any absolute centre. It should appear, that the weight of bodies depends on their configuration, as well external as internal, which gives them that form of action which is called gravitation. Thus, for instance, a piece of lead, spherically formed, falls quickly and direct : reduce this ball into very thin plates, it will be sustained in the air for a much longer time: apply to it the action of fire, this lead will rise in the atmosphere: here, then, the same metal, variously modified, has very different modes of action.

A very simple observation would have sufficed to make the philosophers, antecedent to Newton, feel the inadequateness of the causes they admitted to operate with such powerful effect. They had a sufficiency to convince themselves, in the collision of two bodies, which they could contemplate, and in the known laws of that motion, which these always communicate by reason of their greater or less compactness; from whence they ought to have inferred, that the density of *subtle* or *ethereal* matter, being considerably less than that of the planets, it could only communicate to them a very feeble motion, quite insufficient to produce that velocity of action, of which they could not possibly avoid being the witnesses.

If Nature had been viewed uninfluenced by prejudice, they must have been long since convinced that matter acts by its own peculiar activity; that it needs no exterior communicative force to set it in motion. They might have perceived that whenever mixed bodies were placed in a situation to act on each other, motion was instantly excited; and that these mixtures acted with a force capable of producing the most surprising results.

If particles of iron, sulphur, and water be mixed together, these bodies thus capacitated to act on each other, are heated by degrees, and ultimately produce a violent combustion. If flour be wetted with water, and the mixture closed up, it will be found, after some lapse of time, (by the aid of a microscope) to have produced organized beings that enjoy life, of of which the water and the flour were believed incapable: it is thus that inanimate matter can pass into life, or animate matter, which is in itself only an assemblage of motion.

Reasoning from analogy, which the philosophers of the present day do not hold incompatible, the production of a man, independent of the ordinary means, would not be more astonishing than that of an insect with flour and water. Fermentation and putrid substances, evidently produce living animals. We have here the principle ; with proper materials, principles can always be brought into action. That generation which is styled *uncertain* is only so for those who do not reflect, or who do not permit themselves, attentively, to observe the operations of Nature.

The generative of motion, and its developement, as well as the energy of matter, may be seen every where ; more particularly in those unitions in which fire, air, and water, find themselves combined. These elements, or rather these mixed bodies, are the most volatile, the most fugitive of beings ; nevertheless in the hands of Nature, they are the essential agents employed to produce the most striking phenomena. To these we must ascribe the effects of thunder, the eruption of volcanoes, earthquakes, &c. Science offers to our consideration an agent of astonishing force, in gunpowder, the instant it comes in contact with fire. In short, the most terrible effects result from the combination of matter, which is generally believed to be dead and inert.

These facts prove, beyond a doubt, that motion is produced, is augmented, is accelerated in matter, without the help of any exterior agent: therefore it is

reasonable to conclude that motion is the necessary
consequence of immutable laws, resulting from the
essence, from the properties existing in the different
elements, and the various combinations of these
elements. Are we not justified, then, in concluding,
from these precedents, that there may be an infinity
of other combinations, with which we are unacquainted, competent to produce a great variety of
motion in matter, without being under the necessity
of having recourse, for the explanation, to agents
who are more difficult to comprehend than even the
effects which are attributed to them?

Had man but paid proper attention to what passed
under his review, he would not have sought out of
Nature, a power distinguished from herself, to set
her in action, and without which he believes she
cannot move. If, indeed, by Nature is meant a heap
of dead matter, destitute of peculiar qualities purely
passive, we must unquestionably seek out of this
Nature the principle of her motion. But if by Nature be understood, what it really is, a whole, of
which the numerous parts are endowed with various
properties, which oblige them to act according to
these properties; which are in a perpetual ternate-
ness of action and re-action; which press, which
gravitate towards a common center, whilst others
depart from and fly off towards the periphery, or
circumference; which attract and repel; which by
continual approximation and constant collision, produce and decompose all the bodies we behold; then,
I say, there is no necessity to have recourse to supernatural powers, to account for the formation of
things, and those extraordinary appearances which
are the result of motion.

28   SYSTEM OF NATURE.

Those who admit a cause exterior to matter, are obliged to believe that this cause produced all the motion by which matter is agitated in giving it existence.   This belief rests on another, namely, that matter could begin to exist ; an hypothesis that, until this moment, has never been satisfactorily demonstrated.   To produce from nothing, or the CREATION, is a term that cannot give us the least idea of the formation of the universe ; it presents no sense, upon which the mind can rely.   In fact, the human mind is not adequate to conceive a moment of non-existence, or when all shall have passed away ; even admitting this to be a truth, it is no truth for us, because by the very nature of our organization, we cannot admit positions as facts, of which no evidence can be adduced that has relation to our senses : we may, indeed, consent to believe it, because others say it;   but will any rational being be satisfied with such an admission ? Can any moral good spring from such blind assurance ?   Is it consistent with sound doctrine, with philosophy, or with reason ?   Do we, in fact, pay any respect to the intellectual powers of another, when we say to him, " I will believe this, because in all the attempts you have ventured, for the purpose of proving what you say, you have entirely failed ; and have been at last obliged to acknowledge you know nothing about the matter ?"   What moral reliance ought we to have on such people ?   Hypothesis may succeed hypothesis ; system may destroy system : a new set of ideas may overturn the ideas of a former day.   Other Gallileos may be condemned to death — other Newtons may arise — we may reason — argue — dispute — quarrel — punish and destroy : nay, we may even exterminate those who differ from us in opinion ; but when we have done all this, we shall be obliged to fall back upon our original darkness—to confess, that that which has no relation with our senses, that which cannot manifest itself to us by some of the ordinary modes by which other things are manifested, has no existence for us—is not comprehensible by us—can never entirely remove our doubt—can never seize on our stedfast belief; seeing it is that of which we cannot form even a notion ; in short, that it is that, which as long as we remain what we are, must be hidden from us by a veil, which no power, no faculty, no energy, we possess, is able to remove.   All who are not enslaved by prejudice agree to the truth of the position, that *nothing can be made of nothing.*

Many theologians have acknowledged Nature to be an active whole.   Almost all the ancient philosophers were agreed to regard the world as eternal. OCELLUS LUCANUS, speaking of the universe, says, " *it has always been, and it always will be.*" VATABLE and GROTIUS assure us, that to render the Hebrew phrase in the first chapter of GENESIS correctly, we must say, " *when God made heaven and earth, matter was without form.*"   If this be true, and every Hebraist can judge for himself, then the word which has been rendered *created*, means only to fashion, form, arrange.   We know that the Greek words *create* and *form*, have always indicated the same thing.   According to ST. JEROME, *creare* has the same meaning as *condere*, to found, to build. The Bible does not any where say in a clear manner, that the world was made of nothing.   TER-

30   SYSTEM OF NATURE.

TULLIAN and the father PETAU both admit, that
" *this is a truth established more by reason than
by authority.*" ST. JUSTIN seems to have contem-
plated matter as eternal, since he commends PLATO
for having said, that " *God, in the creation of the
world, only gave impulse to matter, and fashioned
it.*" BURNET and PYTHAGORAS were entirely of
this opinion, and even our Church Service may be
adduced in support ; for although it admits by im-
plication a beginning, it expressly denies an end :
" *As it was in the beginning, is now, and ever
shall be, world without end.*" It is easy to perceive that that which cannot cease to exist, must
have always been.

Motion becomes still more obscure, when creation,
or the formation of matter, is attributed to a SPI-
RITUAL being ; that is to say, to a being which has
no analogy, no point of contact, with it—to a being
which has neither extent or parts, and cannot, therefore, be susceptible of motion, as we understand the
term ; this being only the change of one body, relatively to another body, in which the body moved
presents successively different parts to different points
of space. Moreover, as all the world are nearly
agreed that matter can never be totally annihilated,
or cease to exist ; by what reasoning, I would ask,
do they comprehend—how understand—that that
which cannot cease to be, could ever have had a beginning.

If, therefore, it be asked, whence came matter ? it
is very reasonable to say it has always existed. If it
be inquired, whence proceeds the motion that agi-
tates matter ? the same reasoning furnishes the answer ; namely, that as motion is coeval with matter,

it must have existed from all eternity, seeing that
motion is the necessary consequence of its existence—of its essence—of its primitive properties, such
as its extent, its gravity, its impenetrability, its
figure, &c. By virtue of these essential constituent
properties, inherent in all matter, and without which
it is impossible to form an idea of it, the various
matter of which the universe is composed must from
all eternity have pressed against each other—have
gravitated towards a center—have clashed—have
come in contact—have been attracted—have been
repelled—have been combined — have been separated: in short, must have acted and moved according to the essence and energy peculiar to each genus,
and to each of its combinations.

★   ★   ★   ★

[p. 34]

                                          In
short, Nature is but an immense chain of causes and
effects, which unceasingly flow from each other.
The motion of particular beings depends on the
general motion, which is itself maintained by individual motion. This is strengthened or weakened,
accelerated or retarded, simplified or complicated,
procreated or destroyed, by a variety of combinations and circumstances, which every moment
change the directions, the tendency, the modes of
existing, and of acting, of the different beings that
receive its impulse.

If it were true, as has been asserted by some
philosophers, that every thing has a tendency to form
one unique or single mass, and in that unique mass
the instant should arrive when all was in *nisus*, all

would eternally remain in this state; to all eternity there would be no more than one Being and one effort: this would be eternal and universal death.

If we desire to go beyond this, to find the principle of action in matter, to trace the origin of things, it is for ever to fall back upon difficulties; it is absolutely to abridge the evidence of our senses; by which only we can understand, by which alone we can judge of the causes acting upon them, or the impulse by which they are set in action.

Let us, therefore, content ourselves with saying WHAT is supported by our experience, and by all the evidence we are capable of understanding; against the truth of which not a shadow of proof, such as our reason can admit, has ever been adduced—which has been maintained by philosophers in every age—which theologians themselves have not denied, but which many of them have upheld; namely, that *matter always existed; that it moves by virtue of its essence; that all the phenomena of Nature is ascribable to the diversified motion of the variety of matter she contains; and which, like the phœnix, is continually regenerating out of its own ashes.*

★   ★   ★   ★

[p. 46]

Be this as it may, whenever we see a cause act, we look upon its effect as natural: when this cause becomes familiar to the sight, when we are accustomed to it, we think we understand it, and its effects surprise us no longer.   Whenever any unusual effect is perceived, without our discovering the cause, the mind sets to work, becomes uneasy ; this uneasiness increases in proportion to its extent: as soon as it is believed to threaten our preservation, we become completely agitated ; we seek after the cause with an earnestness proportioned to our alarm ; our perplexity augments in a ratio equivalent to the persuasion we are under: how essentially requisite it is, we should become acquainted with the cause that has affected us in so lively a manner.   As it frequently happens that our senses can teach us nothing respecting this cause which so deeply interests us—which we seek with so much ardour, we have recourse to our imagination ; this, disturbed with alarm, enervated by fear, becomes a suspicious, a fallacious guide : we create chimeras, fictitious causes, to whom we give the credit, to whom we ascribe the honour of those phenomena by which we have been so much alarmed. It is to this disposition of the human mind that must be attributed, as will be seen in the sequel, the religious errors of man, who, despairing of the capability to trace the natural causes of those perplexing phenomena to which he was the witness, and sometimes the victim, created in his brain (heated with terror) imaginary causes, which have become to him a source of the most extravagant folly.

In Nature, however, there can be only natural causes and effects ; all motion excited in this Nature,

SYSTEM OF NATURE. 47

follows constant and necessary laws: the natural operations, to the knowledge of which we are competent, of which we are in a capacity to judge, are of themselves sufficient to enable us to discover those which elude our sight; we can at least judge of them by analogy. If we study Nature with attention, the modes of action which she displays to our senses will teach us not to be disconcerted by those which she refuses to discover. Those causes which are the most remote from their effects, unquestionably act by intermediate causes; by the aid of these, we can frequently trace out the first. If in the chain of these causes we sometimes meet with obstacles that oppose themselves to our research, we ought to endeavour by patience and diligence to overcome them; when it so happens we cannot surmount the difficulties that occur, we still are never justified in concluding the chain to be broken, or that the cause which acts is SUPER-NATURAL. Let us, then, be content with an honest avowal, that Nature contains resources of which we are ignorant; but never let us substitute phantoms, fictions, or imaginary causes, senseless terms, for those causes which escape our research; because, by such means we only confirm ourselves in ignorance, impede our enquiries, and obstinately remain in error.

★   ★   ★   ★

[Vol 2, p. 100]

The first theology of man was grounded on fear, modelled by ignorance: either afflicted or benefitted by the elements, he adored these elements themselves; by a parity of reasoning, if reasoning it can be called, he extended his reverence to every material, coarse object; he afterwards rendered his

homage to the agents he supposed presiding over
these elements ; to powerful genii ; to inferior genii ;
to heroes ; to men endowed with either great or
striking qualities. Time, aided by reflection, with
here and there a slight corruscution of truth, induced
him in some places to relinquish his original ideas ;
he believed he simplified the thing by lessening the
number of his gods,-but he achieved nothing by this
towards attaining to the truth ; in recurring from
cause to cause man finished by losing sight of every
thing ; in this obscurity, in this dark abyss, his
mind still laboured, he formed new chimeras, ho
made new gods, or rather he formed a very complex
machinery ; still, as before, whenever he could not
account for any phenomenon that struck his sight,
he was unwilling to ascribe it to physical causes;
and the name of his divinity, whatever that might
happen to be, was always brought in to supply his
own ignorance of natural causes. _

   If a faithful account was rendered of man's ideas
upon the Divinity, he would be obliged to acknowledge, that for the most part the word *Gods* has
been used to express the concealed, remote, unknown
causes of the effects he witnessed ; that he applies
this term when the spring of natural, the source of
known causes ceases to be visible : as soon as he loses
the thread of these causes, or as soon as his mind
can no longer follow the chain, he solves the
difficulty, terminates his research, by ascribing it
to his gods ; thus giving a vague definition to an
unknown cause, at which either his idleness, or his
limited knowledge, obliges hi u to stop. When,
therefore, he ascribes to his gods the production of
some phenomenon, the novelty or the extent of which

102   SYSTEM OF NATURE.

strikes him with wonder, but of which his ignorance
precludes him from unravelling the true cause, or
which he believes the natural powers with which he
is acquainted are inadequate to bring forth ; does he,
in fact, do any thing more than substitute for the
darkness of his own mind, a sound to which he has
been accustomed to listen with reverential awe?
Ignorance may be said to be the inheritance of the
generality of men; these attribute to their gods not
only those uncommon effects that burst upon their
senses with an astounding force, but also the most
simple events, the causes of which are the most easy
to be known to whoever shall be willing to meditate
upon them. In short, man has always respected
those unknown causes, those surprising effects
which his ignorance prevented him from fathoming.

But does this afford us one single, correct idea of
the *Divinity* ? Can it be possible we are acting rationally, thus eternally to make him the agent of our
stupidity, of our sloth, of our want of information
on natural causes? Do we, in fact, pay any kind
of adoration to this being, by thus bringing him
forth on every trifling occasion, to solve the difficulties
ignorance throws in our way? Of whatever na-
ture this great *Cause of causes* may be, it is evident
to the slightest reflection that he has been sedulous
to conceal himself from our view ; that he has rendered it impossible for us to have the least acquaintance with him, except through the medium of
nature, which he has unquestionably rendered
competent to every thing : this is the rich banquet
spread before man; he is invited to partake, with a
welcome he has no right to dispute ; to enjoy therefore is to obey ; to be happy is to render that worship

which must make him most acceptable ; *to be happy himself is to make others happy ; to make others happy is to be virtuous ; to be virtuous he must revere truth : to know what truth is, he must examine with caution, scrutinize with severity, every opinion he adopts :* this granted, is it at all consistent with the majesty of the Divinity, is it not insulting to such a being to clothe him with our wayward passions ; to ascribe to him designs similar to our narrow view of things ; to give him our filthy desires ; to suppose he can be guided by our finite conceptions ; to bring him on a level with frail humanity, by investing him with our qualities, however much we may exaggerate them ; to indulge an opinion that he can either act or think as we do ; to imagine he can in any manner resemble such a feeble play-thing, as is the greatest, the most distinguished man? No! it is to degrade him in the eye of reason; to violate every regard for truth ; to set moral decency at defiance ; to fall back into the depth of cimmerian darkness. Let man therefore sit down cheerfully to the feast; let him contentedly partake of what he finds; but let him not worry the Divinity with his useless prayers, with his shallow-sighted requests, to solicit at his hands that which, if granted, would in all probability be the most injurious for himself : these supplications are, in fact, at once to say, that with our limited experience, with our slender knowledge, we better understand what is suitable to our condition, what is convenient to our welfare, than the mighty *Cause of all causes* who has left us in the hands of nature: it is to be presumptuous in the highest degree of presumption ; it is impiously to endeavour to lift up a

104   SYSTEM OF NATURE.

veil which it is evidently forbidden man to touch; that even his most strenuous efforts attempt in vain.

It remains, then, to inquire, if man can reasonably flatter himself with obtaining a perfect knowledge of the power of nature ; of the properties of the beings she contains; of the effects which may result from their various combinations? Do we know why the magnet attracts iron? Are we better acquainted with the cause of polar attraction? Are we in a condition to explain the phenomena of light, electricity, elasticity? Do we understand the mechanism by which that modification of our brain, which we cal volition, puts our arm or our legs into motion? Can we render to ourselves an account of the manner in which our eyes behold objects, in which our ears receive sounds, in which our mind conceives ideas? All we know upon these subjects is, that they are so. If then we are incapable of accounting for the most ordinary phonomena, which nature daily exhibits to us, by what chain of reasoning do we refuse to her the power of producing other effects equally incomprehensible to us? Shall we be more instructed, when every time we behold an effect of which we are not in a capacity to develope the cause, we may idly say, this effect is produced by the power, by the will of God? Undoubtedly it is the great *Cause of causes* must have produced every thing; but is it not lessening the true dignity of the Divinity, to introduce him as interfering in every operation of nature; nay, in every action of so insignificant a creature as man? as a mere agent executing his own eternal, immutable laws ; when experience, when reflection, when the evidence of all we contemplate, warrants the idea, that this ineffable being has rendered nature compe-

tent to every effect, by giving her those irrevocable
laws, that eternal, unchangeable system, according
to which all the beings she contains must eternally
act?   Is it not more worthy the exalted mind of the
GREAT PARENT OF PARENTS, *ens entium*, more consistent with truth, to suppose that his wisdom in
giving these immutable, these eternal laws to the
macrocosm, foresaw every thing that could possibly
be requisite for the happiness of the beings contained
in it-; that therefore he left it to the invariable operation of a system which never can produce any effect
that is not the best possible that circumstances however viewed will admit: that consequently the natural
activity of the human mind, which is itself the result
of this eternal action, was purposely given to man,
that he might endeavour to fathom, that he might
strive to unravel, that he might seek out the concate-
nation of these laws, in order to furnish remedies
against the evils produced by ignorance.   How many
discoveries in the great science of natural philosophy
has mankind progressively made, which the ignorant
prejudices of our forefathers on their first announce-
ment considered as impious, as displeasing to the
Divinity, as heretical profanations, which could only
be expiated by the sacrifice of the enquiring individuals; to whose labour their posterity owes such
an infinity of gratitude?   Even in modern days we
have seen a SOCRATES destroyed, a GALILEO condemned, whilst multitudes of other benefactors to
mankind have been held in contempt by their unin-
formed cotemporaries, for those very researches into
nature which the present generation hold in the
highest veneration.   *Whenever ignorant priests are
permitted to guide the opinions of nations, science*

can make but a very slender progress: natural discoveries will be always held inimical to the interest
of bigotted superstitious men.   It may, to the minds
of infatuated mortals, to the shallow comprehension
of prejudiced beings, appear very pious to reply on
every occasion our gods do this, our gods do that;
but to the contemplative philosopher, to the man of
reason, to the real adorers of the great *Cause of
causes,* it will never be convincing that a sound, a
mere word, can attach the reason of things; can
have more than a fixed sense; can suffice to explain
problems.   The word GOD is for the most part used
to denote the impenetrable cause of those effects
which astonish mankind; which man is not competent to explain.   But is not this wilful idleness?   Is
it not inconsistent with our nature?   Is it not
being truly impious, to sit down with those fine
faculties we have received, and give the answer of
a child to every thing we do not understand; or
rather which our own sloth, or our own want of industry has prevented us from knowing?   Ought we
not rather to redouble our efforts to penetrate the
cause of those phenomena which strike our mind?
Is not this, in fact, the duty we owe to the great, the
universal Parent?   When we have given this answer, what have we said? nothing but what every
one knows.   Could the great *Cause of causes* make
the whole, without also making its part?   But does
it of necessity follow that he executes every trifling
operation, when he has so noble an agent as his own
nature, whose laws he has rendered unchangeable,
whose scale of operations can never deviate from the
eternal routine he has marked out for her and all the
beings she embraces?   Whose secrets, if sought out,

contain the true balsam of life—the sovereign remedy for all the diseases of man.

When we shall be ingenuous with ourselves, we
shall be obliged to agree that it was uniformly the
ignorance in which our ancestors were involved;
their want of knowledge of natural causes, their un-
enlightened ideas on the powers of nature, which
gave birth to the gods they worshipped ; that it is,
again, the impossibility which the greater part of
mankind find to withdraw themselves out of this ignorance, the difficulty they consequently find to form
to themselves simple ideas of the formation of things,
the labour that is required to discover the true
sources of those events, which they either admire or
fear, that makes them believe these ideas are necessary to enable them to render an account of those
phenomena, to which their own sluggishness renders them incompetent to recur. Here, without
doubt, is the reason they treat all those as irrational
who do not see the necessity of admitting an unknown agent, or some secret energy, which for want
of being acquainted with Nature, they have placed
out of herself.

The phenomena of nature necessarily breed various sentiments in man : some he thinks favorable to
him, some prejudicial, while the whole is only what
it can be. Some excite his love, his admiration, his
gratitude ; others fill him with trouble, cause aver-
sion, drive him to despair. According to the various
sensations he experiences, he either loves or fears
the causes to which he attributes the effects, which
produce in him these different passions : these sentiments are commensurate with the effects he experiences; his admiration is enhanced, his fears are aug-

198   SYSTEM OF NATURE.

mented, in the same ratio as the phenomena which
strikes his senses are more or less extensive, more or
less irresistible or interesting to him. Man necessarily
makes himself the centre of nature; indeed he can
only judge of things, as he is himself affected by them;
he can only love that which he thinks favorable to
his being; he hates, he fears every thing which
causes him to suffer : in short, as we have seen in the
former volume, he calls confusion every thing that
deranges the economy of his machine ; he believes all
is in order, as soon as he experiences nothing but
what is suitable to his peculiar mode of existence.
By a necessary consequence of these ideas, man
firmly believes that the entire of nature was made for
him alone; that it was only himself which she had
in view in all her works ; or rather that the powerful
cause to which this nature was subordinate, had only
for object man and his convenience, in all the stupendous effects which are produced in the universe.

If there existed on this earth other thinking beings
besides man, they would fall exactly into similar prejudices with himself; it is a sentiment founded upon
that predilection which each individual necessarily
has for himself; a predilection that will subsist until
reason, aided by experience, in pointing out the
truth, shall have rectified his errors.

17. Soame Jenyns (1704-1787)

'On the Chain of Universal Being' (1782)
From Jenyns, *Works* (London, 1790), vol. 3, 179-185

[179]

DISQUISITION I.

ON THE CHAIN OF UNIVERSAL BEING.

THE farther we inquire into the works of our great Creator, the more evident marks we shall discover of his infinite wisdom and power, and perhaps in none more remarkable, than in that wonderful chain of beings, with which this terrestrial globe is furnished; rising above each other, from the senseless clod, to the brightest genius of human kind, in which, though the chain itself is sufficiently visible, the links, which compose it, are so minute, and so finely wrought, that they are quite imperceptible to our eyes. The various qualities, with which these various beings are endued, we perceive without difficulty, but the boundaries of those qualities, which form this chain of subordination, are so mixed, that where one ends, and the next begins, we are unable

N 2   to

[180]

to discover. The manner by which this is performed, is a subject well worthy of our consideration, though I do not remember to have seen it much considered; but on an accurate examination appears to be this.

In order to diffuse all possible happiness, God has been pleased to fill this earth with innumerable orders of beings, superior to each other in proportion to the qualities and faculties which he has thought proper to bestow upon them; to mere matter he has given extension, solidity, and gravity; to plants, vegetation; to animals, life and instinct; and to man, reason; each of which superior qualities augments the excellence and dignity of the possessor, and places him higher in the scale of universal existence. In all these, it is remarkable, that he has not formed this necessary and beautiful subordination, by placing beings of quite different natures above each other, but by granting some additional quality to each superior order, in conjunction with all those possessed by their inferiors; so that, though

[181]

though they rife above each other in excellence, by means of thefe additional qualities, one mode of exiftence is common to them all, without which they never could have coalefced in one uniform and regular fyftem.

Thus, for inftance, in plants we find all the qualities of mere matter, the only order below them, folidity, extenfion, and gravity, with the addition of vegetation; in animals, all the properties of matter, together with the vegetation of plants, to which is added, life and inftinct; and in man we find all the properties of matter, the vegetation of plants, the life and inftinct of animals, to all which is fuperadded reafon.

That man is endued with thefe properties of all inferior orders, will plainly appear by a flight examination of his compofition; his body is material, and has all the properties of mere matter, folidity, extenfion, and gravity; it is alfo vefted with the quality of plants, that is, a power of vegetation, which it inceffantly exercifes without any knowledge

N 3   or

[182]

or confent of his; it is fown, grows up, expands, comes to maturity, withers, and dies, like all other vegetables: he poffeffes likewife the qualities of lower animals, and fhares their fate; like them, he is called into life without his knowledge or confent; like them, he is compelled by irrefiftible inftincts, to anfwer the purpofes for which he was defigned; like them, he performs his deftined courfe, partakes of its bleffings, and endures its fufferings for a fhort time, then dies, and is feen no more: in him inftinct is not lefs powerful than in them, though lefs vifible, by being confounded with reafon, which it fometimes concurs with, and fometimes counteracts; by this, with the concurrence of reafon, he is taught the belief of a God, of a future ftate, and the difference between moral good and evil; to purfue happinefs, to avoid danger, and to take care of himfelf and his offspring; by this too he is frequently impelled, in contradiction to reafon, to relinquifh eafe and fafety, to traverfe inhofpitable deferts and tempeftuous feas, to inflict and fuffer all the miferies of war, and,

[183]

and, like the herring and the mackarel, to hasten to his own destruction, for the public benefit, which he neither understands or cares for. Thus is this wonderful chain extended from the lowest to the highest order of terrestrial beings, by links so nicely fitted, that the beginning and end of each is invisible to the most inquisitive eye, and yet they altogether compose one vast and beautiful system of subordination.

The manner by which the consummate wisdom of the divine artificer has formed this gradation, so extensive in the whole, and so imperceptible in the parts, is this :— He constantly unites the highest degree of the qualities of each inferior order to the lowest degree of the same qualities, belonging to the order next above it ; by which means, like the colours of a skilful painter, they are so blended together, and shaded off into each other, that no line of distinction is any were to be seen. Thus, for instance, the qualities solidity, extension, and gravity, of

N 4

of

[184]

of mere matter, being united with the lowest degree of vegetation, compose a stone ; from whence this vegetative power ascending through an infinite variety of herbs, flowers, plants, and trees to its greatest perfection in the sensitive plant, joins there the lowest degree of animal life in the shell-fish, which adheres to the rock ; and it is difficult to distinguish which possesses the greatest share, as the one shews it only by shrinking from the finger, and the other by opening to receive the water which surrounds it. In the same manner this animal life rises from this low beginning in the shell-fish, through innumerable species of insects, fishes, birds, and beasts to the confines of reason, where, in the dog, the monkey, and chimpanzè, it unites so closely with the lowest degree of that quality in man, that they cannot easily be distinguished from each other. From this lowest degree in the brutal Hottentot, reason, with the assistance of learning and science, advances, through the various stages

of

[185]

of human underſtanding, which riſe above each other, till in a Bacon or a Newton it attains the ſummit.

Here we muſt ſtop, being unable to pur-ſue the progreſs of this aſtoniſhing chain be-yond the limits of this terreſtrial globe with the naked eye ; but through the perſpective of analogy and conjecture, we may perceive that it aſcends a great deal higher, to the in-habitants of other planets, to angels, and archangels, the loweſt orders of whom may be united by a like eaſy tranſition with the higheſt of our own, in whom to reaſon may be added intuitive knowledge, inſight into futurity, with innumerable other faculties of which we are unable to form the leaſt idea ; through whom it may aſcend, by gradations almoſt infinite, to thoſe moſt exalted of created beings, who are ſeated on the foot-ſtool of the celeſtial throne.

DIS-

18. Joseph Priestley (1733-1804)

Letters to a Philosophical Unbeliever (Bath, 1780)
Pp. 105-125

LETTER IX.

An Examination of Mr. Hume's DIALOGUES on NATURAL RELIGION.

DEAR SIR,

I Am glad to find that you think there is at leaſt ſome appearance of weight in what, at your requeſt, I have urged, in anſwer to the objections againſt the belief of a God and a providence; and I am confident the more attention you give to the ſubject, the ſtronger will thoſe arguments appear, and the more trifling and undeſerving of regard you will think the cavils of atheiſts, ancient or modern. You wiſh, however, to know diſtinctly what I think of *Mr. Hume's poſthumous Dialogues on Natural Religion*; becauſe, coming from a writer of ſome note, that work is frequently a topic of converſation in the ſocieties you frequent.

With

With respect to *Mr. Hume's metaphysical writings* in general, my opinion is, that, on the whole, the world is very little the wiser for them. For though, when the merits of any question were on his side, few men ever wrote with more perspicuity, the arrangement of his thoughts being natural, and his illustrations peculiarly happy; yet I can hardly think that we are indebted to him for the least real advance in the knowledge of the human mind. Indeed, according to his own very frank confession, his object was mere *literary reputation**. It was not the *pursuit of truth*, or the advancement of virtue and happiness; and it was much more easy to make a figure by disturbing the systems of others, than by erecting any of his own. All schemes have their respective weak sides, which a man who has nothing of his own to risk may more easily find, and expose.

In many of his *Essays* (which, in general, are excessively wire-drawn) Mr. Hume seems to have had nothing in view but to *amuse*

* See his Life, written by himself, p. 32, 33.

his readers, which he generally does agreeably enough; proposing doubts to received hypotheses, leaving them without any solution, and altogether unconcerned about it. In short, he is to be considered in these *Essays* as a mere *writer* or *declaimer*, even more than Cicero in his book of Tusculan Questions,

He seems not to have given himself the trouble so much as to read *Dr. Hartley's Observations on Man*, a work which he could not but have heard of, and which it certainly behoved him to study. The doctrine of *association of ideas*, as explained and extended by Dr. Hartley, supplies materials for the most satisfactory solution of almost all the difficulties he has started, as I could easily shew if I thought it of any consequence; so that to a person acquainted with this theory of the human mind, *Hume's Essays* appear the merest trifling. Compared with Dr. Hartley, I consider Mr. Hume as not even a child.

Now, I will frankly tell you, that this last performance of Mr. Hume has by no means changed favour of the theift, the victory is clearly on the fide of the atheift. I therefore fhall not be furprifed if this work fhould have a confiderable effect in promoting the caufe of atheifm, with thofe whofe *general turn of thinking*, and *habits of life*, make them no ill-wifhers to that fcheme.

To fatisfy your wifhes, I fhall recite what I think has moft of the appearance of ftrength, or plaufibility, in what Mr. Hume has advanced on the atheiftical fide of the queftion, though it will necefarily lead me to repeat fome things that I have obferved already; but I fhall endeavour to do it in fuch a manner, that you will not deem it quite idle and ufelefs repetition.

With refpect to the general argument for the being of God, from the marks of defign in the univerfe, he fays, p. 65, " Will any " man tell me, with a ferious countenance, " that an orderly univerfe muft arife from " fome thought and art, like the human, " becaufe we have experience of it. To
afcertain

changed for the better the idea I had before formed of him as a metaphyfical writer. The dialogue is ingenioufly and artfully conducted. Philo, who evidently fpeaks the fentiments of the writer, is not made to fay all the good things that are advanced, his opponents are not made to fay any thing that is very palpably abfurd, and every thing is made to pafs with great decency and decorum.

But though Philo, in the moft interefting part of the debate, advances nothing but common-place objections againft the belief of a God, and hackneyed declamation againft the plan of providence, his antagonifts are feldom reprefented as making any fatisfactory reply. And when, at the laft, evidently to fave appearances, he relinquifhes the argument, on which he had expatiated with fo much triumph, it is without alledging any fufficient reafon; fo that his arguments are left, as no doubt the writer intended, to have their full effect on the mind of the reader. And though the debate feemingly clofes in favour

" ascertain this reasoning, it were requisite
" that we had experience of the origin of
" worlds, and it is not sufficient, surely, that
" we have seen ships and cities arise from
" human art and contrivance."

Now, if it be admitted that there are marks of design in the universe, as numberless fitnesses of things to things prove beyond all dispute, is it not a necessary consequence, that if it had a cause at all, it must be one that is capable of design? Will any person say that an eye could have been constructed by a being who had no knowledge of optics, who did not know the nature of light, or the laws of refraction? And must not the universe have had a cause, as well as any thing else, that is finite and incapable of comprehending itself?

We might just as reasonably say, that any particular ship, or city, any particular horse, or man, had nothing existing superior to it, as that the visible universe had nothing superior to it, if the universe be no more capable

of comprehending itself than a ship, or a city, a horse, or a man. There can be no charm in the words *world* or *universe*, so that they should require no cause when they stand in precisely the same predicament with other things that evidently *do* require a superior cause, and could not have existed without one.

All that Mr. Hume says on the difficulty of stopping at the idea of an uncaused being, is on the supposition that this uncaused being is a *finite one*, incapable of comprehending itself, and, therefore, in the same predicament with a ship or a house, a horse or a man, which it is impossible to conceive to have existed without a superior cause. " How " shall we satisfy ourselves," says he, p. 93, &c. " concerning the cause of that being " whom you suppose the author of nature.— " If we stop and go no farther, why go so far, " why not stop at the material world. How " can we satisfy ourselves without going on in " infinitum.—By supposing it to contain the " principle of order within itself, we really " assert

" affert it to be God, and the fooner we ar-
" rive at that Divine Being, fo much the
" better. When you go one ftep beyond
" the mundane fyftem, you only excite an
" inquifitive humour, which it is impoffible
" ever to fatisfy."

It is very true, that no perfon can fatisfy himfelf with going backwards *in infinitum* from one thing that requires a fuperior caufe, to another that equally requires a fuperior caufe. But any perfon may be fufficiently fatisfied with going back through finite caufes as far as he has evidence of the exiftence of intermediate finite caufes; and then, feeing that it is abfurd to go on *in infinitum* in this manner, to conclude that, whether he can comprehend it or not, there *muft* be fome *uncaufed intelligent being*, the original and defigning caufe of all other beings. For other-wife, what we *fee* and *experience* could not have exifted. It is true that we cannot conceive *how* this fhould be, but we are able to acquiefce in this ignorance, becaufe there is no *contradiction* in it.

He

"He fays, p. 15, " Motion, in many in-
" ftances from gravity, from elafticity, from
" electricity, begins in matter without any
" known voluntary agent; and to fuppofe
" always in thefe cafes an unknown voluntary
" agent, is mere hypothefis, and hypothefis
" attended with no advantage." He alfo fays,
" p. 118, " Why may not motion have been pro-
" pagated by impulfe through all eternity?"

I will admit that the powers of gravity, elafticity, and electricity, might have been in bodies from all eternity, without any fupe-rior caufe, if the bodies in which we find them were capable of knowing that they had fuch powers, of that *defign* which has proportioned them to one another, and of combining them in the wonderful and ufeful manner in which they are actually propor-tioned and combined in nature. But when I fee that they are as evidently incapable of this as I am of properly producing a plant or an animal, I am under a neceffity of looking for a higher caufe; and I cannot reft till I come to a being *effentially different* from all vifible beings

I

beings whatever, so as not to be in the predicament that they are in, of requiring a superior cause. Also, if motion could have been in the universe without any cause, it must have been in consequence of bodies being possessed of the power of *gravity*, &c. from eternity, without a cause. But as they could not have had those powers without communication from a superior and intelligent being, capable of proportioning them, in the exact and useful manner in which they are possessed, the thing is manifestly *impossible*.

What Mr. Hume says with respect to the *origin of the world* in the following paragraph, which I think unworthy of a philosopher, and miserably trifling on so serious a subject, goes intirely upon the idea of the supreme cause resembling such beings as do themselves require a superior cause, and not (which, however, *must* be the case) a being that can have no superior in wisdom or power. I, therefore, think it requires no particular animadversion.

"Many

"Many worlds," he says p. 106, "might "have been botched and bungled throughout "an eternity ere this system was struck out, "much labour lost, many fruitless trials "made, and a flow, but continued improve- "ment, carried on during infinite ages in the "art of world making."

"A man who follows your hypothesis," p. 111, "is able perhaps to assert, or con- "jecture, that the universe some time arose "from something like design; but beyond "that position he cannot ascertain one single "circumstance, and is left afterwards to fix "every point of his theology by the utmost "licence of fancy and hypothesis. This "world, for ought we know, is very faulty "and imperfect, compared to a superior "standard, and was only the first rude essay "of some infant deity, who afterwards aban- "doned it, ashamed of his own performance. "It is the work only of some dependent "inferior deity, and is the object of derision "to his superiors. It is the production of "old age and dotage, in some superannuated

I 2   " deity,

" deity, and ever since his death has run on
" at adventures, from the first impulse and
" active force, which it received from him."

In reading *Mr. Hume's life*, written by himself, one might be surprised to find no mention of a *God*, or of a *providence*, which conducted him through it; but this cannot be any longer wonderful, when we find that, for any thing he certainly believed to the contrary, he himself might be the most considerable being in the universe. His maker, if he had any, was either a careless playful infant, a trifling forgetful dotard, or was, perhaps, dead and buried, without leaving any other to take care of his affairs. All that he believed of his maker was, that he was capable of *something like design*, but of his own comprehensive intellectual powers he could have no doubt,

Neither can we think it at all extraordinary that Mr. Hume should have recourse to *amusing books* in the last period of his life, when he considered the author of nature himself

himself as never having had any serious object in view, and when he neither left any thing behind him, nor had any thing before him, that was deserving of his care. How can it be supposed that the man, who scrupled not to ridicule his maker, should consider the human race, or the world, in any other light than as objects of ridicule, or pity. And well satisfied might he be to have been so fortunate in his passage through the world, and his easy escape out of it, when it was deserted by its maker, and was continually exposed to some unforeseen and dreadful catastrophe. How poor a consolation, however, must have been his *literary fame*, with such gloomy prospects as these!

What Mr. Hume says with respect to the deficiency in the proof of the *proper infinity* of the divine attributes, and of a probable *multiplicity of deities*, all goes on the same idea, viz. that the ultimate cause of the universe is such a being as must himself require a superior cause; whereas, nothing can be more evident, how incomprehensible soever it may be,

I 3

be, than that the being which has existed from eternity, and is the cause of all that does exist, must be one that *cannot* have a superior, and, therefore, must be infinite in knowledge and power, and consequently, as I have endeavoured to shew before, can be but *one*.

" As the cause," he says, p. 104, " ought " only to be proportioned to the effect, and " the effect, so far as it falls under our cog-" nizance, is not infinite, what pretensions " have we to ascribe that attribute to the " Divine Being ?—By sharing the work " among several we may so much farther " limit the attributes of each, and get rid of " that extensive power and knowledge which " must be supposed in one deity."—This I think unworthy of a philosopher on so grave and interesting a subject.

It is owing to the same inattention to this one consideration, that, in order to get rid of the idea of a supreme intelligent cause of all things, Mr. Hume urges the superior pro-bability

bability of the universe resembling a *plant*, or an *animal*. " If the universe," says he, p. 129, " bears a greater likeness to animal bo-" dies, and to vegetables, than to the works of " human art, it is more probable that its cause " resembles the cause of the former than that " of the latter; and its origin ought rather to " be ascribed to generation, or vegetation, " than to reason or design."

On this, Demea, the orthodox speaker, very properly observes, p. 137, " Whence could " arise so wonderful a faculty but from de-" sign, or how can order spring from any " thing which perceives not that order which " it bestows." In reply to which Philo contents himself with saying, ib. " A tree " bestows order, and organization, on that " tree which springs from it, without know-" ing the order; an animal, in the same man-" ner, on its offspring," and p. 140, " Judging " by our limited and imperfect experience, " generation has some privileges above rea-" son; for we see every day the latter to arise " from

I 4

" from the former, never the former from the " latter."

Manifestly unsatisfactory as this reply is, nothing is advanced in answer to it by either of the other disputants. But it is obvious to remark, that, if an animal has marks of design in its construction, a design which itself cannot comprehend, it hardly possible for any person to imagine that it was originally produced without a power superior to itself, and capable of comprehending its structure, though he was not himself present at the original formation of it, and, therefore, could not see it. Can we possibly believe that any particular *horse* that we know, originated without a superior cause? Equally impossible is it to believe, that the *species of horses* should have existed without a superior cause.

How little then does it avail Mr. Hume to say, p. 135, that " reason, instinct, genera-" tion, vegetation, are similar to each other, " and the causes of similar effects;" as if *instinct, generation,* and *vegetation,* did not necessarily

cessarily imply *design,* or reason, as the cause of them. He might with equal reason have placed other powers in nature, as *gravity, elasticity,* &c. in the same rank with these; whereas all these must equally have proceeded from reason, or design, and could not have had any existence independent of it. For design is conspicuous in all those powers, and especially in the proportion and distribution of them.

Pursuing the analogy of plants and animals, he says, p. 152, " In like manner as a " tree sheds its seeds into the neighbouring " fields, and produces other trees; so the " great vegetable the world, or this planetary " system, produces within itself certain seeds, " which being scattered into the surrounding " chaos, vegetate into new worlds. A comet, " for instance, is the seed of a world, and " after it has been fully ripened by passing " from sun to sun, and star to star, it is at " last tossed into the unformed elements, " which every where surround this universe, " and

122   LETTERS TO A

" and immediately fprouts up into a new
" fyftem."

" Or, if we fhould fuppofe this world to
" be an *animal*, a comet is the *egg* of this
" animal ; and in like manner as an oftrich
" lays its egg in the fand, which, without
" any farther care, hatches the egg, and pro-
" duces a new animal ; fo ———— Does not a
" plant or an animal," p. 134, " which
" fprings from vegetation or generation, bear
" a ftronger refemblance to the world, than
" does any artificial machine, which arifes
" from reafon and defign ?"

Had any friend of religion advanced an
idea fo completely abfurd as this, what would
not Mr. Hume have faid to turn it into ridicule. With juft as much probability might
he have faid that Glafgow grew from a feed
yielded by Edinburgh, or that London and
Edinburgh, marrying, by natural generation,
produced York, which lies between them.
With much more probability might he have
faid that *pamphlets* are the productions of
large

PHILOSOPHICAL UNBELIEVER.   123

large *books*, that *boats* are young *fhips*, and
that *piftols* will grow into great *guns*; and
that either there never were any firft towns,
books, fhips, or guns, or that, if there were,
they had no makers.

How it could come into any man's head
to imagine that a thing fo complex as this
world, confifting of land and water, earths
and metals, plants and animals, &c. &c. &c.
fhould produce a feed, or egg, containing
within it the elements of all its innumerable
parts, is beyond my power of conception.

What muft have been that man's knowledge of philofophy and nature, who could
fuppofe for a moment, that a comet could
poffibly be the feed of a world? Do comets
fpring from worlds, carrying with them the
feeds of all the plants, &c. that they contain? Do comets travel from fun to fun, or
from ftar to ftar? By what force are they
toffed into the *unformed elements*, which
Mr. Hume fuppofes every where to furround
the univerfe? What are thofe elements?
and

and what evidence has he of their exiftence? or, fuppofing the comet to arrive among them, whence could arife its power of vegetating into a new fyftem?

What Mr. Hume objects to the arguments for the *benevolence* of the deity is fuch mere cavilling, and admits of fuch eafy anfwers, that I am furprifed that a man whofe fole object was even *literary reputation* fhould have advanced it.

" The caufe of nature, p. 186, " tends " not to human or animal felicity, therefore " it is not eftablifhed for that purpofe." He might as well have faid that *health* is not agreeable to the ends of nature, as that en-joyment and *happinefs* is not, fince the one is the neceffary confequence of the other. " It " is contrary," he fays, in fact, p. 193, " to " every one's feeling and experience to main-" tain a continued exiftence in this world to " be eligible and defirable. It is contrary " to an authority fo eftablifhed as nothing " can fubvert." And yet almoft all animals and

and all men *do* defire life, and, according to his own account, his own life was a fin-gularly happy and enviable one.

" You muft prove," p. 195, " thefe pure " unmixed and uncontrollable attributes from " the prefent mixed and confufed pheno-" mena, and from thefe alone : a hopeful un-" dertaking." If *evil* was not, in a thoufand ways, neceffarily connected with, and fub-fervient to *good*, the undertaking would be hopelefs, but not otherwife.

" It feems plainly poffible," p. 205, " to " carry on the bufinefs of life without any " pain. Why then is any animal ever rendered " fufceptible of fuch a fenfation?" But pain, *as fuch*, we have feen to be excellently ufeful, as a guard againft more pain, and greater evils; and no man can pretend to fay that the fame end *could* have been attained by any other means.

19. William Paley (1743-1805)

Natural Theology; or Evidences of the Existence and Attributes of the Deity, collected from the Appearances of Nature (London, 1802)
From the 19th edition (London, 1819), pp. 69-71, 212-219

CHAPTER VI.

THE ARGUMENT CUMULATIVE.

WERE there no example in the world, of contrivance, except that of the *eye*, it would be alone sufficient to support the conclusion which we draw from it, as to the necessity of an intelligent Creator. It could never be got rid of; because it could not be accounted for by any other supposition, which did not contradict all the principles we possess of knowledge; the principles, according to which, things do, as often as they can be brought to the test of experience, turn out to be true or false. Its coats and humours, constructed, as the lenses of a telescope are constructed, for the refraction of rays of light to a point, which forms the proper action of the organ; the provision in its muscular tendons for turning its pupil to the object, similar to that which is given to the telescope by screws, and upon which power of direction in the eye, the exercise of its office as an optical instrument depends: the further provision for its defence, for its constant lubricity and moisture; which we see in its socket and its lids, in its gland for the secretion of the matter of tears, its outlet or communication with the nose for carrying off the liquid after the eye is washed with it; these provisions compose

70   THE ARGUMENT CUMULATIVE.

altogether an apparatus, a system of parts, a preparation of means, so manifest in their design, so exquisite in their contrivance, so successful in their
issue, so precious, and so infinitely beneficial in
their use, as, in my opinion, to bear down all doubt
that can be raised upon the subject.   And what I
wish, under the title of the present chapter, to observe is, that if other parts of nature were inaccessi-
ble to our inquiries, or even if other parts of nature
presented nothing to our examination but disorder
and confusion, the validity of this example would
remain the same.   If there were but one watch in
the world, it would not be less certain that it had a
maker.   If we had never in our lives seen any but
one single kind of hydraulic machine, yet, if of that
one kind, we understood the mechanism and use,
we should be as perfectly assured that it proceeded
from the hand, and thought, and skill, of a work-
man, as if we visited a museum of the arts, and saw
collected there twenty different kinds of machines
for drawing water, or a thousand different kinds for
other purposes.   Of this point, each machine is a
proof, independently of all the rest.   So it is with
the evidences of a Divine agency.   The proof is
not a conclusion which lies at the end of a chain of
reasoning, of which chain each instance of contrivance is only a link, and of which, if one link fail,
the whole falls; but it is an argument separately
supplied by every separate example.   An error in
stating an example, affects only that example.   The
argument is cumulative, in the fullest sense of that
term.   The eye proves it without the ear; the ear

THE ARGUMENT CUMULATIVE. 71

without the eye. The proof in each example is complete; for when the design of the part, and the conduciveness of its structure to that design is shown, the mind may set itself at rest; no future consideration can detract any thing from the force of the example.

[p. 212]

CHAPTER XIV.

PROSPECTIVE CONTRIVANCES.

I can hardly imagine to myself a more distinguishing mark, and consequently a more certain proof of design, than *preparation*, *i. e.* the providing of things beforehand which are not to be used until a considerable time afterwards; for this implies a contemplation of the future, which belongs only to intelligence.

Of these *prospective* contrivances, the bodies of animals furnish various examples.

I. The human teeth afford an instance, not only of prospective contrivance, but of the completion of the contrivance being designedly suspended. They are formed within the gums, and there they stop; the fact being, that their further advance to maturity would not only be useless to the new-born animal, but extremely in its way; as it is evident that the act of *sucking*, by which it is for some time to be nourished, will be performed with more ease both to the nurse and to the infant, whilst the inside of the mouth, and edges of the gums, are smooth and soft, than if set with hard pointed bones. By the time they are wanted, the teeth are ready. They have been lodged within the gums for some months past, but detained, as it were in their sockets, so long as their further protrusion would interfere with the office to which the mouth is destined. Nature, namely, that intelligence which was employed in creation, looked beyond the first year of the infant's life; yet, whilst she was providing for functions which were after that term to become necessary, was careful not to incommode those which preceded them. What renders it more probable that this is the effect of design, is, that the teeth are imperfect, whilst all other parts of the mouth are perfect. The lips are perfect, the tongue is perfect; the cheeks, the jaws, the palate, the pharynx, the larynx, are all perfect; the teeth alone are not so. This is the fact with respect to the human mouth: the fact also is, that the parts above enumerated are called into use from the beginning; whereas the teeth would be only so many obstacles and annoyances, if they were there. When a contrary order is necessary, a contrary order prevails. In the worm of the beetle, as hatched from the egg, the teeth are the first things which arrive at perfection. The insect begins to gnaw as soon as it escapes from the shell, though its other parts be only gradually advancing to their maturity.

What has been observed of the teeth is true of the *horns* of animals, and for the same reason. The horn of a calf or a lamb does not bud, or at least does not sprout to any considerable length, until the animal be capable of browsing upon its pasture; because such a substance upon the forehead of the young animal, would very much incommode the teat of the dam in the office of giving suck.

But in the case of the *teeth,*—of the human teeth at least, the prospective contrivance looks still further. A succession of crops is provided, and provided from the beginning; a second tier being originally formed beneath the first, which do not come into use till several years afterwards. And this double or suppletory provision meets a difficulty in the mechanism of the mouth, which would have appeared almost insurmountable. The expansion of the jaw (the consequence of the proportionable growth of the animal, and of its skull), necessarily separates the teeth of the first set, however compactly disposed, to a distance from one another, which would be very inconvenient. In due time, therefore, *i. e.* when the jaw has attained a great part of its dimensions, a new set of teeth springs up (loosening and pushing out the old ones before them), more exactly fitted to the space which they are to occupy, and rising also in such close ranks, as to allow for any extension of line which the subsequent enlargement of the head may occasion.

II. It is not very easy to conceive a more evidently prospective contrivance than that which, in all viviparous animals, is found in the *milk* of the female parent. At the moment the young animal enters the world, there is its maintenance ready for it. The particulars to be remarked in the economy are neither few nor slight. We have the first nutritious quality of the fluid, unlike, in this respect, every other excretion of the body : and in which nature hitherto remains unimitated, neither cookery nor chymistry having been able to make milk out of grass; we have, secondly, the organ for its reception and retention; we have, thirdly, the excretory duct annexed to that organ; and we have, lastly, the determination of the milk to the breast, at the particular juncture when it is about to be wanted. We have all these properties in the subject before us; and they are all indications of design. The last circumstance is the strongest of any. If I had been to guess before-hand, I should have conjectured, that at the time when there was an extraordinary demand for nourishment in one part of the system there would be the least likelihood of a redundancy to supply another part. The advanced pregnancy of the female has no intelligible tendency to fill the breasts with milk. The lacteal system is a constant wonder ; and it adds to other causes of our admiration, that the number of the teats or paps in each species is found to bear a proportion to the number of the young. In the sow, the

216   PROSPECTIVE CONTRIVANCES.

bitch, the rabbit, the cat, the rat, which have numerous litters, the paps are numerous, and are
disposed along the whole length of the belly: in
the cow and mare, they are few. The most simple account of this, is to refer it to a designing
Creator.

BUT, in the argument before us, we are entitled
to consider not only animal bodies when framed,
but the circumstances under which they are framed: and in this view of the subject, the constitution of many of their parts is most strictly prospective.

III. The eye is of no use at the time when it is
formed. It is an optical instrument made in a dun-
geon; constructed for the refraction of light to a
focus, and perfect for its purpose before a ray of
light has had access to it; geometrically adapted
to the properties and action of an element with
which it has no communication. It is about indeed
to enter into that communication; and this is precisely the thing which evidences intention. It is
providing for the *future* in the closest sense which
can be given to these terms; for it is providing for
a future change, not for the then-subsisting condition of the animal, nor for any gradual progress or
advance in that same condition, but for a new state,
the consequence of a great and sudden alteration,
which the animal is to undergo at its birth. Is it to
be believed that the eye was formed, or, which is
the same thing, that the series of causes was fixed
by which the eye is formed, without a view to this

5

PROSPECTIVE CONTRIVANCES. 217

change; without a prospect of that condition, in which its fabric, of no use at present, is about to be of the greatest; without a consideration of the qualities of that element, hitherto entirely excluded, but with which it was hereafter to hold so intimate a relation. A young man makes a pair of spectacles for himself against he grows old; for which spectacles he has no want or use whatever at the time he makes them. Could this be done without knowing and considering the defect of vision to which advanced age is subject? Would not the precise suitableness of the instrument to its purpose, of the remedy to the defect, of the convex lens to the flattened eye, establish the certainty of the conclusion, that the case, afterwards to arise, had been considered beforehand, speculated upon, provided for? all which are exclusively the acts of a reasoning mind. The eye formed in one state, for use only in another state, and in a different state, affords a proof no less clear of destination to a future purpose, and a proof proportionably stronger, as the machinery is more complicated, and the adaptation more exact.

IV. What has been said of the eye holds equally true of the lungs. Composed of air-vessels, where there is no air; elaborately constructed for the alternate admission and expulsion of an elastic fluid, where no such fluid exists; this great organ, with the whole apparatus belonging to it, lies collapsed in the fœtal thorax, yet in order, and in readiness for action, the first moment that the occasion requires its service. This is having a machine locked up in store for future use: which incontestably proves, that the case was expected to occur, in which this use might be experienced : but expectation is the proper act of intelligence. Considering the state in which an animal exists before its birth, I should look for nothing less in its body than a system of lungs. It is like finding a pair of bellows in the bottom of the sea ; of no sort of use in the situation in which they are found ; formed for an action which was impossible to be exerted ; holding no relation or fitness to the element which surrounds them, but both to another element in another place.

As part and parcel of the same plan, ought to be mentioned, in speaking of the lungs, the provisionary contrivances of *foramen ovale* and *ductus arteriosus.* In the fœtus, pipes are laid for the passage of the blood through the lungs ; but, until the lungs be inflated by the inspiration of air, that passage is impervious, or in a great degree obstructed. What then is to be done ? what would an artist, what would a master do upon the occasion ? He would endeavour, most probably, to provide a *temporary* passage, which might carry on the communication required, until the other was open. Now this is the thing which is actually done in the heart : instead of the circuitous route through the lungs, which the blood afterwards takes before it get from one auricle of the heart to the other, a portion of the blood passes immediately from the right auricle to the left, through a hole placed in the partition which separates these cavities. This hole anatomists call the *foramen ovale.* There is likewise an-

PROSPECTIVE CONTRIVANCES. 219

other cross cut answering the same purpose, by what is called the *ductus arteriosus*, lying between the pulmonary artery and the aörta. But both expedients are so strictly temporary, that after birth the one passage is closed, and the tube which forms the other shrivelled up into a ligament. If this be not contrivance, what is?

But, forasmuch as the action of the air upon the blood in the lungs appears to be necessary to the perfect concoction of that fluid, *i. e.* to the life and health of the animal (otherwise the shortest route might still be the best), how comes it to pass that the *fœtus* lives, and grows, and thrives, without it? The answer is, that the blood of the fœtus is the mother's; that it has undergone that action in her habit; that one pair of lungs serves for both. When the animals are separated, a new necessity arises; and to meet this necessity as soon as it occurs an organization is prepared. It is ready for its purpose; it only waits for the atmosphere; it begins to play the moment the air is admitted to it.

20. Joseph Townsend (1739-1816)

The Character of Moses Established for Veracity as an Historian Recording Events from the Creation to the Deluge (Bath, 1813)
Title page, pp. 94-96, 398-403, 430-436

THE

CHARACTER OF MOSES

ESTABLISHED FOR VERACITY AS AN HISTORIAN,

RECORDING EVENTS

From the Creation to the Deluge

BY THE REV. JOSEPH TOWNSEND, M. A. RECTOR OF PEWSEY, WILTS.

BATH:

PRINTED BY M. GYE, MARKET-PLACE,

AND PUBLISHED BY LONGMAN, HURST, REES, ORME AND BROWN, PATERNOSTER-ROW, LONDON.

1813.

[p. 94]

SUBJECT VI.

OF THE DELUGE.

TRADITIONAL reports of an universal Deluge have been diffused and noticed in every nation upon earth. Yet these reports, whilst they agree as to the fact, are so various, and attended with such improbable circumstances, they carry with them such evident marks of fiction, that, although we remain persuaded of the general truth, we are compelled to disregard particulars, and to search for authentic records, by which we may gain more perfect information as to the nature and extent, the causes and consequences of this wonderful event.

The *Chinese* and *Japanese* annually celebrate their feast of waters, in which they traverse the rivers in their gondolas, crying " Peirun, " Peirun."

This *Peirun* was a wise and virtuous king, whose throne was established in a very fertile island, and whose subjects became so vicious, that they drew down the vengeance of heaven, in consequence of which

95

the island was swallowed up by the sea. The prince, however, favoured by the gods, and forewarned of the dire event, saved himself and family in a ship, and having sailed to another country, disappeared, leaving no traces of himself behind.*

Among the *American* Indians, who are settled near Churchill River on the North-West coast of Hudson's Bay, we find the worship of two superior beings; the one good, the other evil. Of these, Ukkemah, the good deity, made the first parents of mankind; three males, and as many females, of different colours.

With this imperfect account of the origin of the human race, these savages retain traditional reports of the deluge, but here they substitute a beaver for the dove.†

In *Greenland* a mutilated tradition of the deluge has been noticed by Crantz, in which it is stated, that the world was overset, and that all mankind, except one, were drowned. Father Lafitau has given us a similar tradition, as preserved among the IROQUOIS INDIANS of North America, and Clavigero assures us that the MEXICANS had some notion of the same event.

Similar traditions prevailed among the nations of ancient Europe. This appears in Josephus, who quotes from Berosus, from Nicholas of Damascus, and from an Egyptian author, who wrote the Phœnician Antiquities.

To illustrate the same event, Eusebius quotes Abydenus, and Cyril refers to Alexander Polyhistor. Plato makes mention of a *general*

* Kempfer's Hist. of Japan. † Phil. Trans. vol. 60, p. 129.

96

deluge, and Plutarch speaks of a dove sent out from the ark by Deucalion.   Ovid certainly represents his deluge as universal, and ascribes to Deucalion the character which belongs to Noah, and, like Moses, the Roman poet states, that the human race was thus punished for their incorrigible wickedness.

Traditional reports have been collected and brought forwards by every apologist for revelation, from the first ages of Christianity to the present day, and may be referred to in Stillingfleet, Gale, and Ramsay: but independently of divine authority, the most convincing evidence is to be sought for in the records which remain engraved in the deepest mines, and on the most elevated mountains.

In the display I am about to make of this natural evidence, scattered over the surface of the earth, I shall simply state my facts, and then examine what inferences may fairly be derived from them. And for this purpose, I shall first explore one small tract of country, that the attention of the young geologist may not be distracted by a multiplicity of objects crowding at once upon his view.   When he has surveyed this island, he may be the better qualified for more distant excursions, and be able to compare its strata and extraneous fossils with those of every other portion of the globe.   He will be thus prepared to follow me in my general conclusion, and will be convinced that the Mosaic account of the deluge is agreeable to truth.

★   ★   ★   ★

[p. 398]

GEOLOGICAL CHRONOMETERS.

M. DE LUC, to whom geology is indebted for more numerous facts, than have ever been presented to the world, before he brought them forward to our view, is the first philosopher, who thought of looking to this habitable earth itself for the record of its birth.   He has examined, with more than common sagacity, numerous physical chronometers, and demonstrated, that these agree with revelation. By. their means we may ascertain the era of the grand revolution, which has happened to our globe, and bring it, as nearly as it is requisite, to that, which Moses himself assigned to this marvelous event.

In all his labours, his principal object has been to promote the happiness of men by the confirmation of their hopes, and he was well aware, that this purpose will be effectually answered by the examination of these natural chronometers, which cannot possibly deceive us.

Deltas, at the mouths of rivers, may be regarded as the first of these, because we cannot refer beyond a given time the date of their commencement.   Such accretions I particularly remarked in

399

my Spanish travels at the mouth of the Ebro, and such, from re-mote antiquity, have been noticed at the mouths of the Nile.

The *great lakes* exhibit similar accretions at the entrance of rivers into them. Thus it is in the Lake of Geneva, as particularly noticed by M. de Luc. This forms an excellent chronometer. For had our continents existed, myriads of ages before the time assigned by Moses for the Deluge; the Lake of Geneva, had been long since, filled with the sediments of its waters and had become one exten-sive plain; because not an atom of this sediment either escapes out of the lake, or is deposited at any considerable distance from its entrance into it. The Rhone, at its departure from Geneva, having deposited all its impurities, is perfectly limpid, and, although thirty feet deep, does not appear to have the depth of thirty inches.

Lesser lakes have been successively filled, and have been con-verted first into marshes and then into meadows. M. de Luc has given in the first volume of his Geological Travels, a most interest-ing description of numerous lakes in Mecklenburg and Sleswigh, which in process of time have become dry meadows.

He remarks, that in this conversion, reeds are the most power-ful agents, and in the progress of conversion always form the van. The reason is obvious, for it is universally observed, that they raise themselves above the water, from a greater depth, than any other aquatic plant. In the second zone we find scirpus cæspitosus, scirpus maritimus, scirpus pauciflorus eriophorum polystaehyon, eriophorum vaginatum, equisetum palustre, equisetum fluviatile and equisetum hyemale, with numerous bog plants.

400

Among the plants which appear in proportion as the mass becomes more solid, are, ledum palustre, vaccinium oxycoccos, comarum palustre, erica tetralix, and some of the aquatic grasses, then the poas and the meadow plants.

When the sphagnum palustre has established itself in wet land above a bed of clay; *peat* begins to grow, and constantly increases. Near Lough Erne, at Sir James Caldwell's, I saw an extensive bed of peat, ten feet in thickness, covering a Roman pavement; and M. de Luc refers us to one in the Duvels Moer, near Bremen, which is forty feet thick, black in the bottom, and, when dry, resembles coal, both in its fracture and in its combustibility.*

The old people near the Baltic remember lakes, which, having been filled with peat, are become good meadow land; and, when sand has been driven by the wind over their surface, have been converted into rich arable land.

These peat meads, therefore, are good chronometers, because the lesser lakes have been long since filled, and the greater lakes are in the act of being filled.

Such likewise are *bays* and *creeks*, because these, in process of time, become choaked with sand or slime, and are converted into marshes. This operation is regularly and constantly proceeding, and its progress will assist us to establish infallible chronometers.

It is well known that navigable rivers, like the Thames, require constant attention, and very expensive operations to preserve them

* Geol. Travels, vol. I.

401

free from shoals. It is equally notorious, that bays and harbours, if neglected, become dangerous to navigation, and are at last filled up to such a degree, as to be no longer bays, but sea beaches, covered only by high tides.

Estuaries are certainly among the best chronometers, because as long as the present continents have subsisted, so long have the waters of the sea and of the land united to replenish them, and to convert them into salt marshes. In consequence of this operation, cities which, like Truro, in Cornwall, once were sea-ports, now carry on their trade in small craft; and others, which formerly were accessible at all times, are now, like Mevagizey, dependent on the tides, and at low water see all their vessels laid dry upon the strand. In process of time Mevagizey will be reduced to the same state with Truro, and every estuary will cease to feel the influence of tides.

In conformity with these observations of M. de Luc, are those of Dr. Jameson, who says—In the Baltic many bays, which were navigable within the memory of man, are now filled and covered with grass. Several harbours in Lapland, that formerly admitted vessels, are now between three and four thousand paces from the sea; and at Helsingor are iron works, in places which were covered by the sea about eighty years ago. The whole of the ancient kingdom of Prussia appears to have been formed in this manner. It is said that the sea reached as far as Culm within the period of human history, and the city of Dantzic, several hundred years ago, was close to the sea shore.

3 f

402

Drift sands, in given circumstances, form good chronometers. For this observation we are indebted to M. de Luc, the younger, who, describing the operation of the Lybian sands, which, driven over the Western borders of the Nile, cover the most elevated structures of villages and cities with their surrounding plains, observes— " These sands, anciently far remote from Egypt, now doom to sterility " a land which was once remarkable for its fertility." If, then, our continents were as ancient as Dr. Hutton represents them to be, no traces of the habitation of man would appear on the Western margin of the Nile. When Egypt was the granary of the East, and fed the Western provinces of Asia, these Lybian sands had not approached her borders.

Bordering upon Egypt we find another chronometer. For when Alexandria was the emporium of the world, the navigation of the red sea was not attended with danger on its coasts, nor were its ports blocked up with reefs of *coral*. But now shoals have progressively increased, and in process of time the Isis ochrasia, with other zoophytes, will wholly obstruct the navigation of this gulf. The *reefs*, therefore, formed by the numerous genera of zoophytes, are a good chronometer.

Mouldering cliffs are excellent chronometers. Each has an accumulation of fragments constantly rising against the scarp. This in time will vanish, and instead of cliffs there will be hills, occupied by woods, by pasture, or by tillage. Were the continents as ancient as Dr. Hutton conceived them to be, there would be now no cliffs, and the whole earth had long since arrived at its quiescent state.

403

From all these chronometers, consisting in effects, which result from known causes, operating since the existence of our continents, and of which the progress within known times are indicated by monuments, we may safely draw this conclusion, that our continents are not of a more remote antiquity than has been assigned to them by the sacred historian in the beginning of his Pentateuch.

★　　★　　★　　★

[p. 430]

X.—The science of geology becomes of infinite importance, when we consider it as connected with our immortal hopes.　These depend on the truth of revelation, and the whole system of revealed religion is ultimately connected with the veracity of Moses.

The divine legation of Christ and of the Jewish Lawgiver must stand or fall together.　If the Mosaic account of the creation and of the deluge is true, and consequently the promises recorded by him well founded, we may retain our hopes; but, should the former be given up as false, we must renounce the latter.

It has been objected to his account of the deluge, that had the whole atmosphere been converted into rain, it could have raised the water only thirty feet, the height to which a column of water can be raised by the pressure of the atmosphere.　This therefore would not have

431

been sufficient to reach the summits of our most moderate hills.—
Mathematicians have even calculated with much labor how many
oceans of water would be required to cover the tops of our most
lofty mountains, and have perplexed themselves with difficulties of
their own creating. But when we consider that the fountains of the
great deep were broken up, and that the ocean poured its whole
contents upon the earth, it must be clear to us, that a sufficient
quantity of water could not be wanting for the destruction of a guilty
world.

The description of Moses, short as it is, corresponds exactly with
the phœnomena produced by this grand convulsion. The accounts
we have received of volcanic eruptions, exhibit a deluge in miniature,
with its occasional causes and consequent effects. These are commonly attended by incessant rain; the fountains of the great deep are
broken up; the waters overflow; and in their retreat they have been
observed *going* and *returning* by alternations, as particularly noticed
at Kingston, in Jamaica, at Callao, and more recently at Lisbon.
This part of the subject has been so skilfully handled by Whitehurst,
that subsequent writers can do little more than copy his judicious
observations. I shall therefor content myself with having demonstrated by a reference to facts, that the earth has been overwhelmed
by an universal deluge.

Some vain pretenders to science, have been ambitious to display
their knowledge and sagacity, by an appeal to natural evidence for
the antiquity of the present system, in opposition to the Chronology
of Moses. This evidence they have endeavoured to produce from

432

the numerous beds of vegetable earth interposed between the several eruptions of Ætna and Vesuvius. The most distinguished hero in this field of infidelity, was the Cannon Recupero, and his idle observations have been recorded by a traveller of no mean talents in composition, although ill qualified to estimate the value of an opinion, which he has thought proper to communicate.

It is well known, that the materials ejected by volcanoes, at various intervals, are extremely various; some, being apt to moulder, are readily decomposed and quickly converted into soil, whilst other substances are so refractory, as to remain unchanged for ages, and others again remain for ever barren.

There is no vestige of vegetable earth over the whole of Mount Castagna, and very little in Campo Blanco, although their origin was anterior to all our records. The lava of Ætna ejected, A. D. 1329, was covered eight inches with earth before the year 1776—that of Ischia, which issued in 1302, had produced no vegetable earth at the end of the last century. Even to the present day it continues to preserve its hardness and sterility. Another current of lava in Catania, at the end of two thousand years remains precisely in the same condition.* No fewer than six alterations of lava and of volcanic ashes, which immediately admit of vegetation, appear over Herculaneum, the destruction of which is recent.

When I was travelling in Arragon, I remarked, that in a whole day's journey no trace of vegetable soil was to be seen.

---

* Spalanzani's Two Sicilies tom. 8vo. 1798.

433

In addition to what I have said upon this subject, I must here repeat an observation already made, that from chalk, through all the intermediate strata incumbent on the granite, in all our perforations, no vestige of vegetable soil is to be seen, excepting on the surface of the earth.

Our infidel traveller is mistaken, not merely in the application of his rule, but in the rule itself. His hypothesis was idle, and his application of that hypothesis absurd.

It remains therefore as a fact, that we have *one* bed of vegetable earth, formed by the hand of time, since the grand convulsion which turned the dry land into barrenness, and the bed of the ocean into a fertile field.

It has been a favorite notion with a certain description of philosophers, that the ocean is progressively shifting its bed, retreating in one direction and advancing in the other; swallowing up old continents, whilst others are incessantly protruded from beneath its waves.

These distinguished sages, however, do not agree.

Buffon, because it happened to suit his system, conceived, that the sea is moving from East to West, gaining on the Eastern coasts, and losing on the Western.

Professor Link, on the contrary, persuades himself that the sea strives unremittingly to extend its dominion from West to East.

Unfortunately for the credit of these wise men, all our most elevated mountains in every part of the earth, have respectively the same dates. Granite in the Alps, Andes, and Tartarian mountains, consists of quartz, field spar, and mica. The superincumbent sand-

3 K

434

stone is disintigrated granite.   The attendant lime-stone is uniformly composed of the spoils of zoophytes, of encrinus, and of corals, with certain species of anomiæ.   All other rock strata are characterized by their distinctive fossils.   Coal beds, throughout the globe, are found only in the neighbourhood of the mountain lime-stone.   Chalk is every where the same substance, and preserves its situation with respect to other strata.   The detritus of all these constitutes our soil, and this, with the spoils of animals and vegetables, forms our vegetable earth, which, like the rock strata, every where in Europe, Asia, Africa, and America, refers us to one date.

Where then has nature been detected in producing these substances, or any one of them?

Supposing her operations in their formation, and in bringing them to light to have been constant and progressive; such successive operations could not have escaped the observation of mankind.   Our records, from early ages, would have noticed the rise and progress of new granitic peaks; new mountains of lime-stone, containing different species of marine productions, would have made their appearance in the ocean, and the natural history of both chalk and flints could not be, as they are at present, hid from us.

The statement of De Luc respecting the church of St. Marc, in Venice, and of the cathedral in the Isle of Torcello, with the concession of Dr. Hutton, in regard to the port of Byzantium, and the Isthmus of Corinth, being the same as they were two or three thousand years ago; these things prove, that the hypothesis, above referred to, is inconsistent with acknowledged facts.

435

But could we even grant, that the ocean is constantly robbing the continents in one direction, and depositing their spoils in the opposite direction, whether East or West, this would not account for the dip of strata from the high granitic chains.

From the observation, that the bones of elephants and of other animals, inhabitants of the torrid zone, have been discovered in high Northern latitudes, philosophers have hastily concluded, that the earth has been regularly and incessantly shifting her poles, and changing her climates. In fact the teeth, tusks, and bones of the Asiatic elephant and of the mammouth, have been found in the wide expanse of mountains from 50°. North latitude to as many South, that is, from the Ohio to Patagonia.

But then it must be observed, that the ivory in all these teeth and tusks, so widely scattered over distant climates, refers us nearly to the same date, and that date not more remote than numerous other facts enable us to fix on, as the epoch of the universal deluge. The ivory is so well preserved as to be fit for use; those spoils of terrene animals are discovered in alluvial strata, and with them we find, as at Walton in Essex, shells, fish-bones, and other productions of the ocean.

We are informed, that in Siberia, Professor Pallas met with the carcase of a rhinoceros, which still retained in part the skin and hair unchanged.

Now had this and other animals of a warm climate died on the spot, where these carcases appear, and had the temperature been gradually and slowly changed from heat to cold; the whole corruptible substance would have submitted to the laws of nature, and

3 κ 2

436

must have either perished by putrifaction or been devoured by worms. But, when, at the grand convulsion, such a perishable substance had been conveyed into the frigid zone; it there remained and will remain unchanged.

It is remarkable, that in the Ural mountains the bones of the mammouth are confined to the alluvial strata, and appear chiefly in the elevated tract of country watered by rivers, which fall into the Tobol, and the Obi. Some few indeed appear near Lake Ischernoi, whose waters ultimately flow into the Volga. But this lake is nearly contiguous to the river Tagil, which falls into the Toura, as that does into the Tobol. The district in which they have been noticed, is one of the most lofty portions of Siberia, and the source of its great rivers, whether flowing towards the Caspian to the South, or towards the Frozen Ocean to the North.

Thus have I demonstrated, that the Mosaic account of the Deluge, does not merely accord with traditional reports universally diffused through civilized and savage nations; but is confirmed by infallible records inscribed on our Alpine rocks, and legible on all the strata, discovered by our deepest excavations in the bowels of the earth.

The veracity of Moses, as an historian, stands therefore unimpeached by the natural evidence to be derived from the actual condition of our globe.

In my next work, should I live to finish it, I shall examine the languages, customs and manners of the human race, as described in the Pentateuch, and in the most venerable records of the Pagan World.

FINIS.

21. William Buckland (1784-1856)

Vindiciae Geologicae (Oxford, 1820)
Title page, Dedication, pp. 22-38

VINDICIÆ GEOLOGICÆ;

OR THE

CONNEXION OF GEOLOGY WITH RELIGION

EXPLAINED,

IN

AN INAUGURAL LECTURE

DELIVERED

BEFORE THE UNIVERSITY OF OXFORD, MAY 15, 1819,

ON THE

ENDOWMENT OF A READERSHIP IN GEOLOGY

BY

HIS ROYAL HIGHNESS THE PRINCE REGENT.

BY THE

REV. WILLIAM BUCKLAND, B. D. F. R. S. M. G. S.

FELLOW OF THE IMPERIAL SOCIETIES OF MINERALOGY AND NATURAL HISTORY AT
PETERSBURG AND MOSCOW, FELLOW OF CORPUS CHRISTI COLLEGE, OXFORD,
AND READER IN MINERALOGY AND GEOLOGY IN THE SAME UNIVERSITY.

Tantum abest, ut causæ physicæ homines a Deo et providentiâ abducant, ut contra potius philosophi illi in iisdem eruendis occupati fuerunt, nullum exitum rei reperiant, nisi postremo ad Deum et providentiam confugiant. *Bac. de Augm. Scient.* iii. 5.

OXFORD,

AT THE UNIVERSITY PRESS FOR THE AUTHOR;

SOLD BY R. BLISS, OXFORD; LONGMAN, HURST, REES, ORME, AND BROWN;
AND MESSRS. WHITTAKERS, LONDON.

1820.

TO THE RIGHT HONOURABLE

WILLIAM WYNDHAM, BARON GRENVILLE,

F. R. S.

CHANCELLOR OF THE UNIVERSITY OF OXFORD,

ETC. ETC. ETC.

FROM A FIRM CONVICTION OF HIS SINCERE REGARD FOR THE

INSEPARABLE INTERESTS OF SCIENCE AND RELIGION ;

AND FROM FEELINGS OF

GRATITUDE AND HIGH PERSONAL RESPECT ;

THIS ATTEMPT TO SHEW THAT THE STUDY OF GEOLOGY

HAS A TENDENCY TO CONFIRM THE EVIDENCES OF

NATURAL RELIGION ;

AND

THAT THE FACTS DEVELOPED BY IT ARE CONSISTENT WITH

THE ACCOUNTS OF THE CREATION AND DELUGE

RECORDED IN

THE MOSAIC WRITINGS,

IS,

WITH PERMISSION, HUMBLY DEDICATED

BY HIS LORDSHIP'S

MOST OBEDIENT AND FAITHFUL SERVANT,

WILLIAM BUCKLAND.

[p. 22]

Let us now proceed to the second part of our inquiry, and examine in what degree the results of Geological investigations appear to have affected the evidences of revelation, by bringing to notice facts, which may seem at first sight to be inconsistent with the literal interpretation of the Mosaic records.

Unfortunately for the interests of philosophy, it has happened that a minute examination of the structure and composition of the earth has given rise to a difficulty from an apparent nonconformity of certain Geological phenomena with the literal and popular account of the creation, as it is presented to us in the book of Genesis, and in which the truth of that record seems at first sight to be implicated.

If the fact I now allude to were not so generally notorious, that a recent Author[g] in one of our northern Universities has thought the subject of sufficient importance to devote a chapter of his work on the Evidences of Christianity to what he calls the scepticism of Geologists; it might have been superfluous to introduce the mention of this subject before those who know the strength of the irrefragable moral evidence, on which the general authority of the sacred writings is established, and which cannot be invalidated by occasional differences touching minute details of historical

[g] The Rev. Dr. Chalmers.

23

events, or by objections on grounds so hypothetical and uncertain, as those afforded by the yet imperfect science of Geology. But to many who have not examined the detail of these evidences, and who look only to natural phenomena, an apparent inconsistency of tangible facts with the popular and literal interpretation of Scripture history presents difficulties, which have been supposed, however inconsiderately, to invalidate the truth of the Mosaic records.

Though it cannot be denied that some slight difficulties may exist, it is satisfactory to find that the evidence of facts unequivocally confirms the statement of these records in all points of most essential importance; and that our science stands on the same ground which astronomy occupied on the first publication of the system of Copernicus. It has added largely to the evidences of natural religion in that kingdom of nature, where proofs of design and order are most obscurely developed to the ordinary observer, and have been most frequently overlooked, and even denied; and with respect to those points, on which the declaration of Scripture is positive and decisive, as, for instance, in asserting the low antiquity of the human race; the evidence of all facts that have yet been established in Geology coincides with the records of Sacred History and Profane Tradition to confirm the conclusion, that *the existence of mankind* can on no account be supposed to have taken its beginning before that time which is assigned to it in the Mosaic writings.

Again, the grand fact of *an universal deluge* at no very remote period is proved on grounds so decisive and incontrovertible, that, had we never heard of such an event from Scripture, or any other authority, Geology of itself must have called in the assistance of some such catastrophe, to explain the phenomena of diluvian action

24

which are universally presented to us, and which are unintelligible without recourse to a deluge exerting its ravages at a period not more ancient than that announced in the Book of Genesis.

It is highly satisfactory to find the following strong statement on this subject, published by one who deservedly ranks in the very first class of natural observers, and in the very centre of continental philosophy. " It may be seen," says Cuvier, " that nature every " where distinctly informs us that the commencement of *the present* " *order of things cannot be dated at a very remote period;* and it is " remarkable that mankind every where speak the same language " with nature." And in another place he adds, " I am of opinion " with M. Deluc and M. Dolomieu, that if there is any circum- " stance thoroughly established in Geology, it is that the crust of " our globe has been subjected to a great and sudden revolution, " the epoch of which cannot be dated much farther back than five " or six thousand years ago; and that this revolution had buried all " the countries *which were before inhabited by men and by the other* " *animals that are now best known.*" Theory of the Earth, §. 34.

The two great points then of the low antiquity of the human race, and the universality of a recent deluge, are most satisfactorily confirmed by every thing that has yet been brought to light by Geological investigations; and as far as it goes, the Mosaic account is in perfect harmony with the discoveries of modern science. If Geology goes further, and shews that the present system of this planet is built on the wreck and ruins of one more ancient, there is nothing in this inconsistent with the Mosaic declaration, that the whole material universe was created in the beginning by the Almighty: and though Moses confines the detail of his history to the preparation of this globe for the reception of the human race, he does not deny the prior existence of another system of things,

25

of which it was quite foreign to his purpose to make mention, as having no reference to the destiny or to the moral conduct of created man.

The true state of the question respecting the difficulties that arise from the periods of time in which the creation is said to have taken place, has been set forth with much ability and fairness by Mr. Sumner, a divine whose rational and sober piety no person will venture to dispute, and whose admirable work on the Records of Creation, from its originality of sentiment, accuracy of argument, and elegance of writing, ranks amongst the most able productions of the present day.

" Any curious information as to the structure of the earth " ought not," he says, " to be expected by any one acquainted " with the general character of the Mosaic records. There is no- " thing in them to gratify the curiosity or repress the researches " of mankind, when brought in the progress of cultivation to cal- " culate the motions of the heavenly bodies, or speculate on the " formation of the globe. The expressions of Moses are evidently " accommodated to the first and familiar notions derived from the " sensible appearances of the earth and heavens; and the absurdity " of supposing that the literal interpretation of terms in Scripture " ought to interfere with philosophical inquiry would have been as " generally forgotten as renounced, if the oppressors of Galileo " had not found a place in history. The concessions, if they may " be so called, of believers in Revelation on this point have been " amply remunerated by the sublime discoveries as to the pro- " spective wisdom of the Creator, which have been gradually " unfolded by the progressive improvements in astronomical " knowledge. We may trust with the same confidence as to any " future results from Geology, if this science should ever find its " Newton, and break through the various obstacles peculiar to

E

26

" that study, which have hitherto precluded any general solution
" of its numerous and opposite phenomena."

After following up these general remarks with a more detailed
exposition of the harmony which subsists between the facts observable in the structure of the earth, and a fair and liberal interpretation of the Mosaic account of the creation, Mr. Sumner concludes his statement with the following satisfactory result of his investigations.

" All that I am concerned to establish is the unreasonableness
" of supposing that Geological discoveries, as far as they have
" hitherto proceeded, are hostile to the Mosaic account of the
" creation. No rational naturalist would attempt to describe, either
" from the brief narration in Genesis or otherwise, the process by
" which our system was brought from confusion into a regular
" and habitable state. No rational theologian will direct his hos-
" tility against any theory, which, acknowledging the agency of
" the Creator, only attempts to point out the secondary instru-
" ments he has employed. It may be safely affirmed, that no
" Geological theory has yet been proposed, which is not less re-
" concileable to ascertained facts and conflicting phenomena, than
" to the Mosaic history.

" According to that history, we are bound to admit, that only
" one general destruction or revolution of the globe has taken
" place since the period of that creation which Moses records,
" and of which Adam and Eve were the first inhabitants. The
" certainty of one event of that kind would appear from the dis-
" coveries of geologers, even if it were not declared by the sacred
" historian. *But we are not called upon to deny the possible ex-*
" *istence of previous worlds, from the wreck of which our globe*
" *was organized, and the ruins of which are now furnishing matter*

27

" *to our curiosity.* The belief of their existence is indeed con-
" sistent with rational probability, and somewhat confirmed by
" the discoveries of Astronomy, as to the plurality of worlds [h]."

A similar exposition of the acceptation in which we ought to receive the opinions expressed or implied in the sacred writings on
subjects connected with the discoveries of modern Physics, has
been still more strongly given by the illustrious Bishop Horsley in many of his sermons, and more especially in that preached
before the Humane Society [i].

Buffon also, in the results which were continually arising from
his endless investigations into natural history, declares that he
discovered no inconsistency between these phenomena and the
statements of the Mosaic records [k].

It cannot however be denied, that examples of its abuse have for
a long time caused the study of the Physical sciences, and in later
days more particularly the pursuit of inquiries into Geology, to lie
under the imputation of being dangerous to Religion.

When it was attempted to explain every thing by the sole
agency of second causes, without any reference whatever to the
first ; when nature was set up as an original source of being, distinct and independent of the Almighty ; when it was taught that
matter possessed an existence which he never gave it, and that the
elements had differences and qualities independent of him : these
surely were grounds sufficient to excite alarm in all persons who
were zealous for the cause of religion, and the preservation of the

[h] Vid. Records of Creation, vol. 2. p. 356.
[i] Horsley's Sermons, 8vo. 1816, vol. 3. Serm. 39.
[k] Histoire Naturelle, tom. 12. Des Epoques de la Nature.

28

best interests of mankind. But the doctrines which gave Philosophy its formidable aspect have now been almost utterly abandoned: and if we will calmly allow reason to subdue the first alarm which excessive zeal excites in good and pious minds, it will teach us, that nothing can be more unjust than the apprehension lest the study of nature, when *rightly* pursued, or in other words, the contemplation of the attributes of the Creator, as they are displayed through the medium of his works, should in any way be destructive of the credibility of those things, which he has disclosed to us in the revelation of his will.

The existence of this feeling of unnecessary alarm, and the injustice and unreasonableness of entertaining it, have been admirably marked out by the great master of modern science, where he is describing the obstacles which in his time were opposed to its advancement, and shewing the absurdity, if not impiety of dissolving that union, by which Philosophy becomes associated in its natural and just office, as the faithful auxiliary and handmaid of Religion. " Naturalem enim Philosophiam, (post verbum Dei cer-" tissimam superstitionis medicinam,) eandem probatissimum fidei " alimentum esse. Itaque merito religioni, tanquam fidissimam " et acceptissimam ancillam, attribui, cum altera voluntatem Dei " altera potestatem manifestet."

It was seen distinctly, and felt experimentally by that great Philosopher whose words I have now quoted, that the illustration of the divine attributes, and the advancement of Religion, are the great objects which stamp value upon natural knowledge, and that it is something very different from fair investigation that will conduct its followers to infidelity; and I cannot better conclude this part of my subject, than in his own impressive words: " Let no " man upon a weak conceit of sobriety or ill applied moderation " think or maintain that a man can search too far, or be too well

29

" studied ' in the Book of God's Word,' or the ' Book of God's
" Works;' but rather let men endeavour an endless progress
" and proficiency in both: only let them beware that they apply
" both to charity, and not to swelling; to use, and not to ostenta-
" tion; and again, that they do not unwisely mingle or confound
" these learnings together[1]."

Having premised thus much as to the general state of the question, let us proceed to view the case before us, and examine how
far the phenomena developed by Geological investigations can be
shewn to be in no way inconsistent with the true spirit of the Mosaic cosmogony.

We find the primitive rocks on the greater portion of the
earth's surface, (*i. e.* rocks which contain no remains of animal
or vegetable life, or fragments of other rocks,) covered by an
accumulation of derivative or secondary strata, the greatest perpendicular thickness of which cannot be estimated at less than
two miles.

These strata do not appear to have been deposited hastily and
suddenly; on the contrary, the phenomena attendant on them are
such as prove that their formation was slow and gradual, going on
during successive periods of tranquillity and great disturbance; and
being in some cases entirely produced from the destruction of
more ancient rocks, which had been consolidated, and again
broken up by violent convulsions antecedent to the deposition of
those more modern or secondary strata which are sometimes in
great measure derivative from their exuviæ.

The differences also of the organic remains both of animals and

---

[1] Advancement of Learning, lib. 1.

30

vegetables, contained in the different strata successively deposited upon each other, and again their non-agreement with now existing species, seem to indicate that great changes have taken place in animated nature, and that new races of organized beings have successively arisen and become extinct during the periods at which these strata were formed; and thus to point out a series of revolutions, to the last of which the present system of the earth and its inhabitants belongs [m].

It seems therefore impossible to ascribe the formation of these strata to a period so short as the single year occupied by the Mosaic deluge; which was an opinion at first naturally adopted by those who observed the occurrence of marine shells in inland countries at great elevations above the present ocean, but who were ignorant of the enormous masses, and subdivisions of distinct secondary strata, above alluded to, and of the facts which prove their slow, gradual, and successive deposition. The deluge has indeed left traces of its operation deeply sculptured on every stratum of the earth, but they are such as differ most essentially from those we are now considering; and prove the deposition of these strata to have been antecedent to that catastrophe; which as it is recorded in Scripture merely as a work of destruction, so has it left behind it undeniable evidences that its tendency was only to destroy. But the strata we have been considering, although they bear on their *surface* unequivocal marks of the agency of that convulsion, were evidently not produced, but partially destroyed by it, and must be referred for their origin to periods of much higher antiquity.

[m] For a concise and able statement of the leading phenomena as yet observed, which prove that numerous revolutions have affected the surface of the earth, both before and since the creation of living beings; and of the successive changes that have taken place in animal nature, during the progress of these revolutions; see Cuvier's admirable Essay on the Theory of the Earth.

31

It has been supposed therefore by others, with greater plausibility, that these strata have been formed at the bottom of the antediluvian ocean during the interval between the Mosaic Creation and the Deluge; and that, at the time of that deluge, portions of the globe, which had been previously elevated above the level of the sea, and formed the antediluvian continents, were suddenly submerged with their inhabitants, while the ancient bed of the ocean rose to supply their place. This hypothesis, it has been said, has the advantage of explaining the cause why the remains imbedded in the strata are principally those of marine animals: but it labours under considerable objections. It should rather appear from the little that is said in Scripture, that the antediluvian continents were the same with the present: and a similar conclusion is to be derived from the universal diffusion of the bones of *land* animals in those superficial depositions of gravel, which seem to have resulted from the deluge, in almost every valley of the earth that has been made the subject of geological investigations. As these bones are remarkably perfect, and seldom have signs of having been much rolled, or transported from a distance, they appear to have belonged to animals that lived and died near the spots where they are now found: those places consequently must have formed parts not of the ocean of the antediluvian world, but of its continents.

A third hypothesis may be suggested, which supposes the word " beginning" as applied by Moses in the first verse of the Book of Genesis, to express an undefined period of time which was antecedent to the last great change that affected the surface of the earth, and to the creation of its present animal and vegetable inhabitants; during which period a long series of operations and revolutions may have been going on, which, as they are wholly unconnected with the history of the human race, are passed over in silence by the sacred historian, whose only concern with them

32

was barely to state, that the matter of the universe is not eternal and self-existent, but was originally created by the power of the Almighty.

A fourth hypothesis is that which follows the opinion previously adopted by many learned and pious men, on grounds very different from those of Geology, that the days of the Mosaic creation are not to be strictly construed as implying the same length of time which is at present occupied by a single revolution of our globe, but PERIODS of a much longer extent. And Bishop Horsley, while he insists that the day in the Mosaic account could only signify a revolution of the earth round its axis, still adds these remarkable words, which do, in fact, admit the whole of this hypothesis; "That " this revolution was performed in the same space of time in the " beginning of the world and now, I could not over-confidently " affirm [n]."

To the first and second of these solutions there seem to be, as I have already stated, some considerable objections.

The first is both at variance with the Sacred Records, and still more inconsistent with the phenomena of Nature.

The second, and I say it with diffidence, as it has received the countenance of very high authority, while it derives assuredly no support from the Sacred Records, is also, on the side of natural appearances, liable to objections not yet sufficiently removed.

And if, by the assistance of either of the two last, (and perhaps more particularly of the third,) we may be enabled to remove the leading difficulties which the infant state of Geology as yet can-

[n] Vol. ii. Serm. 23. On the Sabbath.

33

not but present to us; if from these conjectures no detriment can be shewn to arise to the faith of the most pious individual; if they have, in fact, been maintained by some of the ablest divines and writers of the English Church, men uninterested in Geology, but interested in Religion; no danger surely can be apprehended from their admission: nor shall we think it necessary to discard them, until some stronger reason shall be brought for their rejection, or until some happier Genius shall have arisen to shed new light upon our inquiries.

Difficulties indeed will still present themselves, but difficulties by which neither will the ardor of science be discouraged, nor the full confidence of religious faith be shaken; difficulties such as those of which the whole moral and material world is full, and without the existence of which, in the opinion of the celebrated Pascal, it were not easy to believe that this world which we inhabit is the production of that mysterious Being, " whose ways are " unsearchable, and his works past finding out."

[p. 35]

A P P E N D I X,

*Containing a brief Summary of the Proofs afforded by Geology, of
the Mosaic Deluge.*

———◆———

I HAVE been induced to draw up the following Appendix in consequence
of an article which appeared in the Quarterly Review of May 1819, on
Mr. Gisborne's Testimony of Natural Theology to Christianity.

With the learned writer of this Review I fully coincide in every sentiment of the highest respect for the character of Mr. Gisborne, and in every
opinion which he has expressed with so much ability on the Geological
error which his work contains.

There is, however, one point of vital importance, on which it is sufficiently apparent, from the preceding Lecture, that I entirely differ from
the writer of this Review, namely, in the belief he entertains, on the authority of Linnæus, that Geology affords no proofs of the Mosaic Deluge: and
this difference may be the more securely stated, as the general attachment
of the Quarterly Review to the cause of Revelation is so decided; and as the
very paper in question contains the strongest assertions of the truth of the
Mosaic History: it is simply therefore a matter of science, on which our
opinions are at variance.

That Linnæus himself should have held such opinions at a period when
Geology was in its first infancy, and many of its most important phenomena were totally unknown; and when it was impossible for him to
distinguish those effects which are attributable simply to the action of the
Mosaic Deluge, from the more numerous cases of analogous disturbances

F 2

36

which the earth appears to have undergone before the creation of man; is a circumstance which can excite in us no surprise. But I am at a loss to conceive how any person who has evidently read the works of Cuvier with so much attention as the writer of this Review, and who reproaches Mr. Gisborne for want of knowledge of this author, could have been induced to revert to the premature opinion of so infantine a Geologist as Linnæus, and have overlooked that most important conclusion which I have before quoted, in which Cuvier himself sums up the results of his own valuable observations [a].

In every thing that I have been able to observe myself, or to collect from others whose opinions on such subjects I most highly respect, I find a series of numerous and widely varied facts; a certain class of which bears as unequivocal evidence to the existence of a Deluge, at or near the period assigned to it by Moses; as the phenomena of stratification afford, on the other hand, of a succession of different and more ancient revolutions affecting our planet before the existence of the human race. And it is from want of accuracy in distinguishing between these facts, that errors have prevailed. such as those into which Linnæus fell.

On the detail of those evidences of a recent diluvian action which are afforded in the neighbourhood of Oxford, and in some of the central parts of England, I have recently spoken more at large in another place, to which it seems more peculiarly adapted [b]. It may be sufficient here to state very summarily the main reasons which confirm me in the opinion which I have always entertained.

The proofs then of the Mosaic Deluge presented by natural phenomena are in my opinion these.

[a] See p. 24. of the above Lecture, and Sect. 34. of Jameson's translations of Cuvier's Theory of the Earth.

[b] See paper on the evidences of a recent Deluge afforded by the gravel beds and state of the plains and valleys of the central parts of England, presented to the Geological Society by myself in November 1819; and also another memoir laid before the same Society by the Rev. W. D. Conybeare and myself, on the coal districts of Somerset and S. Gloucestershire, in which the decisive evidences of diluvian action presented in those counties are given in considerable detail.

37

1. The general shape and position of hills and valleys; the former having their sides and surfaces universally modified by the action of violent waters, and presenting often the same alternation of salient and retiring angles that mark the course of a common river. And the latter, in those cases, which are called valleys of denudation, being attended with such phenomena as shew them to owe their existence entirely to excavation under the action of a retiring flood of waters.

2. The almost universal confluence and successive inosculations of minor valleys with each other, and final termination of them all in some main trunk which conducts them to the sea; and the rare interruption of their courses by transverse barriers producing lakes.

3. The occurrence of detached insulated masses of horizontal strata called *outliers*, at considerable distances from the beds of which they once evidently formed a continuous part, and from which they have been at a recent period separated by deep and precipitous valleys of denudation.

4. The immense deposits of gravel that occur occasionally on the summits of hills, and almost universally in valleys over the whole world; in situations to which no torrents or rivers such as are now in action could ever have drifted them.

5. The nature of this gravel, being in part composed of the wreck of the neighbouring hills, and partly of fragments and blocks that have been transported from very distant regions.

6. The nature and condition of the organic remains deposited in this gravel, many, though not all of them, being identical with species that now exist, and very few having undergone the smallest process of mineralization. Their condition resembles rather that of common grave bones, than of those fossil bones which are found imbedded in the regular strata, being in so recent a state, and having undergone so little decay, that if the records of history, and the circumstances that attend them, did not absolutely forbid such a supposition, we should be inclined to attribute them even to a much later period than the Mosaic Deluge: and certainly there is, in my opinion,

38

no single fact connected with them, that should lead us to date their origin from any more ancient era.

7. The total impossibility of referring any one of these appearances to the action of ancient or modern rivers, or any other causes, that are now, or appear ever to have been in action since the last retreat of the diluvian waters.

8. The analogous occurrence of similar phenomena in almost all the regions of the world, that have hitherto been scientifically investigated, presenting a series of facts that are uniformly consistent with the hypothesis of a contemporaneous and diluvian origin.

9. The perfect harmony and consistency in the circumstances of those few changes that now go on, (e. g. the formation of ravines and gravel by mountain torrents; the depth and continual growth of peat bogs; the formation of tufa, sand-banks, and deltas; and the filling up of lakes, estuaries, and marshes,) with the hypothesis which dates the commencement of all such operations at a period not more ancient than the Mosaic Deluge.

All these, whether considered collectively or separately, present such a general conformity of facts, tending to establish the universality of a recent Deluge, as no difficulties or objections that have hitherto arisen are in any way sufficient to overrule.

In the full confidence that these difficulties will at length be removed, however slowly, by the gradual progress and extension of science, we may for the present rest satisfied with the argument, that numberless phenomena have been already ascertained, which, without the admission of a recent and universal Deluge, it seems not easy, nay, utterly impossible to explain.

22. William Buckland (1784-1856)

Reliquiae Diluvianae (London, 1823)
Title page, pp. 10-24, 37-48, Plate 3

RELIQUIÆ DILUVIANÆ;

OR,

OBSERVATIONS

ON THE

ORGANIC REMAINS

CONTAINED IN

CAVES, FISSURES, AND DILUVIAL GRAVEL,

AND ON

OTHER GEOLOGICAL PHENOMENA,

ATTESTING THE ACTION OF AN

UNIVERSAL DELUGE.

_____

BY THE REV. WILLIAM BUCKLAND, B.D. F.R.S.F.L.S.

MEMBER OF THE GEOLOGICAL SOCIETY OF LONDON; OF THE IMPERIAL SOCIETIES OF MINERALOGY AND NATURAL HISTORY AT PETERSBURG AND MOSCOW; AND OF THE NATURAL HISTORY SOCIETY AT HALLE: HONORARY MEMBER OF THE AMERICAN GEOLOGICAL SOCIETY; CORRESPONDENT OF THE MUSEUM OF NATURAL HISTORY OF FRANCE; FELLOW OF C.C.C. AND PROFESSOR OF MINERALOGY AND GEOLOGY IN THE UNIVERSITY OF OXFORD.

_____

LONDON:

JOHN MURRAY, ALBEMARLE-STREET.

1823.

[p. 10]

On entering the cave at Kirkdale (see Plate II. fig. 2.), the first thing observed was a sediment of soft mud or loam, covering entirely its whole bottom to the average depth of about a foot, and concealing the subjacent rock, or actual floor of the cavern. Not a particle of mud was found attached either to the sides or roof; nor was there a trace of it adhering to the sides or upper portions of the transverse fissures, or any thing to suggest the idea that it entered through them. The surface of this sediment when the cave was first opened was nearly smooth and level, except in those parts where its regularity had been broken by the accumulation of stalagmite above it, or ruffled by the dripping of water: its substance is an argillaceous and slightly micaceous loam, composed of such minute particles as would easily be suspended in muddy water, and mixed with much calcareous matter, that seems to have been derived in part from the dripping of the roof, and in part from comminuted bones. At about 100 feet within the cave's mouth the sediment became more coarse and sandy, and partially covered with an incrustation of black manganese ore.

Above this mud, on advancing some way into the cave, the roof and sides were found to be partially studded and cased over with a coating of stalactite, which was most abundant in those parts where the transverse fissures occur, but in small quantity where the rock is compact and devoid of fissures. Thus far it resembled the stalactite of ordinary caverns; but on tracing it downwards to the surface of the mud, it was there found to turn off at right angles from the sides of the cave, and form above the mud a plate or crust, shooting across like ice on the surface of water, or cream on a pan of milk. (See Plate II. fig. 2.)   The thickness and quantity of this crust varied with that found on the roof and sides, being most abundant, and covering the mud entirely where there was much stalactite on the sides, and more scanty in those places where the roof or sides presented but little: in many parts it was totally wanting both on the roof and surface of the mud and of the subjacent floor.   Great portion of this crust had been destroyed in digging up the mud to extract the bones before my arrival; it still remained, however, projecting partially in some few places along the sides; and in one or two, where it was very thick, it formed, when I visited the cave, a continuous bridge over the mud entirely across from one side to the other.   In the outer portion of the cave, there was originally a mass of this kind which had been accumulated so high as to obstruct the passage, so that a man could not enter till it had been dug away.

These horizontal incrustations have been formed by the water which, trickling down the sides, was forced to ooze off laterally as soon as it came into contact with the mud; in other parts, where it fell in drops from the roof, stalagmitic accumulations have been raised on its surface, some of which are very large and flat, resembling a cake of bees wax, but more commonly they are of the size and shape of a cow's pap, a name which the workmen have applied to them. There is no alternation of mud with any repeated beds of stalactite, but simply a partial deposit of the latter on the floor beneath it; and it was chiefly in the lower part of the earthy sediment, and in the stalagmitic matter beneath it, that the animal remains were found:

there was nowhere any black earth or admixture of animal matter, except an infinity of extremely minute particles of undecomposed bone.   In the whole extent of the cave, only a very few large bones have been discovered that are tolerably perfect; most of them are broken into small angular fragments and chips, the greater part of which lay separately in the mud, whilst others were wholly or partially invested with stalagmite; and others again mixed with masses of still smaller fragments and cemented by stalagmite, so as to form an osseous breccia.   In some few places where the mud was shallow, and the heaps of teeth and bones considerable, parts of the latter were elevated some inches above the surface of the mud and its stalagmitic crust; and the upper ends of the bones thus projecting like the legs of pigeons through a pie-crust into the void space above, have become thinly covered with stalagmitic drippings, whilst their lower extremities have no such incrustation, and have simply the mud adhering to them in which they have been imbedded; an horizontal crust of stalagmite, about an inch thick, crosses the middle of these bones, and retains them firmly in the position they occupied at the bottom of the cave.   A large flat plate of stalagmite, corresponding in all respects with the above description, and containing three long bones fixed so as to form almost a right angle with the plane of the stalagmite, is in the collection of the Rev. Mr. Smith, of Kirby Moorside.   The same gentleman has also, among many other valuable specimens, a fragment of the thigh bone of an elephant, which is the largest I have seen from this cave.

The effect of the loam and stalagmite in preserving the bones from decomposition, by protecting them from all access of atmospheric

air, has been very remarkable; some that had lain uncovered in the
cave for a long time before the introduction of the loam were in various stages of decomposition; but even in these the further progress
of decay appears to have been arrested as soon as they became
covered with it; and in the greater number, little or no destruction
of their form, and scarcely any of their substance, has taken place.   I
have found, on immersing fragments of these bones in an acid till
the phosphate and carbonate of lime were removed, that nearly the
whole of their original gelatine has been preserved.   Analogous
cases of animal remains preserved from decay by the protection of
similar diluvial mud occur on the coast of Essex, near Walton, and
at Lawford, near Rugby, in Warwickshire; here the bones of the
same species of elephant, rhinoceros, and other diluvial animals occur
in a state of freshness and perfection even exceeding that of those in
the cave at Kirkdale; and from a similar cause, viz. their having been
guarded from the access of atmospheric air, or the percolation of
water, by the argillaceous matrix in which they have been imbedded:
whilst other bones that have lain the same length of time in diluvial
sand, or gravel, and been subject to the constant percolation of
water, have lost their compactness and strength, and great part
of their gelatine, and are often ready to fall to pieces on the slightest
touch; and this where the beds of clay and gravel in question alternate in the same quarry, as at Lawford.

The workmen on first discovering the bones at Kirkdale, supposed them to have belonged to cattle that died by a murrain in this
district a few years ago, and they were for some time neglected, and
thrown on the roads with the common limestone; they were at length

noticed by Mr. Harrison, a medical gentleman of Kirby Moorside, and have since been collected and dispersed amongst so many individuals, that it is probable nearly all the specimens will in a few years be lost, with the exception of such as may be deposited in public collections.   By the kindness and liberality of the Bishop of Oxford (to whom I am also indebted for my first information of the existence of this cave) and of C. Duncombe, Esq. and Lady Charlotte Duncombe, of Duncombe Park, a nearly complete series of the teeth discovered in it has been presented to the Museum at Oxford; whilst a still better collection, both of teeth and bones, is in the possession of J. Gibson, Esq. of Stratford in Essex, to whose exertions we owe the preservation of many valuable specimens, and who has presented a series of them to several public collections in London *. W.. Salmond, Esq. also, of York, has been engaged with much zeal and activity in measuring and exploring new branches of the cave, and making large collections of the teeth and bones, from which he has sent specimens to the Royal Institution of London and to M. Cuvier.   He has recently deposited the bulk of his collection at the newly-established Philosophical Society at York.   I am indebted to him for the annexed ground plan of the cave, and its ramifications,

* The British Museum, the Royal College of Surgeons, and the Geological Society have all been enriched by the liberality of Mr. Gibson.   The Geological Society possesses also a magnificent collection of the remains of elephant, rhinoceros, ox, elk, and other anteluvian animals found in the diluvian gravel beds of various parts of England, together with some fine specimens of bones from the caverns of Germany: their collection also of the organic remains found in the secondary strata of England, and of specimens of the strata themselves, is arranged in a manner which affords to the members of that society the most ready access to a knowledge of the physical changes which the country we inhabit has undergone, and of general geology.

DISCOVERED AT KIRKDALE, IN YORKSHIRE. 15

(Plate II. fig. 3.)   Drawings by Mr. Clift, of some of the most perfect of Mr. Gibson's specimens, have been sent to M. Cuvier, for the new edition of his work on fossil animals; copies of these have been made for me by the kindness of Miss Morland, and appear in the annexed plates, with many other drawings, for which I am indebted to the pencil of Miss Duncombe; and the Rev. George Young, and Mr. Bird of Whitby, in their History of the Geology of the Coast of Yorkshire, have given engravings of some other teeth and a few bones in their possession.

It appears that the teeth and bones which have as yet been discovered in the cave at Kirkdale are referable to the following 23 species of animals.

6 Carnivora.—Hyæna, Tiger, Bear, Wolf, Fox, Weasel. (See Plates III. IV. V. VI. and XIII.)

4 Pachydermata.—Elephant, Rhinoceros, Hippopotamus, and Horse. (See Plates VII. X. and XIII.)

4 Ruminantia.—Ox, and three species of Deer. (See Plates VIII. IX. and X.)

4 Rodentia.—Hare, Rabbit, Water-rat, and Mouse. (See Plates X. XI. and XIII.)

5 Birds.—Raven, Pigeon, Lark, a small species of Duck, resembling the anas sponsor, or summer duck, and a Bird not ascertained, being about the size of a thrush. (See Plate XI. fig. 19 to 29, and Plate XIII. fig. 11, 12.)

The bottom of the cave, on first removing the mud, was found to

be strewed all over like a dog-kennel, from one end to the other, with
hundreds of teeth and bones, or rather broken and splintered fragments of bones, of all the animals above enumerated; they were
found in greatest quantity near its mouth, simply because its area in
this part was most capacious; those of the larger animals, elephant,
rhinoceros, &c. were found co-extensively with all the rest, even in
the inmost and smallest recesses. (See Plate II. fig. 3.*) Scarcely a
single bone has escaped fracture, with the exception of the astragalus,
and other hard and solid bones of the tarsus and carpus joints, and
those of the feet. (See Plate X. fig. 1 to 5, and fig. 7 to 10, and
Plate V. fig. 5 to 12.) On some of the bones, marks may be traced,
which, on applying one to the other, appear exactly to fit the form
of the canine teeth of the hyæna that occur in the cave. The
hyæna's bones have been broken, and apparently gnawed equally
with those of the other animals. Heaps of small splinters, and
highly comminuted, yet angular fragments of bone, mixed with teeth
of all the varieties of animals above enumerated, lay in the bottom of
the den, occasionally adhering together by stalagmite, and forming, as
has been before mentioned, an osseous breccia. Many insulated
fragments also are wholly or partially enveloped with stalagmite, both
externally and internally. Not one skull is to be found entire; and
it is so rare to find a large bone of any kind that has not been more
or less broken, that there is no hope of obtaining materials for the
construction of a single limb, and still less of an entire skeleton.
The jaw bones also, even of the hyænas, are broken to pieces like the
rest; and in the case of all the animals, the number of teeth and of
solid bones of the tarsus and carpus is more than twenty times as

great as could have been supplied by the individuals whose other bones we find mixed with them.

Fragments of jaw bones are by no means common; the greatest number I saw belong to the deer, hyæna, and water-rat, and retain their teeth; in all the jaws both teeth and bone are in an equal state of high preservation, and show that their fracture has been the effect of violence, and not of natural decay. I have seen but ten fragments of deers' jaws, and about forty of hyænas, and as many of rats. (See Plate III. fig. 3, 4, 5, and Plate IV. fig. 2, 3). The ordinary fate of the jaw bones, as of all the rest, appears to have been to be broken to pieces.

The greatest number of teeth are those of hyænas, and the ruminantia. Mr. Gibson alone collected more than 300 canine teeth of the hyæna, which at the least must have belonged to 75 individuals, and adding to these the canine teeth I have seen in other collections, I cannot calculate the total number of hyænas of which there is evidence, at less than 200 or 300. I have already stated, that many of these animals had died before the first set, or milk teeth, had been shed; these teeth are represented in Plate VI. fig. 15 to 27: the state of their fangs shows that they had not fallen out by absorption. The only remains that have been found of the tiger species (see Plate VI. fig. 5, 6, 7) are two large canine teeth, each four inches in length, and a few molar teeth, one of which is in my possession; these exceed in size that of the largest lion or Bengal tiger. There is one tusk only of a bear (see Plate VI. fig. 1), which exactly resembles those of the extinct ursus spelæus of the caves of Germany, the size of which M. Cuvier says must have equalled that of a large

D

horse.   Of the fox there are many teeth (see Plate VI. fig. 8 to 14).
Of the wolf I do not recollect that I have seen more than one large
molar tooth (see Plate XIII. fig. 5, 6) ; the smaller molars of the wolf
however are very like some of the first set of the young hyæna.   A
few jaws and teeth have also been found belonging to the weasel.
(Plate VI. fig. 28, 29).   Teeth of the larger pachydermatous animals
are not abundant.   I have information of about ten elephants' teeth,
but of no tusk ; most of these teeth are broken, and as very few of
them exceed three inches in their longest diameter, they must have
belonged to extremely young animals.   (See Plate VII. fig. 1 and 2).
I have seen but six molar teeth of the hippopotamus, and a few
fragments of its canine and incisor teeth, the best of which are in the
possession of Mr. Thorpe, of York.   (See Plate VII. fig. 8, 9, 10,
and Plate XIII. fig. 7).   Teeth of the rhinoceros are not so rare : I
have seen at least 50, some of them very large, and apparently from
aged animals.   (See Plate VII. fig. 3, 4, 5, 6).   I have heard of only
two or three teeth belonging to the horse.   Of the teeth of deer
there are at least three species (see Plate VIII. fig. 9, 11, 13), the
smallest being very nearly of the size and form of those of a fallow
deer, the largest agreeing in size, but differing in form from those of
the modern elk; and a third being of an intermediate size, and
approaching that of a large stag or red deer.   I have not ascertained
how many species there are of ox, but apparently there are two.
But the teeth which occur perhaps in greatest abundance are those
of the water-rat (see Plate XI. fig. 1 to 6, and 11 to 18) ; for in almost
every specimen I have collected or seen of the osseous breccia, there
are teeth or broken fragments of the bones of this little animal mixed

DISCOVERED AT KIRKDALE, IN YORKSHIRE. 19

with and adhering to the fragments of all the larger bones. These rats may be supposed to have abounded on the edge of the lake, which I have shown probably existed at that time in this neighbourhood: there are also the jaw of a hare, and a few teeth and bones of rabbits and mice. (Plate X. fig. 14, 15, 16, 17, 18, Plate XI. fig. 7, 8, 9, 10, and Plate XIII. fig. 8).

Besides the teeth and bones already described, the cave contained also fragments of horns of at least two species of deer. (See Plate IX. fig. 3, 4, and 5). One of these resembles the horn of the common stag or red deer, the circumference of the base measuring $9\frac{3}{4}$ inches, which is about the size of our largest stag. A second (fig. 4) measures $7\frac{3}{4}$ inches at the same part, and both have two antlers, that rise very near the base. In a smaller species the lowest antler is $3\frac{1}{2}$ inches above the base, the circumference of which is 8 inches. (See fig. 5). No horns are found entire, but fragments only, and these apparently gnawed to pieces like the bones: their lower extremity nearest the head is that which has generally escaped destruction: and it is a curious fact, that this portion of all the horns I have seen from the cave shows, by the rounded state of the base, that they had fallen off by absorption or necrosis, and been shed from the head on which they grew, and not broken off by violence.

It must already appear probable, from the facts above described, particularly from the comminuted state and apparently gnawed condition of the bones, that the cave at Kirkdale was, during a long succession of years, inhabited as a den by hyænas, and that they dragged into its recesses the other animal bodies whose remains are found mixed indiscriminately with their own: this conjecture is ren-

D 2

dered almost certain by the discovery I made, of many small balls of the solid calcareous excrement of an animal that had fed on bones, resembling the substance known in the old Materia Medica by the name of album græcum (see Plate X. fig. 6): its external form is that of a sphere, irregularly compressed, as in the fæces of sheep, and varying from half an inch to an inch and half in diameter; its colour is yellowish white, its fracture is usually earthy and compact, resembling steatite, and sometimes granular; when compact, it is interspersed with small cellular cavities, and in some of the balls there are undigested minute fragments of the enamel of teeth. It was at first sight recognised by the keeper of the Menagerie at Exeter Change, as resembling, both in form and appearance, the fæces of the spotted or Cape hyæna, which he stated to be greedy of bones beyond all other beasts under his care. This information I owe to Dr. Wollaston, who has also made an analysis of the substance under discussion, and finds it to be composed of the ingredients that might be expected in fæcal-matter derived from bones, viz. phosphate of lime, carbonate of lime, and a very small proportion of the triple phosphate of ammonia and magnesia; it retains no animal matter, and its originally earthy nature and affinity to bone will account for its perfect state of preservation*.

I do not know what more conclusive evidence than this can be added to the facts already enumerated, to show that the hyænas

* I have one ball of this substance that is in great part invested with a thin circular case or crust of stalagmite. This must have been formed round it whilst it lay loose and exposed to the dripping of water on the bottom of the cave, before the introduction of the mud.

DISCOVERED AT KIRKDALE, IN YORKSHIRE.

inhabited this cave, and were the agents by which the teeth and bones of the other animals were there collected; it may be useful therefore to consider, in this part of our inquiry, what are the habits of modern hyænas, and how far they illustrate the case before us.

The modern hyæna (of which there are only three known species, all of them smaller and different from the fossil one) is an inhabitant exclusively of hot climates; the most savage, or striped species, abounds in Abyssinia, Nubia, and the adjacent parts of Africa and Asia. The less ferocious, or spotted one, inhabits the Cape of Good Hope, and lives principally on carrion. He is seldom seen by day, but prowls by night, and clears the plains of the carcasses, and even skeletons, which the vultures have picked clean, in preference to attacking any living creature. In the structure of its bones this animal approaches more nearly than the striped hyæna to the fossil species: to these M. Cuvier adds a third, the red hyæna, which is very rare.

The structure of these animals places them in an intermediate class between the cat and dog tribes; not feeding, like the former, almost exclusively on living prey, but like the latter, being greedy of putrid flesh and bones*: their love of putrid flesh induces them to follow armies, and dig up human bodies from the grave. They inhabit holes in the earth, and chasms of rocks; are fierce, and of obstinate courage, attacking stronger quadrupeds than themselves, and even repelling lions. Johnson says of them, in his Field Sports,

* It is quite impossible to mistake the jaw of any species of hyæna for that of the wolf or tiger kind; the latter having three molar teeth only in the lower jaw, and the former seven; whilst all the hyæna tribe have four. (See Plate IV. fig. 1, 2, 3).

that " they feed on small animals and carrion, and often come in for
the prey left by tigers and leopards after their appetites have been
satiated: they are great enemies of dogs, and kill numbers of them.
They make no earths of their own, but lie under rocks, or resort to
the earths of wolves, as foxes do to those of badgers; and it is not
uncommon to find wolves and hyænas in the same bed of earths."
Their habit of digging human bodies from the grave, and dragging
them to their den, and of accumulating around it the bones of all
kinds of animals, is thus described by Busbequius, where he is
speaking of the Turkish mode of burial in Anatolia, and their custom
of laying large stones upon their graves to protect them from the
hyænas.   " Hyæna regionibus iis satis frequens; sepulchra suffodit,
extrahitque cadavera, portatque ad suam speluncam; juxta quam
videre est ingentem cumulum ossium humanorum ' veterinariorum' *
et reliquorum omne genus animalium." (Busbeq. Epist. 1 Leg. Turc.†)
Brown, also, in his Travels to Darfur, describes the hyænas' manner
of taking off their prey in the following words:—" they come in
herds of six, eight, and often more, into the villages at night, and
carry off with them whatever they are able to master; they will kill
dogs and asses even within the enclosure of houses, and fail not to
assemble wherever a dead camel or other animal is thrown, which,
acting in concert, they sometimes drag to a prodigious distance."

* Veterinam bestiam jumentum CATO appellavit a vehendo: (quasi veheterinus vel
veterinus.) Pomp. Fest.

† This evidence is the more valuable, from the accuracy and delight with which it
appears, from his own testimony, that Busbequius used to watch the habits of wild
animals, which he kept for this purpose in his menagerie at Constantinople, where he
resided many years as ambassador from the Emperor of Germany.

DISCOVERED AT KIRKDALE, IN YORKSHIRE.   23

Sparman and Pennant mention that a single hyæna has been known to carry off a living man or woman in the vicinity of the Cape *.

The strength of the hyæna's jaw is such, that in attacking a dog, he begins by biting off his leg at a single snap. The capacity of his teeth, for such an operation, is sufficiently obvious from simple inspection; and, consistent with this strength of teeth and jaw, is the

---

* It appears from the discussions of the learned Bochart, in his Hierozoicon, on the hyæna, that the peculiar habits of this animal had attracted the attention of the earliest naturalists, more especially his savage voracity, and practice of digging human bodies from their graves for the purpose of devouring them. He quotes the following passages: Aristotelis Hist. lib. viii. cap. 5. " Τυμβωρυχεῖ δὲ ἐφιέμενον Ἰῆς σαρκοφαγίας Ἰῶν ἀνϑρώπων."—Plinius, lib. viii. cap. 30. " Ab uno animali sepulchra erui (traduntur) inquisitione corporum."—Solinus, " Eadem hyæna inquisitione corporum sepultorum busta eruit."—Hieronymus in Esaiam, capite lxv. " Semper cadavera persequitur et vivit succo et sanie corporum mortuorum."—Et in Ieremiam, capite xiii. " Vivit cadaveribus mortuorum, et de sepulchris solet effodere corpora."

Bochart shows also that certain parts of the body of this animal, particularly the atlas or first vertebra of the neck, which they called the " nodus," were used by the ancient enchanters in the ceremonies of their magical incantations.

> " Huc quicquid fœtu genuit natura sinistro
> Miscetur: non spuma canum, quibus unda timori est;
> Viscera non lyncis, non diræ nodus hyænæ
> Defuit."
>
> *Lucanus*, Lib. VI. v. 673.

And contends that the same animal is also alluded to in the Old Testament, in 1 Samuel, ch. 13. v. 18, and Jeremiah, ch. 12. v. 9.

In the former of these passages he is of opinion with Aquila, that the " Valley of Zeboim" ought to have been translated the " Valley of Hyænas;" and in the latter he thinks with the Septuagint, that the words which in our version are rendered " sheckled bird," should have been " ravenous spotted beast," i. e. hyæna. The Septuagint have it, " Μὴ σπήλαιον ὑαίνης ἢ κληρονομία με ἐμοί." Mr. Parkhurst, also, and Scheuzer are for establishing the hyæna in this passage.

The proverbial enmity supposed to subsist between this animal and the dog is also mentioned by Oppian, Pliny, and Ælian, and alluded to in Ecclesiasticus, ch. xiii. 18. " Τίς εἰρήνη ὑαίνη πρὸς κύνα;"—" What agreement is there between the hyæna and a dog?"

24   ACCOUNT OF FOSSIL TEETH AND BONES

state of the muscles of his neck, being so full and strong, that in early times this animal was fabled to have but one cervical vertebra. They live by day in dens, and seek their prey by night, having large prominent eyes, adapted, like those of the rat and mouse, for seeing in the dark.   To animals of such a class, our cave at Kirkdale would afford a most convenient habitation; and the circumstances we find developed in it are entirely consistent with the habits above enumerated.

★   ★   ★   ★

[p. 37]

Should it be asked why, amidst the remains of so many hundred animals, not a single skeleton of any kind has been found entire, we see an obvious answer, in the power and known habit of hyænas to devour the bones of their prey; and the gnawed fragments on the one hand, and album græcum on the other, afford double evidence of their having largely gratified this natural propensity: the exception of the teeth and numerous small bones of the lower joints and extremities, that remain unbroken, as having been too hard and solid to afford inducement for mastication, is entirely consistent with this solution*.   And should it be further asked, why we do not find, at

---

* Since this paper was first published, I have had an opportunity of seeing a Cape hyæna at Oxford, in the travelling collection of Mr. Wombwell, the keeper of which confirmed in every particular the evidence given to Dr. Wollaston by the keeper at Exeter 'Change.   I was enabled also to observe the animal's mode of proceeding in the destruction of bones: the shin bone of an ox being presented to this hyæna, he began to bite off with his molar teeth large fragments from its upper extremity, and swallowed them whole as fast as they were broken off.   On his reaching the medullary cavity, the bone split into angular fragments, many of which he caught up greedily and swallowed

least, the entire skeleton of the one or more hyænas that died last and left no survivors to devour them; we find a sufficient reply to this question, in the circumstance of the probable destruction of the last individuals by the diluvian waters: on the rise of these, had there been any hyænas in the den, they would have rushed out, and fled for safety to the hills; and if absent, they could by no possibility have returned to it from the higher levels: that they were extirpated by this catastrophe is obvious, from the discovery of their bones in the diluvial gravel both of England and Germany. The same circum-

---

entire: he went on cracking it till he had extracted all the marrow, licking out the lowest portion of it with his tongue: this done, he left untouched the lower condyle, which contains no marrow, and is very hard. The state and form of this residuary fragment are precisely like those of similar bones at Kirkdale; the marks of teeth on it are very few, as the bone usually gave off a splinter before the large conical teeth had forced a hole through it; these few, however, entirely resemble the impressions we find on the bones at Kirkdale; the small splinters also in form and size, and manner of fracture, are not distinguishable from the fossil ones. I preserve all the fragments and the gnawed portions of this bone for the sake of comparison by the side of those I have from the antediluvian den in Yorkshire: there is absolutely no difference between them, except in point of age. The animal left untouched the solid bones of the tarsus and carpus, and such parts of the cylindrical bones, as we find untouched at Kirkdale, and devoured only the parts analogous to those which are there deficient. The keeper pursuing this experiment to its final result, presented me the next morning with a large quantity of album græcum, disposed in balls, that agree entirely in size, shape, and substance with those that were found in the den at Kirkdale. I gave the animal successively three shin bones of a sheep; he snapped them asunder in a moment, dividing each in two parts only, which he swallowed entire, without the smallest mastication. On the keeper putting a spar of wood, two inches in diameter, into his den, he cracked it in pieces as if it had been touchwood, and in a minute the whole was reduced to a mass of splinters. The power of his jaws far exceeded any animal force of the kind I ever saw exerted, and reminded me of nothing so much as of a miner's crushing mill, or the scissars with which they cut off bars of iron and copper in the metal founderies.

stance will also explain the reason why there are no heaps of bones found on the outside of the Kirkdale cave, as described by Busbequius on the outside of the hyænas' dens in Anatolia; for every thing that lay without, on the antediluvian surface, must have been swept far away, and scattered by the violence of the diluvian waters; and there is no reason for believing that hyænas, or any other animals whatever, have occupied the den subsequently to that catastrophe*.

Although the evidence to prove the cave to have been inhabited as a den by successive generations of hyænas appears thus direct, it may be as well to consider what other hypotheses can be suggested, to explain the collection of bones assembled in it.

1st. It may be said, that the various animals had entered the cave spontaneously to die, or had fled into it as a refuge from some general convulsion: but the diameter of the cave, as has been mentioned before, compared with the bulk of the elephant and rhinoceros, renders this solution impossible as to the larger animals; and with respect to the smaller, we can imagine no circumstances that would collect together, spontaneously, animals of such dissimilar habits as hyænas, tigers, bears, wolves, foxes, horses, oxen, deer, rabbits, water-rats, mice, weasels, and birds.

2d. It may be suggested, that they were drifted in by the waters

---

* It has been suggested further, that there is no proof that this individual cave was actually occupied at the precise point of time at which the waters began to rise, although it certainly had been so during several generations not long preceding. It may have been abandoned a short time prior to it, and at that moment have been untenanted; for modern hunters do not always find their game exactly on the same spot, nor is there any thing to prevent hyænas as well as other wild animals from occasionally changing their quarters. *Quarterly Review*, Oct. 1822, p. 468.

of a flood : if so, either the carcasses floated in entire; or the bones
alone were drifted in after separation from the flesh : in the first of
these cases, the larger carcasses, as we have already stated, could not
have entered at all; and of the smaller ones, the cave could not have
contained a sufficient number to supply one-twentieth part of the
teeth and bones; moreover, the bones would not have been broken
to pieces, nor in different stages of decay. And had they been washed
in by a succession of floods, we should have had a succession of beds
of sediment and stalactite, and the cave would have been filled up by
the second or third repetition of such an operation as that which introduced the single stratum of mud, which alone occurs in it.   On
the other hypothesis, that they were drifted in after separation from
the flesh, they would have been mixed with gravel, and at least
slightly rolled on their passage; and it would still remain to be shown
by what means they were split and broken to pieces, and the dispro-
portion created which exists between the numbers of the teeth and
bones.   They could not have fallen in through the fissures, for these
are closed upwards in the substance of the rock, and do not reach to
the surface.

The 3rd, and only remaining hypothesis that occurs to me is, that
they were dragged in for food by the hyænas, who caught their prey
in the immediate vicinity of their den; and as they could not have
dragged it home from any very great distances, it follows, that the
animals they fed on all lived and died not far from the spot where
their remains are found.

The accumulation of these bones, then, appears to have been a
long process, going on during a succession of years, whilst all the

animals in question were natives of this country. The general dispersion of bones of the same animals through the diluvian gravel of high latitudes, over great part of the northern hemisphere, shows that the period in which they inhabited these regions was that immediately preceding the formation of this gravel, and that they perished by the same waters which produced it. M. Cuvier has moreover ascertained, that the fossil elephant, rhinoceros, hippopotamus, and hyæna, belong to species now unknown; and as there is no evidence that they have at any time, subsequent to the formation of the diluvium, existed in these regions, we may conclude that the period, at which the bones of these extinct species were introduced into the cave at Kirkdale, was antediluvian. Had these species ever re-established themselves in the northern portions of the world since the deluge, it is probable their remains would have been found, like those of the ox, horse, deer, hog, &c. preserved in the postdiluvian accumulations of gravel, sand, silt, mud, and peat, which are referable to causes still in operation, and which, by careful examination of their relations to the adjacent country, can be readily distinguished from those which are of diluvian origin.

The teeth and fragments of bones above described seem to have lain a long time scattered irregularly over the bottom of the den, and to have been continually accumulating until the introduction of the sediment in which they are now imbedded, and to the protection of which they owe that high state of preservation they possess. Those that lay long uncovered at the bottom of the den have undergone a decay proportionate to the time of their exposure; others, that have

G

lain only a short time before the introduction of the diluvian mud, have been preserved by it almost from even incipient decomposition.

Thus the phenomena of this cave seem referable to a period immediately antecedent to the last inundation of the earth, and in which the world was inhabited by land animals, almost all bearing a generic and many a specific resemblance to those which now exist; but so completely has the violence of that tremendous convulsion destroyed and remodelled the form of the antediluvian surface, that it is only in caverns that have been protected from its ravages that we may hope to find undisturbed evidence of events in the period immediately preceding it. The bones already described, and the stalagmite formed before the introduction of the diluvial mud, are what I consider to be the products of the period in question. It was indeed probable, before the discovery of this cave, from the abundance in which the remains of similar species occur in superficial gravel beds, which cannot be referred to any other than a diluvial origin, that such animals were the antediluvian inhabitants not only of this country, but generally of all those northern latitudes in which their remains are found (but the proof was imperfect, as it was possible they might have been drifted or floated hither by the waters from the warmer regions of the earth); but the facts developed in this charnel-house of the antediluvian forests of Yorkshire demonstrate that there was a long succession of years in which the elephant, rhinoceros, and hippopotamus had been the prey of the hyænas, which, like themselves, inhabited England in the period immediately preceding the formation of the diluvial gravel; and if they inhabited this country, it follows as a

DISCOVERED AT KIRKDALE, IN YORKSHIRE.   43

corollary, that they also inhabited all those other regions of the northern hemisphere in which similar bones have been found under precisely the same circumstances, not mineralised, but simply in the state of grave bones imbedded in loam, or clay, or gravel, over great part of northern Europe, as well as North America and Siberia. The catastrophe producing this gravel appears to have been the last event that has operated generally to modify the surface of the earth, and the few local and partial changes that have succeeded it, such as the formation of deltas, terraces, tufa, torrent-gravel and peat-bogs, all conspire to show, that the period of their commencement was subsequent to that at which the dilivium was formed *.

* It was stated in describing the locality of the cave at Kirkdale, and on comparing it with the fact of its containing the remains of large and small aquatic animals, that there was probably a lake in this part of the country at the period when they inhabited it; and this hypothesis is rendered probable by the form and disposition of the hills that still encircle the Vale of Pickering. (See Map, Plate I.)

Inclosed on the south, the west, north-west, and north, by the lofty ranges of the Wolds, the Howardian hills, the Hambleton hills, and Eastern Moorlands, the waters of this vale must either run eastward to Filey Bay, or inland towards York; and such is the superior elevation of the strata along the coast, that the sources of the Derwent, rising almost close to the sea, near Scarborough and Filey, are forced to run west and southward fifty miles inland away from the sea, till falling into the Ouse, they finally reach it by turning again eastward through the Humber. The only outlet by which this drainage is accomplished is the gorge at New Malton; and though it is not possible to ascertain what was the precise extent of this antediluvian lake, or how much of the low districts, now constituting the Vale of Pickering, may have been excavated by the same diluvian waters that produced the gorge, it is obvious, that without the existence of this gorge, much of the district within it would be laid under water; and it is not till within these few years that a large tract of this land has been recovered from a state of swamp and marsh by an artificial canal, called the Muston Drainage, which runs inland from the sea westward along the valley of the Derwent, from Muston, near Filey Bay, to the gorge of New Malton; it is equally obvious, that this gorge is referable to the agency of diluvial denudation, the ravages of which have not, perhaps, left a single portion of

44   ACCOUNT OF FOSSIL TEETH AND BONES

It is in the highest degree curious to observe, that four of the genera of animals whose bones are thus widely diffused over the temperate, and even polar regions of the northern hemisphere, should at present exist only in tropical climates, and chiefly south of the equator; and that the only country in which the elephant, rhinoceros, hippopotamus, and hyæn aare now associated is Southern Africa. In the immediate neighbourhood of the Cape they all live and die together, as they formerly did in Britain; whilst the hippopotamus is now confined exclusively to Africa, and the elephant, rhinoceros, and hyæna are also diffused widely over the continent of Asia.

To the question which here so naturally presents itself, as to what might have been the climate of the northern hemisphere when peopled with genera of animals which are now confined to the warmer regions of the earth, it is not essential to the point before me to find a solution; my object is to establish the fact, that the animals lived and died in the regions where their remains are now found, and were not drifted thither by the diluvian waters from other latitudes. The state of the climate in which these extinct species may have

the antediluvian surface of the whole earth, which is not excavated and re-modelled, so as to have lost all traces of the exact features it bore antecedently to the operations of the deluge.

It is probable, that inland lakes were much more numerous than they are at present, before the excavation of the many gorges by which our modern rivers make their escape; and this is consistent with the frequent occurrence of the remains of the hippopotamus in the diluvian gravel of England, and of various parts of Europe, particularly in the Val d'Arno. It is not unlikely that, in this antediluvian period, England was connected with the Continent, and that the excavation of the shallow channel of the Straits of Dover, and of a considerable portion of that part of the German ocean which lies between the east coast of England and the mouths of the Elbe and Rhine, may have been the effect of diluvial denudation. The average depth of all this tract of water is said to be less than thirty fathoms.

lived antecedently to the great inundation by which they were extirpated is a distinct matter of inquiry, on which the highest authorities are by no means agreed. It is the opinion of Cuvier, on the one hand, that as some of the fossil animals differ from existing species of the genera to which they belong, it is probable they had a constitution adapted to endure the rigours of a northern winter; and this opinion derives support from the Siberian elephant's carcase, discovered with all its flesh entire, in the ice of Tungusia, and its skin partially covered by long hair and wool; and from the hairy rhinoceros found in 1771 in the same country, in the frozen gravel of Vilhoui, having its flesh and skin still perfect, and of which the head and feet are now preserved at Petersburg, together with the skeleton of the elephant above alluded to, and a large quantity of its wool; to which Cuvier adds the further fact, that there are genera of existing animals, e. g. the fox tribe, which have species adapted to the extremes both of polar and tropical climates.

On the other hand, it is contended that the abundant occurrence of fossil crocodiles and tortoises, and of vegetables and shells (e. g. the nautilus), nearly allied in structure and character to those which are now peculiar to hot climates, in the secondary strata, as well as in the diluvium of high north latitudes, renders it more probable that the climate was warm in which these plants and animals lived and died, than that a change of constitution and habit should have taken place in so many animal and vegetable genera, the existing members of which are rarely found except in the warmer regions of the present earth. To this argument, I would add a still greater objection arising from the difficulty of maintaining such animals as those we are considering

46   ACCOUNT OF FOSSIL TEETH AND BONES

amid the rigours of a polar winter; and this difficulty cannot be solved by supposing them to have migrated periodically, like the musk ox and rein deer of Melville Island; for in the case of crocodiles and tortoises extensive emigration is almost impossible, and not less so to such an unwieldy animal as the hippopotamus when out of water.   It is equally difficult to imagine that they could have passed their winters in lakes or rivers frozen up with ice; and though the elephant and rhinoceros, if clothed in wool, may have fed themselves on branches of trees and brushwood during the extreme severities of winter, still I see not how even these were to be obtained in the frozen regions of Siberia, which at present produce little more than moss and lichens, which during great part of the year are buried under impenetrable ice and snow; yet it is in these regions of extreme cold, on the utmost verge of the now habitable world, that the bones of elephants are found occasionally crowded in heaps along the shores of the icy sea from Archangel to Behring's Straits, forming whole islands composed of bones and mud at the mouth of the Lena, and encased in icebergs, from which they are melted out by the solar heat of their short summer, along the coast of Tungusia, in sufficient numbers to form an important article of commerce *.

* "Lieutenant Kotzebue has discovered, in the western part of the gulf to the north of Behring's Straits, a mountain covered with verdure (moss and grass) composed interiorly of solid ice. On arriving at a place where the shore rises almost perpendicularly from the sea to the height of 100 feet, and continues afterwards to extend with a gradual inclination, they observed masses of the purest ice 100 feet high, preserved under the above vegetable carpet. The portion exposed to the sun was melting and sending much water into the sea. An undoubted proof of this ice being primitive (i. e. not formed by any causes now in action), was afforded by the great number of bones and teeth of mammoths which make their appearance when it is melted. The soil of these

Between these two conflicting opinions we are compelled to make our choice: there seems to be no third or intermediate state with which both may be compatible. It is not, however, to my present purpose to discuss the difficulties that will occur on both sides, till the further progress of geological science shall have afforded us more ample information as to the structure of our globe, and have supplied those data, without which all opinions that can be advanced on the subject must be premature, and amount to no more than plausible conjecture. At present I am concerned only to establish two important facts, 1st, that there has been a recent and general inundation of the globe; and, 2d, that the animals whose remains are found interred in the wreck of that inundation were natives of high north latitudes, and not drifted to their present place from equatorial regions by the waters that caused their destruction. One thing, however, is nearly certain, viz. that if any change of climate has taken place, it took place suddenly; for how otherwise could the elephant's carcase, found entire in ice at the mouth of the Lena, have been preserved from putrefaction till it was frozen up with the waters of the then existing ocean? Nor is it less probable that this supposed change was contemporaneous with, and produced by, the same cause which brought on the inundation. What this cause was, whether a change in the inclination in the earth's axis, or the near approach of a comet, or any other cause or combination of causes purely astrono-

mountains, which, to a certain height, are covered with an abundant herbage, is only half a foot thick; it is composed of a mixture of clay, earth, sand, and mould; the ice melts gradually beneath it, the carpet falls downwards and continues to thrive; the latitude is 66° 15' 36" N."—*Gilbert's* Annalen, 1821, quoted in the Journal of Science and the Arts, No. 27, page 236.

48 CHRONOLOGICAL INFERENCES FROM

mical, is a question the discussion of which is foreign to the object of the present memoir.

★ ★ ★ ★

260 EXPLANATION OF THE PLATES.

PLATE III.

1. Portion of the left upper jaw of the modern hyæna from the Cape.

2. Inside view of No. 1.

3. Analogous portion of the left upper jaw of the fossil hyæna from Kirkdale.

4. Inside view of No. 3, with the tooth of a water-rat adhering by stalagmite to a broken portion of the palate.

5. Fragment from Kirkdale, showing five incisor teeth of the upper jaw, much worn down, and the inside of the palate.

Pl. 3.

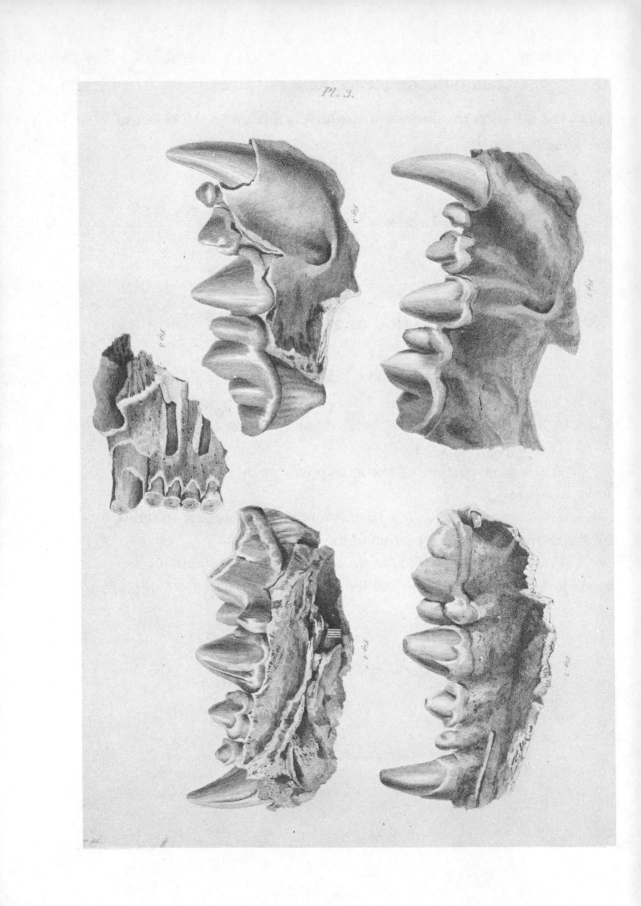

23. Thomas Chalmers (1780-1847)

On the Power, Wisdom, and Goodness of God as Manifested in the Adaptation of External Nature to the Moral and Intellectual Constitution of Man, 2 vols. (London, 1833)
Vol. 1, ix-xi and 44-56; vol. 2, 282-293

[Vol. 1, p. ix]

NOTICE.

THE series of Treatises, of which the present is one, is published under the following circumstances:

The RIGHT HONOURABLE and REVEREND FRANCIS HENRY, EARL of BRIDGEWATER, died in the month of February, 1829; and by his last Will and Testament, bearing date the 25th of February, 1825, he directed certain Trustees therein named to invest in the public funds the sum of Eight thousand pounds sterling; this sum, with the accruing dividends thereon, to be held at the disposal of the President, for the time being, of the Royal Society of London, to be paid to the person or persons nominated by him. The Testator further directed, that the person or persons selected by the said President should be appointed to write, print, and publish one thousand copies of a work *On the Power, Wisdom, and Goodness of God, as manifested in the Creation; illustrating such work by all reasonable arguments, as for instance the variety and formation of God's creatures in the animal, vegetable, and mineral kingdoms; the effect of digestion, and thereby of conversion; the construction of the hand of man, and an infinite variety of other arguments; as also by discoveries ancient and modern, in arts, sciences, and the whole extent of literature.* He desired, moreover, that the profits arising from the sale of the works so published should be paid to the authors of the works.

X

The late President of the Royal Society, Davies Gilbert, Esq. requested the assistance of his Grace the Archbishop of Canterbury and of the Bishop of London, in determining upon the best mode of carrying into effect the intentions of the Testator.   Acting with their advice, and with the concurrence of a nobleman immediately connected with the deceased, Mr. Davies Gilbert appointed the following eight gentlemen to write separate Treatises on the different branches of the subject as here stated:

THE REV. THOMAS CHALMERS, D.D.

PROFESSOR OF DIVINITY IN THE UNIVERSITY OF EDINBURGH.

ON THE ADAPTATION OF EXTERNAL NATURE TO THE MORAL AND INTELLECTUAL CONSTITUTION OF MAN.

JOHN KIDD, M.D. F.R.S.

REGIUS PROFESSOR OF MEDICINE IN THE UNIVERSITY OF OXFORD.

ON THE ADAPTATION OF EXTERNAL NATURE TO THE PHYSICAL CONDITION OF MAN.

THE REV. WILLIAM WHEWELL, M.A. F.R.S.

FELLOW OF TRINITY COLLEGE, CAMBRIDGE.

ON ASTRONOMY AND GENERAL PHYSICS.

SIR CHARLES BELL, K.H. F.R.S.

THE HAND: ITS MECHANISM AND VITAL ENDOWMENTS AS EVINCING DESIGN.

PETER MARK ROGET, M.D.

FELLOW OF AND SECRETARY TO THE ROYAL SOCIETY.

ON ANIMAL AND VEGETABLE PHYSIOLOGY.

xi

THE REV. WILLIAM BUCKLAND, D. D. F. R. S.

CANON OF CHRIST CHURCH, AND PROFESSOR OF GEOLOGY IN THE
UNIVERSITY OF OXFORD.

ON GEOLOGY AND MINERALOGY.

THE REV. WILLIAM KIRBY, M. A. F. R. S.

ON THE HISTORY, HABITS, AND INSTINCTS OF ANIMALS.

WILLIAM PROUT, M. D. F. R. S.

ON CHEMISTRY, METEOROLOGY, AND THE FUNCTION OF DIGESTION.

His Royal Highness the Duke of Sussex, President of the Royal Society, having desired that no unnecessary delay should take place in the publication of the above mentioned treatises, they will appear at short intervals, as they are ready for publication.

[Vol. I, p. 44]

27. The great object of philosophy is to ascertain the simple or ultimate principles, into which all the phenomena of nature may by analysis be resolved. But it often happens that in this attempt she stops short at a secondary law, which might be demonstrated by further analysis to be itself a complex derivative of the primitive or elementary laws. Until this work of analysis be completed, we shall often mistake what is compound for what is simple, both in the philosophy of mind and the philosophy of matter—being frequently exposed to intractable substances or intractable phenomena in both, which long withstand every effort that science makes for their decomposition. It is thus that the time is not yet come, and may never come, when we

shall fully understand, what be all the simple
elements or simple laws of matter ; and what be
all the distinct elementary laws, or, as they have
sometimes been termed, the ultimate facts in the
constitution of the human mind.   But we do not
need to wait for this communication, ere we can
trace, in either department, the wisdom and
beneficence of a Deity—for many are both the
material and the mental processes which might
be recognized as pregnant with utility, and so,
pregnant with evidence for a God, long before
the processes themselves are analyzed.   The
truth is, that a secondary law, if it do not exhibit
any additional proof of design, in a distinct useful principle, exhibits that proof in a distinct and
useful disposition of parts—for, generally speaking, a secondary law is the result of an operation by
some primitive law, in peculiar and new circumstances.   For example, the law of the tides is a
secondary law, resolvable into one more general
and elementary—even the law of gravitation.
But we might imagine a state of things, in which
the discovery of this connection would have
been impossible,—as a sky perpetually mantled
with a cloudy evelopement, which, while it did
not intercept the light either of the sun or moon,
still hid these bodies from our direct observation.
In these circumstances, the law of the tides and
the law of gravitation, though identical in themselves, could not have been identified by us ;

and so, we might have ascribed this wholesome
agitation of the sea and of the atmosphere to a
distinct power or principle in nature—affording
the distinct indication of both a kind and intelligent Creator. Now this inference is not
annihilated—it is not even enfeebled by the
discovery in question; for although the good
arising from tides in the ocean and tides in the
air, is not referable to a peculiar law—it is at
least referable to a peculiar collocation. And
this holds of all the useful secondary laws in the
material world.   If they cannot be alleged in
evidence for the number of beneficial principles
in nature—they can at least be alleged in
evidence for the number of nature's beneficial
arrangements.   If they do not attest the multitude of useful properties, they at the least attest
the multitude of useful parts in nature; and the
skill, guided by benevolence which has been
put forth in the distribution of them. So that
long ere the philosophy of matter is perfected,
or all its phenomena and its secondary laws have
been resolved into their original and constituent
principles—may we, in their obvious and immediate utility alone, detect as many separate
evidences in nature as there are separate facts
in nature, for a wise and benevolent Deity.

28. And the same will be found true of the
secondary laws in the mental world, which, if
not as many distinct beneficial principles in the

INTRODUCTORY CHAPTER.   47

constitution of the mind, are the effect of as
many distinct and beneficial arrangements in
the objects or circumstances by which it is surrounded. We have not to wait the completion
of its still more subtle and difficult analysis,
ere we come within sight of those varied indications of benevolent design which are so abundantly to be met with, both in the constitution
of the mind itself, and in the adaptation thereto
of external nature. Some there are, for example, who contend that the laws of taste are
not primitive but secondary ; that our admiration
of beauty in material objects is resolvable into
other and original emotions, and, more especially, by means of the associating principle,
into our admiration of moral excellence. Let
the justness of this doctrine be admitted ; and
its only effect on our peculiar argument is, that
the benevolence of God in thus multiplying our
enjoyments, instead of being indicated by a distinct law for suiting the human mind to the
objects which surround it, is indicated both by
the distribution of these objects and by their
investment with such qualities as suit them to
the previous constitution of the mind—that he
hath pencilled them with the very colours, or
moulded them into the very shapes which suggest either the graceful or the noble of human
character ; that he hath imparted to the violet its
hue of modesty, and clothed the lily in its robe

48   INTRODUCTORY CHAPTER.

of purest innocence, and given to the trees of the forest their respective attitudes of strength or delicacy, and made the whole face of nature one bright reflection of those virtues which the mind and character of man had originally radiated. If it be not by the implantation of a peculiar law in mind, it is at least by a peculiar disposition of tints and forms in external nature, that he hath spread so diversified a loveliness over the panorama of visible things; and thrown so many walks of enchantment around us; and turned the sights and the sounds of rural scenery into the ministers of so much and such exquisite enjoyment; and caused the outer world of matter to image forth in such profusion those various qualities, which at first had pleased or powerfully affected us in the inner world of consciousness and thought. It is by the modifying operation of circumstances that a primary is transmuted into a secondary law; and if the blessings which we enjoy under it cannot be ascribed to the insertion of a distinct principle in the nature of man, they can at least be ascribed to a useful disposition of circumstances in the theatre around him.

29. It is thus that philosophical discovery, which is felt by many to enfeeble the argument for a God, when it reduces two or more subordinate to simpler and anterior laws, does in fact leave that argument as entire as before—for if,

by analysis, it diminish the number of beneficial properties in matter, it replaces the injury which it may be supposed to have done in this way to the cause of theism, by presenting us with as great an additional number of beneficial arrangements in nature. And further, it may not be out of place to observe, that there appear to be two distinct ways by which an artificer might make manifest the wisdom of his contrivances. He may either be conceived of, as forming a substance and endowing it with the fit properties; or as finding a substance with certain given properties, and arranging it into fit dispositions for the accomplishment of some desirable end. Both the former and the latter of these we ascribe to the divine artificer—of whom we imagine, that He is the Creator as well as the Disposer of all things. It is only the latter that we can ascribe to the human artificer, who creates no substance, and ordains no property; but finds the substance with all its properties ready made and put into his hands, as the raw material out of which he fashions his implements and rears his structures of various design and workmanship. Now it is a commonly received, and has indeed been raised into a sort of universal maxim, that the highest property of wisdom is to achieve the most desirable end, or the greatest amount of good, by the fewest possible means, or by the simplest machinery. When this test is applied to the laws of

50   INTRODUCTORY CHAPTER.

nature—then we esteem it, as enhancing the
manifestation of intelligence, that one single law,
as gravitation, should, as from a central and commanding eminence, subordinate to itself a whole
host of most important phenomena ; or that from
one great and parent property, so vast a family
of beneficial consequences should spring.   And
when the same test is applied to the dispositions,
whether of nature or art—then it enhances the
manifestation of wisdom, when some great end is
brought about with a less complex or cumbersome
instrumentality, as often takes place in the simplification of machines, when, by the device of
some ingenious ligament or wheel, the apparatus
is made equally, perhaps more effective, whilst
less unwieldy or less intricate than before.   Yet
there is one way in which, along with an exceeding complication in the mechanism, there might
be given the impression, of the very highest skill
and capacity having been put forth on the contrivance of it.   It is when, by means of a very
operose and complex instrumentality, the triumph of art has been made all the more conspicuous, by a very marvellous result having
been obtained out of very unpromising materials.
It is true, that, in this case too, a still higher
impression of skill would be given, if the same or
a more striking result were arrived at, even after
the intricacy of the machine had been reduced,
by some happy device, in virtue of which, certain

INTRODUCTORY CHAPTER. 51

of its parts or circumvolutions had been super-
seded; and thus, without injury to the final
effect, so much of the complication had been
dispensed with. Still, however, the substance,
whether of the machine or the manufacture, may
be conceived so very intractable as to put an
absolute limit on any further simplification, or
as to create an absolute necessity for all the
manifold contrivance which had been expended
on it. When this idea predominates in the mind
—then all the complexity which we may behold
does not reduce our admiration of the artist,
but rather deepens the sense that we have, both
of the reconditeness of his wisdom, and of the
wondrous vastness and variety of his resources.
It is the extreme wideness of the contrast, between the sluggishness of matter and the fineness
of the results in physiology, which so enhances
our veneration for the great Architect of Nature,
when we behold the exquisite organizations of
the animal and vegetable kingdoms.* The two
exhibitions are wholly distinct from each other—
yet each of them may be perfect in its own way.
The first is held forth to us, when one law of
pervading generality is found to scatter a myriad
of beneficent consequences in its train. The
second is held forth, when, by an infinite com-

* Dr. Paley would state the problem thus. The laws of matter
being given, so to organize it, as that it shall produce or sustain
the phenomena, whether of vegetation or of life.

52   INTRODUCTORY CHAPTER.

plexity of means, a countless variety of expedients with their multiform combinations, some one design, such as the upholding of life in plants or animals is accomplished. Creation presents us in marvellous profusion with specimens of both these—at once confirming the doctrine, and illustrating the significancy of the expression in which Scripture hath conveyed it to us, when it tells of the *manifold* wisdom of God.

30. But while, on a principle already often recognised, this multitude of necessary conditions to the accomplishment of a given end, enhances the argument for a God, because each separate condition reduces the hypothesis of chance to a more violent improbability than before; yet it must not be disguised that there is a certain transcendental mystery which it has the effect of aggravating, and which it leaves unresolved. We can understand the complex machinery and the circuitous processes to which a human artist must resort, that he might overcome the else uncomplying obstinacy of inert matter, and bend it in subserviency to his special designs. But that the Divine artist who first created the matter and ordained its laws, should find the same complication necessary for the accomplishment of his purposes; that such an elaborate workmanship, for example, should be required to establish the functions of sight and hearing in the animal economy,

INTRODUCTORY CHAPTER. 53

is very like the lavish or ostensible ingenuity of a Being employed in conquering the difficulty which himself had raised. It is true, the one immediate purpose is served by it which we have just noticed,—that of presenting, as it were, to the eye of enquirers a more manifold inscription of the Divinity. But if, instead of being the object of inference, it had pleased God to make himself the object of a direct manifestation, then for the mere purpose of becoming known to his creatures, this reflex or circuitous method of revelation would have been altogether uncalled for. That under the actual system of creation, and with its actual proofs, he has made his existence most decisively known to us, we most thankfully admit. But when question is made between the actual and the conceivable systems of creation which God might have emanated, we are forced to confess, that the very circumstances which, in the existing order of things, have brightened and enhanced the evidence of His being, have also cast a deeper secrecy over what may be termed the general policy of His government and ways. And this is but one of the many difficulties, which men of unbridled speculation and unobservant of that sound philosophy that keeps within the limits of human observation, will find it abundantly possible to conjure up on the field of natural theism. It does look an impracticable enigma that the Omnipotent God, who could have grafted all the capacities of thought and feeling on an elementary atom, should have deemed fit to incorporate the human soul in the midst of so curious and complicated a frame-work. For what a variegated structure is man's animal economy. What an apparatus of vessels and bones and ligaments. What a complex mechanism. What an elaborate chemistry. What a multitude of parts in the anatomy, and of processes in the physiology of this marvellous system. What a medley, we had almost said, what a package of contents. What an unwearied play of secretions and circulations and other changes incessant and innumerable. In short, what a laborious complication ; and all to uphold a living principle, which, one might think, could by a simple fiat of omnipotence, have sprung forth at once from the great source and centre of the spiritual system, and mingled with the world of spirits—just as each new particle of light is sent forth by the emanation of a sunbeam, to play and glisten among fields of radiance.

31. But to recall ourselves from this digression among the possibilities of what might have been, to the realities of the mental system, such as it actually is. Ere we bring the very general observations of this chapter to a close, we would briefly notice an analogy between the realities of the mental and those of the corporeal system.

INTRODUCTORY CHAPTER. **55**

The enquirers into the latter have found it of
substantial benefit to their science, to have
mixed up with the prosecution of it a reference
to final causes. Their reasoning on the likely
uses of a part in anatomy, has, in some instances, suggested or served as a guide to speculations, which have been at length verified by a
discovery. We believe, in like manner, that
reasoning on the likely or obvious uses of a principle in the constitution of the human mind,
might lead, if not to the discovery, at least to
the confirmation of important truth—not perhaps
in the science itself, but in certain of the cognate
sciences which stand in no very distant relation
to it. For example, we think it should rectify
certain errors which have been committed both
in jurisprudence and political economy, if it can
be demonstrated that some of the undoubted
laws of human nature are traversed by them;
and so, that violence is thereby done to the
obvious designs of the Author of Nature. We
shall not hold it out of place, though we notice
one or two of these instances, by which it might
be seen that the mental philosophy, when
studied in connection with the palpable views
of Him by whom all its principles and processes
were ordained, is fitted to enlighten the practice
of legislation, and more especially to determine
the wisdom of certain arrangements which have

for their object the economic well-being of society.

32. We feel the arduousness of our peculiar task, and the feeling is not at all alleviated by our sense of its surpassing dignity. The superiority of mind to matter has often been the theme of eloquence to moralists. For what were all the wonders of the latter and all its glories, without a spectator mind that could intelligently view and that could tastefully admire them? Let every eye be irrevocably closed, and this were equivalent to the entire annihilation in nature of the element of light; and in like manner, if the light of all consciousness were put out in the world of mind, the world of matter, though as rich in beauty, and in the means of benevolence as before, were thereby reduced to a virtual nonentity. In these circumstances, the lighting up again of even but one mind would restore its being, or at least its significancy, to that system of materialism, which, untouched itself, had just been desolated of all those beings in whom it could kindle reflection, or to whom it could minister the sense of enjoyment. It were tantamount to the second creation of it,—or, in other words, one living intelligent spirit is of higher reckoning and mightier import than a dead universe.

[Vol. 2, p. 282]

21. There is a confused imagination with many, that every new accession, whether of evidence or of doctrine, made to the Natural, tends in so far, to reduce the claims or to depreciate the importance of the Christian Theology. The apprehension is, that, as the latter was designed to supplement the insufficiency of the former,—then, the more that the arguments of Natural Theology are strengthened, or its truths are multiplied ; the more are the lessons of the Christian Theology unneeded and uncalled for. It is thus that the discoveries of reason are held as superseding, or as casting a shade of insignificance, and even of discredit over the discoveries

of revelation. There is a certain dread or jealousy, with some humble Christians, of all that incense which is offered at the shrine of the divinity by human science—whose daring incursion on the field of theology, it is thought, will, in very proportion to the brilliancy of its success, administer both to the proud independence of the infidel, and to the pious alarm of the believer.

22. But to mitigate this disquietude, it should be recollected, in the first place, that, if Christianity have real and independent evidence of being a message from God, it will be all the more humbly and respectfully deferred to, should a previous natural theology have assured us of His existence, and thrown the radiance of a clear and satisfying demonstration over the perfections of His character. However plausible its credentials may be, we should feel no great interest in its statements or its overtures, if we doubted the reality of that Being from whom it professes to have come ; and it is precisely in as far as we are preoccupied with the conviction of a throne in heaven, and of a God sitting upon that throne, that we should receive what bore the signatures of an embassy from Him with awful reverence.

23. But there is another consideration still more decisive of the place and importance of Christianity, notwithstanding every possible

achievement by the light of nature. There are many discoveries which, so far from alleviating, serve but to enhance the difficulties of the question. For example, though science has made known to us the magnitude of the universe, it has not thereby advanced one footstep towards the secret of God's moral administration; but has, in fact, receded to a greater distance, from this now more hopeless, because now more complex and unmanageable problem than before. To multiply the data of a question, is not always the way to facilitate its solution; but often the way, rather, to make it more inextricable. And this is precisely the effect of all the discoveries that can be made by natural theology, on that problem which it is the special office of Christianity to resolve. With every new argument by which philosophy enhances the goodness and greatness of the Supreme Being, does it deepen still more the guilt and ingratitude of those who have revolted against Him. The more emphatically it can demonstrate the care and benevolence of God—the more emphatically, along with this, does it demonstrate the worthlessness of man. The same light which irradiates the perfections of the divine nature, irradiates, with more fearful manifestation than ever, the moral disease and depravation into which humanity has fallen. Had natural theology been altogether extinct, and there had been no sense of a law or law-giver among men, we should have been unconscious of any difficulty to be re-dressed, of any dilemma from which we needed extrication. But the theology of nature and con-science tells us of a law; and in proportion as it multiplies the claims of the Law-giver in heaven, does it aggravate the criminality of its subjects upon earth. With the rebellious phenomenon of a depraved species before our eyes, every new discovery of God, but deepens the enigma of man's condition in time, and of his prospects in eternity; and so makes the louder call for that remedial system, which it is the very pur-pose of Christianity to introduce into the world.

24. We hold that the theology of nature sheds powerful light on the being of a God; and that, even from its unaided demonstrations, we can reach a considerable degree of probability, both for His moral and natural attributes. But when it undertakes the question between God and man, this is what it finds to be impracticable. It is here where the main helplessness of nature lies. It is baffled in all its attempts to decipher the state and the prospects of man, viewed in the relation of an offending subject to an offended sovereign. In a word, its chief obscurity, and which it is wholly unable to disperse, is that which rests on the hopes and the destiny of our species. There is in it enough of manifestation to awaken the fears of guilt, but not enough

again to appease them. It emits, and audibly
emits, a note of terror; but in vain do we listen
for one authentic word of comfort from any of
its oracles. It is able to see the danger, but not
the deliverance. It can excite the forebodings
of the human spirit, but cannot quell them—
knowing just enough to stir the perplexity, but
not enough to set the perplexity at rest. It can
state the difficulty, but cannot unriddle the difficulty—having just as much knowledge as to
enunciate the problem, but not so much as might
lead to the solution of the problem. There must
be a measure of light, we do allow; but, like the
lurid gleam of a volcano, it is not a light which
guides, but which bewilders and terrifies. It
prompts the question, but cannot frame or furnish the reply. Natural theology may see as
much as shall draw forth the anxious interro-
gation, "What shall I do to be saved?" The
answer to this comes from a higher theology.

25. These are the grounds on which we would
affirm the insufficiency of that academic theism,
which is sometimes set forth in such an aspect
of completeness and certainty, as might seem to
leave a revelation or a gospel wholly uncalled
for. Many there are who would gloss over the
difficulties of the question; and who, in the
midst of all that undoubted outrage which has
been inflicted by sinful creatures on the truth
and the holiness and the justice of God, would,

by merging all the attributes of the Divinity
into a placid and undistinguishing tenderness,
still keep their resolute hold of heaven, as at
least the splendid imagination, by which to irra-
diate the destinies of our species. It is thus that
an airy unsupported romance has been held
forth as the vehicle, on which to embark all the
hopes and the hazards of eternity. We would
not disguise the meagreness of such a system.
We would not deliver the lessons of natural
theology, without telling at the same time of its
limits. We abjure the cruelty of that senti-
mentalism, which, to hush the alarms of guilty
man, would rob the Deity of his perfections,
and stamp a degrading mockery upon his law.
When expounding the arguments of natural
theology, along with the doctrines which it
dimly shadows forth, we must speak of the
difficulties which itself suggests but which it
cannot dispose of; we must make mention of
the obscurities into which it runs, but which it is
unable to dissipate—of its unresolved doubts—of
the mysteries through which it vainly tries to
grope its uncertain way—of its weary and fruitless efforts—of its unutterable longings. And
should, on the one hand, the speculations of
human ingenuity, and, on the other, the certainties of a well accredited revelation, come
forth to illuminate this scene of darkness—we
must not so idolize the light or the sufficiency of

nature, as to turn from the firmament's meridian blaze, that we might witness and admire the tiny lustre of a glow-worm.

26. The two positions are perfectly reconcileable—first of the insufficiency of natural religion ; and secondly, the great actual importance of it. It is the wise and profound saying of D'Alembert, that, ' man has too little sagacity to resolve an infinity of questions, which he has yet sagacity enough to make.' Now this marks the degree, in which natural theology is sagacious—being able, from its own resources, to construct a number of cases, which at the same time it is not able to reduce. These must be handed up for solution to a higher calculus ; and thus it is, that the theology of nature and of the schools, the theology of the ethical class—though most unsatisfactory, when treated as a terminating science—is most important, and the germ of developements at once precious and delightful, when treated as a rudimental one. It is a science, not so much of dicta as of desiderata ; and, from the way in which these are met by the counterpart doctrines of the gospel, the light of a powerful and most pleasing evidence is struck out by the comparison between them. It is that species of evidence which arises from the adaptation of a mould to its counterpart form ; for there is precisely this sort of fitting, in the adjustment which

obtains, between the questions of the natural and the responses of the supernatural theology. For the problem which natural theology cannot resolve, the precise difficulty which it is wholly unable to meet or to overcome, is the restoration of sinners to acceptance and favour with a God of justice. All the resources and expedients of natural theology are incompetent for this solution—it being, in fact, the great desideratum which it cannot satisfy. Still it performs an important part in making us sensible of the desideratum. It makes known to us our sin; but it cannot make known to us salvation. Let us not overlook the importance of that which it does, in its utter helplessness as to that which it does not. It puts the question, though it cannot answer the question; and nowhere so much as at this turning-point, are both the uses and the defects of natural theology so conspicuously blended.

27. Natural theology then, however little to be trusted as an informer, yet as an enquirer, or rather as a prompter to enquiry, is of inestimable service. It is a high function that she discharges, for though not able to satisfy the search, she impels to the search. We are apt to undervalue, if not to set her aside altogether, when we compare her obscure and imperfect notices with the lustre and the fulness of revelation. But this is because we overlook the virtue that lies in the probabilities of a subject

—a virtue, either, on the one hand, to fasten the attention; or, on the other hand, to condemn the want of it. This we hold to be the precise office of natural theology—and an office too, which she performs, not merely as the theology of science among those who listen to her demonstrations in the academic hall; but which she also performs with powerful and practical effect, as the theology of conscience, throughout all the classes of our general population. It is this initial work which makes her so useful, we should say so indispensable, as a preliminary to the gospel. Natural theology is quite overrated by those who would represent it as the foundation of the edifice. It is not that, but rather the taper by which we must grope our way to the edifice. The stability of a fabric is not greater than the stability of that upon which it rests; and it were ascribing a general infirmity to revelation, to set it forth, as leaning upon natural theism, in the way that a mathematical doctrine leans upon the axioms or first principles of the science. Christianity rests on its own proper evidence; and if, instead of this, she be made to rest on an antecedent natural religion, she becomes weak throughout, because weak radically. It is true that in theology, the natural goes before the revealed, even as the cry of weakness or distress goes before the relief to which it aspires, and which it is prompted to seek after. It goes before, not synthetically in the order of demonstration, but historically in the mind of the enquirer. It is not that natural religion is the premises, and Christianity the conclusion ; but it is that natural religion creates an appetite which it cannot quell ; and he who is urged thereby, seeks for a rest and a satisfaction which he can only obtain in the fulness of the gospel. Natural theology has been called the basis of Christianity. It would accord better with our own views of the place which it occupies, and of the high purpose which it undoubtedly serves —if it were called the basis of Christianization.

28. The most important exemplification of the way in which natural religion bears upon Christianity, is furnished by the question of a sinner's acceptance with God. Natural religion can suggest to man the apprehension of his guilt ; for however dim her objective view of the Deity, there is no such dimness in her ethical notion of what is due even to an uncertain God. Without having seriously resolved the question, we may stand convicted to our own minds of a hardened and habitual carelessness of the question. If our whole lives long have been spent in the midst of created things, without any serious or sustained effort of our spirits in quest of a Creator—if, as our consciences can tell, the whole drift and practical earnestness of our thoughts are towards the gifts, with but a rare and occasional anxiety towards the Giver—if the sense of

Him touch but lightly on our spirits, and we, by
our perpetual lapses from the sacred to the secu-
lar, prove that our gravitation is to earth, and
that in truth our best-loved element is atheism—
if the notices of a God, however indistinct wherewith we are surrounded, instead of fastening our
regards on this high contemplation, do but disturb without at all influencing the general tenor
of our engagements—these are things of which
the light of Nature can take cognizance; and
these are things because of which, and of their felt
unworthiness, nature is visited by the misgivings
both of remorse and of terror. She has data
enough on which to found the demonstration
and the sense of her own unworthiness; and
hence a general feeling of insecurity among all
spirits, a secret but strong apprehension that all
is not right between them and God.

29. This is not a matter of mere sensitive and
popular impression; but in strict accordance
with the views of a calm and intelligent jurisprudence. It enters into the very essence of our
conception of a moral government, that it must
have sanctions—which could not have place,
were there either to be no dispensation of re-
wards and punishments; or were the penalties,
though denounced with all the parade and pro-
clamation of law, to be never executed. It is
not the lesson of conscience, that God would,
under the mere impulse of a parental fondness

for the creatures whom He had made, let down the high state and sovereignty which belong to Him ; or that He would forbear the infliction of the penalty, because of any soft or timid shrinking from the pain it would give to the objects of His displeasure.   There is nothing either in history or nature, which countenances such an imagination of the Deity, as that, in the relentings of mere tenderness, He would stoop to any weak or unworthy compromise with guilt. The actual sufferings of life speak loudly and experimentally against the supposition ; and when one looks to the disease and the agony of spirit, and above all the hideous and unsparing death, with its painful struggles and gloomy forebodings, which are spread universally over the face of the earth—we cannot but imagine of the God who presides over such an economy, that He is not a being who will falter from the imposition of any severity, which might serve the objects of a high administration. Else all steadfastness of purpose, and steadfastness of principle were fallen from.   God would stand forth to the eye of His own creatures, a spectacle of outraged dignity.   And He of whom we image that He dwells in an unviolable sanctuary, the august monarch of heaven and earth —with a law by subjects dishonoured, by the sovereign unavenged—would possess but the semblance and the mockery of a throne.

24. Adam Sedgwick (1785-1873)

A Discourse on the Studies of the University of Cambridge, 5th edition (London and Cambridge, 1850)
Pp. xvi-xxvii

that we have no right to speak of a Creator or of a creative power; because the links of nature's chain may be infinite in number, and the order of nature may have been eternal. With such a view of nature we may end in downright atheism; or, if we accept the indications of intelligence in the natural world, we may perhaps advance one step farther, and try to satisfy the longings of the mind in some cold scheme of pantheism. As a matter of fact, views, like those just pointed at, have been brought forward again and again by men who have denied the being of a God; or, if they could not bring themselves so far to belie their inner nature as to deny the being of a God, were at least resolved to deprive him of his personality, of his creative power and will, and of his providential government. To combat such opinions is not the immediate purpose of this Preface; for I wish to deal with facts rather than opinions. Whatever semblance of truth they may have, while we arrest ourselves among the laws of dead matter, they are utterly without meaning when applied to the forms of organic life: for it is now beyond dispute, and is proved by the physical records of the earth, *that all the visible forms of organic life had a beginning in time.* To have established this point is the glory of Geology.

§ 2. *Theory of Spontaneous Generation, Transmutation of Species, &c.*

To combat or explain away the previous conclusion a new scheme of nature was invented. It was con-

It may be true that we can form no adequate conception of creative power; neither, on the other hand, have we any adequate conception of the sustaining power, whereby the order of the natural world is upheld. It may also be true that in the mind and will of the intelligent First Cause there is no distinction between the exercise of a creative and a sustaining power. Of this we know absolutely nothing; and what do we gain by such a speculation? It is irreverent, and out of the reach of sound philosophy: for we cannot, to use the words of Bacon, "fly up to the secrets of the senses." When applied to nature all our language is inadequate, and but feebly shadows out such ultimate truths of the material world as would express the will and purpose of the great First Cause. But our knowledge is not unreal because it is limited; provided it be only the expression of that form of truth which defines the reflexion of the natural world in the mind of man, while he is honestly employed upon the materials surrounding him, and neither forgets his own faculties, nor oversteps the evidence that is before him.

To meet such views as these, it has been affirmed, that we behold in nature only a chain of second causes of which we know neither the beginning nor the end;

tended that we know nothing but second causes, and that they are all in all—that the commencement of organic life was nothing more than one of the material changes in the endless cycle of movements going on continually before our eyes—a new material combination produced by the elemental powers of the natural world; and as purely natural as any new mechanical deposit or any new chemical combination. This view of the commencement of the organic world was called *spontaneous generation.*

But our theorists were not content to rest at this point. They further assumed that the humblest forms of organic life, having thus begun, had also a natural tendency to breed upwards, so as to ascend (by a law of progressive development) on a natural scale of organic forms:—that a monad thus passed by natural means (and by natural means only) into the more complicated form of some zoophyte—the zoophyte into a mollusk—the mollusk, by a like succession of natural steps, into a fish, a reptile, a bird, and a mammal:—and lastly, that by a like natural progression (in which all idea of creative power is excluded) some inferior mammal passed into a monkey, and a monkey into a man. The successive changes, implied in this theory, were not sudden, but slow and gradual, and brought about, during the lapse of ages, by the insensible sliding of one species into another. Thus by the simple operation of second causes we obtain, on the principles of this theory, two classes of phenomena, one defined by the words *spontaneous generation,* the other by such terms as *progressive*

development, or *transmutation of species :* and thus we are supposed naturally to account for all the phenomena of organic life and the whole sequence of animated nature.

The authors and early defenders of this theory were, perhaps without exception, unbelievers in every form of Revealed Truth. They were materialists in the rankest sense of that term. They denied all distinction between material and moral phenomena—regarding them both as nothing more than the varied manifestations of the powers of second causes. Most of them formally denied all proofs of design in nature, and all indications of an overruling Providence; and thus struck at the foundation of Natural Religion. But a doctrine may be true, and yet may be turned to evil purposes. The first questions for discussion are the following:—Is this doctrine true? Has the animal kingdom been first produced by *spontaneous generation,* and afterwards perfected by *transmutation and progressive development ?*

The Author of the *Vestiges of the Natural History of Creation,* has adopted the whole scheme which has been sketched in the preceding sentences; and to a comment on his principles I must devote a portion of this Preface. His work is written in a dogmatic spirit, and in good language. It is written also in the words of seeming reverence, and takes for granted the indications of a Final Cause; though its principles and language were invented and affirmed by those who did their best to cheat us out of our conceptions of a Creator, and denied the whole doctrine of Final Causes. The Author proved, by the numerous mistakes of his must be some such power within the natural range of things." Satisfactorily shewn that there must be some power in nature independent of our experience! The Author while using this language is speaking of second causes; and seems never to have learnt that there are not, and never can be, any probabilities in nature that are not suggested by experience. I now pass on to his system.

(1) He assumes the truth of the Nebular Hypothesis. It is his first link in the chain of natural causes. But has this hypothesis been confirmed by the progress of discovery? Is it passing into the condition of a sound physical theory? I think the contrary. On this subject I request the academic reader (for to such readers the following little work is still addressed) to turn to note (D) of the Appendix (*infra*, p. 118*.) I cannot pause to notice the author's violation of every rule of sober and severe induction in his extravagant extension of the hypothesis.

(2) After a series of natural transformations, he at length finds a world fit for the support of animal life, and animal life begins. Spontaneous generation and a gradual transformation of species on an ascending scale are now to bring about all the phenomena of the organic world†. He allows of no creative will distinct

* See also Supplement to the Appendix No. I.

† In using these words I refer to no particular scheme of arrangement for the organic kingdoms. The reasoning of the text applies to every scheme, linear or circular, simple or complicated. Every scheme, however, implies an ascent from beings of a low organic structure to beings of a higher; and it is a matter of indifference to the argument, whether this ascent take place upon one line or upon a thousand.

early editions, that he was neither well acquainted with the first principles of physics, nor well read in any sound work on physiology. Hence, his book was received with no respect and favour by men of science. On this point I can, even now, speak with the utmost confidence. But it was new in the popular literature of this country; and more than this, it was systematical and positive, and seemed to offer to the smatterers in natural science a kind of short and royal road to universal knowledge. By such persons it has been received with no common favour.

The Author is not only unacquainted with any of the severe lessons of inductive knowledge, but has a mind apparently incapable of comprehending them. Without this supposition it would be hardly possible to acquit him of insincerity. No moral accusation is, however, brought against him. He writes in good faith, and had imposed upon himself before he unconsciously attempted to deceive others. The misinterpreted facts, to which he first clung to support his argument, may be rescued from his grasp, one after another. But he will not easily change or modify his first opinions: for, speaking of specific transmutations, he has told us—that though there never may have been an instance of it since the beginning of the human race, "yet the doctrine may be shewn, on grounds altogether apart, to have a strong probability on its side." ... "And though this knowledge were never to be clearly attained, it would not much affect the present argument, provided it be satisfactorily shewn that there my firm conviction. All the Author's instances are drawn from the dark corners of nature's kingdom, where it is almost physically impossible to trace the progress of her workmanship. Sober philosophy would tell him, in such cases, to be guided by analogy ; and all analogy is against him. We may presume that he has selected such instances as are best suited to fortify his argument. And what are they?—The *Hydatid*, which sometimes affects the domestic pig, and is supposed not to attack the wild animal ; the *Larva* of the *Œnopota cellaris*, which lives nowhere but in wine and beer ; an *insect* which feeds only on chocolate ; a *Tinea*, which only attacks dressed wool ; and the *Pimelodes cyclopum*, which are only found in subterranean lakes in the old craters of the Andes. How are the negations implied in the three first instances to be proved? How, for example, is it possible to prove that no wild boar is ever attacked by the *Hydatid?* The domestic animals are constantly before us, the wild animals are not. The *Tinea* attacks the fleece, as well as the prepared and manufactured wool. And were the Author's statement true to the letter it would start no new difficulty ; for sheep in the wild state must cast their wool, which, when scoured by the elements, might become a proper nidus for the *Tinea*. The case of the *Pimelodes cyclopum* is only one example, out of many, of animals with a confined habitat : neither is it fairly stated ; for those who have described these fishes tell us that they are found in the streams on the mountain-sides as well as in the old craters of the Andes. They are not more difficult

from the vulgar action of second causes—no distinction between mind and matter—*material and moral* :—and man (with all his powers, physical and intellectual, his responsibilities as a social being, his expectations of moral progress, and his hopes of future good) is, so far as regards causation, a phenomenon of the same order with the incrustation on a culinary vessel, the salt formed in a chemist's laboratory, or the crystal in a mineral vein. Should we gain in clearness of conception, or be more philosophical in our use of general terms, by linking together (as the supposed products of a common material causation) phenomena so different in kind, and so widely asunder in every manifestation they make to the mind of man? Is there any sobriety or truth in such a scheme as this? On the contrary, I think it shallow, mischievous, and untrue.

(3) All natural knowledge is based on inductive reasoning. We have learnt to comprehend the mechanical movement of the heavens by first learning the laws of motion upon the earth. In like manner, we have learnt to speculate securely on the functions of organized being, during the old conditions of the earth, by first studying the laws of organic life among the phenomena of living nature. In every instance we must begin with what is known and present to us, before we can speculate about what is unknown and remote. To this rule we know of no exception.

(4) What proof, then, have we of the doctrine of spontaneous generation in the living world? In replying that we are utterly without proof, I only state

to account for than the trout and other fishes so commonly found in the high mountain-lakes of Europe.

The *Entozoa* are, beyond comparison, the cases most difficult to account for: but the whole history of many species has been well explained in conformity with the common laws of generation: and, speaking generally, we may ask, if these creatures spring spontaneously without ova, how comes it to pass that nature has provided a means for the continuance of their species, and that some of them are almost incredibly prolific*?

But it was affirmed, within the last few years, that a *new animal* had been produced by a direct galvanic experiment, and without any pre-existing germs of animal life. If so, we should have one instance of the commencement of organic life, in conformity with the hypothesis of spontaneous generation. It turned out, however, that this new marvel of nature's chemistry was but an old and wellknown species of *Acarus*, of which the *ova*, in tens of thousands, probably existed in the dusty corners of the very room where the first experiments were carried on. The creatures thus produced were not (as they ought to have been) low in the organic scale, but were of a very complicated structure; and one of the pretended creations was a female well filled with eggs. If galvanism could thus create animals, no wonder it should also exercise over them a fecundating influence! But is there so much as one good

* See Professor Owen's Lectures on the Invertebrate Animals (1843, pp. 76—81), and the *Edinburgh Review* (July, 1845, pp. 68—72). The ova in one individual of the Entozoa amount to sixty-four millions!

physiologist or chemist who now adopts the first interpretation of these galvanic experiments? I believe not so much as one. Ridicule is the only weapon we can condescend to use against the outrage on common sense and universal experience implied in this mockery of a creative power. One thing, however, is proved by this history, that to be an intrepid vindicator of rash hypotheses a man must be first endowed by nature with an ample capacity of belief*.

(5) Have we any proof of *specific transmutations* in the living world? We have not, so far as I understand the question, so much as the shadow of any proof of them. The constancy of organic forms—like species producing like according to a fixed law of generation— is the obvious and certain fact. These laws are to the organic world what the laws of elective affinity are to chemical combinations. Varieties there are—the limits of species are not well known—the riches of nature are so great that, in the almost boundless varieties of animal forms created on a common plan, one species often comes close upon another. As an inevitable consequence, naturalists have made many blunders; and their vanity may sometimes have led them to give new specific names, where the new names were not called for. But the mistakes of naturalists alter not the laws of nature. Art has been pushed to the utmost in modifying the natural forms of organic life: but not so much as one true specific change has been ever brought about, so as to raise the progeny of any known animal to a

* See Supplement to the Appendix No. II.

S. D.

higher grade on the organic scale. These are the broad conclusions we arrive at from all the facts and analogies offered to our senses. In this instance it will not serve our purpose to entrench ourselves among the dark corners of the animal kingdom; where, (as in the case of the *Entozoa*,) from the inevitable want of evidence, we may, by casting away analogy, affirm that generation is ambiguous, and that species are inconstant. The Author's theory demands specific transmutations on the whole ascending scale, from a monad to a man. To suppose that specific transmutations are now going on at the bottom of the scale, where our senses fail us, and we can have no good evidence of the fact; while no transmutations are going on in the upper steps of the organic scale, where we have good evidence, is to stultify the whole argument, and to suppose an inconstancy in nature's workmanship, abhorrent from any conception we can form of a true organic law.

A good theory embodies in verbal propositions our conceptions of natural laws; and these conceptions are all based on observation, experiment, or good analogy. Does the hypothesis of *spontaneous generation and transmutation of species* deserve the name of a theory? It is not suggested, but contradicted, by the broad and obvious facts of nature; and I know of no good analogy to help it out. A hypothetical spirit may do good service, provided it urge us on to make new experiments; but if we rest content with it, and, above all, if it lead us, as it has too often done, to shut our eyes against facts, and to take from nature no response but such as suits our

fanatical belief of what nature ought to be, it must do deadly mischief to the cause of inductive truth.

25. Charles Darwin (1809-1882)

On the Origin of Species by means of Natural Selection, or the Preservation of Favoured Races in the Struggle for Life (London, 1859)
Pp. 459-490

CHAPTER XIV.

RECAPITULATION AND CONCLUSION.

Recapitulation of the difficulties on the theory of Natural Selection — Recapitulation of the general and special circumstances in its favour — Causes of the general belief in the immutability of species — How far the theory of natural selection may be extended — Effects of its adoption on the study of Natural history — Concluding remarks.

As this whole volume is one long argument, it may be convenient to the reader to have the leading facts and inferences briefly recapitulated.

That many and grave objections may be advanced against the theory of descent with modification through natural selection, I do not deny. I have endeavoured to give to them their full force. Nothing at first can appear more difficult to believe than that the more complex organs and instincts should have been perfected, not by means superior to, though analogous with, human reason, but by the accumulation of innumerable slight variations, each good for the individual possessor. Nevertheless, this difficulty, though appearing to our imagination insuperably great, cannot be considered real if we admit the following propositions, namely,—that gradations in the perfection of any organ or instinct, which we may consider, either do now exist or could have existed, each good of its kind,—that all organs and instincts are, in ever so slight a degree, variable,—and, lastly, that there is a struggle for existence leading to the preservation of each profitable deviation of structure or instinct. The truth of these propositions cannot, I think, be disputed.

X 2

It is, no doubt, extremely difficult even to conjecture by what gradations many structures have been perfected, more especially amongst broken and failing groups of organic beings; but we see so many strange gradations in nature, as is proclaimed by the canon, "Natura non facit saltum," that we ought to be extremely cautious in saying that any organ or instinct, or any whole being, could not have arrived at its present state by many graduated steps. There are, it must be admitted, cases of special difficulty on the theory of natural selection; and one of the most curious of these is the existence of two or three defined castes of workers or sterile females in the same community of ants; but I have attempted to show how this difficulty can be mastered.

With respect to the almost universal sterility of species when first crossed, which forms so remarkable a contrast with the almost universal fertility of varieties when crossed, I must refer the reader to the recapitulation of the facts given at the end of the eighth chapter, which seem to me conclusively to show that this sterility is no more a special endowment than is the incapacity of two trees to be grafted together; but that it is incidental on constitutional differences in the reproductive systems of the intercrossed species. We see the truth of this conclusion in the vast difference in the result, when the same two species are crossed reciprocally; that is, when one species is first used as the father and then as the mother.

The fertility of varieties when intercrossed and of their mongrel offspring cannot be considered as universal; nor is their very general fertility surprising when we remember that it is not likely that either their constitutions or their reproductive systems should have been profoundly modified. Moreover, most of the varieties which have been experimentised on have been produced under domestication; and as domestication apparently tends to eliminate sterility, we ought not to expect it also to produce sterility.

The sterility of hybrids is a very different case from that of first crosses, for their reproductive organs are more or less functionally impotent; whereas in first crosses the organs on both sides are in a perfect condition. As we continually see that organisms of all kinds are rendered in some degree sterile from their constitutions having been disturbed by slightly different and new conditions of life, we need not feel surprise at hybrids being in some degree sterile, for their constitutions can hardly fail to have been disturbed from being compounded of two distinct organisations. This parallelism is supported by another parallel, but directly opposite, class of facts; namely, that the vigour and fertility of all organic beings are increased by slight changes in their conditions of life, and that the offspring of slightly modified forms or varieties acquire from being crossed increased vigour and fertility. So that, on the one hand, considerable changes in the conditions of life and crosses between greatly modified forms, lessen fertility; and on the other hand, lesser changes in the conditions of life and crosses between less modified forms, increase fertility.

Turning to geographical distribution, the difficulties encountered on the theory of descent with modification are grave enough. All the individuals of the same species, and all the species of the same genus, or even higher group, must have descended from common parents; and therefore, in however distant and isolated parts of the world they are now found, they must in the course of successive generations have passed from some one part to the others. We are often wholly unable

even to conjecture how this could have been effected. Yet, as we have reason to believe that some species have retained the same specific form for very long periods, enormously long as measured by years, too much stress ought not to be laid on the occasional wide diffusion of the same species; for during very long periods of time there will always be a good chance for wide migration by many means. A broken or interrupted range may often be accounted for by the extinction of the species in the intermediate regions. It cannot be denied that we are as yet very ignorant of the full extent of the various climatal and geographical changes which have affected the earth during modern periods; and such changes will obviously have greatly facilitated migration. As an example, I have attempted to show how potent has been the influence of the Glacial period on the distribution both of the same and of representative species throughout the world. We are as yet profoundly ignorant of the many occasional means of transport. With respect to distinct species of the same genus inhabiting very distant and isolated regions, as the process of modification has necessarily been slow, all the means of migration will have been possible during a very long period; and consequently the difficulty of the wide diffusion of species of the same genus is in some degree lessened.

As on the theory of natural selection an interminable number of intermediate forms must have existed, linking together all the species in each group by gradations as fine as our present varieties, it may be asked, Why do we not see these linking forms all around us? Why are not all organic beings blended together in an inextricable chaos? With respect to existing forms, we should remember that we have no right to expect (excepting in rare cases) to discover *directly* connecting links between them, but only between each and some extinct and supplanted form. Even on a wide area, which has during a long period remained continuous, and of which the climate and other conditions of life change insensibly in going from a district occupied by one species into another district occupied by a closely allied species, we have no just right to expect often to find intermediate varieties in the intermediate zone. For we have reason to believe that only a few species are undergoing change at any one period; and all changes are slowly effected. I have also shown that the intermediate varieties which will at first probably exist in the intermediate zones, will be liable to be supplanted by the allied forms on either hand; and the latter, from existing in greater numbers, will generally be modified and improved at a quicker rate than the intermediate varieties, which exist in lesser numbers; so that the intermediate varieties will, in the long run, be supplanted and exterminated.

On this doctrine of the extermination of an infinitude of connecting links, between the living and extinct inhabitants of the world, and at each successive period between the extinct and still older species, why is not every geological formation charged with such links? Why does not every collection of fossil remains afford plain evidence of the gradation and mutation of the forms of life? We meet with no such evidence, and this is the most obvious and forcible of the many objections which may be urged against my theory. Why, again, do whole groups of allied species appear, though certainly they often falsely appear, to have come in suddenly on the several geological stages? Why do we not find great piles of strata beneath the Silurian system, stored with the remains of the progenitors of the Silurian groups of fossils? For certainly on my theory such

strata must somewhere have been deposited at these ancient and utterly unknown epochs in the world's history.

I can answer these questions and grave objections only on the supposition that the geological record is far more imperfect than most geologists believe. It cannot be objected that there has not been time sufficient for any amount of organic change; for the lapse of time has been so great as to be utterly inappreciable by the human intellect. The number of specimens in all our museums is absolutely as nothing compared with the countless generations of countless species which certainly have existed. We should not be able to recognise a species as the parent of any one or more species if we were to examine them ever so closely, unless we likewise possessed many of the intermediate links between their past or parent and present states; and these many links we could hardly ever expect to discover, owing to the imperfection of the geological record. Numerous existing doubtful forms could be named which are probably varieties; but who will pretend that in future ages so many fossil links will be discovered, that naturalists will be able to decide, on the common view, whether or not these doubtful forms are varieties? As long as most of the links between any two species are unknown, if any one link or intermediate variety be discovered, it will simply be classed as another and distinct species. Only a small portion of the world has been geologically explored. Only organic beings of certain classes can be preserved in a fossil condition, at least in any great number. Widely ranging species vary most, and varieties are often at first local,—both causes rendering the discovery of intermediate links less likely. Local varieties will not spread into other and distant regions until they are considerably modified and improved; and when they do spread, if discovered in a geological formation, they will appear as if suddenly created there, and will be simply classed as new species. Most formations have been intermittent in their accumulation; and their duration, I am inclined to believe, has been shorter than the average duration of specific forms. Successive formations are separated from each other by enormous blank intervals of time; for fossiliferous formations, thick enough to resist future degradation, can be accumulated only where much sediment is deposited on the subsiding bed of the sea. During the alternate periods of elevation and of stationary level the record will be blank. During these latter periods there will probably be more variability in the forms of life; during periods of subsidence, more extinction.

With respect to the absence of fossiliferous formations beneath the lowest Silurian strata, I can only recur to the hypothesis given in the ninth chapter. That the geological record is imperfect all will admit; but that it is imperfect to the degree which I require, few will be inclined to admit. If we look to long enough intervals of time, geology plainly declares that all species have changed; and they have changed in the manner which my theory requires, for they have changed slowly and in a graduated manner. We clearly see this in the fossil remains from consecutive formations invariably being much more closely related to each other, than are the fossils from formations distant from each other in time.

Such is the sum of the several chief objections and difficulties which may justly be urged against my theory; and I have now briefly recapitulated the answers and explanations which can be given to them. I have felt these difficulties far too heavily during many years to

x 3

doubt their weight. But it deserves especial notice that the more important objections relate to questions on which we are confessedly ignorant; nor do we know how ignorant we are. We do not know all the possible transitional gradations between the simplest and the most perfect organs; it cannot be pretended that we know all the varied means of Distribution during the long lapse of years, or that we know how imperfect the Geological Record is. Grave as these several difficulties are, in my judgment they do not overthrow the theory of descent with modification.

Now let us turn to the other side of the argument. Under domestication we see much variability. This seems to be mainly due to the reproductive system being eminently susceptible to changes in the conditions of life; so that this system, when not rendered impotent, fails to reproduce offspring exactly like the parent-form. Variability is governed by many complex laws,—by correlation of growth, by use and disuse, and by the direct action of the physical conditions of life. There is much difficulty in ascertaining how much modification our domestic productions have undergone; but we may safely infer that the amount has been large, and that modifications can be inherited for long periods. As long as the conditions of life remain the same, we have reason to believe that a modification, which has already been inherited for many generations, may continue to be inherited for an almost infinite number of generations. On the other hand we have evidence that variability, when it has once come into play, does not wholly cease; for new varieties are still occasionally produced by our most anciently domesticated productions.

Man does not actually produce variability; he only

unintentionally exposes organic beings to new conditions of life, and then nature acts on the organisation, and causes variability. But man can and does select the variations given to him by nature, and thus accumulate them in any desired manner. He thus adapts animals and plants for his own benefit or pleasure. He may do this methodically, or he may do it unconsciously by preserving the individuals most useful to him at the time, without any thought of altering the breed. It is certain that he can largely influence the character of a breed by selecting, in each successive generation, individual differences so slight as to be quite inappreciable by an uneducated eye. This process of selection has been the great agency in the production of the most distinct and useful domestic breeds. That many of the breeds produced by man have to a large extent the character of natural species, is shown by the inextricable doubts whether very many of them are varieties or aboriginal species.

There is no obvious reason why the principles which have acted so efficiently under domestication should not have acted under nature. In the preservation of favoured individuals and races, during the constantly-recurrent Struggle for Existence, we see the most powerful and ever-acting means of selection. The struggle for existence inevitably follows from the high geometrical ratio of increase which is common to all organic beings. This high rate of increase is proved by calculation, by the effects of a succession of peculiar seasons, and by the results of naturalisation, as explained in the third chapter. More individuals are born than can possibly survive. A grain in the balance will determine which individual shall live and which shall die,—which variety or species shall increase in number, and which shall decrease, or finally become extinct. As the indi-

viduals of the same species come in all respects into the closest competition with each other, the struggle will generally be most severe between them; it will be almost equally severe between the varieties of the same species, and next in severity between the species of the same genus. But the struggle will often be very severe between beings most remote in the scale of nature. The slightest advantage in one being, at any age or during any season, over those with which it comes into competition, or better adaptation in however slight a degree to the surrounding physical conditions, will turn the balance.

With animals having separated sexes there will in most cases be a struggle between the males for possession of the females. The most vigorous individuals, or those which have most successfully struggled with their conditions of life, will generally leave most progeny. But success will often depend on having special weapons or means of defence, or on the charms of the males; and the slightest advantage will lead to victory.

As geology plainly proclaims that each land has undergone great physical changes, we might have expected that organic beings would have varied under nature, in the same way as they generally have varied under the changed conditions of domestication. And if there be any variability under nature, it would be an unaccountable fact if natural selection had not come into play. It has often been asserted, but the assertion is quite incapable of proof, that the amount of variation under nature is a strictly limited quantity. Man, though acting on external characters alone and often capriciously, can produce within a short period a great result by adding up mere individual differences in his domestic productions; and every one admits that there are at least individual differences in species under nature. But, besides such differences, all naturalists have admitted the existence of varieties, which they think sufficiently distinct to be worthy of record in systematic works. No one can draw any clear distinction between individual differences and slight varieties; or between more plainly marked varieties and sub-species, and species. Let it be observed how naturalists differ in the rank which they assign to the many representative forms in Europe and North America.

If then we have under nature variability and a powerful agent always ready to act and select, why should we doubt that variations in any way useful to beings, under their excessively complex relations of life, would be preserved, accumulated, and inherited? Why, if man can by patience select variations most useful to himself, should nature fail in selecting variations useful, under changing conditions of life, to her living products? What limit can be put to this power, acting during long ages and rigidly scrutinising the whole constitution, structure, and habits of each creature,—favouring the good and rejecting the bad? I can see no limit to this power, in slowly and beautifully adapting each form to the most complex relations of life. The theory of natural selection, even if we looked no further than this, seems to me to be in itself probable. I have already recapitulated, as fairly as I could, the opposed difficulties and objections: now let us turn to the special facts and arguments in favour of the theory.

On the view that species are only strongly marked and permanent varieties, and that each species first existed as a variety, we can see why it is that no line of demarcation can be drawn between species, commonly supposed to have been produced by special acts of creation, and varieties which are acknowledged to have been produced by secondary laws. On this same view we can understand how it is that in each region

where many species of a genus have been produced, and where they now flourish, these same species should present many varieties; for where the manufactory of species has been active, we might expect, as a general rule, to find it still in action; and this is the case if varieties be incipient species. Moreover, the species of the larger genera, which afford the greater number of varieties or incipient species, retain to a certain degree the character of varieties; for they differ from each other by a less amount of difference than do the species of smaller genera. The closely allied species also of the larger genera apparently have restricted ranges, and they are clustered in little groups round other species—in which respects they resemble varieties. These are strange relations on the view of each species having been independently created, but are intelligible if all species first existed as varieties.

As each species tends by its geometrical ratio of reproduction to increase inordinately in number; and as the modified descendants of each species will be enabled to increase by so much the more as they become more diversified in habits and structure, so as to be enabled to seize on many and widely different places in the economy of nature, there will be a constant tendency in natural selection to preserve the most divergent offspring of any one species. Hence during a long-continued course of modification, the slight differences, characteristic of varieties of the same species, tend to be augmented into the greater differences characteristic of species of the same genus. New and improved varieties will inevitably supplant and exterminate the older, less improved and intermediate varieties; and thus species are rendered to a large extent defined and distinct objects. Dominant species belonging to the larger groups tend to give birth to new and dominant forms; so that each large group tends to become still larger, and at the same time more divergent in character. But as all groups cannot thus succeed in increasing in size, for the world would not hold them, the more dominant groups beat the less dominant. This tendency in the large groups to go on increasing in size and diverging in character, together with the almost inevitable contingency of much extinction, explains the arrangement of all the forms of life, in groups subordinate to groups, all within a few great classes, which we now see everywhere around us, and which has prevailed throughout all time. This grand fact of the grouping of all organic beings seems to me utterly inexplicable on the theory of creation.

As natural selection acts solely by accumulating slight, successive, favourable variations, it can produce no great or sudden modification; it can act only by very short and slow steps. Hence the canon of " Natura non facit saltum," which every fresh addition to our knowledge tends to make more strictly correct, is on this theory simply intelligible. We can plainly see why nature is prodigal in variety, though niggard in innovation. But why this should be a law of nature if each species has been independently created, no man can explain.

Many other facts are, as it seems to me, explicable on this theory. How strange it is that a bird, under the form of woodpecker, should have been created to prey on insects on the ground; that upland geese, which never or rarely swim, should have been created with webbed feet; that a thrush should have been created to dive and feed on sub-aquatic insects; and that a petrel should have been created with habits and structure fitting it for the life of an auk or grebe! and so on in endless other cases. But on the view of each

species constantly trying to increase in number, with natural selection always ready to adapt the slowly varying descendants of each to any unoccupied or ill-occupied place in nature, these facts cease to be strange, or perhaps might even have been anticipated.

As natural selection acts by competition, it adapts the inhabitants of each country only in relation to the degree of perfection of their associates; so that we need feel no surprise at the inhabitants of any one country, although on the ordinary view supposed to have been specially created and adapted for that country, being beaten and supplanted by the naturalised productions from another land. Nor ought we to marvel if all the contrivances in nature be not, as far as we can judge, absolutely perfect; and if some of them be abhorrent to our ideas of fitness. We need not marvel at the sting of the bee causing the bee's own death; at drones being produced in such vast numbers for one single act, and being then slaughtered by their sterile sisters; at the astonishing waste of pollen by our fir-trees; at the instinctive hatred of the queen bee for her own fertile daughters; at ichneumonidæ feeding within the live bodies of caterpillars; and at other such cases. The wonder indeed is, on the theory of natural selection, that more cases of the want of absolute perfection have not been observed.

The complex and little known laws governing variation are the same, as far as we can see, with the laws which have governed the production of so-called specific forms. In both cases physical conditions seem to have produced but little direct effect; yet when varieties enter any zone, they occasionally assume some of the characters of the species proper to that zone. In both varieties and species, use and disuse seem to have produced some effect; for it is difficult to resist this conclusion when we look, for instance, at the logger-headed duck, which has wings incapable of flight, in nearly the same condition as in the domestic duck; or when we look at the burrowing tucutucu, which is occasionally blind, and then at certain moles, which are habitually blind and have their eyes covered with skin; or when we look at the blind animals inhabiting the dark caves of America and Europe. In both varieties and species correlation of growth seems to have played a most important part, so that when one part has been modified other parts are necessarily modified. In both varieties and species reversions to long-lost characters occur. How inexplicable on the theory of creation is the occasional appearance of stripes on the shoulder and legs of the several species of the horse-genus and in their hybrids! How simply is this fact explained if we believe that these species have descended from a striped progenitor, in the same manner as the several domestic breeds of pigeon have descended from the blue and barred rock-pigeon!

On the ordinary view of each species having been independently created, why should the specific characters, or those by which the species of the same genus differ from each other, be more variable than the generic characters in which they all agree? Why, for instance, should the colour of a flower be more likely to vary in any one species of a genus, if the other species, supposed to have been created independently, have differently coloured flowers, than if all the species of the genus have the same coloured flowers? If species are only well-marked varieties, of which the characters have become in a high degree permanent, we can understand this fact; for they have already varied since they branched off from a common progenitor in certain characters, by which they have come to be specifically distinct from each other;

and therefore these same characters would be more likely still to be variable than the generic characters which have been inherited without change for an enormous period. It is inexplicable on the theory of creation why a part developed in a very unusual manner in any one species of a genus, and therefore, as we may naturally infer, of great importance to the species, should be eminently liable to variation; but, on my view, this part has undergone, since the several species branched off from a common progenitor, an unusual amount of variability and modification, and therefore we might expect this part generally to be still variable. But a part may be developed in the most unusual manner, like the wing of a bat, and yet not be more variable than any other structure, if the part be common to many subordinate forms, that is, if it has been inherited for a very long period; for in this case it will have been rendered constant by long-continued natural selection.

Glancing at instincts, marvellous as some are, they offer no greater difficulty than does corporeal structure on the theory of the natural selection of successive, slight, but profitable modifications. We can thus understand why nature moves by graduated steps in endowing different animals of the same class with their several instincts. I have attempted to show how much light the principle of gradation throws on the admirable architectural powers of the hive-bee. Habit no doubt sometimes comes into play in modifying instincts; but it certainly is not indispensable, as we see, in the case of neuter insects, which leave no progeny to inherit the effects of long-continued habit. On the view of all the species of the same genus having descended from a common parent, and having inherited much in common, we can understand how it is that allied species, when placed under considerably different conditions of life, yet should follow nearly the same instincts; why the thrush of South America, for instance, lines her nest with mud like our British species. On the view of instincts having been slowly acquired through natural selection we need not marvel at some instincts being apparently not perfect and liable to mistakes, and at many instincts causing other animals to suffer.

If species be only well-marked and permanent varieties, we can at once see why their crossed offspring should follow the same complex laws in their degrees and kinds of resemblance to their parents,—in being absorbed into each other by successive crosses, and in other such points,—as do the crossed offspring of acknowledged varieties. On the other hand, these would be strange facts if species have been independently created, and varieties have been produced by secondary laws.

If we admit that the geological record is imperfect in an extreme degree, then such facts as the record gives, support the theory of descent with modification. New species have come on the stage slowly and at successive intervals; and the amount of change, after equal intervals of time, is widely different in different groups. The extinction of species and of whole groups of species, which has played so conspicuous a part in the history of the organic world, almost inevitably follows on the principle of natural selection; for old forms will be supplanted by new and improved forms. Neither single species nor groups of species reappear when the chain of ordinary generation has once been broken. The gradual diffusion of dominant forms, with the slow modification of their descendants, causes the forms of life, after long intervals of time, to appear as if they had changed simultaneously throughout the world. The fact of the fossil remains of each formation being in some degree intermediate in character between the

fossils in the formations above and below, is simply explained by their intermediate position in the chain of descent. The grand fact that all extinct organic beings belong to the same system with recent beings, falling either into the same or into intermediate groups, follows from the living and the extinct being the offspring of common parents. As the groups which have descended from an ancient progenitor have generally diverged in character, the progenitor with its early descendants will often be intermediate in character in comparison with its later descendants; and thus we can see why the more ancient a fossil is, the oftener it stands in some degree intermediate between existing and allied groups. Recent forms are generally looked at as being, in some vague sense, higher than ancient and extinct forms; and they are in so far higher as the later and more improved forms have conquered the older and less improved organic beings in the struggle for life. Lastly, the law of the long endurance of allied forms on the same continent,—of marsupials in Australia, of edentata in America, and other such cases,—is intelligible, for within a confined country, the recent and the extinct will naturally be allied by descent.

Looking to geographical distribution, if we admit that there has been during the long course of ages much migration from one part of the world to another, owing to former climatal and geographical changes and to the many occasional and unknown means of dispersal, then we can understand, on the theory of descent with modification, most of the great leading facts in Distribution. We can see why there should be so striking a parallelism in the distribution of organic beings throughout space, and in their geological succession throughout time; for in both cases the beings have been connected by the bond of ordinary generation, and the means of modification have been the same. We see the full meaning of the wonderful fact, which must have struck every traveller, namely, that on the same continent, under the most diverse conditions, under heat and cold, on mountain and lowland, on deserts and marshes, most of the inhabitants within each great class are plainly related; for they will generally be descendants of the same progenitors and early colonists. On this same principle of former migration, combined in most cases with modification, we can understand, by the aid of the Glacial period, the identity of some few plants, and the close alliance of many others, on the most distant mountains, under the most different climates; and likewise the close alliance of some of the inhabitants of the sea in the northern and southern temperate zones, though separated by the whole intertropical ocean. Although two areas may present the same physical conditions of life, we need feel no surprise at their inhabitants being widely different, if they have been for a long period completely separated from each other; for as the relation of organism to organism is the most important of all relations, and as the two areas will have received colonists from some third source or from each other, at various periods and in different proportions, the course of modification in the two areas will inevitably be different.

On this view of migration, with subsequent modification, we can see why oceanic islands should be inhabited by few species, but of these, that many should be peculiar. We can clearly see why those animals which cannot cross wide spaces of ocean, as frogs and terrestrial mammals, should not inhabit oceanic islands; and why, on the other hand, new and peculiar species of bats, which can traverse the ocean, should so often be found on islands far distant from any continent. Such facts

as the presence of peculiar species of bats, and the absence of all other mammals, on oceanic islands, are utterly inexplicable on the theory of independent acts of creation.

The existence of closely allied or representative species in any two areas, implies, on the theory of descent with modification, that the same parents formerly inhabited both areas; and we almost invariably find that wherever many closely allied species inhabit two areas, some identical species common to both still exist. Wherever many closely allied yet distinct species occur, many doubtful forms and varieties of the same species likewise occur. It is a rule of high generality that the inhabitants of each area are related to the inhabitants of the nearest source whence immigrants might have been derived. We see this in nearly all the plants and animals of the Galapagos archipelago, of Juan Fernandez, and of the other American islands being related in the most striking manner to the plants and animals of the neighbouring American mainland; and those of the Cape de Verde archipelago and other African islands to the African mainland. It must be admitted that these facts receive no explanation on the theory of creation.

The fact, as we have seen, that all past and present organic beings constitute one grand natural system, with group subordinate to group, and with extinct groups often falling in between recent groups, is intelligible on the theory of natural selection with its contingencies of extinction and divergence of character. On these same principles we see how it is, that the mutual affinities of the species and genera within each class are so complex and circuitous. We see why certain characters are far more serviceable than others for classification;—why adaptive characters, though of paramount importance to the being, are of hardly any importance in classification; why characters derived from rudimentary parts, though of no service to the being, are often of high classificatory value; and why embryological characters are the most valuable of all. The real affinities of all organic beings are due to inheritance or community of descent. The natural system is a genealogical arrangement, in which we have to discover the lines of descent by the most permanent characters, however slight their vital importance may be.

The framework of bones being the same in the hand of a man, wing of a bat, fin of the porpoise, and leg of the horse,—the same number of vertebræ forming the neck of the giraffe and of the elephant,—and innumerable other such facts, at once explain themselves on the theory of descent with slow and slight successive modifications. The similarity of pattern in the wing and leg of a bat, though used for such different purpose,—in the jaws and legs of a crab,—in the petals, stamens, and pistils of a flower, is likewise intelligible on the view of the gradual modification of parts or organs, which were alike in the early progenitor of each class. On the principle of successive variations not always supervening at an early age, and being inherited at a corresponding not early period of life, we can clearly see why the embryos of mammals, birds, reptiles, and fishes should be so closely alike, and should be so unlike the adult forms. We may cease marvelling at the embryo of an air-breathing mammal or bird having branchial slits and arteries running in loops, like those in a fish which has to breathe the air dissolved in water, by the aid of well-developed branchiæ.

Disuse, aided sometimes by natural selection, will often tend to reduce an organ, when it has become useless by changed habits or under changed conditions

of life; and we can clearly understand on this view the meaning of rudimentary organs. But disuse and selection will generally act on each creature, when it has come to maturity and has to play its full part in the struggle for existence, and will thus have little power of acting on an organ during early life; hence the organ will not be much reduced or rendered rudimentary at this early age. The calf, for instance, has inherited teeth, which never cut through the gums of the upper jaw, from an early progenitor having well-developed teeth; and we may believe, that the teeth in the mature animal were reduced, during successive generations, by disuse or by the tongue and palate having been fitted by natural selection to browse without their aid; whereas in the calf, the teeth have been left untouched by selection or disuse, and on the principle of inheritance at corresponding ages have been inherited from a remote period to the present day. On the view of each organic being and each separate organ having been specially created, how utterly inexplicable it is that parts, like the teeth in the embryonic calf or like the shrivelled wings under the soldered wing-covers of some beetles, should thus so frequently bear the plain stamp of inutility! Nature may be said to have taken pains to reveal, by rudimentary organs and by homologous structures, her scheme of modification, which it seems that we wilfully will not understand.

I have now recapitulated the chief facts and considerations which have thoroughly convinced me that species have changed, and are still slowly changing by the preservation and accumulation of successive slight favourable variations. Why, it may be asked, have all the most eminent living naturalists and geologists rejected this view of the mutability of species? It cannot be to hide our ignorance under such expressions as the "plan of creation," "unity of design," &c., and to think that we give an explanation when we only restate a fact. Any one whose disposition leads him to attach more weight to unexplained difficulties than to the explanation of a certain number of facts will certainly reject my theory. A few naturalists, endowed with much flexibility of mind, and who have already begun to doubt on the immutability of species, may be influenced by this volume; but I look with confidence to the future, to young and rising naturalists, who will be able to view both sides of the question with impartiality. Whoever is led to believe that species are mutable will do good service by conscientiously expressing his conviction; for only thus can the load of prejudice by which this subject is overwhelmed be removed.

Several eminent naturalists have of late published their belief that a multitude of reputed species in each genus are not real species; but that other species are real, that is, have been independently created. This seems to me a strange conclusion to arrive at. They admit that a multitude of forms, which till lately they themselves thought were special creations, and which are still thus looked at by the majority of naturalists, and which consequently have every external characteristic feature of true species,—they admit that these have been produced by variation, but they refuse to extend the same view to other and very slightly different forms. Nevertheless they do not pretend that they can define, or even conjecture, which are the created forms of life, and which are those produced by secondary laws. They admit variation as a *vera causa* in one case, they arbitrarily reject it in another, without assigning any distinction in the two cases. The day will come when this will be given as a curious illustration of

asserted that organic beings in a state of nature are subject to no variation; it cannot be proved that the amount of variation in the course of long ages is a limited quantity; no clear distinction has been, or can be, drawn between species and well-marked varieties. It cannot be maintained that species when intercrossed are invariably sterile, and varieties invariably fertile; or that sterility is a special endowment and sign of creation. The belief that species were immutable productions was almost unavoidable as long as the history of the world was thought to be of short duration; and now that we have acquired some idea of the lapse of time, we are too apt to assume, without proof, that the geological record is so perfect that it would have afforded us plain evidence of the mutation of species, if they had undergone mutation.

But the chief cause of our natural unwillingness to admit that one species has given birth to other and distinct species, is that we are always slow in admitting any great change of which we do not see the intermediate steps. The difficulty is the same as that felt by so many geologists, when Lyell first insisted that long lines of inland cliffs had been formed, and great valleys excavated, by the slow action of the coast-waves. The mind cannot possibly grasp the full meaning of the term of a hundred million years; it cannot add up and perceive the full effects of many slight variations, accumulated during an almost infinite number of generations.

Although I am fully convinced of the truth of the views given in this volume under the form of an abstract, I by no means expect to convince experienced naturalists whose minds are stocked with a multitude of facts all viewed, during a long course of years, from a point of view directly opposite to mine. It is so easy

Y

the blindness of preconceived opinion. These authors seem no more startled at a miraculous act of creation than at an ordinary birth. But do they really believe that at innumerable periods in the earth's history certain elemental atoms have been commanded suddenly to flash into living tissues? Do they believe that at each supposed act of creation one individual or many were produced? Were all the infinitely numerous kinds of animals and plants created as eggs or seed, or as full grown? and in the case of mammals, were they created bearing the false marks of nourishment from the mother's womb? Although naturalists very properly demand a full explanation of every difficulty from those who believe in the mutability of species, on their own side they ignore the whole subject of the first appearance of species in what they consider reverent silence.

It may be asked how far I extend the doctrine of the modification of species. The question is difficult to answer, because the more distinct the forms are which we may consider, by so much the arguments fall away in force. But some arguments of the greatest weight extend very far. All the members of whole classes can be connected together by chains of affinities, and all can be classified on the same principle, in groups subordinate to groups. Fossil remains sometimes tend to fill up very wide intervals between existing orders. Organs in a rudimentary condition plainly show that an early progenitor had the organ in a fully developed state; and this in some instances necessarily implies an enormous amount of modification in the descendants. Throughout whole classes various structures are formed on the same pattern, and at an embryonic age the species closely resemble each other. Therefore I cannot doubt that the theory of descent with modification

y 2

embraces all the members of the same class. I believe that animals have descended from at most only four or five progenitors, and plants from an equal or lesser number.

Analogy would lead me one step further, namely, to the belief that all animals and plants have descended from some one prototype. But analogy may be a deceitful guide. Nevertheless all living things have much in common, in their chemical composition, their germinal vesicles, their cellular structure, and their laws of growth and reproduction. We see this even in so trifling a circumstance as that the same poison often similarly affects plants and animals; or that the poison secreted by the gall-fly produces monstrous growths on the wild rose or oak-tree. Therefore I should infer from analogy that probably all the organic beings which have ever lived on this earth have descended from some one primordial form, into which life was first breathed.

When the views entertained in this volume on the origin of species, or when analogous views are generally admitted, we can dimly foresee that there will be a considerable revolution in natural history. Systematists will be able to pursue their labours as at present; but they will not be incessantly haunted by the shadowy doubt whether this or that form be in essence a species. This I feel sure, and I speak after experience, will be no slight relief. The endless disputes whether or not some fifty species of British brambles are true species will cease. Systematists will have only to decide (not that this will be easy) whether any form be sufficiently constant and distinct from other forms, to be capable of definition; and if definable, whether the differences be sufficiently important to deserve a specific name. This latter point will become a far more essential consideration than it is at present; for differences, however slight, between any two forms, if not blended by intermediate gradations, are looked at by most naturalists as sufficient to raise both forms to the rank of species. Hereafter we shall be compelled to acknowledge that the only distinction between species and well-marked varieties is, that the latter are known, or believed, to be connected at the present day by intermediate gradations, whereas species were formerly thus connected. Hence, without quite rejecting the consideration of the present existence of intermediate gradations between any two forms, we shall be led to weigh more carefully and to value higher the actual amount of difference between them. It is quite possible that forms now generally acknowledged to be merely varieties may hereafter be thought worthy of specific names, as with the primrose and cowslip; and in this case scientific and common language will come into accordance. In short, we shall have to treat species in the same manner as those naturalists treat genera, who admit that genera are merely artificial combinations made for convenience. This may not be a cheering prospect; but we shall at least be freed from the vain search for the undiscovered and undiscoverable essence of the term species.

The other and more general departments of natural history will rise greatly in interest. The terms used by naturalists of affinity, relationship, community of type, paternity, morphology, adaptive characters, rudimentary and aborted organs, &c., will cease to be metaphorical, and will have a plain signification. When we no longer look at an organic being as a savage looks at a ship, as at something wholly beyond his comprehension; when we regard every production of nature as one which has had a history; when we contemplate every complex structure

and instinct as the summing up of many contrivances, each useful to the possessor, nearly in the same way as when we look at any great mechanical invention as the summing up of the labour, the experience, the reason, and even the blunders of numerous workmen; when we thus view each organic being, how far more interesting, I speak from experience, will the study of natural history become!

A grand and almost untrodden field of inquiry will be opened, on the causes and laws of variation, on correlation of growth, on the effects of use and disuse, on the direct action of external conditions, and so forth. The study of domestic productions will rise immensely in value. A new variety raised by man will be a far more important and interesting subject for study than one more species added to the infinitude of already recorded species. Our classifications will come to be, as far as they can be so made, genealogies; and will then truly give what may be called the plan of creation. The rules for classifying will no doubt become simpler when we have a definite object in view. We possess no pedigrees or armorial bearings; and we have to discover and trace the many diverging lines of descent in our natural genealogies, by characters of any kind which have long been inherited. Rudimentary organs will speak infallibly with respect to the nature of long-lost structures. Species and groups of species, which are called aberrant, and which may fancifully be called living fossils, will aid us in forming a picture of the ancient forms of life. Embryology will reveal to us the structure, in some degree obscured, of the prototypes of each great class.

When we can feel assured that all the individuals of the same species, and all the closely allied species of most genera, have within a not very remote period descended from one parent, and have migrated from some one birthplace; and when we better know the many means of migration, then, by the light which geology now throws, and will continue to throw, on former changes of climate and of the level of the land, we shall surely be enabled to trace in an admirable manner the former migrations of the inhabitants of the whole world. Even at present, by comparing the differences of the inhabitants of the sea on the opposite sides of a continent, and the nature of the various inhabitants of that continent in relation to their apparent means of immigration, some light can be thrown on ancient geography.

The noble science of Geology loses glory from the extreme imperfection of the record. The crust of the earth with its embedded remains must not be looked at as a well-filled museum, but as a poor collection made at hazard and at rare intervals. The accumulation of each great fossiliferous formation will be recognised as having depended on an unusual concurrence of circumstances, and the blank intervals between the successive stages as having been of vast duration. But we shall be able to gauge with some security the duration of these intervals by a comparison of the preceding and succeeding organic forms. We must be cautious in attempting to correlate as strictly contemporaneous two formations, which include few identical species, by the general succession of their forms of life. As species are produced and exterminated by slowly acting and still existing causes, and not by miraculous acts of creation and by catastrophes; and as the most important of all causes of organic change is one which is almost independent of altered and perhaps suddenly altered physical conditions, namely, the mutual relation of organism to organism,—the improvement or the extermination of

others; it follows, that the amount of organic change in the fossils of consecutive formations probably serves as a fair measure of the lapse of actual time. A number of species, however, keeping in a body might remain for a long period unchanged, whilst within this same period, several of these species, by migrating into new countries and coming into competition with foreign associates, might become modified; so that we must not overrate the accuracy of organic change as a measure of time. During early periods of the earth's history, when the forms of life were probably fewer and simpler, the rate of change was probably slower; and at the first dawn of life, when very few forms of the simplest structure existed, the rate of change may have been slow in an extreme degree. The whole history of the world, as at present known, although of a length quite incomprehensible by us, will hereafter be recognised as a mere fragment of time, compared with the ages which have elapsed since the first creature, the progenitor of innumerable extinct and living descendants, was created.

In the distant future I see open fields for far more important researches. Psychology will be based on a new foundation, that of the necessary acquirement of each mental power and capacity by gradation. Light will be thrown on the origin of man and his history.

Authors of the highest eminence seem to be fully satisfied with the view that each species has been independently created. To my mind it accords better with what we know of the laws impressed on matter by the Creator, that the production and extinction of the past and present inhabitants of the world should have been due to secondary causes, like those determining the birth and death of the individual. When I view all beings not as special creations, but as the lineal descendants of some few beings which lived long before the first bed of the Silurian system was deposited, they seem to me to become ennobled. Judging from the past, we may safely infer that not one living species will transmit its unaltered likeness to a distant futurity. And of the species now living very few will transmit progeny of any kind to a far distant futurity; for the manner in which all organic beings are grouped, shows that the greater number of species of each genus, and all the species of many genera, have left no descendants, but have become utterly extinct. We can so far take a prophetic glance into futurity as to foretel that it will be the common and widely-spread species, belonging to the larger and dominant groups, which will ultimately prevail and procreate new and dominant species. As all the living forms of life are the lineal descendants of those which lived long before the Silurian epoch, we may feel certain that the ordinary succession by generation has never once been broken, and that no cataclysm has desolated the whole world. Hence we may look with some confidence to a secure future of equally inappreciable length. And as natural selection works solely by and for the good of each being, all corporeal and mental endowments will tend to progress towards perfection.

It is interesting to contemplate an entangled bank, clothed with many plants of many kinds, with birds singing on the bushes, with various insects flitting about, and with worms crawling through the damp earth, and to reflect that these elaborately constructed forms, so different from each other, and dependent on each other in so complex a manner, have all been produced by laws acting around us. These laws, taken in the largest sense, being Growth with Reproduction; Inheritance which is almost implied by reproduction; Variability from the indirect and direct action of the external con-

ditions of life, and from use and disuse; a Ratio of Increase so high as to lead to a Struggle for Life, and as a consequence to Natural Selection, entailing Divergence of Character and the Extinction of less-improved forms. Thus, from the war of nature, from famine and death, the most exalted object which we are capable of conceiving, namely, the production of the higher animals, directly follows. There is grandeur in this view of life, with its several powers, having been originally breathed into a few forms or into one; and that, whilst this planet has gone cycling on according to the fixed law of gravity, from so simple a beginning endless forms most beautiful and most wonderful have been, and are being, evolved.

26. Thomas Henry Huxley (1825-1895)

'On the Reception of the "Origin of Species" '
From *The Life and Letters of Charles Darwin, including an Auto-*
biographical Chapter, edited by Francis Darwin, 3 vols.
(London ,1887), vol. 2, 179-204

(179)

CHAPTER V.

BY PROFESSOR HUXLEY.

ON THE RECEPTION OF THE 'ORIGIN OF SPECIES.'

To the present generation, that is to say, the people a few
years on the hither and thither side of thirty, the name of
Charles Darwin stands alongside of those of Isaac Newton and
Michael Faraday ; and, like them, calls up the grand ideal of
a searcher after truth and interpreter of Nature.   They think
of him who bore it as a rare combination of genius, industry,
and unswerving veracity, who earned his place among the
most famous men of the age by sheer native power, in the
teeth of a gale of popular prejudice, and uncheered by a
sign of favour or appreciation from the official fountains of
honour ; as one who, in spite of an acute sensitiveness to
praise and blame, and notwithstanding provocations which
might have excused any outbreak, kept himself clear of all
envy, hatred, and malice, nor dealt otherwise than fairly and
justly with the unfairness and injustice which was showered
upon him ; while, to the end of his days, he was ready to
listen with patience and respect to the most insignificant of
reasonable objectors.

And with respect to that theory of the origin of the forms of
life peopling our globe, with which Darwin's name is bound up
as closely as that of Newton with the theory of gravitation,
nothing seems to be further from the mind of the present
generation than any attempt to smother it with ridicule or
to crush it by vehemence of denunciation.   " The struggle for

N 2

existence," and " Natural selection," have become household words and every-day conceptions. The reality and the importance of the natural processes on which Darwin founds his deductions are no more doubted than those of growth and multiplication ; and, whether the full potency attributed to them is admitted or not, no one doubts their vast and far-reaching significance. Wherever the biological sciences are studied, the 'Origin of Species' lights the path of the investigator ; wherever they are taught it permeates the course of instruction. Nor has the influence of Darwinian ideas been less profound, beyond the realms of Biology. The oldest of all philosophies, that of Evolution, was bound hand and foot and cast into utter darkness during the millennium of theological scholasticism. But Darwin poured new life-blood into the ancient frame; the bonds burst, and the revivified thought of ancient Greece has proved itself to be a more adequate expression of the universal order of things than any of the schemes which have been accepted by the credulity and welcomed by the superstition of seventy later generations of men.

To any one who studies the signs of the times, the emergence of the philosophy of Evolution, in the attitude of claimant to the throne of the world of thought, from the limbo of hated and, as many hoped, forgotten things, is the most portentous event of the nineteenth century. But the most effective weapons of the modern champions of Evolution were fabricated by Darwin ; and the 'Origin of Species' has enlisted a formidable body of combatants, trained in the severe school of Physical Science, whose ears might have long remained deaf to the speculations of *a priori* philosophers.

I do not think that any candid or instructed person will deny the truth of that which has just been asserted. He may hate the very name of Evolution, and may deny its pretensions as vehemently as a Jacobite denied those of George the Second. But there it is—not only as solidly seated as the Hanoverian

dynasty, but happily independent of Parliamentary sanction—
and the dullest antagonists have come to see that they have
to deal with an adversary whose bones are to be broken by
no amount of bad words.

Even the theologians have almost ceased to pit the plain
meaning of Genesis against the no less plain meaning of
Nature. Their more candid, or more cautious, representatives
have given up dealing with Evolution as if it were a damnable
heresy, and have taken refuge in one of two courses. Either
they deny that Genesis was meant to teach scientific truth,
and thus save the veracity of the record at the expense of its
authority; or they expend their energies in devising the cruel
ingenuities of the reconciler, and torture texts in the vain
hope of making them confess the creed of Science. But when
the *peine forte et dure* is over, the antique sincerity of the venerable sufferer always reasserts itself. Genesis is honest to the
core, and professes to be no more than it is, a repository of
venerable traditions of unknown origin, claiming no scientific
authority and possessing none.

As my pen finishes these passages, I can but be
amused to think what a terrible hubbub would have been
made (in truth was made) about any similar expressions of
opinion a quarter of a century ago. In fact, the contrast
between the present condition of public opinion upon the
Darwinian question; between the estimation in which
Darwin's views are now held in the scientific world; between
the acquiescence, or at least quiescence, of the theologians of
the self-respecting order at the present day and the out-
burst of antagonism on all sides in 1858–9, when the new
theory respecting the origin of species first became known to
the older generation to which I belong, is so startling that,
except for documentary evidence, I should be sometimes
inclined to think my memories dreams. I have a great
respect for the younger generation myself (they can write our
lives, and ravel out all our follies, if they choose to take the

182   ON THE RECEPTION OF

trouble, by and by), and I should be glad to be assured that the feeling is reciprocal ; but I am afraid that the story of our dealings with Darwin may prove a great hindrance to that veneration for our wisdom which I should like them to display. We have not even the excuse that, thirty years ago, Mr. Darwin was an obscure novice, who had no claims on our attention. On the contrary, his remarkable zoological and geological investigations had long given him an assured position among the most eminent and original investigators of the day ; while his charming 'Voyage of a Naturalist' had justly earned him a wide-spread reputation among the general public. I doubt if there was any man then living who had a better right to expect that anything he might choose to say on such a question as the Origin of Species would be listened to with profound attention, and discussed with respect ; and there was certainly no man whose personal character should have afforded a better safeguard against attacks, instinct with malignity and spiced with shameless impertinences.

Yet such was the portion of one of the kindest and truest men that it was ever my good fortune to know ; and years had to pass away before misrepresentation, ridicule, and denunciation, ceased to be the most notable constituents of the majority of the multitudinous criticisms of his work which poured from the press. I am loth to rake any of these ancient scandals from their well-deserved oblivion ; but I must make good a statement which may seem overcharged to the present generation, and there is no *pièce justificative* more apt for the purpose, or more worthy of such dishonour, than the article in the 'Quarterly Review' for July 1860.* Since Lord Brougham

---

* I was not aware when I wrote these passages that the authorship of the article had been publicly acknowledged. Confession unaccompanied by penitence, however, affords no ground for mitigation of judgment ; and the kindliness with which Mr. Darwin speaks of his assailant, Bishop Wilberforce (Vol. II. pp. 325, 329, 332), is so striking an exemplification of his singular gentleness and modesty, that it rather increases one's indignation against the presumption of his critic.

assailed Dr. Young, the world has seen no such specimen of
the insolence of a shallow pretender to a Master in Science as
this remarkable production, in which one of the most exact
of observers, most cautious of reasoners, and most candid of
expositors, of this or any other age, is held up to scorn
as a " flighty " person, who endeavours " to prop up his utterly
rotten fabric of guess and speculation," and whose " mode of
dealing with nature " is reprobated as " utterly dishonourable
to Natural Science."   And all this high and mighty talk, which
would have been indecent in one of Mr. Darwin's equals,
proceeds from a writer whose want of intelligence, or of conscience, or of both, is so great, that, by way of an objection to
Mr. Darwin's views, he can ask, " Is it credible that all favourable varieties of turnips are tending to become men ; " who is
so ignorant of paleontology, that he can talk of the " flowers
and fruits " of the plants of the carboniferous epoch ; of com-
parative anatomy, that he can gravely affirm the poison apparatus of the venomous snakes to be " entirely separate from
the ordinary laws of animal life, and peculiar to themselves ; "
of the rudiments of physiology, that he can ask, " what
advantage of life could alter the shape of the corpuscles into
which the blood can be evaporated ? "   Nor does the reviewer
fail to flavour this outpouring of preposterous incapacity with
a little stimulation of the *odium theologicum*. Some inkling
of the history of the conflicts between Astronomy, Geology,
and Theology, leads him to keep a retreat open by the
proviso that he cannot " consent to test the truth of Natural
Science by the word of Revelation ; " but, for all that, he
devotes pages to the exposition of his conviction that Mr.
Darwin's theory " contradicts the revealed relation of the
creation to its Creator," and is " inconsistent with the fulness
of his glory."

If I confine my retrospect of the reception of the 'Origin
of Species ' to a twelvemonth, or thereabouts, from the time

of its publication, I do not recollect anything quite so foolish and unmannerly as the 'Quarterly Review' article, unless, perhaps, the address of a Reverend Professor to the Dublin Geological Society might enter into competition with it.   But a large proportion of Mr. Darwin's critics had a lamentable resemblance to the 'Quarterly' reviewer, in so far as they lacked either the will, or the wit, to make themselves masters of his doctrine ; hardly any possessed the knowledge required to follow him through the immense range of biological and geological science which the 'Origin' covered ; while, too commonly, they had prejudged the case on theological grounds, and, as seems to be inevitable when this happens, eked out lack of reason by superfluity of railing.

But it will be more pleasant and more profitable to consider those criticisms, which were acknowledged by writers of scientific authority, or which bore internal evidence of the greater or less competency and, often, of the good faith, of their authors.   Restricting my survey to a twelvemonth, or thereabouts, after the publication of the 'Origin,' I find among such critics Louis Agassiz ; * Murray, an excellent entomologist ; Harvey, a botanist of considerable repute ; and the author of an article in the 'Edinburgh Review,' all strongly adverse to Darwin.   Pictet, the distinguished and widely learned paleontologist of Geneva, treats Mr. Darwin with a respect which forms a grateful contrast to the tone of some of the preceding writers, but consents to go with him

* "The arguments presented by Darwin in favor of a universal derivation from one primary form of all the peculiarities existing now among living beings have not made the slightest impression on my mind.

"Until the facts of Nature are shown to have been mistaken by those who have collected them, and that they have a different meaning from that now generally assigned to them, I shall therefore consider the transmutation theory as a scientific mistake, untrue in its facts, unscientific in its method, and mischievous in its tendency."—Silliman's 'Journal,' July 1860, pp. 143, 154.   Extract from the 3rd vol. of 'Contributions to the Natural History of the United States.'

THE 'ORIGIN OF SPECIES.'   185

only a very little way.* On the other hand, Lyell, up to that time a pillar of the anti-transmutationists (who regarded him, ever afterwards, as Pallas Athene may have looked at Dian, after the Endymion affair), declared himself a Darwinian, though not without putting in a serious *caveat*. Nevertheless, he was a tower of strength, and his courageous stand for truth as against consistency, did him infinite honour.   As evolutionists, *sans phrase*, I do not call to mind among the biologists more than Asa Gray, who fought the battle splendidly in the United States ; Hooker, who was no less vigorous here ; the present Sir John Lubbock and my-self.   Wallace was far away in the Malay Archipelago ; but, apart from his direct share in the promulgation of the theory of natural selection, no enumeration of the influences at work, at the time I am speaking of, would be com-plete without the mention of his powerful essay ' On the Law which has regulated the Introduction of New Species,' which was published in 1855.   On reading it afresh, I have been astonished to recollect how small was the impression it made.

In France, the influence of Elie de Beaumont and of Flourens, —the former of whom is said to have " damned himself to everlasting fame" by inventing the nickname of "*la science moussante*" for Evolutionism,†—to say nothing of the ill-will of other powerful members of the Institut, produced for a

* " I see no serious objections to the formation of varieties by natural selection in the existing world, and that, so far as earlier epochs are con-cerned, this law may be assumed to explain the origin of closely allied species, supposing for this purpose a very long period of time.

" With regard to simple varieties and closely allied species, I believe that Mr. Darwin's theory may explain many things, and throw a great light upon numerous ques-tions."—' Sur l'Origine de l'Espèce. Par Charles Darwin.' 'Archives des Sc. de la Bibliothèque Universelle de Genève,' pp. 242, 243, Mars 1860.

† One is reminded of the effect of another small academic epigram. The so-called vertebral theory of the skull is said to have been nipped in the bud in France by the whisper of an academician to his neighbour, that, in that case, one's head was a "*vertèbre pensante*."

long time the effect of a conspiracy of silence; and many years passed before the Academy redeemed itself from the reproach that the name of Darwin was not to be found on the list of its members.   However, an accomplished writer, out of the range of academical influences, M. Laugel, gave an excellent and appreciative notice of the 'Origin' in the 'Revue des Deux Mondes.'   Germany took time to consider; Bronn produced a slightly Bowdlerized translation of the 'Origin'; and 'Kladderadatsch' cut his jokes upon the ape origin of man; but I do not call to mind that any scientific notability declared himself publicly in 1860.*   None of us dreamed that, in the course of a few years, the strength (and perhaps I may add the weakness) of "Darwinismus" would have its most extensive and most brilliant illustrations in the land of learning. If a foreigner may presume to speculate on the cause of this curious interval of silence, I fancy it was that one moiety of the German biologists were orthodox at any price, and the other moiety as distinctly heterodox.   The latter were evolutionists, *a priori*, already, and they must have felt the disgust natural to deductive philosophers at being offered an inductive and experimental foundation for a conviction which they had reached by a shorter cut.   It is undoubtedly trying to learn that, though your conclusions may be all right, your reasons for them are all wrong, or, at any rate, insufficient.

On the whole, then, the supporters of Mr. Darwin's views in 1860 were numerically extremely insignificant.   There is not the slightest doubt that, if a general council of the Church scientific had been held at that time, we should have been condemned by an overwhelming majority.   And there is as little doubt that, if such a council gathered now, the decree would be of an exactly contrary nature.   It would indicate a lack

* However, the man who stands next to Darwin in his influence on modern biologists, K. E. von Bär, wrote to me, in August 1860, expressing his general assent to evolutionist views.   His phrase, "J'ai énoncé les mêmes idées . . . que M. Darwin" (vol. ii. p. 329), is shown by his subsequent writings to mean no more than this.

of sense, as well as of modesty, to ascribe to the men of that generation less capacity or less honesty than their successors possess. What, then, are the causes which led instructed and fair-judging men of that day to arrive at a judgment so different from that which seems just and fair to those who follow them ? That is really one of the most interesting of all questions connected with the history of science, and I shall try to answer it. I am afraid that in order to do so I must run the risk of appearing egotistical.   However, if I tell my own story it is only because I know it better than that of other people.

I think I must have read the 'Vestiges' before I left England in 1846 ; but, if I did, the book made very little impression upon me, and I was not brought into serious contact with the 'Species' question until after 1850.   At that time, I had long done with the Pentateuchal cosmogony, which had been impressed upon my childish understanding as Divine truth, with all the authority of parents and instructors, and from which it had cost me many a struggle to get free.   But my mind was unbiassed in respect of any doctrine which presented itself, if it professed to be based on purely philosophical and scientific reasoning.   It seemed to me then (as it does now) that "creation," in the ordinary sense of the word, is perfectly conceivable.   I find no difficulty in imagining that, at some former period, this universe was not in existence ; and that it made its appearance in six days (or instantaneously, if that is preferred), in consequence of the volition of some pre-existent Being.   Then, as now, the so-called *a priori* arguments against Theism, and, given a Deity, against the possibility of creative acts, appeared to me to be devoid of reasonable foundation.   I had not then, and I have not now, the smallest *a priori* objection to raise to the account of the creation of animals and plants given in 'Paradise Lost,' in which Milton so vividly embodies the natural sense of Genesis. Far be it from me to say that it is untrue because it is impossible. I confine myself to what must be regarded as a modest and reasonable request for some particle of evidence that the existing species of animals and plants did originate in that way, as a condition of my belief in a statement which appears to me to be highly improbable.

And, by way of being perfectly fair, I had exactly the same answer to give to the evolutionists of 1851-8. Within the ranks of the biologists, at that time, I met with nobody, except Dr. Grant, of University College, who had a word to say for Evolution—and his advocacy was not calculated to advance the cause. Outside these ranks, the only person known to me whose knowledge and capacity compelled respect, and who was, at the same time, a thorough-going evolutionist, was Mr. Herbert Spencer, whose acquaintance I made, I think, in 1852, and then entered into the bonds of a friendship which, I am happy to think, has known no interruption. Many and prolonged were the battles we fought on this topic. But even my friend's rare dialectic skill and copiousness of apt illustration could not drive me from my agnostic position. I took my stand upon two grounds : firstly, that up to that time, the evidence in favour of transmutation was wholly insufficient ; and, secondly, that no suggestion respecting the causes of the transmutation assumed, which had been made, was in any way adequate to explain the phenomena. Looking back at the state of knowledge at that time, I really do not see that any other conclusion was justifiable.

In those days I had never even heard of Treviranus' 'Biologie.' However, I had studied Lamarck attentively and I had read the 'Vestiges' with due care ; but neither of them afforded me any good ground for changing my negative and critical attitude. As for the 'Vestiges,' I confess that the book simply irritated me by the prodigious ignorance and thoroughly unscientific habit of mind manifested by the writer. If it had any influence on me at all, it set me against Evolution ; and the only review I ever have qualms of conscience about, on the ground of needless savagery, is one I wrote on the 'Vestiges' while under that influence.

With respect to the 'Philosophie Zoologique,' it is no reproach to Lamarck to say that the discussion of the Species question in that work, whatever might be said for it in 1809, was miserably below the level of the knowledge of half a century later. In that interval of time the elucidation of the structure of the lower animals and plants had given rise to wholly new conceptions of their relations ; histology and embryology, in the modern sense, had been created ; physiology had been reconstituted ; the facts of distribution, geological and geographical, had been prodigiously multiplied and reduced to order. To any biologist whose studies had carried him beyond mere species-mongering in 1850, one-half of Lamarck's arguments were obsolete and the other half erroneous, or defective, in virtue of omitting to deal with the various classes of evidence which had been brought to light since his time. Moreover his one suggestion as to the cause of the gradual modification of species—effort excited by change of conditions—was, on the face of it, inapplicable to the whole vegetable world. I do not think that any impartial judge who reads the 'Philosophie Zoologique' now, and who afterwards takes up Lyell's trenchant and effectual criticism (published as far back as 1830), will be disposed to allot to Lamarck a much higher place in the establishment of biological evolution than that which Bacon assigns to himself in relation to physical science generally,—*buccinator tantum.**

But, by a curious irony of fate, the same influence which led me to put as little faith in modern speculations on this subject, as in the venerable traditions recorded in the first two chapters of Genesis, was perhaps more potent than any other

* Erasmus Darwin first promulgated Lamarck's fundamental conceptions, and, with greater logical consistency, he had applied them to plants. But the advocates of his claims have failed to show that he, in any respect, anticipated the central idea of the 'Origin of Species.'

in keeping alive a sort of pious conviction that Evolution, after all, would turn out true. I have recently read afresh the first edition of the 'Principles of Geology'; and when I consider that this remarkable book had been nearly thirty years in everybody's hands, and that it brings home to any reader of ordinary intelligence a great principle and a great fact—the principle, that the past must be explained by the present, unless good cause be shown to the contrary ; and the fact, that, so far as our knowledge of the past history of life on our globe goes, no such cause can be shown *—I cannot but believe that Lyell, for others, as for myself, was the chief agent in smoothing the road for Darwin. For consistent uniformitarianism postulates evolution as much in the organic as in the inorganic world. The origin of a new species by other than ordinary agencies would be a vastly greater "catastrophe" than any of those which Lyell successfully eliminated from sober geological speculation.

In fact, no one was better aware of this than Lyell himself.† If one reads any of the earlier editions of the 'Principles' carefully (especially by the light of the interesting series of letters recently published by Sir Charles Lyell's biographer), it is easy to see that, with all his energetic opposition to Lamarck,

* The same principle and the same fact guide and result from all sound historical investigation. Grote's ' History of Greece' is a product of the same intellectual movement as Lyell's ' Principles.'

† Lyell, with perfect right, claims this position for himself. He speaks of having " advocated a law of continuity even in the organic world, so far as possible without adopting Lamarck's theory of transmutation. . . .

" But while I taught that as often as certain forms of animals and plants disappeared, for reasons quite intelligible to us, others took their place by virtue of a causation which was beyond our comprehension ; it remained for Darwin to accumulate proof that there is no break between the incoming and the outgoing species, that they are the work of evolution, and not of special creation. . . .

" I had certainly prepared the way in this country, in six editions of my work before the 'Vestiges of Creation' appeared in 1842 [1844], for the reception of Darwin's gradual and insensible evolution of species." —'Life and Letters,' Letter to Haeckel, vol. ii. p. 436. Nov. 23, 1868.

on the one hand, and to the ideal quasi-progressionism of Agassiz, on the other, Lyell, in his own mind, was strongly disposed to account for the origination of all past and present species of living things by natural causes. But he would have liked, at the same time, to keep the name of creation for a natural process which he imagined to be incomprehensible.

In a letter addressed to Mantell (dated March 2, 1827), Lyell speaks of having just read Lamarck ; he expresses his delight at Lamarck's theories, and his personal freedom from any objections based on theological grounds. And though he is evidently alarmed at the pithecoid origin of man involved in Lamarck's doctrine, he observes :—

"But, after all, what changes species may really undergo! How impossible will it be to distinguish and lay down a line, beyond which some of the so-called extinct species have never passed into recent ones."

Again, the following remarkable passage occurs in the post-script of a letter addressed to Sir John Herschel in 1836 :—

"In regard to the origination of new species, I am very glad to find that you think it probable that it may be carried on through the intervention of intermediate causes. I left this rather to be inferred, not thinking it worth while to offend a certain class of persons by embodying in words what would only be a speculation." * He goes on to refer to the criticisms which have been directed against him on the ground that, by leaving species to be originated by miracle, he is inconsistent with his own doctrine of uniformitarianism ; and he leaves it

* In the same sense, see the letter to Whewell, March 7, 1837, vol. ii., p. 5 :—
"In regard to this last subject [the changes from one set of animal and vegetable species to another]... you remember what Herschel said in his letter to me. If I had stated as plainly as he has done the possibility of the introduction or origination of fresh species being a natural, in contradistinction to a miraculous process, I should have raised a host of prejudices against me, which are unfortunately opposed at every step to any philosopher who attempts to address the public on these mysterious subjects." See also letter to Sedgwick, Jan. 20, 1838, vol. ii. p. 35.

to be understood that he had not replied, on the ground of his general objection to controversy.

Lyell's contemporaries were not without some inkling of his esoteric doctrine. Whewell's 'History of the Inductive Sciences,' whatever its philosophical value, is always worth reading and always interesting, if under no other aspect than that of an evidence of the speculative limits within which a highly-placed divine might, at that time, safely range at will. In the course of his discussion of uniformitarianism, the encyclopædic Master of Trinity observes :—

" Mr. Lyell, indeed, has spoken of an hypothesis that 'the successive creation of species may constitute a regular part of the economy of nature,' but he has nowhere, I think, so described this process as to make it appear in what department of science we are to place the hypothesis. Are these new species created by the production, at long intervals, of an offspring different in species from the parents? Or are the species so created produced without parents? Are they gradually evolved from some embryo substance? Or do they suddenly start from the ground, as in the creation of the poet? . . .

"Some selection of one of these forms of the hypothesis, rather than the others, with evidence for the selection, is requisite to entitle us to place it among the known causes of change, which in this chapter we are considering. The bare conviction that a creation of species has taken place, whether once or many times, so long as it is unconnected with our organical sciences, is a tenet of Natural Theology rather than of Physical Philosophy." *

The earlier part of this criticism appears perfectly just and appropriate ; but, from the concluding paragraph, Whewell evidently imagines that by " creation " Lyell means a preternatural intervention of the Deity ; whereas the letter to Herschel shows that, in his own mind, Lyell meant natural

* Whewell's ' History,' vol. iii. p. 639–640 (ed. 2, 1847).

THE 'ORIGIN OF SPECIES.'   193

causation ; and I see no reason to doubt * that, if Sir Charles could have avoided the inevitable corollary of the pithecoid origin of man—for which, to the end of his life, he entertained a profound antipathy—he would have advocated the efficiency of causes now in operation to bring about the condition of the organic world, as stoutly as he championed that doctrine in reference to inorganic nature.

The fact is, that a discerning eye might have seen that some form or other of the doctrine of transmutation was inevitable, from the time when the truth enunciated by William

* The following passages in Lyell's letters appear to me decisive on this point :—

To Darwin, Oct. 3, 1859 (ii. 325), on first reading the ' Origin.'

" I have long seen most clearly that if any concession is made, all that you claim in your concluding pages will follow.

" It is this which has made me so long hesitate, always feeling that the case of Man and his Races, and of other animals, and that of plants, is one and the same, and that if a *vera causa* be admitted for one instant, [instead] of a purely un-known and imaginary one, such as the word ' creation,' all the conse-quences must follow."

To Darwin, March 15, 1863 (vol. ii. p. 365).

" I remember that it was the con-clusion he [Lamarck] came to about man that fortified me thirty years ago against the great impression which his arguments at first made on my mind, all the greater because Constant Prévost, a pupil of Cuvier's forty years ago, told me his con-viction ' that Cuvier thought species not real, but that science could not advance without assuming that they were so.' "

To Hooker, March 9, 1863 (vol. ii. p. 361), in reference to Darwin's feeling about the ' Antiquity of Man.'

" He [Darwin] seems much dis-appointed that I do not go farther with him, or do not speak out more. I can only say that I have spoken out to the full extent of my present convictions, and even beyond my state of *feeling* as to man's un-broken descent from the brutes, and I find I am half converting not a few who were in arms against Dar-win, and are even now against Huxley." He speaks of having had to abandon " old and long cherished ideas, which constituted the charm to me of the theoretical part of the science in my earlier days, when I believed with Pascal in the theory, as Hallam terms it, of ' the arch-angel ruined.' "

See the same sentiment in the letter to Darwin, March 11, 1863, p. 363 :—

" I think the old ' creation ' is almost as much required as ever, but of course it takes a new form if Lamarck's views improved by yours are adopted.",

VOL. II.   O

Smith, that successive strata are characterised by different. kinds of fossil remains, became a firmly established law of nature. No one has set forth the speculative consequences of this generalisation better than the historian of the 'Inductive Sciences':—

"But the study of geology opens to us the spectacle of many groups of species which have, in the course of the earth's history, succeeded each other at vast intervals of time; one set of animals and plants disappearing, as it would seem, from the face of our planet, and others, which did not before exist, becoming the only occupants of the globe. And the dilemma then presents itself to us anew:—either we must accept the doctrine of the transmutation of species, and must suppose that the organized species of one geological epoch were transmuted into those of another by some long-continued agency of natural causes; or else, we must believe in many successive acts of creation and extinction of species, out of the common course of nature; acts which, therefore, we may properly call miraculous." *

Dr. Whewell decides in favour of the latter conclusion. And if any one had plied him with the four questions which he puts to Lyell in the passage already cited, all that can be said now is that he would certainly have rejected the first. But would he really have had the courage to say that a *Rhinoceros tichorhinus*, for instance, "was produced without parents;" or was "evolved from some embryo substance;" or that it suddenly started from the ground like Milton's lion "pawing to get free his hinder parts"? I permit myself to doubt whether even the Master of Trinity's well-tried courage—physical, intellectual, and moral—would have been equal to this feat. No doubt the sudden concurrence of half-a-ton of inorganic molecules into a live rhinoceros is conceivable, and therefore may be possible. But does such an event lie

* Whewell's 'History of the In-   vol. iii. p. 624–625. See, for the
ductive Sciences.' Ed. ii., 1847,   author's verdict, pp. 638–39.

sufficiently within the bounds of probability to justify the belief in its occurrence on the strength of any attainable, or, indeed, imaginable, evidence?

In view of the assertion (often repeated in the early days of the opposition to Darwin) that he had added nothing to Lamarck, it is very interesting to observe that the possibility of a fifth alternative, in addition to the four he has stated, has not dawned upon Dr. Whewell's mind. The suggestion that new species may result from the selective action of external conditions upon the variations from their specific type which individuals present—and which we call "spontaneous," because we are ignorant of their causation—is as wholly unknown to the historian of scientific ideas as it was to biological specialists before 1858. But that suggestion is the central idea of the 'Origin of Species,' and contains the quintessence of Darwinism.

Thus, looking back into the past, it seems to me that my own position of critical expectancy was just and reasonable, and must have been taken up, on the same grounds, by many other persons. If Agassiz told me that the forms of life which had successively tenanted the globe were the incarnations of successive thoughts of the Deity; and that He had wiped out one set of these embodiments by an appalling geological catastrophe as soon as His ideas took a more advanced shape, I found myself not only unable to admit the accuracy of the deductions from the facts of paleontology, upon which this astounding hypothesis was founded, but I had to confess my want of any means of testing the correctness of his explanation of them. And besides that, I could by no means see what the explanation explained. Neither did it help me to be told by an eminent anatomist that species had succeeded one another in time, in virtue of "a continuously operative creational law." That seemed to me to be no more than saying that species had succeeded one another, in the form of a vote-catching resolution, with "law" to please the man of science, and "creational" to draw the orthodox. So I took refuge in that "*thätige Skepsis*" which Goethe has so well defined ; and, reversing the apostolic precept to be all things to all men, I usually defended the tenability of the received doctrines, when I had to do with the transmutationists ; and stood up for the possibility of transmutation among the orthodox—thereby, no doubt, increasing an already current, but quite undeserved, reputation for needless combativeness.

I remember, in the course of my first interview with Mr. Darwin, expressing my belief in the sharpness of the lines of demarcation between natural groups and in the absence of transitional forms, with all the confidence of youth and imperfect knowledge. I was not aware, at that time, that he had then been many years brooding over the species-question ; and the humorous smile which accompanied his gentle answer, that such was not altogether his view, long haunted and puzzled me. But it would seem that four or five years' hard work had enabled me to understand what it meant ; for Lyell,* writing to Sir Charles Bunbury (under date of April 30, 1856), says :—

"When Huxley, Hooker, and Wollaston were at Darwin's last week they (all four of them) ran a tilt against species— further, I believe, than they are prepared to go."

I recollect nothing of this beyond the fact of meeting Mr. Wollaston ; and except for Sir Charles' distinct assurance as to "all four," I should have thought my *outrecuidance* was probably a counterblast to Wollaston's conservatism. With regard to Hooker, he was already, like Voltaire's Habakkuk, "*capable de tout*" in the way of advocating Evolution.

As I have already said, I imagine that most of those of my contemporaries who thought seriously about the matter, were very much in my own state of mind—inclined to say to both Mosaists and Evolutionists, "a plague on both your

* 'Life and Letters,' vol. ii p. 212.

THE 'ORIGIN OF SPECIES.'   197

houses !" and disposed to turn aside from an interminable and apparently fruitless discussion, to labour in the fertile fields of ascertainable fact.   And I may, therefore, further suppose that the publication of the Darwin and Wallace papers in 1858, and still more that of the 'Origin' in 1859, had the effect upon them of the flash of light, which to a man who has lost himself in a dark night, suddenly reveals a road which, whether it takes him straight home or not, certainly goes his way.   That which we were looking for, and could not find, was a hypothesis respecting the origin of known organic forms, which assumed the operation of no causes but such as could be proved to be actually at work.   We wanted, not to pin our faith to that or any other speculation, but to get hold of clear and definite conceptions which could be brought face to face with facts and have their validity tested. The 'Origin' provided us with the working hypothesis we sought.   Moreover, it did the immense service of freeing us for ever from the dilemma—refuse to accept the creation hypothesis, and what have you to propose that can be accepted by any cautious reasoner?   In 1857, I had no answer ready, and I do not think that any one else had.   A year later, we reproached ourselves with dulness for being perplexed by such an inquiry.   My reflection, when I first made myself master of the central idea of the 'Origin,' was, "How extremely stupid not to have thought of that!"   I suppose that Columbus' companions said much the same when he made the egg stand on end.   The facts of variability, of the struggle for existence, of adaptation to conditions, were notorious enough ; but none of us had suspected that the road to the heart of the species problem lay through them, until Darwin and Wallace dispelled the darkness, and the beacon-fire of the 'Origin' guided the benighted.

Whether the particular shape which the doctrine of evolution, as applied to the organic world, took in Darwin's hands, would prove to be final or not, was, to me, a matter of indifference. In my earliest criticisms of the 'Origin' I ventured to point out that its logical foundation was insecure so long as experiments in selective breeding had not produced varieties which were more or less infertile ; and that insecurity remains up to the present time. But, with any and every critical doubt which my sceptical ingenuity could suggest, the Darwinian hypothesis remained incomparably more probable than the creation hypothesis. And if we had none of us been able to discern the paramount significance of some of the most patent and notorious of natural facts, until they were, so to speak, thrust under our noses, what force remained in the dilemma— creation or nothing? It was obvious that, hereafter, the probability would be immensely greater, that the links of natural causation were hidden from our purblind eyes, than that natural causation should be incompetent to produce all the phenomena of nature. The only rational course for those who had no other object than the attainment of truth, was to accept "Darwinism" as a working hypothesis, and see what could be made of it. Either it would prove its capacity to elucidate the facts of organic life, or it would break down under the strain. This was surely the dictate of common sense ; and, for once, common sense carried the day. The result has been that complete *volte-face* of the whole scientific world, which must seem so surprising to the present generation. I do not mean to say that all the leaders of biological science have avowed themselves Darwinians ; but I do not think that there is a single zoologist, or botanist, or palæontologist, among the multitude of active workers of this generation, who is other than an evolutionist, profoundly influenced by Darwin's views. Whatever may be the ultimate fate of the particular theory put forth by Darwin, I venture to affirm that, so far as my knowledge goes, all the ingenuity and all the learning of hostile critics has not enabled them to adduce a solitary fact, of which it can be said, this is irreconcilable with the Darwinian theory. In the prodigious variety and com-

THOMAS HENRY HUXLEY 477

plexity of organic nature, there are multitudes of phenomena which are not deducible from any generalisations we have yet reached. But the same may be said of every other class of natural objects. I believe that astronomers cannot yet get the moon's motions into perfect accordance with the theory of gravitation.

It would be inappropriate, even if it were possible, to discuss the difficulties and unresolved problems which have hitherto met the evolutionist, and which will probably continue to puzzle him for many generations to come, in the course of this brief history of the reception of Mr. Darwin's great work. But there are two or three objections of a more general character, based, or supposed to be based, upon philosophical and theological foundations, which were loudly expressed in the early days of the Darwinian controversy, and which, though they have been answered over and over again, crop up now and then at the present day.

The most singular of these, perhaps immortal, fallacies, which live on, Tithonus-like, when sense and force have long deserted them, is that which charges Mr. Darwin with having attempted to reinstate the old pagan goddess, Chance. It is said that he supposes variations to come about "by chance," and that the fittest survive the "chances" of the struggle for existence, and thus "chance" is substituted for providential design.

It is not a little wonderful that such an accusation as this should be brought against a writer who has, over and over again, warned his readers that when he uses the word "spontaneous," he merely means that he is ignorant of the cause of that which is so termed; and whose whole theory crumbles to pieces if the uniformity and regularity of natural causation for illimitable past ages is denied. But probably the best answer to those who talk of Darwinism meaning the reign of "chance," is to ask them what they themselves understand by "chance." Do they believe that anything in this universe happens without reason or without a cause? Do they really conceive that any event has no cause, and could not have been predicted by any one who had a sufficient insight into the order of Nature? If they do, it is they who are the inheritors of antique superstition and ignorance, and whose minds have never been illumined by a ray of scientific thought. The one act of faith in the convert to science, is the confession of the universality of order and of the absolute validity, in all times and under all circumstances, of the law of causation. This confession is an act of faith, because, by the nature of the case, the truth of such propositions is not susceptible of proof. But such faith is not blind, but reasonable; because it is invariably confirmed by experience, and constitutes the sole trustworthy foundation for all action.

If one of these people, in whom the chance-worship of our remoter ancestors thus strangely survives, should be within reach of the sea when a heavy gale is blowing, let him betake himself to the shore and watch the scene. Let him note the infinite variety of form and size of the tossing waves out at sea; or of the curves of their foam-crested breakers, as they dash against the rocks; let him listen to the roar and scream of the shingle as it is cast up and torn down the beach; or look at the flakes of foam as they drive hither and thither before the wind; or note the play of colours, which answers a gleam of sunshine as it falls upon their myriad bubbles. Surely here, if anywhere, he will say that chance is supreme, and bend the knee as one who has entered the very penetralia of his divinity. But the man of science knows that here, as everywhere, perfect order is manifested; that there is not a curve of the waves, not a note in the howling chorus, not a rainbow-glint on a bubble, which is other than a necessary consequence of the ascertained laws of nature; and that with a sufficient knowledge of the conditions, competent physico-mathematical skill could account for, and indeed predict, every one of these "chance" events.

A second very common objection to Mr. Darwin's views was (and is), that they abolish Teleology, and eviscerate the argument from design. It is nearly twenty years since I ventured to offer some remarks on this subject, and as my arguments have as yet received no refutation, I hope I may be excused for reproducing them. I observed, "that the doctrine of Evolution is the most formidable opponent of all the commoner and coarser forms of Teleology. But perhaps the most remarkable service to the philosophy of Biology rendered by Mr. Darwin is the reconciliation of Teleology and Morphology, and the explanation of the facts of both, which his views offer. The teleology which supposes that the eye, such as we see it in man, or one of the higher vertebrata, was made with the precise structure it exhibits, for the purpose of enabling the animal which possesses it to see, has undoubtedly received its death-blow. Nevertheless, it is necessary to remember that there is a wider teleology which is not touched by the doctrine of Evolution, but is actually based upon the fundamental proposition of Evolution. This proposition is that the whole world, living and not living, is the result of the mutual interaction, according to definite laws, of the forces * possessed by the molecules of which the primitive nebulosity of the universe was composed. If this be true, it is no less certain that the existing world lay potentially in the cosmic vapour, and that a sufficient intelligence could, from a knowledge of the properties of the molecules of that vapour, have predicted, say the state of the fauna of Britain in 1869, with as much certainty as one can say what will happen to the vapour of the breath on a cold winter's day. . . . .

. . . . The teleological and the mechanical views of nature are not, necessarily, mutually exclusive. On the contrary, the more purely a mechanist the speculator is, the more firmly

* I should now like to substitute the word powers for "forces."

does he assume a primordial molecular arrangement of which all the phenomena of the universe are the consequences,. and the more completely is he thereby at the mercy of the teleologist, who can always defy him to disprove that this primordial molecular arrangement was not intended to evolve the phenomena of the universe." *

The acute champion of Teleology, Paley, saw no difficulty in admitting that the "production of things" may be the result of trains of mechanical dispositions fixed beforehand by intelligent appointment and kept in action by a power at the centre, † that is to say, he proleptically accepted the modern doctrine of Evolution ; and his successors might do well to follow their leader, or at any rate to attend to his weighty reasonings, before rushing into an antagonism which has no reasonable foundation.

Having got rid of the belief in chance and the disbelief in design, as in no sense appurtenances of Evolution, the third libel upon that doctrine, that it is anti-theistic, might perhaps be left to shift for itself. But the persistence with which many people refuse to draw the plainest consequences from the propositions they profess to accept, renders it advisable to remark that the doctrine of Evolution is neither Anti-theistic nor Theistic. It simply has no more to do with Theism than the first book of Euclid has. It is quite certain that a normal fresh-laid egg contains neither cock nor hen ; and it is also as certain as any proposition in physics or morals, that if such an egg is kept under proper conditions for three weeks, a cock or hen chicken will be found in it. It is also quite certain that if the shell were transparent we should be able to watch the formation of the young fowl, day by day,. by a process of evolution, from a microscopic cellular germ to its full size and complication of structure. Therefore

* The " Genealogy of Animals "   † 'Natural   Theology,' chap. ('The Academy,' 1869), reprinted   xxiii. in ' Critiques and Addresses.'

Evolution, in the strictest sense, is actually going on in this and analogous millions and millions of instances, wherever living creatures exist. Therefore, to borrow an argument from Butler, as that which now happens must be consistent with the attributes of the Deity, if such a Being exists, Evolution must be consistent with those attributes. And, if so, the evolution of the universe, which is neither more nor less explicable than that of a chicken, must also be consistent with them. The doctrine of Evolution, therefore, does not even come into contact with Theism, considered as a philosophical doctrine. That with which it does collide, and with which it is absolutely inconsistent, is the conception of creation, which theological speculators have based upon the history narrated in the opening of the book of Genesis.

There is a great deal of talk and not a little lamentation about the so-called religious difficulties which physical science has created. In theological science, as a matter of fact, it has created none. Not a solitary problem presents itself to the philosophical Theist, at the present day, which has not existed from the time that philosophers began to think out the logical grounds and the logical consequences of Theism. All the real or imaginary perplexities which flow from the conception of the universe as a determinate mechanism, are equally involved in the assumption of an Eternal, Omnipotent and Omniscient Deity. The theological equivalent of the scientific conception of order is Providence ; and the doctrine of determinism follows as surely from the attributes of foreknowledge assumed by the theologian, as from the universality of natural causation assumed by the man of science. The angels in 'Paradise Lost' would have found the task of enlightening Adam upon the mysteries of "Fate, Foreknowledge, and Free-will," not a whit more difficult, if their pupil had been educated in a "Real-schule" and trained in every laboratory of a modern university. In respect of the great problems of Philosophy, the post-Darwinian generation is,

204   ON THE RECEPTION OF THE 'ORIGIN OF SPECIES.'

in one sense, exactly where the præ-Darwinian generations were. They remain insoluble. But the present generation has the advantage of being better provided with the means of freeing itself from the tyranny of certain sham solutions.

The known is finite, the unknown infinite ; intellectually we stand on an islet in the midst of an illimitable ocean of inexplicability. Our business in every generation is to reclaim a little more land, to add something to the extent and the solidity of our possessions. And even a cursory glance at the history of the biological sciences during the last quarter of a century is sufficient to justify the assertion, that the most potent instrument for the extension of the realm of natural knowledge which has come into men's hands, since the publication of Newton's 'Principia,' is Darwin's 'Origin of Species.'

It was badly received by the generation to which it was first addressed, and the outpouring of angry nonsense to which it gave rise is sad to think upon. But the present generation will probably behave just as badly if another Darwin should arise, and inflict upon them that which the generality of mankind most hate—the necessity of revising their convictions. Let them, then, be charitable to us ancients ; and if they behave no better than the men of my day to some new benefactor, let them recollect that, after all, our wrath did not come to much, and vented itself chiefly in the bad language of sanctimonious scolds. Let them as speedily perform a strategic right-about-face, and follow the truth wherever it leads. The opponents of the new truth will discover, as those of Darwin are doing, that, after all, theories do not alter facts, and that the universe remains unaffected even though texts crumble. Or, it may be, that, as history repeats itself, their happy ingenuity will also discover that the new wine is exactly of the same vintage as the old, and that (rightly viewed) the old bottles prove to have been expressly made for holding it.